Lecture Notes in Computer Science   5247

Commenced Publication in 1973
Founding and Former Series Editors:
Gerhard Goos, Juris Hartmanis, and Jan van Leeuwen

Peter Forbrig   Fabio Paternò (Eds.)

Engineering Interactive Systems 2008

Second Conference on
Human-Centered Software Engineering, HCSE 2008 and
7th International Workshop on
Task Models and Diagrams, TAMODIA 2008
Pisa, Italy, September 25-26, 2008
Proceedings

 Springer

Volume Editors

Peter Forbrig
University of Rostock, Department of Computer Science
Albert-Einstein-Str. 21, 18051 Rostock, Germany
E-mail: peter.forbrig@uni-rostock.de

Fabio Paternò
ISTI-CNR
Via G. Moruzzi 1, 56124 Pisa, Italy
E-mail: fabio.paterno@isti.cnr.it

Library of Congress Control Number: 2008935025

CR Subject Classification (1998): H.5.2, H.5, D.2, D.3, F.3, I.6, K.6

LNCS Sublibrary: SL 2 – Programming and Software Engineering

ISSN   0302-9743
ISBN-10   3-540-85991-8 Springer Berlin Heidelberg New York
ISBN-13   978-3-540-85991-8 Springer Berlin Heidelberg New York

Springer is a part of Springer Science+Business Media

springer.com

© IFIP International Federation for Information Processing 2008
Printed in Germany

Typesetting: Camera-ready by author, data conversion by Scientific Publishing Services, Chennai, India
Printed on acid-free paper   SPIN: 12513901   06/3180   5 4 3 2 1 0

Preface

Engineering Interactive Systems (EIS) 2008 was an international event combining the 2nd working conference on Human-Centred Software Engineering (HCSE 2008) and the 7th International Workshop on TAsk MOdels and DIAgrams (TAMODIA 2008).

HCSE is a working conference that brings together researchers and practitioners interested in strengthening the scientific foundations of user interface design and examining the relationship between software engineering and human-computer interaction and how to strengthen user-centred design as an essential part of software engineering processes. As a working conference, substantial time is devoted to the open and lively discussion of papers. TAMODIA is an international workshop on models, such as task models and visual representations in Human-Computer Interaction (one of the most widely used notations in this area, ConcurTaskTrees, was developed in the town that hosted this year's event). It focuses on notations used to describe user tasks ranging from textual and graphical forms to interactive, multimodal and multimedia tools.

The pervasiveness of software applications requires user interfaces able to support a wide variety of tasks, in a wide variety of contexts, and accessible through many possible devices. The user interface component of interactive applications is acquiring ever more importance. This is because, often, many different applications are available to perform similar tasks and users choose those that are easier to understand and interact with and that, consequently, increase efficiency, productivity, and acceptance while reducing errors and the need for training. As designers of tomorrow's technology, we have the responsibility of creating interactive software systems that permit better user experience, so that users may enjoy more satisfying experiences with information and communication technologies. This need has brought about new research areas, such as ambient intelligence, natural interaction, end user development, and social interaction.

The response to the conference was positive in terms of submissions and participation. We received around 60 contributions from 20 countries located on 5 continents. We selected for the final programme 7 full papers and 6 short papers for TAMODIA and 3 full papers and 11 short papers for HCSE, as well as 3 interesting demos. The result is a set of interesting and stimulating papers that address such important issues as task models and interaction, user interfaces for ubiquitous systems, multi-device user interfaces, automated usability evaluation, human-centred design, and intelligent user interfaces. The final programme of the event also included one technical invited speaker: Alan Dix from the University of Lancaster on CHANGE: Getting Things Done and Helping Get Things Done: Automated Task Support.

In general, the continuous development of new research topics in the human-computer interaction area shows how the field is able to dynamically evolve and address both new and old challenges. All the results obtained are never an arrival point but they are the basis for new research and results, and we hope that Engineering Interactive Systems 2008 can contribute to this process.

July 2008
Peter Forbrig
Fabio Paternò

Organization

International Programme Committee

Chairs
Peter Forbrig, *University of Rostock,* and
Fabio Paternò, *ISTI-CNR, Italy*

Members for HCSE 2008

Simone D. J. Barbosa	Informatics Department, PUC-Rio, Brazil
Rémi Bastide	LIIHS - IRIT - Université Toulouse 1, France
David Benyon	Napier University, Edinburgh, UK
Regina Bernhaupt	Universität Salzburg, Austria
Ann Blandford	University College London, UK
Gaelle Calvary	CLIPS-IMAG, France
José C. Campos	DI/CCTC, Universidade do Minho, Portugal
Stéphane Chatty	ENAC, IntuiLab, France
Anke Dittmar	University of Rostock, Germany
Gavin Doherty	Department of Computer Science, Trinity College Dublin, Ireland
Xavier Ferre	Universidad Politecnica de Madrid, Spain
Peter Forbrig	University of Rostock, Germany
Nicholas Graham	School of Computing, Queen's University, Canada
Jan Gulliksen	Uppsala University, Sweden
Judy Hammond	University of Technology, Sydney, Australia
Morten Borup Harning	Dialogical ApS/Priway ApS, Denmark
Michael Harrison	University of Newcastle upon Tyne, UK
Joaquim Jorge	INESC-ID, Technical University of Lisbon, Portugal
Rick Kazman	University of Hawaii, SEI/CMU, USA
Kris Luyten	Hasselt University, Expertise Centre for Digital Media, Belgium
Eduard Metzker	DaimlerChrysler Research and Technology, Germany
Tom Moher	University of Illinois at Chicago, USA
Philippe Palanque	IRIT, Université Toulouse 3, France
Oscar Pastor	Valencia University of Technology, Spain
Fabio Paternò	ISTI-CNR, Italy
Matthias Rauterberg	Industrial Design Department, Technical University Eindhoven, The Netherlands

Carmen Santoro   ISTI-CNR, Italy
Daniel Sinnig   Concordia University Montreal, Canada
Constantine Stephanidis   University of Crete and FORTH-ICS, Greece
Gerrit van der Veer   Vrije Universiteit, Amsterdam, The Netherlands
Janet Wesson   Nelson Mandela Metropolitan University, Port
                 Elizabeth, South Africa
Marco Winckler   LIIHS-IRIT, France
Thomas Ziegert   SAP Research CEC Darmstadt, Germany

Members for Tamodia 2008

Sandrine Balbo   University of Melbourne, Australia
Rémi Bastide   University Toulouse 1, France
Birgit Bomsdorf   University of Hagen, Germany
Gaëlle Calvary   University of Grenoble I, France
Karin Coninx   Hasselt University, Belgium
Anke Ditmar   University of Rostock, Germany
Alan Dix   Lancaster University, UK
Peter Forbrig   University of Rostock, Germany
María-Dolores Lozano   Universidad de Castilla-La Mancha, Spain
Kris Luyten   Hasselt University, Belgium
Philippe Palanque   University Paul Sabatier, France
Fabio Paternò   ISTI-CNR, Italy
Costin Pribeanu   ICI Bucuresti, Romania
Matthias Rauterberg   Eindhoven University of Technology,
                 The Netherlands
Carmen Santoro   ISTI-CNR, Italy
Corina Sas   Lancaster University, UK
Dominique Scapin   INRIA, France
Pavel Slavík   Czech Technical University in Prague,
                 Czech Republic
Christian Stary   University of Linz, Austria
Constantine Stephanidis   University of Crete and FORTH-ICS, Greece
Markus Stolze   IBM, USA
Hallvard Trætteberg   University of Trondheim, Norway
Jean Vanderdonckt   UCL, Belgium
Gerrit Van der Veer   Vrije Universiteit, The Netherlands
Peter Wild   University of Cambridge, UK
Marco Winckler   University Paul Sabatier, France

Table of Contents

Keynote

HCSE Long Papers

HCSE Short Papers

Demonstrations

Tasks = Data + Action + Context: Automated Task Assistance through Data-Oriented Analysis

Alan Dix

Computing Department, InfoLab21, Lancaster University
Lancaster, LA1 4WA, UK
alan@hcibook.com
http://www.hcibook.com/alan/papers/EIS-Tamodia2008/

Abstract. Human activity unfolds partly through planning and learnt sequences of actions, and partly through reaction to the physical objects and digital data in the environment. This paper describes various techniques related to automatic task assistance that take this role of data as central. Although this brings additional complexity, it also offers ways to simplify or bypass problems in task inference that otherwise appear difficult or impossible. Although the focus in this paper is on automated task support, the importance of objects and data in understanding tasks is one that applies to other forms of task analysis in the design process.

Keywords: task inference, data detectors, automated task support, intelligent user interfaces, task as grammar.

1 Introduction

One morning recently, whilst having breakfast, I served a bowl of grapefruit segments and then went to make my tea. While making the tea I went to the fridge to get a pint of milk, but after getting the milk from the fridge I only just stopped myself in time as I was about to pour the milk onto my grapefruit! I am sure everyone reading this has made a similar mistake, but it is not just an amusing anecdote; the analysis of such mistakes is the grist of human error analysis and equally tells us critical things about even error-free tasks.

Note that not all mistakes are equally likely: I would be unlikely to pour the milk onto the bare kitchen worktop or onto a plate of bacon and eggs. This is a form of capture error: the bowl containing the grapefruit might on other occasions hold cornflakes; when that is the case and I am standing in the kitchen with milk in my hand, having just got it out of the fridge, it would be quite appropriate to pour the milk into the bowl.

In all but the most repetitive, routinised, or organisationally prescribed settings, the actual evolution of the goal into human activity is far more complex and situated then we can easily capture in simple task-hierarchies and plans. Real activity involves procedural, reactive and consciously considered actions and for over 20 years, many

P. Forbrig and F. Paternò (Eds.): HCSE/TAMODIA 2008, LNCS 5247, pp. 1–13, 2008.

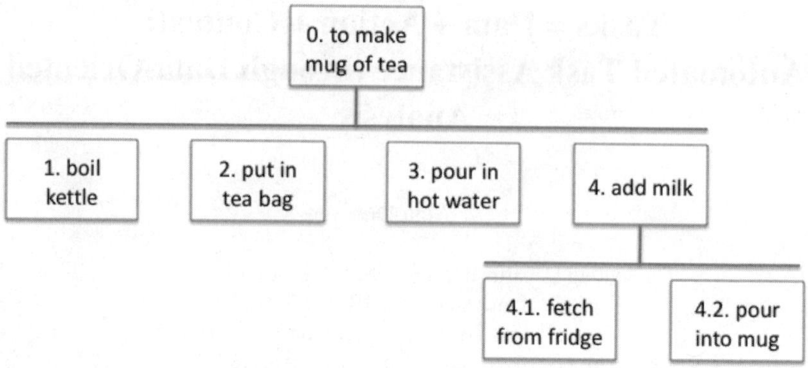

Fig. 1. Making a mug of tea (sorry no teapot)

in HCI have argued that the complexity of 'situated action' renders more formal task or goal analysis incorrect, obsolete and irrelevant. In contrast, in my keynote at the first Tamodia in 2002, I discussed how some of these more contextual or situational elements could be drawn into a formal task model: the role of information, other people, physical artefacts, triggers for action, and placeholders keeping track of where we are in a task [1].

This subtle complexity of real human activity is difficult for a human analyst to adequately describe in more formal terms; even when that formalisation is properly understood to be partial and provisional. However, this is far worse when the 'analyst' is a machine! As a human analyst we can ask what is going on in a user's head, but automated analysis typically has only the trace of user actions available and no real understanding of human activity and purpose.

Over the years I have intermittently worked on aspects of task inference and automated support of user activity. In this paper I will reflect on the relation of this to more human task analysis and the way they inform one another. Many of the techniques described are being worked on together with colleagues at Lancaster, University of Rome "La Sapienza", University of Athens, University of Peloponnese and Universidad Autonoma de Madrid. I will mention other names explicitly in the paper, but in other places when I say "we", this refers to joint work with various colleagues in this group.

2   The Best Laid Plans and Reactions

We'll start by looking in a little more detail at the milk in the grapefruit error. Figure 1 shows a HTA of the task of making a mug of tea. It is subtask 4 that is interesting. It has two further subtasks and one would normally write a plan such as:

```
Plan 4.
        if milk not out do 4.1
        then do 4.2
```

However, maybe it is more like:

> Plan 4.
>> if milk not out do 4.1
>> when milk in hand do 4.2

The capture error is then understandable as the "eat some cereal" task will also have a plan with something like "when milk is in hand pour into bowl".

The first version of the plan is really a 'planned' plan, or maybe a proceduralised one, where the sequence of actions is in some way explicitly or implicitly remembered. However, the second is effectively a stimulus–response reaction based on conditions in the environment – the sequenced and hierarchical structure will still be there, but are maintained because it unfolds as the human actions interact with the environment, not because the order is remembered. Furthermore, the user may even be performing some form of explicit means-end analysis "in order to add milk I need a bottle of milk", … "in order to get a bottle of milk I need to open the fridge".

We can arrange these types of sequenced activity by whether they are explicit or implicit and whether they are pre-planned or environment-driven:

	pre-planned	environment-driven
explicit	(a) following known plan of action	(b) means–end analysis
implicit	(c) proceduralised or routine actions	(d) stimulus–response reaction

From watching a user we often cannot tell which of these is the reason for a particular sequence of observed actions. While these are very different in terms of cognitive activity, they are virtually indistinguishable from behaviour alone.

Now we might assume that a well-practiced user will learn frequently repeated tasks: that is, even if the user starts off with an explicit plan (a) or are means-end driven (b), they will eventually end up with proceduralised or routine actions (c) – practice makes perfect. Certainly this is true of repeated actions in sports and music.

However, theorists advocating strong ideas of the embodied mind would argue that we are creatures fitted most well to a perception–action cycle and where possible are parsimonious with mental representations allowing the environment to encode as much as possible.

> *"In general evolved creatures will neither store nor process information in costly ways when they can use the structure of the environment and their operations on it as a convenient stand-in for the information-processing operations concerned."* ([2] as quoted in [3])

Clark calls this the "007 principle" as it can be summarised as: *"know only as much as you need to know to get the job done"* [3].

In the natural world this means, for example, that we do not need to remember what the weather is like now as we can feel the wind on our cheeks or the rain on our hands. In a more complex setting this can include changes made to the world (e.g. the bowl on the worktop) and even changes made precisely for the reason of offloading information processing or memory (e.g. ticking off the shopping list). Indeed this is one of the main foci of distributed cognition accounts of activity [4].

It is not necessary to take a strong embodied mind or even distributed cognition viewpoint to see that this parsimony is a normal aspect of human behaviour – why bother to remember the precise order of doing things to make my mug of tea when it is obvious what to do when I have milk in my hand and black tea in the mug?

Of curse parsimony of internal representation does *not* mean *no* internal representation. The story of the grapefruit bowl would be less amusing of it happened all the time. While eating breakfast it is not unusual for me to have both a grapefruit bowl and a mug of tea out at the same time – so why don't I make the same mistake every morning? In fact I do have some idea of what follows what (plan) and also have some idea that I am "in the middle of making my tea" (context, schema).

Together these factors: environment, plans, context inform the actions we perform in the world.

We will look at each of these factors and how they impact automatic inference and support of users' tasks.

3 Environment – Data Driven Interaction

In ubiquitous computing, the instrumentation of the environment is a major issue in itself and so inferring user behaviour from the environment is very difficult. In contrast, in the purely digital world of the desktop or web, we have, in principle, relatively easy access to the complete digital environment. This makes certain forms of data-driven interaction particularly easy.

One form of this are "data detectors", which usually use some form of textual analysis to identify potential key terms, dates, etc. in small bodies of text such as email messages, or your current selection. The initial work on data detectors occurred in the late 1990's when there were a number of other data detector projects at Intel (SRA) [5], Apple [6] and Georgia Tech (CyberDesk) [7]. The Apple work led to the inclusion of Apple Data Detectors in the operating systems (and still there albeit often unused). When activated (and when using a compliant application) small contextual menus appear over selected words/phrases in the text of the current document or email.

At around the same time I was involved in the development of onCue [8], a small "intelligent" toolbar. This sat at the side of the screen and watched for changes to the clipboard (through copy-paste); when the clipboard changed, onCue would alter its icons to suggest additional things that the user might like to do with the clipboard contents. For example, if the user selected a person's name various web-based directories would be suggested, if instead a table of numbers were selected, graphs and spreadsheet options would be suggested.

The internal architecture of onCue consisted of two main kinds of components, recognisers and services, linked by a blackboard-like infrastructure. The recognisers examined the clipboard contents to see if they were a recognised type (post-code, name, table, etc.). The services instead responded to data of particular types (e.g. single word for dictionary, post code for mapping web site) and were activated when clipboard contents were recognised to be that type. This separation (itself building on CyberDesk [7]) was an important difference from most other systems where the two were linked as it meant that services could easily be added for previously recognised types adding to the potential for third party additions (through small XML "Qbits").

OnCue used the clipboard as its focus as the clipboard is usually the only truly application-independent source of data on a GUI platform. Ideally onCue would have fitted more closely into applications, but this is hard without per-application coding, even Apple found this despite controlling the platform! For exactly the same reasons, Citrine, another recent application in the data-detector tradition, is based purely on intelligent clipboard-to-clipboard interactions, offering intelligent transformations between types of clipboard content [9].

Citrine is part of a recent small resurgence in work on data detectors, including headlines a few years ago due to disputes about Microsoft SmartTags. Yahoo! also have ways for web developers to include context-sensitive searches into their web pages keyed on phrases in the page contents, and Amazon have recently announced a similar mechanism to link to books and other products. More interesting compared with these more hand-crafted links is the CREO system [10]. CREO takes several large ontologies of general knowledge and uses these to build indices of critical words and phrases. As the user browses the web a plug-in looks for matching words in the web pages visited and adds contextual links to web based interactions concerning the topic of the words. The information for this is also used to allow the user to train the systems to do new actions by example.

The mode of operation of CREO is reminiscent of an older body of work that started over 15 years earlier in the HyperText community, where notions of external linkage were important. Microcosm [11] developed at Southampton pioneered the use of automatic links. This used an index of key terms attached to a particular content. When the user viewed a document any key terms present in the index became live links in the document. Note that, with the exception of CREO, most of the data detectors, including onCue, rely on largely syntactic/lexical matching using regular expressions or other patterns whereas Microcosm was lexicon based.

Snip!t (www.snipit.org) is a web-based system allowing users to bookmark sections of a web page rather than just the URL of the page itself [12]. It has been developed intermittently over a period of about 5 years based on initial user studies of bookmarking that showed that users want to be able to recall a portion of a page [13]. This is now more common in tools such as Google Notebook and various annotation services such as Bricks [14] and MADCOW [15]. Snip!t inherits the recogniser–service architectire of onCue but running server-side rather than on a user's own machine. This allows it to access larger data sources, like Citrine and Microcosm, and so it performs a mixture of lexicon look-up and syntactic recognizing of suitable types, including hybrids. For example if a word matches one of the common names from a US census dataset of first names, it triggers a full syntactic analysis to check whether the surrounding text is really a name.

In many ways these data detector and related services are very much like a butler who, seeing you in the kitchen holding a pint of milk and a mug of black tea, says "would you like me to pour milk in your tea, sir?" However, the above systems all have little if any adaptation to the user, so are like an absent-minded butler who always asks the same even though you never take milk in your tea.

In order to make this kind of data-detector more individual, in the TIM project we are connecting this data detector technology with a personal ontology [16]. A personal ontology is an explicit store of personal information such as friends, work colleagues, projects, papers, and addresses, including the connections between them. There are various usability issues relating to how one encourages a user to produce and maintain such an ontology, but in general the process will be semi-automatic. The GNOWSIS project [17] has found that by mining very explicit desktop data such as address books, email messages etc. it is possible to build at least part of the data we would want to see in such an ontology.

If one assumes that such a personal ontology exists, then the terms in the ontology can be matched in text alongside public information sources such as gazetteers. So as well as recognising that Pisa is a City, it will also recognise that "Fabio" is the first name of an academic in my personal ontology and then be able to suggest things that are appropriate for an academic such as looking him up in DBLP.

4   Context – What to Do and What to Do It to

Of course a human aide would not only know about you as an individual (such as whether you like milk in your tea), but also know something about what is happening to you now (such as making tea or making pancakes).

Context recognition and context awareness have become especially important in ubiquitous and mobile computing where interactions with the world are central, but also in purely digital domains such as adaptive hypertext, and e-learning. It may be useful even in purely digital settings to know, for example, whether the user is stressed or relaxed, with colleagues or on her own. However, this paper will focus on context that can be inferred from the digital domain itself.

To do this, we take the personal ontology and then use spreading activation in order to represent what are the 'hot spots' in the ontology at any particular moment [18]. Spreading activation has its roots in cognitive psychology [19] and so has the potential to model context in a way somewhat resembling a human. The basic idea is that when an event or document refers to some entity in the ontology it becomes 'activated' (say I have an email from Vivi, then the entity representing Vivi gets an initial high activation). The algorithm then 'spreads' the activation by making entities connected to Vivi a little activated, then those connected to these slightly less active entities. There are problems, such as loops in the ontology, which can set up self-reinforcing feedback, but these can be controlled with care in the detailed algorithms.

Now imagine I receive a second email that mentions "George". I may know several people called George, so on its own any form of digital assistant can at best suggest it is one of a long list. However, with the spreading activation, the George who is part of the same project and in the same country as Vivi will be 'hotter; than others and so be the first suggestion. Also if the next action I am performing requires a city name, then an assistant can pre-complete the form with "Athens" as a suggestion as this is the city that is most highly activated.

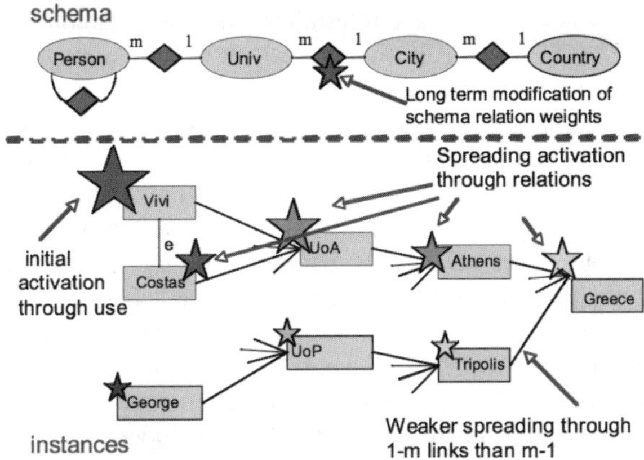

Fig. 2. Spreading activation through a personal ontology

A related approach is being used to create declarative representations of the relationship between web form fields [20]. Whenever a user enters text into form fields an automated system records the contents and then attempts to infer the relationship between the fields. If the fields are completely unrecognised it can do nothing (although this would be an appropriate point to suggest that the users store the data in their personal ontology!) However, if several form fields are found in the personal ontology, then an algorithm searches for 'best' paths between the fields.

There are typically several such paths hence the need for weighting. For example "Lancaster University" is related to "Alan Dix" by being his institution, but also the institution of Devina his work collegue. That is we have two possible paths:

(a) name_of / Person / member / Institution / has_name
(b) name_of / Person / colleague / Person / member / Institution / has_name

The system would give the first of these a higher weight because it is 'shorter' based on number of relationships traversed and their branching factors. Potentially, this could also use the current activation to weight more highly paths through 'hot' entities.

Next time the user comes to the form, the system knows not only what data was entered before (as in standard browser auto-completion), but also the relationship between them in abstract terms. So if the user enters Antonella into the first field, the system traverses path (a) and auto-completes the second field not with "Lancaster University" (the last value entered), but with "University of Rome" as that is the name of the institution that Antonella is a member of.

5   Sequence – From Traces to Plans

Performing a task leads to some observable trace of actions. This trace of real activity is often the meeting point of different views of the world. Even if we disagree on interpretations of events, we can often (although not always!) agree on what actually happened.

For this reason, in earlier work, I have referred to traces as a "ubiquitous semantics" for different user interface formalisms from task analysis to system models [21].

One way to view an HTA is as a grammar over this trace of actions. Personally I have found this a useful way to teach about task analysis, and have included this in the teaching materials for the Human–Computer Interaction textbook (although not yet in the actual text) [22,23]. As an illustration, figure 3 shows a simple HTA of cleaning a house and figure 4 shows how this can be used to build a 'parse tree' of a trace of actual actions (trace on the left, parse tree on the right). Note that unlike a textual grammar, the task grammar includes interleaved activities (the instance of task 4 "empty the dust bag" in the middle of the execution of task 3 "clean the rooms").

This can be applied to practical task analysis. In his thesis work, Stavros Asimakopoulos has used the "HTA as grammar" approach to supply chain forecasting [24]. Interviews with system developers and forecasters included accounts of actual forecasting activity (for the developers, envisaged; for the forecasters, from experience). These (partial) activity sequences were then matched against a normative task analysis based on the literature allowing an analysis of discrepancies between normative and actual tasks.

This approach can be used inductively too, and indeed direct observation is one of the normal sources for task analysis. As an analyst one is looking at a sequence of actual actions and attempting to infer a hierarchical (or other) structure on those actions. To do this the analyst uses a combination of common sense, domain knowledge and interaction with users in order to ascertain that, for example, putting money in a slot is part of parking a car.

```
0. in order to clean the house
     1. get the vacuum cleaner out
     2. get the appropriate attachment
     3. clean the rooms
          3.1. clean the hall
          3.2. clean the living rooms
          3.3. clean the bedrooms
     4. empty the dust bag
     5. put vacuum cleaner and attachments away
```

Fig. 3. HTA for cleaning a house (from [22]

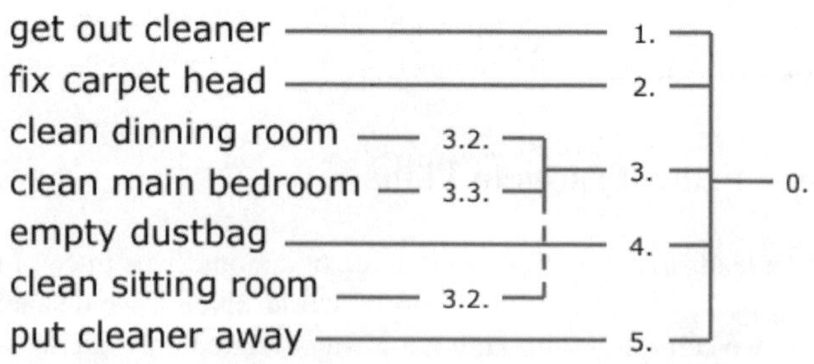

Fig. 4. Parsing a trace using an HTA (from [23] and [24])

For automated analysis this becomes far more complicated – I have been told that the general problem of inferring a hierarchical grammar from a sequence is computationally hard (either NP or at least n^k for some large 'k'!). However, in practice things are not quite as bad as this suggests. Indeed various forms of action/task inference have been common in the literature with the heyday in the early 1990s. The most well known example is Allan Cypher's Eager [25], but there have been many such systems using various algorithms including neural networks and hidden Markov models [26,27,28]. In recent years certain (albeit limited) forms of task inference can be found in commercial systems such as auto-completion of lists in Microsoft Office or form auto-fill features in web browsers … but the former emphasises the need to put any such 'intelligent' features within an appropriate interaction framework. (See "appropriate intelligence" in [29], especially the principle that one should design foremost for the times when the intelligence, inevitably, fails and make interaction graceful at such times.).

In some cases data-focused interactions can give rise to emergent task sequencing: if the output of a basic user action is some form of data, then this becomes the locus for the next action, etc. However, data linkages can also be used to make the job of inferring structure from tasks sequences easier.

One of the problems in inferring task structure from traces of user activity is that we interleave different tasks. I may be writing a paper, but occasionally reading or writing an email while I do so, or maybe taking a break to play a game of solitaire. Email reading on its own is perhaps one of the most challenging domains as perforce the mails arriving are related to different higher-level tasks and yet they typically get read in arrival order not a task at a time.

This is similar to the case in the kitchen where I maybe alternating between making tea, serving grapefruit and chatting to my wife. Although the milk is somewhat problematic, it is obvious that boiling the kettle is connected with making the tea because the water from the kettle goes into the mug not the grapefruit bowl. That is the shared physical objects in the environment can be used to establish links between low-level actions.

We can do the same thing in the digital domain. If we keep track of what digital objects are produced or used by different user actions then this creates a linkage between them. For example, if I copy a date from an event in my calendar and paste it into a hotel booking form, I create an implicit link between the two actions.

If the user types the data, things become more difficult. For example, if the result of a search produced "Miguel" and then I typed "Madrid" into a text box. However, here the algorithm described at the end of the previous section again comes into play and offers a way to establish potential relationships through the personal ontology.

Now, assuming we have these data links between low-level actions, we can start to 'pull out the threads' of tasks from the undifferentiated interleaved sequence of actions. This is a bit like finding one end of a string of pearls in a jewellery box and gently pulling the whole string (see Fig. 5). In principle these data links could take place days, weeks or months later and still be detectable.

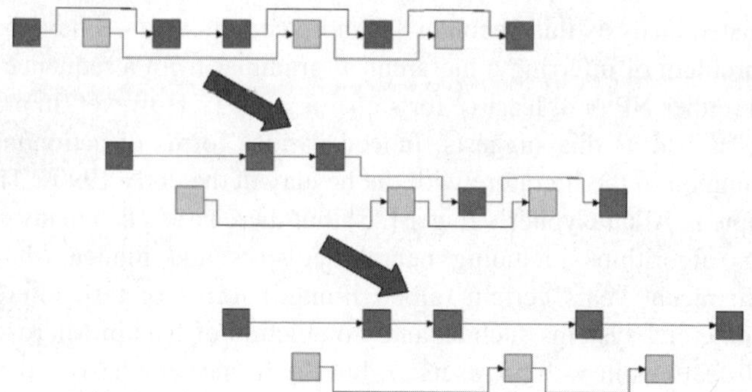

Fig. 5. Pulling out task threads from interleaved user actions

Once this thread has been pulled out we have a task sequence that is not confused by interleaved activities of other kinds and thus far more amenable to further analysis. For example, if a sequence of low-level actions A, B, C is detected and action A is later performed then the option of performing actions B ad C can be proposed. Furthermore the fact that we have the data link between them means we can auto-complete the parameters of the subsequent actions. Of course, given this sequence, some of the more sophisticated inference techniques in the programming by example / by demonstration literature can be used [28]. The crucial thing is that data linkage turns what seems like a near impossible problem into a relatively simple one.

Of course nothing is as trivial as that and there are some complications. The task thread is a data flow and so may not be a simple sequence, but instead DAG (directed acyclic graph) with time-based total ordering. Also any inferred data linkages mean that there is a level of uncertainty associated with the detection of threads, leading to several potential task threads with some level of confidence associated with each.

In principle it would also be possible to infer a level of hierarchical structure, either through the temporal structure, by looking for common sub-sequences of actions; or through the data structure, by looking at branches in the DAG. However, this seems an appropriate level to rely more strongly on the user. When a sequence of actions is suggested an option can be "name it". At this point, the task sequence is being used, and so is an appropriate moment to request small (but optional) additional user effort. If the user does this, it means that (i) the user has effectively agreed that these actions form a meaningful task chunk which can then be treated as atomic in further inference and (ii) the chunk has a meaningful name that can be used in future suggestions, or even to share with others.

6   Discussion

A key theme in this paper has been the interplay between data and action. Taking this seriously allows us to consider various forms of automated task support that would otherwise seem difficult or impossible. This is *not* to say that we should adopt a purely data-oriented view, but by that using data-focused analysis alongside ways to capture or inference more sequential or structured plans, we both create more robust inference and make the detection of structure easier. All of this is set within the context of interaction, some of which we can attempt to infer, and some, such as the deeper intentions of the user, we need to defer to the user's own decisions and control. Indeed, as we saw especially in the final discussion of the preceding section, we are likely to obtain more reliable results if we consider an ongoing dialogue of suggestion and observation rather than a more 'waterfall' approach of observe, infer then automate. Furthermore, such inference processes could easily operate symbiotically alongside more user-initiated scripting such as Apple Automator or Yahoo! Pipes, further increasing user control whilst still offering rich assistance.

With the exception of task threading, the work described in this paper is mostly implemented, but as distinct units, and we are working on bringing this together, within a unified architecture. For various reasons intelligent and adaptive interfaces, whilst continuing to have their strong advocates, got a bad name in the general HCI community for many years. Some of this was due to factors that still need to be treated with care: inappropriate choice of algorithms; the prevailing "user in control" ethos of direct manipulation; and detailed design issues, not least the lack of 'appropriate intelligence' in that often software is designed well for the test cases where it produced good results, but copes less well when the results are less clear. However, some of the problems were simply due to the limited computational power available 15 years ago – intelligent algorithms are typically expensive algorithms. With each PC one thousand times more powerful than during this early blossoming, and the raw computational power in the internet rivalling a (single) human brain, the times seem pregnant for more automated (but not autocratic!) assistance.

While the focus of the work described here is automated task assistance, broader lessons for human analysis and task design also emerge. We started with a non-automated, non-digital example of tea, milk and grapefruit. The focus on artefacts and physical objects as part of the task is central to understanding the errors that occur; and of course are also valuable for re-designing tasks and environments to prevent those errors occurring. The artefact-focus has also proved very powerful in uncovering long-term or complex tasks in the non-digital world [30]. Back in my keynote at the first Tamodia, I emphasised the importance of explicitly including artefacts and environment (both physical and digital) within task analysis. In this paper I have principally shown how taking into account the world of data can help the computer to predict, suggest and automate aspects of user tasks. If this can help the computer, it can help people. While there are exceptions (e.g. [31,32]), many forms of task analysis still portray the user's plans as largely pre-ordained and un-reactive ... effectively a disembodied user thinking and acting without recourse to the world. If the role of artefacts and data is fully represented in task analysis then this could lead to better systems designs that make available prompts and external resources to users; so that users' own choices and actions become easier, less cognitively taxing and less error prone: designing for the embodied user.

Acknowledgements

This paper is drawing on ongoing collaborative work with a number of people including: Tiziana Catarci, Yannis Ioannidis, Azrina Kamaruddin, Akrivi Katifori, Giorgos Lepouras, Nazihah Md.Aki, Estefanía Martín, Miguel Mora, Antonella Poggi, Devina

Ramduny-Ellis, and Costas Vassilakis. It was also supported by the EU funded DELOS Network of Excellence on Digital Libraries.

For links to related work please see:
http://www.hcibook.com/alan/papers/EIS-Tamodia2008/

References

1. Dix, A.: Managing the Ecology of Interaction. In: Pribeanu, C., Vanderdonckt, J. (eds.) Proceedings of Tamodia 2002 - First International Workshop on Task Models and User Interface Design, pp. 1–9. INFOREC Publishing House, Bucharest (2002)
2. Clark, A.: Microcognition,: Philosophy, Cognitive Science and Parallel Processing. MIT Press, Cambridge (1989)
3. Clark, A.: Being There: Putting Brain, Body and the World Together Again. MIT Press, Cambridge (1998)
4. Hollan, J., Hutchins, E., Kirsh, D.: Distributed Cognition: Towards a New Foundation for Human–Computer Interaction Research. In: Carroll, J. (ed.) Human–Computer Interaction in the New Millennium, ch. 4, pp. 75–94. Addison-Wesley Professional, Boston (2002)
5. Pandit, M., Kalbag, S.: The selection recognition agent: Instant access to relevant information and operations. In: Proc. of Intelligent User Interfaces (IUI 1997), pp. 47–52. ACM Press, New York (1997)
6. Nardi, B., Miller, J., Wright, D.: Collaborative, Programmable Intelligent Agents. Communications of the ACM 41(3), 96–104 (1998)
7. Wood, A., Dey, A., Abowd, G.: Cyberdesk: Automated Integration of Desktop and Network Services. In: Proc. of the Conference on Human Factors in Computing Systems (CHI 1997), pp. 552–553. ACM Press, New York (1997)
8. Dix, A., Beale, R., Wood, A.: Architectures to make Simple Visualisations using Simple Systems. In: Proc. of. Advanced Visual Interfaces (AVI 2000), pp. 51–60. ACM Press, New York (2000)
9. Stylos, J., Myers, B., Faulring, A.: Citrine: providing intelligent copy-and-paste. In: Proc. of the 17th Symposium on User Interface Software and Technology (UIST 2004), pp. 185–188. ACM Press, New York (2004)
10. Faaborg, A., Lieberman, H.: A Goal-Oriented Web Browser. In: Proc. of the Conference on Human Factors in Computing Systems (CHI 2006), pp. 751–760. ACM Press, New York (2006)
11. Hall, W., Davis, H., Hutchings, G.: Rethinking Hypermedia: The Microcosm Approach. Kluwer Academic Publishers, Norwell (1996)
12. Dix, A., Catarci, T., Habegger, B., Ioannidis, Y., Kamaruddin, A., Katifori, A., Lepouras, G., Poggi, A., Ramduny-Ellis, D.: Intelligent context-sensitive interactions on desktop and the web. In: Proceedings of the international Workshop in Conjunction with AVI 2006 on Context in Advanced Interfaces, pp. 23–27. ACM Press, New York (2006)
13. Dix, A., Marshall, J.: At the right time: when to sort web history and bookmarks. In: Proc. of HCI International 2003, vol. 1, pp. 758–762 (2003)
14. Haslhofer, B., Hecht, R.: Joining the BRICKS Network - A Piece of Cake. In: The International EVA Conference (2005)
15. Bottoni, P., Civica, R., Levialdi, S., Orso, L., Panizzi, E., Trinchese, R.: MADCOW: a multimedia digital annotation system. In: MADCOW: a multimedia digital annotation system. In Proceedings of the Working Conference on Advanced Visual interfaces, AVI 2004, Gallipoli, Italy, May 25 - 28, 2004, pp. 55–62. ACM, New York (2004)

16. Katifori, A., Vassilakis, C., Daradimos, I., Lepouras, G., Ioannidis, Y., Dix, A., Poggi, A., Catarci, T.: Personal Ontology Creation and Visualization for a Personal Interaction Management System. In: Workshop on The Disappearing Desktop: Personal Information Management 2008. CHI 2008 (2008)
17. Sauermann, L.: The Gnowsis Semantic Desktop for Information Integration. In: The 3rd Conference on Professional Knowledge Management, pp. 39–42 (2005)
18. Katifori, A., Vassilakis, C., Dix, A.: Using Spreading Activation through Ontologies to Support Personal Information Management. In: Common Sense Knowledge and Goal-Oriented Interfaces (CSKGOI 2008) (workshop at 2008 International Conference on Intelligent User Interfaces (IUI 2008). CEUR Workshop Proceedings, vol. 323 (2008)
19. Anderson, J.: A spreading activation theory of memory. Journal of Verbal Learning and Verbal Behaviour 22, 261–295 (1983)
20. Dix, A., Katifori, A., Poggi, A., Catarci, T., Ioannidis, Y., Lepouras, G., Mora, M.: From Information to Interaction: in Pursuit of Task-centred Information Management. In: DELOS Conference 2007 (2007)
21. Dix, A.: Towards a Ubiquitous Semantics of Interaction: phenomenology, scenarios and traces. In: Forbrig, P., Limbourg, Q., Urban, B., Vanderdonckt, J. (eds.) DSV-IS 2002. LNCS, vol. 2545, pp. 238–252. Springer, Heidelberg (2002)
22. Dix, A., Finlay, J., Abowd, G., Beale, R.: Human-Computer Interaction, 3rd edn. Prentice Hall, Harlow (2004)
23. Dix, A., Finlay, J., Abowd, G., Beale, R.: Chaper 15 sides. Online Teaching Resources for Human-Computer Interaction (2004),
    http://www.hcibook.com/e3/resources/
24. Asimakopoulos, S., Fildes, R., Dix, A.: Grammatically interpreted task analysis for supply chain forecasting. In: Proceedings of the 10th British HCI Conference, vol. 2, pp. 235–237. British Computer Society (2005)
25. Cypher., A.: Eager: Programming repetitive tasks by example. In: Proc. of the Conference on Human Factors in Computing Systems (CHI 1991), pp. 33–39. ACM Press, New York (1991)
26. Finlay, J., Beale., R.: Neural networks and pattern recognition in human-computer interaction. ACM SIGCHI Bulletin 25(2), 25–35 (1993)
27. Dix, A., Finlay, J., Beale., R.: Analysis of user behaviour as time series. In: Monk, A., Diaper, D., Harrison, M. (eds.) Proceedings of HCI 1992: People and Computers VII, pp. 429–444. Cambridge University Press, Cambridge (1992)
28. Lieberman, H.: Your wish is my command: programming by example. Morgan Kaufmann, San Francisco (2001)
29. Dix, A., Beale, R., Wood, A.: Architectures to make simple visualisations using simple systems. In: Proceedings of the Working Conference on Advanced Visual interfaces, AVI 2000, pp. 51–60. ACM, New York (2000)
30. Ramduny-Ellis, D., Dix, A., Rayson, P., Onditi, V., Sommerville, I., Ransom, J.: Artefacts as designed, Artefacts as used: resources for uncovering activity dynamics. In: Jones, P., Chisalita, C., van der Veer, G. (eds.) Special Issue on Collaboration in Context: Cognitive and Organizational Artefacts, Cognition, Technology and Work, vol. 7(2), pp. 76–87 (2005)
31. Task Analysis Through Cognitive Archeology Frank Spillers. In: Diaper, D., Stanton, N. (eds.) The Handbook of Task Analysis for Human-Computer Interaction, pp. 279–290. Lawrence Erlbaum Associates, Mahwah (2004)
32. Dix, A., Ramduny-Ellis, D., Wilkinson, J.: Trigger Analysis: Understanding Broken Tasks. In: Diaper, D., Stanton, N. (eds.) The Handbook of Task Analysis for Human-Computer Interaction, pp. 381–400. Lawrence Erlbaum Associates, Mahwah (2004)

Assessment of Object Use for Task Modeling

Sybille Caffiau[1,2], Patrick Girard[1], Dominique L. Scapin[2],
Laurent Guittet[1], and Loe Sanou[1]

[1] Laboratoire d'Informatique Scientifique et Industrielle, Téléport 2-1 avenue Clément Ader,
86961 Futuroscope Cedex, France
{sybille.caffiau,girard,guittet,sanou}@ensma.fr
2 Institut National de Recherche en Informatique et en Automatique, Domaine de Voluceau -
Rocquencourt- B.P. 105
78153, Le Chesnay, France
{Dominique.Scapin}@inria.fr

Abstract. Past research in task modeling suggests the need to introduce objects when using task models for the design of interactive applications. Objects are however rarely included in the task model notations and formalisms. Furthermore, when part of the formalism, their definition is usually informal; and the supporting tool does not generally take them into account for simulation. K-MADe is the first tool that fully uses objects for condition evaluations during task model simulation. This paper presents an evaluation investigating the usage of formal objects with K-MADe. The results show that whilst object concepts seem to be essential in the task model process, their usage and manipulation is not easy.

Keywords: evaluation, task models, objects, K-MADe.

1 Introduction

Designing interactive applications requires a good knowledge of what the users need. One method to gather users requirements is to build task models [1, 2]. Every task model formalism contains different elements to express the user activity such as task categories, scheduling operators and elementary attributes [3]. Many research on task model formalisms pointed out object definition as part of the essential elements in task modeling [4, 5], especially when task models are used to produce interfaces. This work concerns the analysis of the situation [6], the design of interfaces adapted to the context of use [7], or the generation of interfaces from task models [8]. Nonetheless, very few models actually include objects in their formalisms.

One interest of using a task model editor is the ability it offers to validate task scheduling along with the user. In order to facilitate this validation, task model editors contain simulation tools. To reach this aim, objects must be dealt with.

This paper presents an evaluation of the definition and use of task model objects. In order to perform this study, we used K-MADe as a tool support (the corresponding tool of the K-MAD formalism [9]). This tool has been chosen for two main reasons: first the object definition is formal (important aspect to validate task models) and

P. Forbrig and F. Paternò (Eds.): HCSE/TAMODIA 2008, LNCS 5247, pp. 14–28, 2008.

second, it is currently under development thus, the results of this evaluation will be used to improve the tool usability and usage. The first two parts of this paper present the objects used in task models, particularly in the K-MAD formalism and in its associating tool K-MADe. The following parts describe the various steps of the evaluation; going through the goal, participants, procedure, equipment, collected data and, at last, a critical analysis.

2 Objects in Task Models

Task analysis is essential to design interactive applications [10]. In order to facilitate the task analysis process, task models were developed. Due to the wide diversity of task model formalisms and notations, a comparison of the different systems [2] and their components was conducted [1]. This second comparative study highlights the presence of objects in the majority of formalisms to introduce domain models using references, or to embody them in task models. In this paper, we focus our study on task model formalisms that embodied objects.

As stated by Limbourg [1]: "A tool clearly facilitates the task modeling activity, hiding the model notation from the analyst and helping him or her capture it." p137. Moreover our evaluation necessitates the use of a tool. Thus, we looked at the use of objects in task model tools. Five task model formalisms (and their associated tool) correspond to these two criteria: CTT [11] (CTTE), Diane+ [12] (TAMOT), GTA [4] (EUTERPE), MAD* [13, 14] (IMAD) and K-MAD [15] (K-MADe). We will briefly present the use of objects in the tools before comparing them. Then, we describe in further details the use of objects, before comparing the tool we chose for our study, K-MADe.

2.1 Formalismes Using Objects

CTT (CTTE). CTTE objects [16] are a task property. They are characterized by: a **name** (string); a **"class"** among *string, numeric, object, description* or *position*; a **type** among *perceivable* (object presenting any information or allowing action of user) and *application* (intern in the system); an **access mode** (*only reading* or *modification*); a **cardinality** among *low, median* and *high*; and the **platforms** where the object is represented. To our knowledge, no documentation describes in details the concepts of class and cardinality. According to our use of the tool CTTE, we associate the need of the cardinality characteristic with the generation of interfaces [8] based on CTT diagrams. However, the CTTE simulation tool does not take into account objects and we only found some documentation relating to the use of objects for interface generation.

Diane+ (TAMOT[1]). The task model Diane+ integrates objects, named **data**, and uses them to define **conditions**. However, in the associated tool: TAMOT, the only editable condition is the pre-condition, expressed in the form of a string.

GTA (EUTERPE). In EUTERPE, objects are first class components. They are characterized by a **name** (string); a **list of attributes** (each attribute is composed of a

---

[1] http://www.ict.csiro.au/staff/Cecile.Paris/IIT-Track-Record-Past-Projects/Projects/Isolde/Tamot/Index.htm

name (string) and a **value** (string)); and a **list of users** (the users who can manipulate the object). The users are defined as **labeled agent**. Relations can be defined between agents and objects (*owner, create, destroy, use/inspect, change*). An **agent** is defined by a **name** (string); a **type** (*individual, organization* or *computer system*); and a **role** (a *set of tasks* performed by an agent). Moreover, EUTERPE allows the definition of **events**. These are composed of a **name** (string) and the **set of tasks** they are linked with (task set).

MAD* (IMAD). Two types of object are present in MAD*. They correspond to the object-oriented notions of class (**abstract objects**) and instance (**concrete objects**). Each **object** is composed of a **name** (string), a **number** (the *ergonomic number* corresponding to its place in the task tree (integer)), a **list of attributes**. The abstract object attributes are characterized by a **name** (string) and a **type** (*string, boolean, integer*) and concrete object attributes by a **name** (string) and a **value**. Some characteristics are addressed to abstract objects as a meta-class (generalizing link); a sub-class (specializing link); a condition of instance numbering (restriction to one instance). However, in IMAD the two types of objects are not differentiated. The user cannot give a value to IMAD object attributes.

K-MAD (K-MADe). K-MAD allows the definition of **entities** that characterize the environment of the user. These entities either represent what s/he handles or what influences the course of his/her activity. The various types of these entities are: **users** (set of users implicated in the activity); **events** (set of events that can be triggered or caused by the activity); **objects** (set of concepts handled by the user).

As for MAD*, objects can be abstract or concrete. Whilst abstract objects are composed of the characteristics of the objects that are manipulated by users in real world, concrete objects are instances of abstract objects. Each object possesses attributes: abstract attributes (belonging to abstract objects) are their characteristics. Concrete attributes, belonging to concrete objects, aim at associating a value to each characteristic defined by an abstract attribute. These objects are used to define pre-conditions, post-conditions and iteration conditions. K-MAD includes groups of concrete objects, in addition to the definition of the users and the involved events.

In this paper, we present an evaluation of the use of all these elements referred by the term "entities".

2.2 Comparison of Objects in Tools

Table 1 synthesizes the different paradigms used in the five task model tools. Only two of them define the notions of *events* and *users*; EUTERPE and K-MADe. In these two tools, they are associated with the tasks.

With the exception of TAMOT (which does not contain *data* of the model Diane+), all the tools contain the concept of objects and they can be split in two categories. First, the tools considering objects as task attributes (as CTTE), and then the tools considering objects as first class component of the formalism (as EUTERPE, IMAD and K-MADe).

Moreover, in CTTE, a particular object attributes is its cardinality. It is used to help designer define the interactive element presenting this object. In addition, perceivable objects may be a table or a window… thus this tool associates interactive objects to

Table 1. Comparison of concepts in task model tools

Tool	Events	Users	Objects	Conditions
CTTE			*Object*	pre-condition (String)
TAMOT				pre-condition (String)
EUTERPE	Event	Agent	Object	pre-condition (String)
				post-condition(String)
IMAD			Class	pre-condition (String)
				post-condition(String)
K-MADe	Event	Users	Abstract Object	pre-condition (Formal Expression)
			Concrete Object	post-condition (Formal Expression)

tasks. The introduction of these elements (cardinalities and perceivable objects) in task model formalism illustrates the link between objects and interface presentation.

This definition is close to a system point of view, whereas in all others tools, object concepts aim to be closer with to ergonomic point of view. Whilst objects defined in CTTE are concrete (a value is associated to the object since its definition), IMAD does not allow giving a value to object attributes, staying in an abstract level of definition. This level of definition freezes the manipulation of task model objects.

All the formalisms include pre-conditions associated to the tasks. Their validations are mandatory for the execution of the tasks. Then, to allow the validation of task models by the user and thus, the verification the task scheduling (using simulation), these conditions need to be computed. In order to compute them, definitions of objects and conditions have to be formal. Among all the tools, whilst K-MADe allows these formal definitions, all others define conditions using non-computing string.

Due to this possibility of computation of expressions (for instance during the simulation of task models) using these objects, the degree of K-MADe object definition is limited (i.e. object is composed of predefined types) while objects in EUTERPE may be composed of other objects.

After observing two types of object definition in task model formalisms, we can define three groups of tools according to the type of object definitions. Firstly, a group of tools with a low level of formal definition (i.e. containing definitions allowing no verification (as IMAD, TAMOT and CTTE)). Secondly, the medium group, containing EUTERPE, that does not contain formal objects but defines formal relationships between them and tasks. Last, the more formal tool, K-MADe allows formal definition of objects and conditions, which allows using objects during simulation. As we stated in the introduction, this possibility seems essential for our purpose.

3   Presentation of the Tool K-MADe

K-MADe (K-MAD environment) [9, 15] has been developed to model, manipulate, and evaluate the K-MAD formalism. It implements the different characteristics of the K-MAD model. We used it to perform our evaluation of the usage of objects in task models. In section 3.1, we give a general presentation of K-MADe. Section 3.2 outlines the specificities to use objects in the tool.

18   S. Caffiau et al.

3.1 General Presentation

The K-MADe tool is targeted towards people wishing to describe, analyze, and formalize activities of human operators or users. It allows the creation of task models
concerning non-computerized or computerized experiments, real-world or simulated
situation, on the field or in laboratory. Whilst all kinds of profiles are possible, this
environment is particularly intended for ergonomists and HCI specialists. Due to the
wide range of user's background and skills, the tool allows different levels of description, from simple graphics to detailed mathematical expressions using the following
available tools:

- A graphic editor of the K-MAD task model. It uses direct manipulation techniques
  to build, handle and cancel tasks (label 1 in Figure 1).
- Editors of task characteristics (see the list above). Label 2 in Figure 1 indicates
  one of the three representations it provides.
- An editor of abstract objects, users, events and concrete objects. Objects can be
  added, modified and removed. The editing and removal of objects implies the
  modification of all associated objects. *Sheets* (label 3 in the Figure 1) allow to access these object definition editors.
- An editor of expressions for pre-conditions, post-conditions and iterations. The
  tool is able to check the grammar of expressions, and to evaluate them.
- A simulator that allows animating task models.
- Tools for analysis of task models (statistical, coherence, queries…).
- A tool for printing task trees and task characteristics.

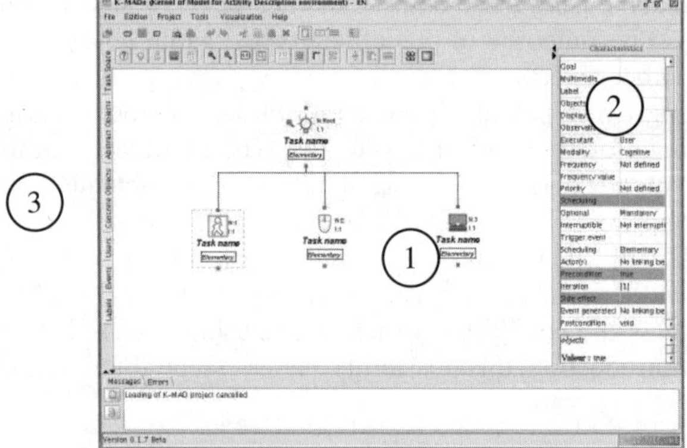

Fig. 1. The main window of K-MADe tool

3.2 Objects in K-MADe

Several K-MADe components are dedicated to the different entities we previously
mentioned. We classify them into two groups; components for editing and components for usage.

Entity edition. Each K-MAD entity is defined using different windows. Editing events and users is equivalent to textually label them and eventually to add a description to them. Contrary to these basic and informal definitions, editing objects is more detailed. Two different windows allow the definition of the two object types; one for abstract objects and one for the concrete ones. The Figure 2 presents the window for editing abstract objects. Types of object attributes (label 1 in Figure 2) are defined among usual programming types (boolean, string, integer). Moreover, concrete objects are accessible only through groups of abstract objects, thus in the abstract object editor, groups are editable (label 2 in Figure 2).

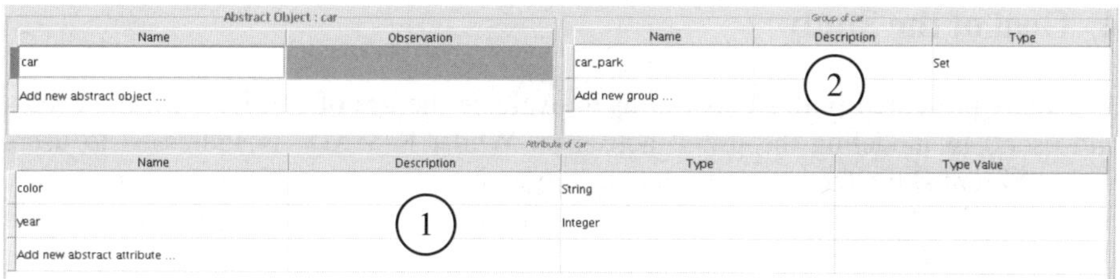

Fig. 2. The K-MADe abstract object editor

The Figure 3 from [15] shows relationships between abstract objects, concrete objects and groups.

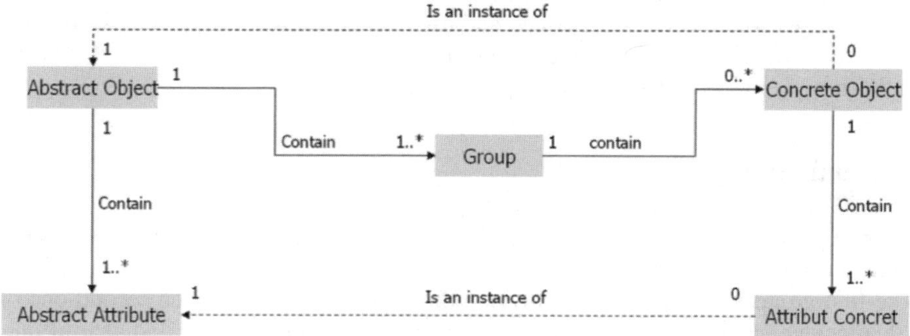

Fig. 3. Relationships between abstract objects, concrete objects and groups

Object usage. K-MADe entities are used to characterize task events (triggered and generated), conditions (pre, post and iteration) and authorized users. The designer chooses from the set of defined ones to associate users and events with task. Conditions (using objects) are edited using the calculator based on B semantics [17]. A special kind of calculator is dedicated to each condition type. Figure 4 shows the calculator for the pre-condition edition. Once edited the conditions can be used to help simulate and consequently validate task models.

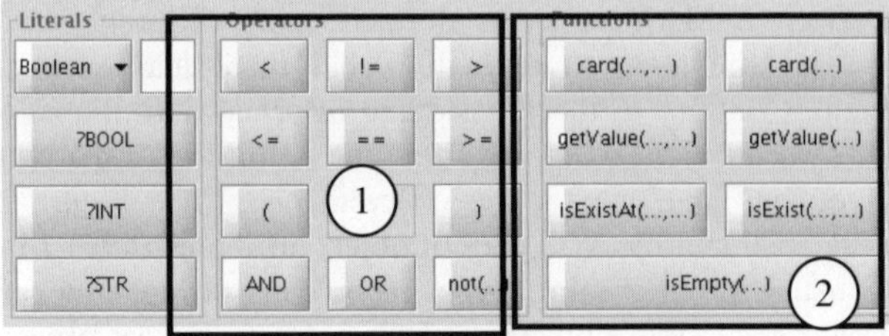

Fig. 4. Pre condition editor calculator

4 Goal of the Study

The study presented in this paper aims to evaluate the use of entities (objects, events and users) in modeling the users' activities. Whilst K-MADe is addressed to users with different skills (computer scientists, ergonomics…), the participants to our study are students in HCI. The target of our evaluation is using task models for application design. K-MAD task model formalism was developed to present the different steps of the task analysis, staying in the task analyst point of view. Thus, the entities are not described using developer vocabulary. For example, the term "class" is not used to identify the abstract object concept. In order to better understand why entities are/can be used, we focus on two aspects: the role they play for users and what consequences their use have on task models. Following these aspects, we separated our study into two evaluations.

The first evaluation aimed at defining schemas of modeling processes focusing on the processes where entities are edited and used. In the second evaluation, we investigated the difficulties related to these concepts: the understanding of the tool, and the definition of models using K-MADe.

5 Participants

All participants were students in their fourth year of French university. There were split into two groups, each participant performing only one of the two evaluations. The first group was composed of 48 bio-informatics students, and the second one of 20 computer science students (studying computer science since their first year of university). Only one computer science student (participant in the second evaluation session) is not French speaker. However, they all attended the same HCI course. This course focuses on user-centred design and where task modeling is presented. The K-MAD formalism was explained in details in the lecture (approximately 4 hours) and students practiced task modeling using K-MADe before the evaluation (approximately 6 hours, performing some task models checked by tutors). Then, even if they are not modeling experts they were more trained to use a task model notation than ergonomic task model experts [18].

The second part of this course was focused on evaluation (basic concepts of evaluation and main methods used in evaluation [19]). As students play the role of evaluators, the protocol applied in this survey is used as an example in order to facilitate their future evaluation workload. However, as this study was their first practical evaluation, their participation was limited to the observation and its annotation. Moreover, their notes were completed with other data.

6 Evaluation Method

In order to perform this evaluation, we used a widely used evaluation technique [19]: real-time expert observation of subjects using the tool. In this part, we will present the experimental procedure, the directives that were given to the participants, and finally, the method used to complete the expert's evaluation.

6.1 General Organization

The two evaluations were performed with a gap of one month between the first and last evaluation. Each evaluation followed the same process. All students were paired. During the first session, one student acted as task model designer (using K-MADe, labeled *user*), while the second acted as the expert (named *observer*). They reversed roles during the second session. Each session lasted one hour and a half with a fifteen minutes break between sessions. The activity to model was the same for all students and it was introduced in French at the beginning of the sessions.

6.2 User Work

The user had to model the activity of completing a volley-ball game marking sheet. Instructions for this activity were given at the beginning of sessions. They were composed of the official instructions of the French Federation of Volley-Ball (FFVB) and two examples of marking sheets (completed and non-completed ones). K-MADe was used to model the tasks to perform.

6.3 Observer Work

During modeling, observers insured that their user verbally described their modeling process, and annotated what they observed concerning the use of the tool by the user (hesitations, exploration in several parts of the software without actions and so on.). In order to help observers in their evaluation, we gave them observation sheets (illustrated in Table 2). These sheets were mainly composed of a three columns table corresponding to the three types of information recorded for each observation:

- The type of the observation among a set of defined categories (user goal (G), tool functionalities (F), functionality utilization (FU) and information (I)).
- The observation in textual form.
- The time of observation.

6.4 User-Logs and Questionnaires

In order to complete the observers' notes and the task model performed, we used two others types of data.

Table 2. Observation sheet example

Type	Observation	Temps
FU	The principal window is not accessible ("simulation" is noted on but the simulation window is not accessible too). => launch again K-MADe	14h32
G	looking for the object definition	14h34 14h37
F	user does not understand the signification of the button with shell-hole	14h40

User-Logs. To complete the observations realized during the evaluation, the users in the first evaluation used a version of K-MADe with sneaks. These ones allowed keeping track of user's actions using timestamps and produced a text-file (the user-log). Particularly, this log indicates when the user enters and exits each K-MADe tool (task space, abstract objects, condition editions (pre, post and iteration)…). Figure 5 shows an example of information in this file.

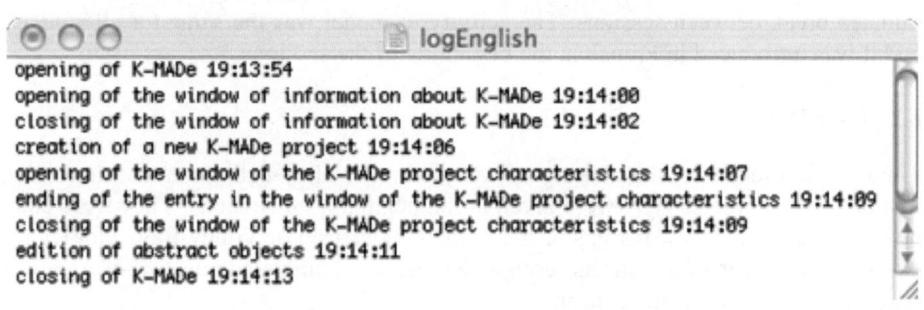

Fig. 5. Illustration of data recorded in the user-log

Questionnaires. Participants were asked to complete a questionnaire in French about the use of objects in the second session of the evaluation. This questionnaire was composed of five questions on definitions, object deletions and conditions.

7   Data

As each of the two evaluations tried to reach different goals, we did not collect the same data for both experiments. In this section, we present the results of each study. Table 3 resumes the data gathered according to the session and the evaluation goal.

7.1   Collected Data

First evaluation. The first evaluation session aimed at analyzing the task modeling process, particularly when the K-MAD entities are defined and manipulated. In order to obtain this information, we used user-logs and notes from the observers. These two types of information allow the collection of two complementary data. While the observer is focused on the user usage, what her/his goals are and how s/he conceptually model, the user-logs give information on how the K-MADe components are used. Using timestamps on both data, we can determine how users use K-MADe tool components.

Moreover, we requested of each student to exploit their notes and the user-log to write an evaluation report. It includes the modeling process of the observed people, his/her use and usage of the tool, and an analysis of the resulting model. Whilst the produced documents were then readable and quite organized, models, observer notes and user-logs were also collected for analysis.

This first evaluation session helped to determine when K-MADe entities were used in the general modeling process. However we did not collect any precise information about their usage, the second session aims to answer this question.

Second evaluation. As for the first evaluation, the user's behavior was reported in the observer notes and a document was written to report clearly their observations. However, user-logs do not gather information about entity usage thus we did not use them for this session. In order to analyze K-MADe entity usage, we considered two types of data: the models and the questionnaires. Verification of entities in the resulting models indicates the degree of understanding of the object concept. Questionnaire analysis (associated with the student report analysis) aims to inform us on the difficulties and the needs of using objects.

Table 3. Data gathered and its goal

Session	Data	Goal
1	- user-log	user activity when modeling
	- observer-student notes	student-user comportment
	- student exploitation document	writing report of the notes
	- model	verification of student analysis
2	- observer-student notes	student-user comportment
	- student exploitation document	redaction of their notes
	- model	validation of object definition and usages
	- questionnaire	object concepts

7.2 Selection of Data

During the first evaluation we collected one folder per user. It included the observer notes, the user-log, the observer exploitation document and the task model. This study aimed at gaining some understanding on the modeling process. The data used to deduce users modeling process was mainly taken from user-logs. This file was automatically generated without any technical problem. However, we did not want to use these user-logs without taking into account the context (reproduced in the observer-student notes and exploitation document). Two of the folders were not complete and therefore were not included into the analysis. We ended up considering 46 out of the 48 folders in our analysis.

The data used for the second evaluation included all the information in the folders, we could therefore only consider the fully-completed folders. However whilst for the first analysis the observer notes, the student exploitation document and the task models were only used to help us give a context to the user-log data, for the second one they were essential. During this evaluation process, we observed that the only non-French speaker student could not understand all the directives (this observation was confirmed when he ought to complete the questionnaire). He was therefore not considered in the analysis. The second part of our evaluation is based on 19 complete folders.

8   Object Definition and Use in Task Modeling Process

Prior to identify the intervention of objects in the task modeling process, we observe that some students did not define objects. Indeed, 26% of users (12/46) of the first session evaluation did not try to define (or use) any K-MAD object. However, we cannot precisely identify why. Two reasons may explain the absence of these elements in task model process: the limited duration of the experiment, or the non-assimilation of object concepts. Student notes and reports did not allow us to identify the main reason. Six participants indicated that the sessions were not long enough but others (6/12) did not give any relevant information on the subject.

From the 34 remaining folders, we identify three main schemas followed by user to perform task models. The most used ones (43,75%) are divided into two steps. Firstly, the user composes the task tree (decomposes tasks). Secondly, s/he iteratively edits entities and associates them with tasks. Steps of the second most used schema (28%) are sequential. The user performs the task decomposition prior to define all entities, and then associate them with the tasks (using conditions). Moreover, an incomplete process (followed by 22% of user-students) is composed by the first two steps of the second schema. The last schema is the iteration of the second one. The Figure 6 resumes the fist and the second schemas.

These observations give us some understanding on the place objects have in the task modeling process. As an example, the concurrent definition of objects and task tree composition indicates that the user associates objects and tasks. On the contrary, when the definition and the use of objects are separated with the task tree composition, we can deduce that the user defines objects only to use them on conditions. Therefore, objects bear the role of associating properties and tasks for some users.

```
task tree composition;
While (time is not finished)
{
    edit objects;
    define    properties    using
them;
}
```

```
task tree composition;
edit objects;
define    properties    using
them;
```

Fig. 6. Schemas of student task modeling process

From the data gathered in both evaluation sessions, we want to identify what are the elements used during the task modeling process. Table 4 shows how many students define each task model component. According to these results, few users integrated the concepts of *events* (20% in the first evaluation and 26% in the second) and *users* (20% and 10,5%) in the task modeling process. On the contrary, the major part of the first evaluation users and all user-students of the second defined the objects (abstract and concrete objects) to model the activity.

Table 4. Users defining each of K-MADe elements

	Event	User	Abstract Object	Concrete Object	Group	Pre	Post	Iteration
1	20%	20%	74%	60%	74%	40%	40%	20%
2	26%	10,5%	100%	100%	100%	84%	89,5%	84%

The definition of event and user objects is textual. Associating them with tasks is easy using selection among the defined elements. On the contrary, the abstract and concrete objects are composed of several concepts. Thus, the difference of the use between these two types of concepts (composed and non-composed ones) cannot be explained by the level of difficulties of the definition.

However, Table 4 indicates also the proportion of users using pre, post and iteration conditions. In the first evaluation session, these three types of object manipulation were widely used in the task modeling process (84% defined at least one pre-condition, 89,5% defined at least one post-condition and 84% defined at least one iteration condition). Prior to edit these conditions, the user needs to define the objects (abstract objects, concrete objects and groups). Then, the objects may be defined only to allow the definition of conditions. Therefore, users did not conceived objects as a part of tasks but as a way to define conditions.

From these numbers, we observe that for the majority of students, it is natural to define objects in order to complete the semantics of scheduling operators. As an example, a volley-ball game ends when one team wins at least 3 sets, no matter of the score of the other team. This condition for the end of a game cannot be expressed using only scheduling operators. All students naturally defined it using objects and conditions.

The study of the proportion of definition of K-MADe concepts of the two sessions shows a difference between the two groups. In the first evaluation, 26% of users do not use any entity. All participants followed the same lecture then, the explication of this gap cannot be found in this teaching. However, these groups do not have the same background. Numbers shown in Table 4, clearly indicate that formal object definitions are easier to be used for computer scientist students.

9 Object Usages

Students use K-MADe in order to define and use entities in task modeling process. Our evaluation aims to understand conceptual and procedural usages of objects. All analysis presented in this part are based on the data gathered in the second evaluation.

9.1 Conceptual Usages

Even if second evaluation students integrated entities in task modeling and used them (in pre, post and iteration conditions), 58% of them noticed that some of these concepts were not understood. These difficulties did not affect the concepts of events and users, used less (26% use events and 10,5% use users) but that were easy to use.

On the contrary, concepts of abstract objects, concrete objects and groups represented respectively 72%, 64% and 27% of difficulties of understanding. Likewise, the use of conditions was not understood by 10,5% of users. 87,5% of users that did not understand the concept of abstract objects (resp. concrete objects), did not also understand the concept of concrete objects either (resp. abstract objects).

The definitions of these two types of objects are very closed, thus the difficulty of using objects seems to be the link between them. This analysis is supported by another observation. Whilst all students indicate that they wanted to edit and use objects, one of them could not describe his definition of objects (abstract, concrete objects and groups).

As we said before, in K-MADe, the manipulation of the concrete objects necessitates the use of groups (label 2 in Figure 2). The role played by the group concept represents a difficulty of conceptual understanding for 67% of users of the second evaluation (we did not collect the point of view of the participants of the first evaluation). Firstly, they indicate that they do not understand why the groups are required for the definition of concrete objects showing the non-understanding of the relationship between concrete objects and groups (shown in Figure 3). Secondly, K-MAD does not allow the definition of the number of elements in groups. Then, the users regret the need to define a group to use only one concrete object.

9.2 K-MADe Object Usages

Our evaluation highlights difficulties from the use of K-MADe to manipulate concepts. Some of users need to edit the K-MAD concepts in several steps. Therefore, 42% of users indicated the need to edit again at least one abstract object and 37% at least one concrete object. Concerning the definition of groups, the proportion is more important because nearly one student out of two (47%) did not define every group at the first attempt.

We did not gather any information about the modifications done during the edition of objects. However, 42% of users indicated that they wanted to delete at least one abstract object, 63% at least one concrete object, and 47% at least one group. These needs seem to indicate that modifications are important on objects. Moreover, they confirm the conceptual understanding difficulties shown preliminarily.

K-MAD (abstract and object) objects are composed of attributes. K-MADe allows to define them with a name and to associate a type of value (or the value for concrete object). The available types of value (label 1 in Figure 2) respectively are boolean, integer and string. These types are used by 58%, 89,5% and 42% of users. The variety of available types are widely used, as only one 37% of users used a unique attribute type to define objects (string or integer).

As users are computer scientists, they are familiar with attribute types. Therefore, they do not find difficulties in understanding and using type attributes. Due to their background, they feel necessary to define other types of attributes such as date, hour or defined objects. Moreover, they indicated the non-understanding of the need of groups to define the concrete objects (58%).

Naming attributes, objects and groups requires the respect of a particular syntax without stresses, underscores and spaces. However, the tool does not indicate these syntactic rules and automatically changes spaces in the names (when the users put them). As these modifications are done automatically (without either any intervention of the users nor any indication), the consequent errors during the condition computations were not understood by the users. 30% of the users indicate they showed this error type during the modeling process.

Then, the last observation concerns the manipulation of objects via calculators. To allow the manipulation of objects and the combination of them, there are operators (label 1 in Figure 4) and defined functions (label 2 in Figure 4). The use of this second type of elements induced some problems. In the tool, there are not any explications either about the sense of the functions, nor to precise what are the order and the type of parameters

10   Conclusion and Future Works

In this paper, we presented an evaluation of the use of the object concept using a task model tool; K-MADe. The data gathered during the evaluation supports the theoretical idea that objects are part of task models. In order to formally express conditions (and complete the scheduling of the task decomposition), the introduction of objects in the modeling process appears intuitive for the participants of our evaluation. However whilst the necessity of the definition of these task entities does not cause any conceptual difficulty for participants, using them is more difficult.

Users indicated some lacks in the tool that influence their task model process: for example, the limitation of object attribute types (no date or hour format) or the impossibility to define an object composed of others (as EUTERPE proposes).

In addition, we observe two major difficulties in the usage of task model objects. Firstly, some of them, the events and the users, are not used and then, do not seem to be understood by users. In the lecture these concepts were presented along with the others thus the lack of usage seems due to the concepts themselves, either to their presentation in the tool or to their definition. No evaluation data allows to precise this fact. Secondly, defining formal conditions using objects is not user-intuitive. Reasons of this difficulty may be the use of the calculator (non-intuitive) or the representation of objects (that need to be naturally manipulated). In order to improve this usage, we need to modify the calculator and presentation of objects.

However, the participant's skills in computer science do not allow us to generalize our observations to all users. Moreover, as we shown before, a minor difference of skills considerably modifies the usage of objects (see Table 4). In order to gain a broader point of view, the same type of evaluations with other background participants has to be performed.

Last, this evaluation aimed at understanding the usage of objects on task modeling process. However in K-MADe, objects are taken into account in the simulator tool then, a research plan of experimental studies will be performed investigating the role of objects in the task model validation step.

References

1. Limbourg, Q., Vanderdonckt, J.: Comparing Task Models for User Interface Design. In: Diaper, D. (ed.) The Handbook of Task Analysis for Humain-Computer Interaction, pp. 135–154 (2004)
2. Balbo, S., Ozkan, N., Paris, C.: Choosing the Right Task-modeling Notation: A Taxonomy. In: Diaper, D., Stanton, N.A. (eds.) The Handbook of Task Analysis for Human-Computer Interaction, pp. 445–466 (2004)
3. Lucquiaud, V.: Sémantique et Outil pour la Modélisation des Tâches Utilisateur: N-MDA. Thesis. Poitiers, 285 (2005)
4. Van Der Veer, G.C.: GTA: Groupware Task Analysis - Modeling Complexity. Acta Psychologica, 297–322 (1996)
5. Dittmar, A., Forbrig, P.: The influence of improved task models on dialogues. In: CADUI, pp. 1–14 (2004)
6. Van Der Veer, G.C., Hoeve, M., Lenting, B.F.: Modeling Complex Work Systems - Method meets Reality. In: Green, T.R.G., Canas, J.J., Warren, C.P. (eds.) 8th European Conference on Cognitive Ergonomics (EACE), INRIA, Le Chesnay, pp. 115–120 (1996)
7. Calvary, G., Coutaz, J., Thevenin, D., Limbourg, Q., Bouillon, L., Vanderdonckt, J.: A unifying reference framework for multi-target user interfaces. Interacting With Computers 15/3, 289–308 (2003)
8. Paternò, F., Santoro, C.: One model, many interfaces. In: Kolski, C., Vanderdonckt, J. (eds.) Computer-Aided Design of User Interfaces (CADUI 2002), Valenciennes, Frances, pp. 143–154 (2002)
9. Baron, M., Lucquiaud, V., Autard, D., Scapin, D.: K-MADe: un environnement pour le noyau du modèle de description de l'activité. In: Robert, J.-M., David, B. (eds.) IHM 2006, Montréal, Canada, pp. 287–288 (2006)
10. Hackos, J.T., Redish, J.C.: User and task analyis for interface design. Wiley, New York (1998)
11. Paternò, F.: Model-Based Design and Evaluation of Interactive Applications (2001)
12. Tarby, J.C., Barthet, M.F.: Analyse et modélisation des tâches dans la conception des systèmes d'information: la méthode Diane+. In: HERMES (eds) Analyse et conception de l'IHM, interaction pour les Systèmes d'Information, vol. 1, Paris (2001)
13. Gamboa, R.F., Scapin, D.L.: Editing MAD* task description for specifying user interfaces, at both semantic and presentation levels. In: Harrison, M.D., Torres, J.C. (eds.) Eurographics Workshop on Design, Specification and Verification of Interactive Systems (DSV-IS 1997), Granada, Spain, pp. 193–208 (1997)
14. Scapin, D., Bastien, J.-M.C.: Analyse des tâches et aide ergonomique à la conception: l'approche MAD*. In: Kolski, C. (ed.) Analyse et conception de l'I.H.M. / Interaction Homme-Machine pour les S.I., Paris, France, vol. 1 (2001)
15. K-MADe electronic reference, `http://kmade.sourceforge.net/`
16. Paterno, F.: ConcurTaskTrees: An Engineered Notation for Task Models. In: Diaper, D., Stanton, N.A. (eds.) The Handbook of tTask Analysis for Human-Computer Interaction, pp. 483–501 (2004)
17. Lano, K.: The B Language Method: A guide to practical Formal Development (1996)
18. Couix, S.: Usages et construction des modèles de tâches dans la pratique de l'ergonomie: une étude exploratoire
19. Nielsen: Usability Engineering (1993) ISBN 0-12-518405-0

Task Model-Based Usability Evaluation
for Smart Environments

Stefan Propp, Gregor Buchholz, and Peter Forbrig

University of Rostock, Institute of Computer Science,
Albert Einstein Str. 21, 18059 Rostock, Germany
{stefan.propp,gregor.buchholz,peter.forbrig}@uni-rostock.de

Abstract. Task models are widely used within the research field of HCI for the model-based development of interactive systems. Recently introduced approaches applied task models further to model the cooperative behavior of people using devices within a smart environment. We describe a method of model-based usability evaluation to evaluate interactive systems, with a particular focus on smart environments, which are developed based on task models. We consider the evaluation in early development stages to interactively walk through the models and in later stages to execute a test case within a real environment. The paper provides results of a prototypical implementation.

Keywords: Model-based Usability Evaluation, Task Models, Smart Environment.

1 Introduction

Today, model-based development methods are well-accepted in the field of designing Human Computer Interaction systems. For instance, models are used to describe the user tasks that are to be supported by the system and to specify various environmental aspects, like involved devices and user roles. Based on such models, user interfaces can be developed in a semi-automatic sequence of transformations preserving the models' structure. We are interested in an integration of usability evaluation in all development stages, and will outline (1) the general model-based approach and (2) existing tool support for usability evaluations and then (3) focus on the specific challenges of task-model based development of smart environments and (4) their evaluation.

1.1 Model-Based Software Development

A primary concern of this methodology is that software engineers and user interface designers base their work on the same models: the task model, user model, business-object model and the device model as a representative of a general environment model. These models are as well the basis for the development of the software developed by software engineers as those for the user interface experts. Software development is seen as a sequence of transformations of models that is not performed in a fully automated way but by humans using interactive tools. In [9], the idea of

P. Forbrig and F. Paternò (Eds.): HCSE/TAMODIA 2008, LNCS 5247, pp. 29–40, 2008.

supporting the development of task models by patterns is shown. Task models in this approach are constructed in CTT (Concurrent Task Trees) [6] notation, describing single actions and their hierarchical and temporal relations. One of the tools called DiaTask [8] allows developing a dialog graph that represents the navigation structure of the interactive system. Such a graph is based on the previous specified task model. A dialog graph consists of a set of nodes, which are called views and a set of transitions. There are several types of views to specify different characteristics in terms of visibility, activation and composition. End views are final points in (sub-) dialogs. Each view is characterized by a set of navigational elements. A transition is a directed relation between an element of a view and a view reflecting navigational aspects of user interfaces. DiaTask allows to assign several different dialog graphs to one task model, thus providing support for the development of systems with different user interfaces for different devices and/or groups of users. Given a task model and one or more dialog graphs a simple WIMP style abstract user interface can be generated wherein each task placed on a view is represented by a button on a XUL window. This prototype is refined by a pattern-based replacement of the buttons with more detailed components that help really fulfilling the tasks symbolized by the buttons. The finished UI still keeps the links to the initially task model intact, thus providing an interface to track the users' actions with the system in terms of executing tasks.

1.2 Model-Based Usability Evaluation

There are some approaches to employ task models in usability evaluations. We will have a look at two of them and afterwards introduce the specifics of model based development of smart environment.

The tool RemUsine with its extension MultiDevice [7] uses task models to describe the expected (planned) behavior of users and compares it to the output of another tool component: the tool logger, which is supposed to be available at client-side. The logging tool stores several types of system events during the test session. To provide automatic analysis of the actual user behavior, possible system events have to be mapped to tasks represented by leaf nodes in the task model. This association has to be done once for several user sessions. The tool then provides assistance in analysis by pointing out, at which parts of the tracked user actions the associated task execution violates temporal or logical relations in the task model. The component MobileLogger protocols different types of system and environment variables and includes a dialog based input form for entering these environment conditions. Finally, the tool supports the evaluator in analyzing this potentially huge amount of data by offering different graphical visualizations.

Another tool, developed closely oriented on the model-based development approach outlined above, is the ReModEl ("REmote MODel-based EvaLuation") client-server system [1]. Herein, no mapping of system events to tasks is necessary. One client-side module captures any task-related events within an application developed following the semi-automatic generation and replacement process. These events are sent to the server as they occur and are stored for subsequent requests. An evaluation expert can connect to the server with the same client software but different modules and observe the events related to one or more specific executions. Thus, same-time but different-place evaluations are provided. The client-module shows several information about the execution, e.g. an animated task tree. There are other modules that allow communication between several clients for example and support subsequent analysis.

1.3 Model-Based Development of Smart Environments

Recent developments aim at transferring the model based development approach into the field of smart environments. We believe that both the actions of users in the smart environment and the functionality of devices within it can be modeled as task models.

The description of each device's capabilities with a task model chunk (device functionality model, DFM) can be found in [12]. The idea is that each time a new device connects to the room's infrastructure its DFM fragment is added to the current task model, referred to as room task model (RTM). Within this process, the combination of available DFMs may provide some new functions, e.g. the conjunction of a scanner and a printer offers a copying functionality. Based on that, the "Task-Constraint Language" (TCL) was introduced in [11]. The actions of every user in the room are described by a task model and constraints specify the modalities of collaboration, e.g. that person "A" finishes his presentation, to give person "B" the floor. Important enhancements have been suggested by Feuerstack et al. [2], extending the task model notation CTT to serve as a runtime model. For that purpose, domain concepts are annotated and an object flow is modeled; different users' task models are synchronized with domain objects.

1.4 Model-Based Usability Evaluation for Smart Environments

Our objective is to provide usability evaluation methods for model based smart environments in all development stages. Because of the models being an inherent part of the system there is no need to parse any log-files in order to extract task-related information. Instead of that we can utilize the task model engine as the source for relevant events. During design time, this engine is used to simulate and animate the underlying models and during run time it acts as the logic within the smart environment providing assistance to the users.

The approach presented in this paper integrates usability evaluation activities in the development process. Furthermore, we believe that software developers and usability experts do not only benefit from working on the same models, but also profit from working in the same environment and interdigitating their work.

Figure 1 shows the process in principle - based on the models (described in section 2) a test case is developed as described in section 3. In section 4 the execution of a test case is explained. Finally, section 5 discusses the analysis of the gathered data.

We define an evaluation scenario as a set of users and devices, each characterized by properties and specific task models. Every user owns one or more roles and all roles are characterized by a certain task model. Every device is associated with one or more types described by a set of properties and a usage model in a CTT like notation, which defines how a device is used. To evaluate a smart environment based on a specific modeling technique the task model chunks to describe user behavior and

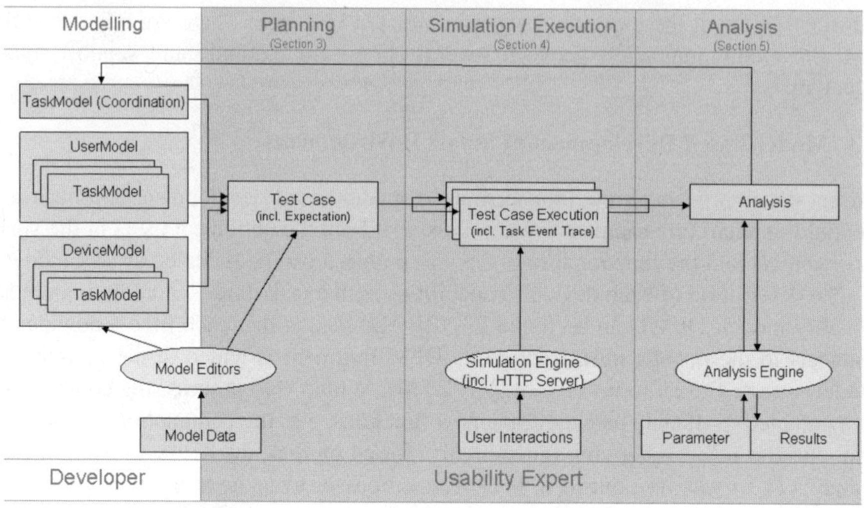

Fig. 1. Usability Evaluation Process

device usage are mapped to CTT notation and additional information is annotated. The aim is to track the interaction between user and environment and validate the interaction according to the model in an analysis stage.

2   Usability within Task Model-Based Software Engineering

In this section we will firstly introduce the vocabulary used in the following. Afterwards, the evaluation approach is presented.

2.1   Disambiguation

According to [6] a task model TM is seen as the sum of possible task traces TT. The hierarchical tree composition from actually executed tasks as leaf nodes and abstract tasks as inner nodes represents the logical structure of the root task that is divided into sub tasks. Within the activities described by a TM there is no contemporaneous execution of any two tasks. At any moment during the execution only one task can be running. This restriction causes some difficulties in describing cooperative work and ongoing activities with several devices in a smart environment. To allow the specification of interactive systems with more than one user acting simultaneously, CTT has been extended to Collaborative ConcurTaskTrees (CCTT) [5]. The main principle in CCTT is to introduce a coordination task tree specifying the relations and interaction between several other task trees that describe the different users or roles involved. In those role-depending task trees a new kind of nodes (connection tasks) is introduced to specify temporal dependencies to connection tasks within another roles' task model. The coordination task model describes these temporal dependencies. In our approach to model the behavior of users and the functionalities of devices we use such separate models for each role and device. Beyond this, Sinnig et al. [11] further extended CCTT in order to consider the fact that each role is typically fulfilled by different users. Therefore, for each user a copy (instance) of the corresponding role task model is created. The various instances are executed concurrently during runtime and the task constrain language (TCL) specifies synchronization points between several instances.

For evaluation purposes the view on the execution of a specific task is more detailed taking into account the different possible states of a task. States can be enabled, disabled, running, suspended, done, and skipped. Each state change of a task, be it a leaf node or inner node, is called a task event and the execution of a model based system is described as a sequence of such events called Task Event Trace (TET). Events occurring as a result of other events (e.g. the finishing of task "A" enables the execution of task "B") are placed beyond the causing event in the sequence.

During the preparation of a usability evaluation of a smart environment system an expected behavior is specified called Expected Task Event Trace (ETET). This ETET is used during the evaluation and the afterwards analysis to compare the actual behavior of users and devices with the expected.

2.2 Brief Overview

This section describes the evaluation process in principle, details of evaluation techniques and visualizations can be found in the subsequent sections.

For smart environments in the development stage we suggest a test setup wherein at least two experimenters act as mediators between the smart environment room and the task model interpreter. Such "Wizard of Oz"- experiments are a common technique for early stage tests of window based software systems and have been conducted within a large number of projects.

The goals of the evaluation can be divided into two sub goals: One aim is to validate the task models (models for roles, devices and the coordination task tree) and the other one is to identify weak points in the environment's sensors and the interpretation of the users' behavior. We will outline the procedure of a usability evaluation and point out, which kinds of problems are addressed.

The evaluation's preparation starts with the definition of a scenario that is to be carried out by one or more users in the smart environment room. Therefore, the task models of all devices and roles participating in the proposed scenario are gathered and an expected behavior has to be developed. This can be done by recording a usage session conducted by experts or by defining a trace manually.

The users taking part in the evaluation are now instructed to fulfill the tasks defined in the scenario. They do not know the complete task models in detail but only the goal and a list of sub goals so as to avoid them to behave more unnatural than inevitable.

During the evaluation the experimenters are provided with all information that is produced by the sensors in the smart environment room, video streams from cameras placed in the SE and an audio stream to keep track of the users' activities. Furthermore, the current states and properties of the devices are displayed. All these data flows are recorded to be used in subsequent analysis, too. We developed an Eclipse plug-in to simulate multiple task trees describing a role's action or a device's capabilities and functions. An experimenter can define a set of task trees for an evaluation and activate the simulations simultaneously. Each time the experimenter observes an action he journalizes it using the task model simulation.

Another expert is responsible for initiating the effects on devices in the SE. Tasks marked as system tasks in the device models are started and stopped in the simulation and delivered as commands to the appropriate devices. Thus, the information flow out of and into the smart environment room is complete: Observed actions are recorded using the manual triggered model simulation and an additional protocol for tasks not modeled so far, and the environment's reactions are simulated by an operator sending the commands to the devices in the smart environment room. The users performing activities in the smart environment room interact with the room devices as if the task model engine was triggering them according to the task models. The subsequent analysis of the recorded events reveals several shortcomings of the SE system developed so far.

The next sections show how to prepare and conduct such an evaluation using the tools that are developed.

3   Planning a Usability Evaluation

Within Eclipse all artefacts and documents necessary to conduct a usability evaluation are defined in a UsabilityTestCase file. This includes a description of the evaluation preparation and environment as well as a definition of the test case that is to be executed. According to [9] the test plan specifies the required resources, focuses the points to test, and serves as a communication tool between the different members of the working team. It includes a high level description of the test's purpose, a list of all the questions and objectives that are to be solved by the test as precise as possible, a description (profile) of all users involved, a detailed description of the test execution, a list of tasks to be carried out by the users in an appropriate level of abstraction, and a description of the used equipment and of the level of participation or neutrality of the test conductors. In the context of model-based smart environments also the task models of both user roles and device types are included, too. The definition of the test executions can include instructions for the usability experts to ask questions to the users during and/or after the test execution. These questions are linked to tasks in the according task model and the links can contain filter criterions to define several questions as to be asked under specific circumstances only.

All information about one single execution of such a UsabilityTestCase is gathered in a UsabilityTestCaseExecution file. Here, the recorded task event traces and the description of the actual setup are stored. It also contains comments and notes made by the usability experts during the evaluation. Figure 2 shows some elements in a usability evaluation: The task models of users and devices as well as some artefacts that are involved in the test case.

4   Conducting a Usability Evaluation (Simulation/Execution)

Now a usability test case is defined, which comprises a description of the test plan, the physical environment (e.g. needed device types) and involved user roles. This abstractly defined test case can be carried out several times with different concrete users and concrete devices, which fit into the defined user roles and device types. Conducting the same test case several times with slightly different parameters ensures the statistical significance of the test result. It further allows identifying infrequently occurring usability issues and comparing the behavior of different users.

4.1 Capturing a Task Event Trace

During the usability evaluation the users are observed and the users' interactions are captured. Capturing can be accomplished at different levels of abstraction, beginning with low level events at the physical level (e.g. mouse clicks and a person changing the location), up to the problem-oriented level (e.g. a person gives a presentation) [3]. We capture the interactions corresponding to an underlying task model, which describes for instance the behavior of a certain user role. Each record of the captured task event trace comprises a time stamp, the conducted test case, the task model, the task, the fired event and the success value. The applied task model simulation engine [8] instantiates a task model and conducts a simulation through receiving events from user interactions and exchanging events between task nodes within the task model. Events cause state changes of the task nodes. For instance a task with the state "enabled" is caused by the event "start" to change the state to "running" and a subsequent event "stop" leads to the state "finished". Depending on the current state of a task, some events are prohibited. For instance a task with the state "enabled" can not react on a "stop" event, because the task has to be started first. In these cases no state change occurs, but nevertheless the event is captured and marked as not successfully processed. Beyond the events which are directly influenced by the user interactions and sent to the leaves of the task tree, there are a lot of events exchanged between inner nodes of the task tree. A task which changes the state sends a notification event to the parent node which updates the own state and sends notifications to the other children and the own parent. We have enhanced the task model simulation engine to capture all these events as a task event trace.

4.2 Simulating and Executing an Evaluation

The task model simulation engine can be used at different stages of the development of the smart environment. In early stages the task models can be simulated to evaluate the content and structure of the task model. In later development stages the task model based developed smart environment can be evaluated. We provide tool support to simulate the execution of a smart environment. The figure below depicts the simulation UI. The left hand side provides the design time view at the usability test case. The right hand side provides the runtime view at the test execution. Every element of the test case on the left is simulated as a task model at the right. A graphical symbol in front of every task within the task tree reflects the current state of the task instance. For instance a red cross marks a task as "disabled", a green circle as "enabled" and a blue tick mark as "finished". The user triggers the simulation progress via context menu. Each leaf task provides a menu to fire the events "run", "start", "stop" and "crash", depending on the current state of a task. "run" is a composition of "start" and "stop". "crash" aborts the execution of a certain task. The different task models are simulated concurrently.

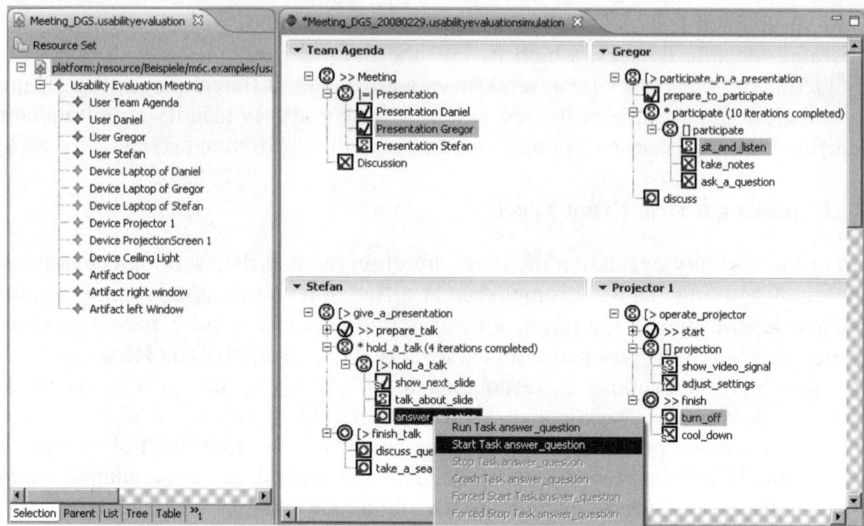

Fig. 2. Usability Evaluation UI to execute a Test Case

To evaluate a real smart environment, the task engine can also be applied. The behavior of the users within the environment, like moving to the presentation zone or switching a projector on, has to be recognized and a corresponding event has to be sent to the task model simulation engine. We provide two complementary ways: on the one hand a HTTP connection to connect external devices to the simulation engine and on the other hand a "Wizard of Oz"-based technique with a human operator.

(1) We enhanced the simulation engine with an HTTP server to receive external events from various sources like a smart environment. A HTTP request from the smart environment contains the destined task and the event. The task is defined by the test case, the task model, and the contained task. A smart environment is equipped with sensors to detect the user behavior and to provide user support accordingly. Therefore the fulfilled tasks are recognized within the normal execution of the environment and subsequently used to trigger the task models executed within the simulation engine. In the case that the smart environment deploys a different modelling technique, the tasks have to be elicted and mapped to models for the simulation engine. Events can only be sent to leaf tasks. The events "start", "stop" and "crash" are supported. A test case execution registers at the server to receive events. For every incoming event, the corresponding test case is determined and the destined task model and task instance. After sending the event the task model engine reacts accordingly and changes the states of the destined task and the dependent tasks. The task event trace is enhanced. If an event is currently prohibited, the event is captured as failed within the event trace. The HTTP response contains optionally a success notification, the resulting set of enabled tasks or the caused events as captured in the task event trace. During the test execution the evaluation UI (figure 2) is concurrently updated to visualize the current state of the environment.

(2) A "Wizard of Oz"-experiment can be conducted alternatively for smart environments which are not directly connected to the simulation engine and therefore are

not able to deliver the recognized user interactions. An additional person observes the interactions within the environment. This observer transfers the user behavior into the simulation engine. The user interface depicted in figure 2 allows to manually trigger the simulation engine. The advantage of this manual process is that an observing person perceives even unexpected situations and copes with them. For example an unforeseen task which was fulfilled by a user can be captured for later analysis. But in a more complex environment the observer might be overstrained by the vast amount of events, which have to be manually processed. Hence we recommend combining both evaluation techniques. Most tasks are fulfilled according to the defined task model and therefore can be captured with the HTTP connection between smart environment and evaluation engine. Some tasks are unforeseeable and can only be captured by a human observer.

When executing a usability evaluation we basically distinguish between three types of tasks according to the task model:

(a) A user fulfills a task which is currently allowed in the task model. The observer triggers the task with the appropriate event in the simulation engine.

(b) A user fulfills a task which is contained within the task model, but currently prohibited due to temporal relationships. In the evaluation UI we provide the option "forced start" to capture the start of a task immediately. The evaluation engine captures the event as failed, but doesn't affect the task model state. A "forced stop" ends a task in an analog way.

(c) A user fulfills a task which is not defined within the task model. The evaluation UI provides the observer with the option to enter an additional task, which is captured as failed event within the task event trace analog to (b).

The evaluation UI depicted in figure 2 can be deployed in different situations. In early development stages it is used to simulate a walk through the task models and to check their consistency. After the smart environment is set up, the HTTP connection to a real environment triggers the evaluation UI and additional manual events can be sent.

5   Analyzing the Results of a Usability Evaluation

During the execution of a test case interactions are captured as task event trace. This data can be analyzed at the same time or later after conducting a test. Conducting the analysis in parallel to the test has the advantage that issues are recognized immediately offering the opportunity of giving support to test users. For instance if an issue is already known from another test, but currently not fixed, it might be beneficial to provide the users with help to save time and discover further issues.

An analysis is based on a single test case and an arbitrarily chosen number of test case executions of the same test case. Hence an analysis can examine both a single test execution in detail and several different executions in comparison to each other. Comparing several executions allows varying a specific parameter for detailed evaluation while preserving the other parameters. Examples are the evaluation of differences of specific user groups (e.g. novice vs. advanced users), under certain context influences (e.g. light intensity, furniture arrangement) or alternative implementations of the smart environment. The task models describe the behavior of people and the potential usage of the devices on an abstract level, leaving out the implementation details. Different implementations can satisfy the specified task models and a comparison identifies individual strengths and weaknesses. We suggest employing some expert users to carry out the test case first and compare their task performances to other users'.

Figure 3 continues the example from section 4 and depicts the analysis in parallel to the evaluation. The left hand side contains the evaluation of a test case, while the right hand side shows a visualization of the current evaluation progress.

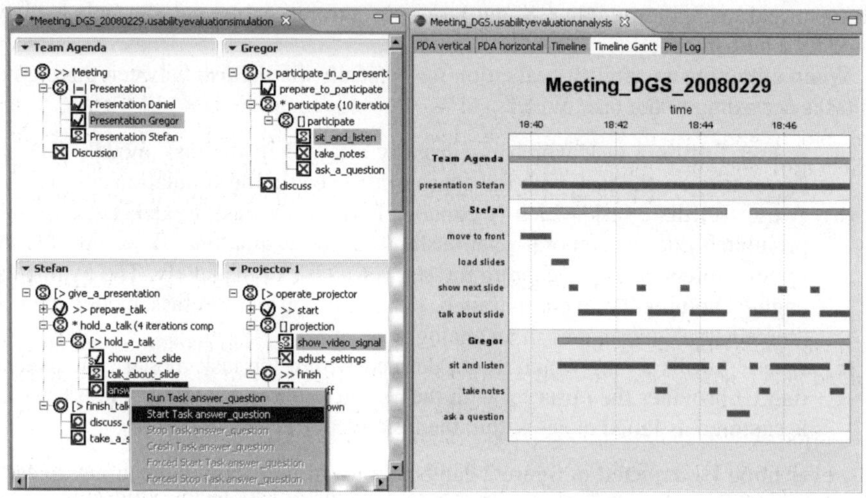

Fig. 3. Analysis of a Usability Test Case

The gantt chart depicts the interactions of the ongoing meeting according to a timeline. The completed tasks are grouped by their task model. A task model is printed in bold case and the duration of executions of the containing tasks is depicted as a green bar. The already started leaf tasks of the task model are depicted as blue bars to indicate their duration. The different task models are executed concurrently.

The captured task event trace serves as basis to derive the input data for the analysis and visualization. The leaf tasks executed by users are extracted and the successfully as well as the failed events are taken into account. Failed event executions reflect a conflict between user behavior and task model, because a user in a smart environment can always choose freely which task to execute. For instance the user can suddenly skip the presentation because of a headache even if the task model doesn't consider this exception. Therefore the evaluation UI allows the observing expert to capture this unexpected task, while the event execution is marked as failed according to the specified task model. Unexpected tasks are depicted as a red bar. A bar depicts the duration of the task execution, while a task is in the state "running". Therefore the events "start", "stop", "crash", "suspend" and "resume" are analyzed.

Depending on the individual interest of the usability evaluation the captured data can be filtered and aggregated. Filter options comprise the filtering according to the minimum and maximum duration of tasks, the start and end time, the involved users and devices. Furthermore data is prepared by aggregation. If there is a huge amount of executed tasks, which are very short and represent a high level of detail, a sequence of leaf tasks with the same parent node within the task model can be aggregated to a higher abstraction level.

An additional normalization step is applied when comparing multiple event traces of different evaluation executions. When different persons fulfill the same task and differ in the needed time, this might be an indicator for a usability issue. But in some cases we faced the problem that the normal working speed was greatly varying and there was no system related issue, e.g. if one tester needs significantly more time for changing slides forth and back with the presenting device. We overcome this problem by normalization of the durations of the task sequence, which proceeds as follows: the expert chooses a task and a certain user. The according time captured during observation is compared to the other users' and for each user is a factor derived. The factor is applied to all tasks of the respective user. As a result the duration of slower users is stretched and the duration of faster users is compressed. We suggest designing a short calibration task and appending it in front of the evaluation. As an alternative all overall durations can be set to the same duration, to compare all users at a 100% basis.

Furthermore timelines are provided to compare different test case executions at a glance. Parallel lanes depict different executions of the same test case with different persons and in addition to [4] the normalization can be applied.

6 Conclusion

In this paper we presented a usability evaluation approach for the task model-based evaluation of interactive systems, particularly for smart environments. Within a smart environment a task can be accomplished cooperatively by a number of users, while changing the devices during executing a task. For instance a user can begin a task on a mobile phone with speech input and fulfill the task on a laptop with keyboard. An interaction trace based only on physical events alone is in this case not sufficient, because it is difficult to compare voice and keyboard input. Therefore we enhanced the physical interaction trace with device independent information on the task level. We defined usability test cases based on task models, to capture task event traces. A subsequent analysis and visualization allows the identification of usability issues. For interactive systems, which are designed with task models, the identified issues within the task models are directly related to the design model. Hence the problem can be tracked back to the cause within the development stage.

To provide tool support we enhanced an existing task model framework with usability evaluation facilities. Hence the evaluation is directly integrated into the model-based development process and allows rapid usability testing at different development stages.

Future research avenues comprise a case study to evaluate our technique within our smart environment. This will help us to discover strengths and weaknesses based on real data.

Acknowledgments. The work of the first author was supported by a grant of the German National Research Foundation (DFG), Graduate School 1424.

References

1. Buchholz, G., Engel, J., Märtin, C., Propp, S.: Model-Based Usability Evaluation - Evaluation of Tool Support. In: HCII 2007, pp. 1043–1052 (2007)
2. Feuerstack, S., Blumendorf, M., Albayrak, S.: Prototyping of Multimodal Interactions for Smart Environments based on Task Models. In: AMI 2007 Workshop on Model-Driven Software Engineering, Darmstadt, Germany (2007)
3. Hilbert, D., Redmiles, D.: Extracting Usability Information from User Interface Events. ACM Computing Surveys 32(4), 384–421 (2000)
4. Malý, I., Slavík, P.: Towards Visual Analysis of Usability Test Logs. In: Coninx, K., Luyten, K., Schneider, K.A. (eds.) TAMODIA 2006. LNCS, vol. 4385, pp. 25–32. Springer, Heidelberg (2007)
5. Mori, G., Paternó, F., Santoro, C.: CTTE: Support for Developing and Analyzing Task Models for Interactive System Design. IEEE Trans. Softw. Eng. 28, 797–813 (2002)
6. Paternò, F.: Model-Based Design and Evaluation of interactive applications. Springer, Heidelberg (1999)
7. Paternò, F., Russino, A., Santoro, C.: Remote evaluation of Mobile Applications. In: Winckler, M., Johnson, H., Palanque, P. (eds.) TAMODIA 2007. LNCS, vol. 4849, pp. 155–168. Springer, Heidelberg (2007)
8. Reichart, D., Forbrig, P., Dittmar, A.: Task Models as Basis for Requirements Engineering and Software Execution. In: Proc. of. TAMODIA, Prague, pp. 51–58 (2004) ISBN 1-59593-000-0
9. Rubin, J.: Handbook of usability testing. In: Hudson, T. (ed.) Wiley technical communication library (1994)
10. Sinnig, D., Gaffar, A., Reichart, D., Forbrig, P., Seffah, A.: Patterns in Model-Based Engineering. In: Proceedings of CADUI 2004, Madeira (2004)
11. Sinnig, D., Wurdel, M., Forbrig, P., Chalin, P., Khendek, F.: Practical Extensions for Task Models. In: Winckler, M., Johnson, H., Palanque, P. (eds.) TAMODIA 2007. LNCS, vol. 4849, pp. 42–55. Springer, Heidelberg (2007)
12. Trapp, M., Schmettow, M.: Consistency in use through Model based User Interface Development. In: Trapp, M., Schmettow, M. (eds.) Workshop at CHI 2006, Montreal, Canada (2006)

From Task to Agent-Oriented Meta-models, and Back Again

Steve Goschnick, Sandrine Balbo, and Liz Sonenberg

Interaction Design Group, Department of Information Systems, University of Melbourne, 3010, Australia
{stevenbg,sandrine,l.sonenberg}@unimelb.edu.au

Abstract. In the research discussed here, in addition to extracting meta-models from numerous existing Agent architectures and frameworks, we looked at several Task meta-models, with the aim of creating a more comprehensive Agent meta-model with respect to the analysis, design and development of computer games. From the agent-oriented perspective gained by examining the resultant extensive agent meta-model – named ShaMAN – we then revisit the Task Analysis research domain, and consider what benefits Task Analysis and Modelling may draw from the Agent-oriented paradigm.

Keywords: Agent-oriented, Task Models, Multi-Agent Systems, Meta-model, Agent Meta-models, Task Meta-models, Software Engineering, Computer game development, Agents in computer games.

1 Introduction

Agent-oriented (AO) architectures and methodologies are the main interest area of the research outlined here, with a focus on the application domain of computer games. In addition to extracting meta-models from numerous existing Agent architectures and frameworks (not covered in this paper), we looked at several Task meta-models, all with the aim of creating a more comprehensive Agent meta-model with respect to the analysis, design and development of computer games. From the agent-oriented perspective gained by examining the resultant extensive agent meta-model – named ShaMAN – we revisit the Task Analysis research domain, and consider what benefits Task Analysis and Modelling may draw from the Agent-oriented paradigm.

1.1 Motivation for Task Models in AO Meta-model Research

A modern sophisticated computer game can be characterised as a mixed-initiative multi-agent system – meaning that interaction happens between the human users/players, and various game-based synthetic characters, which have a high degree of proactive autonomous behaviour. In addition to being multi-agent in nature, such games also involve multiple users, playing alone or in guilds (teams). AO researchers have predominantly been intent on putting intelligence into artefacts (e.g. trading systems, robots, simulations, etc.), with only a small percentage concerned with mixed-initiative human-agent systems [9,11,12], such as computer games.

P. Forbrig and F. Paternò (Eds.): HCSE/TAMODIA 2008, LNCS 5247, pp. 41–57, 2008.
© IFIP International Federation for Information Processing 2008

The specification of goals in agent systems usually begins in analysis with the identification of high-level, motivational goals. Lower level tasks and actions become a focus of endeavour in the AO SDLC when an agent system is being implemented.

Task Analysis (TA) began with a keystroke-level interest in the things that humans do with technology. While the purpose of TA is to understand the user's activity in the context of the whole human-machine system for either an existing or a future system [6], a task model helps the analyst observe, think, record and communicate the user's task activity [18].

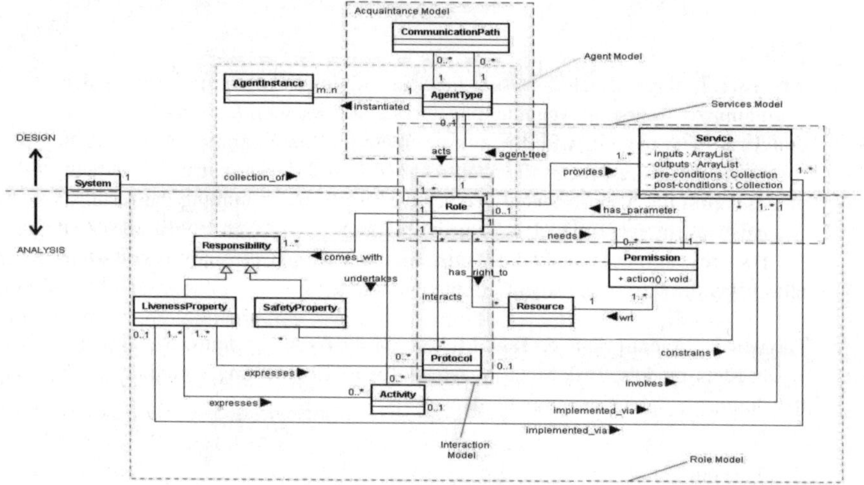

Fig. 1. Meta-model of GAIA V1 in UML, with models superimposed

In a strong sense TA and AO began at the opposite ends of the design spectrum with very different agendas, one bottom-up and people-oriented, the other top-down AI-oriented. While there are several task meta-models that draw from a cognitive top-down perspective, several of which we draw upon in this research – e.g. HTA, TWO, and TKS – there are few agent meta-models that include activities down at the user keystroke level. It seems intuitively obvious that TA ought to have lessons for AO, particularly in mixed-initiate AO systems, including computer games.

1.2 Meta-models

Much of the research discussed here is centred around meta-models expressed in either: UML class diagram notation, or Entity Relation (ER) notation [3], the adoption of which requires a little explanation up front.

Modelling in a Visual Notation, Comparing Meta-models in UML. In agent-oriented research and in computing in general, modelling expressed in some form of visual representation is used to communicate, build and document complex systems and artifacts. In complex systems no single diagram type can most effectively express and communicate all of the concepts and ideas encountered – a particular notation is designed to best encapsulate one or two aspects of the complexity. The UML language for example has no fewer than 13 diagram types from which to choose a representation that best suits a particular aspect and phase of an object-oriented (OO) system or application. Meta-models expressed in UML class diagrams are now commonly used in both the AO [2,13,14] and OO [20] research domains: to represent state-holding entities; to communicate base ideas; and as a useful means to compare different agent systems or architectures [7,14]. To facilitate the process of comparison, it is useful to represent as many aspects of an architecture as possible in a single meta-model diagram.

In the well-known GAIA agent-oriented architecture [28,29] there are distinct models for: Roles, Interaction, Agent, Service and Acquaintances – several with unique notations. However, figure 1 is a single condensed meta-model of GAIA – the dotted lines superimposed over the entities, representing the Roles, Interaction, Agent, Service and Acquaintances models, each a subset of the meta-model.

Agent Concepts. Given that there is no universally accepted single meta-model for AO systems at present, when we first looked to agent concepts and architectures with computer games in mind, we examined the meta-models of several well-known agent architectures and methodologies (AAII [19], GAIA [28,29], Tropos [2,13], TAO/MAS-ML [5], Prometheus [21]) and several that are less well known (ROAD-MAP [16], ShadowBoard [10,11], GoalNet [22]), to explore the commonalities and differences between them. In addition, given our identification of a gap in the AO paradigm down at the input device event level, we included in our study several well-known meta-models from the Task Modelling field. For space reasons this paper discusses the Task meta-models, but not the agent meta-models.

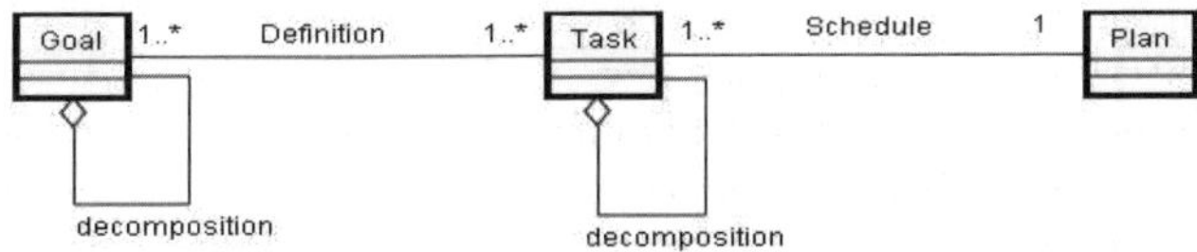

Fig. 2. HTA Task Meta-model in UML notation

Cognitive Task Meta-models Examined. According to Annett [1], HTA is best regarded as "a generic approach to the investigation of problems of human performance within complex, goal-directed control systems". HTA focused on system goals and plans, where other approaches at the time focused on observable aspects of performance. In contrast to a behaviouralist view, the cognitive approach taken by HTA envisaged human behaviour as goal-directed and controlled by feedback. HTA Tasks describe lists of actions needed to achieve a particular goal state. Goals may have sub-goals in a hierarchical fashion. Tasks represent specific user actions in a goal-directed activity. They can be hierarchical with sub-tasks linked to sub-goals (see decomposition relationships in figure 2). Plans are like recipes to achieve a task, controlling sequence and timing.

The Task World Ontology (TWO) model from Groupware Task Analysis (GTA) [26,27], is a generic task analysis model that includes as its primary entities: Event,

Task, Goal, Agent, Role and Object, all of which except Object are like-named entities of primary interest to most Agent meta-modellers. In addition, TWO includes several many-to-many relationships, including Responsible and Plays.

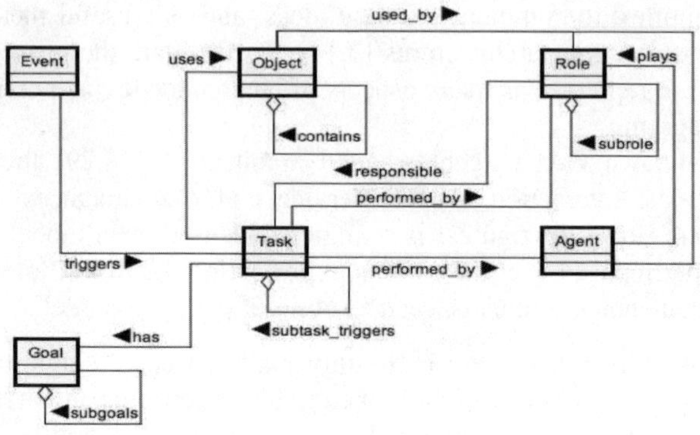

Fig. 3. TWO Task World Ontology model in UML notation (adapted from [27])

The GTA is of specific interest to us, as it stemmed from task analysis in the Computer Supported Cooperative Work (CSCW) field, thereby involving multiple users and complex contexts.

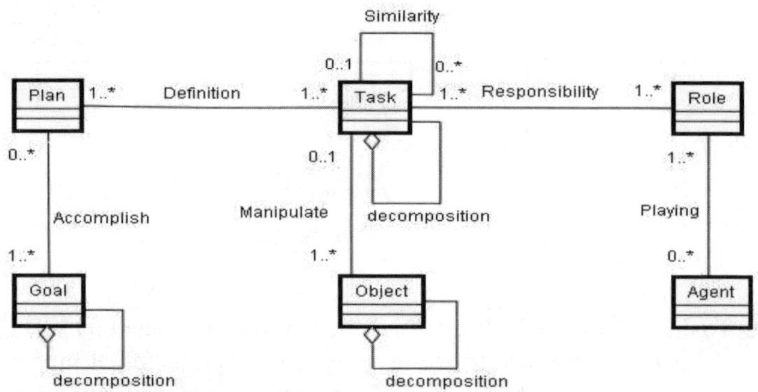

Fig. 4. The Task Knowledge Structure (TKS) Meta-model in UML

Johnson and Johnson [15] developed the Task Knowledge Structure (TKS) model to support the design phase of the SDLC. It details task hierarchies, objects hierarchies (the decomposition relationships in figure 4 represent hierarchies – e.g. subtasks of a task, recursively) and knowledge structures. It aimed to represent the knowledge a user has stored in their head regarding tasks. The user is represented by an Agent in the model. The Role/s that a user takes on, each have Responsibilities that are manifested in a set of Tasks to be done.

Additionally, we looked at GOMS [18] and the DIANE+ [25] task modelling language, which will not be introduced here for brevity sake.

Overview. In Section 2 we introduce the ShaMAN agent meta-model proper. In order to explain the entities in figure 5 efficiently, we present several groupings of the entities from the meta-model in detail, and then describe the flexibility they bring to building applications using the model. In Section 3 we compare some concepts from the ShaMAN meta-model with the Task meta-models investigated. In Section 4 we highlight some challenges that others have raised for Task Modelling. In Section 5 we describe how Task modeling may be enriched by AO concepts, addressing some of those challenges highlighted in Section 4.

2 The ShaMAN Meta-model

At a fundamental level, an agent meta-model is an entity model, thereby abiding by all the conventions of a notation that an application model adheres to. In this research, in a bottom-up design manner, we applied normalisation [17] to a superset of the agent concepts found in the agent meta-models (AAII, Gaia, Roadmap, GoalNet, TAO, Tropos, ShadowBoard and Prometheus), in several task meta-models (HTA, TKS, GOMS and the Task World Ontology (TWO) from Groupware Task Analysis (GTA) together with a few concepts needed by computer games, and arrived at a normalised agent meta-model named ShaMAN, presented in figure 5. (Nb. The normalisation process is not documented here for space reasons).

As a normalised model ShaMAN is both: flexible to ongoing requirements upon the meta-model itself (should it need future enhancements); and is a model least susceptible to anomalies arising from changes of state with respect to the existing concepts represented in it. The following sections describe the main sub-sections of the ShaMAN meta-model in more detail.

2.1 Locales for Computer Games

The domain of applications of interest to us in this research is computer games, which invariably interact with the player through the usage of a human-machine interface, for example a screen of one size or another. The Locale sub-section of the ShaMAN model lets us model the visual metaphors and the screen interaction between player/user and screen characters of a game, right in the AO model itself. It is an abstraction that is suitable for games and other rich media applications, without modelling specific widgets in a UI library. While several of the agent meta-models investigated do have constructs for the agent environment, none specifically model the computer screen as the primary representation of the environment to the user.

In ShaMAN, this screen representation of a sub-section of the agent's environment is called a Locale in homage to Fitzpatrick's [8] definition of a Locale as a generalised abstract representation of where members of a Social World [23] inhabit and interact. Figure 6 represents that sub-section of the ShaMAN meta-model that represents Locales within games. Note: the simplified crows-foot (zero, one or many) ER notation for cardinality, is used in these detailed figures of sub-sections of the meta-model, to increase the general readability.

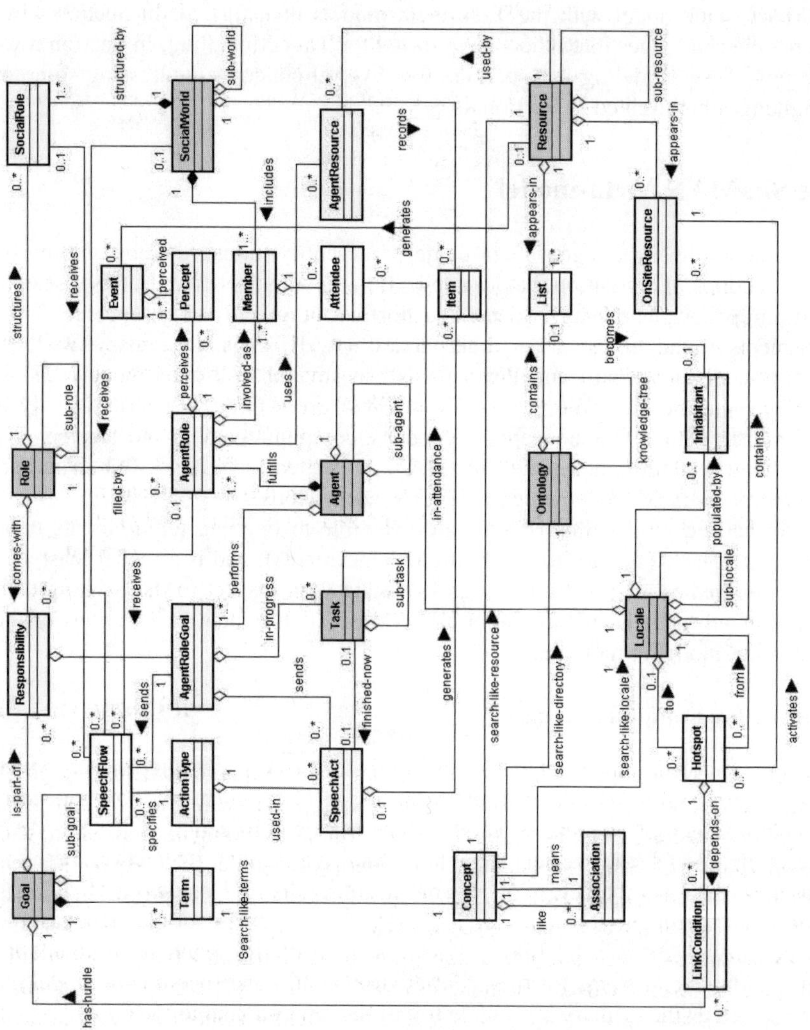

Fig. 5. The ShaMAN Agent Meta-model

The Locale entity may have sub-locales thereby allowing hierarchies of Locales. Locales are a generic concept representing some spatial construct presentable on the screen, e.g. rooms, outdoor areas, sections of a board-game, etc. - suitably broad enough for novel game interfaces. By way of describing the entities in figure 6, we will refer to the game screen in figure 7 as a concrete example of Locale.

The screen depicts the office of the player's character within the game BranchOut, and that room is represented as a Locale in ShaMAN. The HotSpot entity represents any area on the screen that is interactive, in the sense that whenever the user either clicks or passes over that area on the screen (or if a HotSpot has the focus, from a keystroke point-of-view), certain interaction between the user and the game may take place – for example clicking on the filing cabinet draw opens a window that displays the contents of the draw. HotSpots are a generic concept for such screens, whether the game presents a 2D, 3D or something abstract, the interaction with a standard display is 2D and involves area. HotSpot has two relationships with Locale, one named to and the other named from – enabling navigation between Locales.

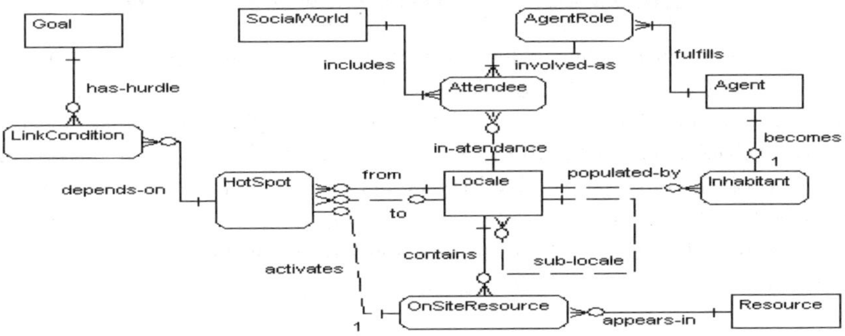

Fig. 6. The Locale sub-section of the meta-model

A HotSpot may also link to an OnSiteResource entity. These are Resources that live in the Resource entity which may involve a hierarchy of Resources. Resources are typically programmed entities that are not Agents in their conception nor development, but they may also represent real objects in the real world. The digital clock on the wall in figure 7 is a fully-functioning clock object, and when clicked-on, displays a fuller interface to the digital clock Resource. OnSiteResource is an associate entity – a representation that allows the same Resource to be used in multiple Locales, e.g. a clock in many rooms drawing upon the same programmed code.

A HotSpot may also have a relationship with the entity LinkCondition, which in turn links to a Goal via a relationship called has-hurdle. This allows the game developer to enforce conditions to be met: e.g. before the player may advance to another Locale, or before they may use a particular Resource.

Locale is also directly linked to two other entities: Attendee and Inhabitant. Attendee is an associative entity that records all occupants in a particular Locale over time, retaining a record of when agents (or human avatars) entered the Locale and when they left it, if they are no longer present. It is linked to the agent's Role during that

Fig. 7. Depiction of a Locale in a Computer Game being developed using ShaMAN

occupation via AgentRole, and also to the SocialWorld they were engaged in when they did so. This history aspect of the Attendee is usefully in providing and recording a back-story for any particular agent-oriented game character – a necessary aspect of realistic game creation. In contrast to Attendee, the Inhabitant entity represents the current occupants of the Locale. It has a direct link to the Agent entity, and is used when the overhead of SocialWorlds and agent Roles are not a concern.

2.2 Communication Via SpeechFlow

Some computer games have large numbers of agents and very often these agents are categorised by the roles they serve. When it comes to communication between agents, there is the need for communication at several levels: one-to-one; one-to-a-group of agents in a particular Social World; one to all agents filling a specific role (e.g. Captain). Note: Human players (human-in-the-loop) are considered to be agents, from the system's point of view. The SpeechFlow sub-section of the ShaMAN meta-model as portrayed in figure 8, addresses these three required levels of communication in gameplay. In addition, it addresses Events from non-agent Resources.

The SpeechFlow entity is at the heart of all interaction within ShaMAN – including events generated by Resources. An agent communicates to other agents or to humans-in-the-loop by generating an instance of SpeechFlow. It does so while acting in some Role, working upon some Goal associated with that Role. The entity that represents the instance of those two things for a particular agent is AgentRoleGoal. While the AgentRoleGoal instance may generate many SpeechFlow instances, each one of them is linked to just one ActionType, which are in turn determined by a particular agent communication language (ACL).

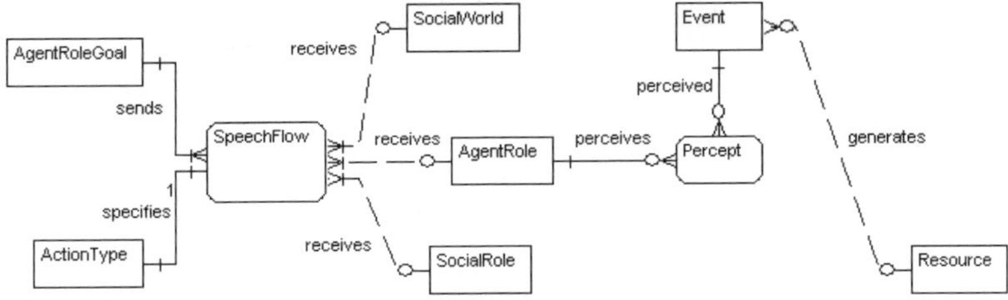

Fig. 8. Message flow within ShaMAN

While a particular instance of AgentRoleGoal is the source of any given instance of SpeechFlow it can have one or more of three possible receivers: AgentRole is a given individual recipient agent while acting in a particular role; SocialWorld means that the message will be broadcast to the whole membership of a social world however many members it has (via Member – see figures 5 or 10); or, SocialRole which is a particular role common to many SocialWorlds, such as 'Treasurer', or, a game example such as 'Captain' – e.g. All 'Captains' of SocialWorld's of type 'Ship'. The three receives relationships are all zero-or-one to many, because they may be either alternative or parallel receivers of a specific message.

Non-agent Events come from Resources (including from UI widgets), and are perceived by Agents through AgentRole as Percepts.

2.3 The Goals, Roles, Responsibilities and Tasks of Agents

Computer games often have the need for intelligent, intentional, proactive and autonomous game characters that interact both with the human players and with other characters in a game. These properties are the harbingers of AO systems, and the sub-group of entities from ShaMAN meta-model in figure 9, represent the entities that appear most frequently (but not consistently) in one form or another, in many of the agent meta-models that we examined.

Figure 9 shows four entities in this sub-model of ShaMAN that have hierarchies of sub-elements of the same type, namely: Goal, Role, Agent and Task. The associate entity between Goal and Role called Responsibility represents the responsibilities of a particular Role. A given Responsibility instance is fulfilled via an instance in the AgentRoleGoal entity, by being enacted or performed by an Agent that takes on that Role. An Agent may have many Roles and the AgentRole entity represents this multiplicity.

In task modeling, a hierarchy of related tasks is performed to achieve a goal that sits at the head (or root) of a task hierarchy. In ShaMAN the AgentRoleGoal entity represents such a root Goal (via Responsibility), while such a task hierarchy is represented by Task together with the self-relationship (a unary relationship) called sub-task.

The completion of a Task may spark a SpeechAct. SpeechActs (zero, one or many of them) may also be generated directly by the AgentRoleGoal entity. Note that SpeechAct is related to the ActionType and SpeechFlow entities that were depicted and described earlier in Section 2.2.

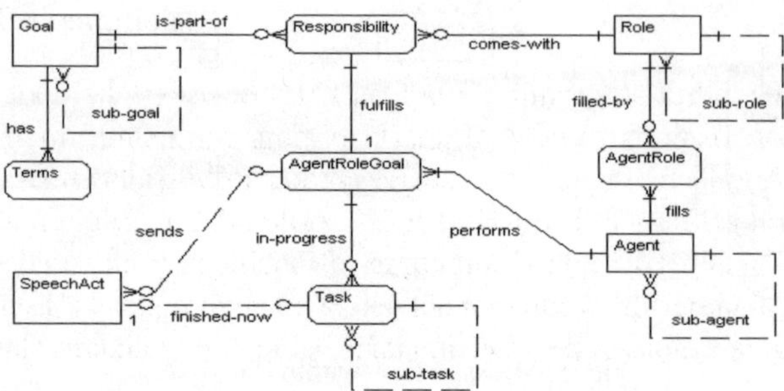

Fig. 9. Goals, Roles and Tasks in ShaMAN

Goals within ShaMAN are expressed as GoalX(term1, term2, … termN), like a predicate in the predicate logic sense. I.e. By setting one or more of the terms to a constant, and leaving one or more of the terms as variables, a logic language such as Prolog will accept such a predicate as a goal, and will set about solving it, without a formal plan. Even though this predicate format for goals conforms with logic languages, it is also an acceptable way to specify methods capable of achieving goals in imperative languages. Likewise, it is an equally acceptable format for expressing RPC-oriented (Remote Procedure Call) web services (WS) and furthermore, database queries in a Query-by-Example format.

In ShaMAN a Term can be a simple variable (or a literal/constant) but it need not be – it may also include constraints. E.g. While the variable Temperature is an acceptable term within a ShaMAN goal, the constraint: during(12 < Temperature < 100) is also acceptable as a term. A term expressed as such is an invariant constraint, meaning that it remains in force for the life of the goal to which it is associated. A second type of constraint can be expressed in a ShaMAN term as follows: before(12 < Temperature < 100) – which means that the constraint must hold before the goal can be begin to be solved. An example of a third form of constraint definition is after(Tempature = 100), representing a constraint that exists following a successful completion of the goal in question. This use of keywords before, during and after within constraints as temporal directives, was proposed by Goschnick & Sterling [12].

Goals will often have sub-goals in a hierarchy of goals to be achieved. One such sub-goal will be associated with a matching sub-role, and an agent will be assigned via an instance of the AgentRole entity. During execution of a ShaMAN application, sub-agents can be called upon in a downward direction via the need to achieve the sub-goals of parent goals, which is termed goal-driven execution. Or, they can be called upon from below, where a SpeechAct has been sent from further down the sub-agent chain, and the upper level goal has to be solved or rerun, termed data-driven execution. Data-driven execution often eventuates when a sub-agent retrieves new information from an external service such as a Web service, or from another agent across agent hierarchies or across Social Worlds. I.e. Even though the groupings of agents within ShaMAN are generally organized in hierarchies, communication and hence cooperation can happen between agents across different agent/sub-agent hierarchies.

2.4 Social Worlds in ShaMAN

Individual Agents can be members of one or more SocialWorlds. Their membership begins with an instance in the Member entity. See figure 10 below. Agents are related to the Member entity via the one-to-many relationship involved-as between their entry in the AgentRole entity and Member, while a SocialWorld includes multiple agents represented in Member via a one-to-many relationship.

   Agents can fill multiple Roles via the AgentRole entity. The Roles that are available within a particular SocialWorld are listed as instances of the SocialRole entity, which sits between Role and SocialWorld. SocialRole is a useful entity in a number of ways: it can be used to specify all the roles that make up a SocialWorld in the design phase, before any Agents become members; and, as we saw in Section 2.2, at execution time SpeechFlow messages can simply be broadcast to all agents in a Social-World that occupy a particular SocialRole such as 'Captain'.

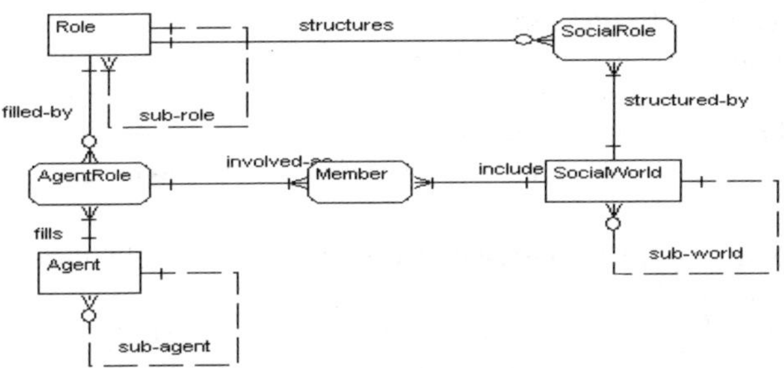

Fig. 10. SocialWorlds within ShaMAN

2.5 Knowledge Tree and Resources

The Knowledge Tree part of ShaMAN (see figure 11) consists of a hierarchy of concepts in the form of an ontology (the entity is called Ontology), but which is then related to lists of Resources (via the ResourceList entity) at each level in the ontology. In the functioning beta instantiated system based on ShaMAN, the Ontology is represented as a file directory structure and the resource list includes a multitude of file types, including image and video files used in a game, through to executable Java objects, such as the Filing Cabinet displayed in figure 7 above and discussed in Section 2.1. It differs from a conventional file directory structure in that any Resource can appear in multiple ResourceLists via the appears-in relationship between them.

   The Resource hierarchy can store any group of objects or resources that are naturally composed in a hierarchical form. For example, a computer consists of motherboard, hard drive/s, memory cards, etc. – which could be logically represented in the Resource tree of ShaMAN. Similarly, a standard GUI screen is a hierarchy of on-screen components/widgets, that can be represented as a part of a Resource hierarchy used by a Locale that represents that screen, and linked by the OnSiteResource entity depicted at the bottom of figure 6.

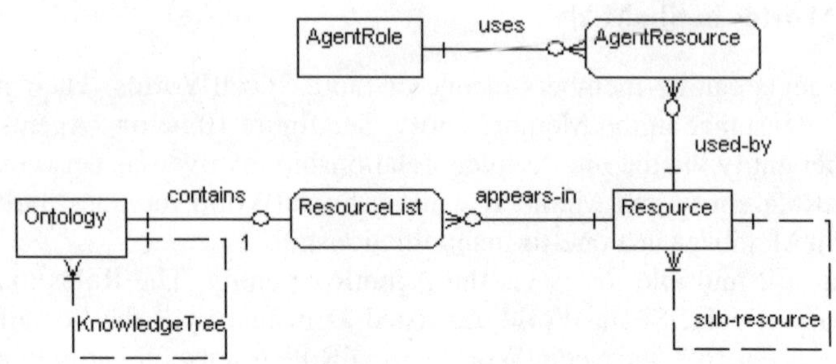

Fig. 11. The ShaMAN Knowledge Tree

3   A Comparison of ShaMAN with Task Meta-models

Our motivation for collecting and comparing agent meta-models was for their agent concepts as the primary input into a normalisation process, to arrive at a well-formed agent meta-model. So our initial interest in the comparison was analytic only.

Table 1 below is a comparative format representing the original set of agent concepts from the Task meta-models that were used as input into the meta-model normalisation process in deriving ShaMAN (see first table column). Nb. There is a similar comparitive table of ShaMAN concepts against the agent meta-models used as input, but it is not in this paper for space reasons.

While a particular comparison in the table, such as ShaMAN's Goal(tree) and TWO's Goal(tree) approximately equates the concepts, the comparison is a gross simplification. A TWO Goal is different from a ShaMAN Goal, in that a TWO Task has a Goal as an attribute, while a ShaMAN Goal leads to a number of Tasks. Sometimes the table comparison is close in meaning, other times it is close in name but distant in meaning, and sometimes there is wide variance in both name and the semantics. However, such a table is useful to begin the cross-model discussion.

What is common to ShaMAN and all the Task models examined is that task represents a unit of work. An analogy that we will use here, is a model-neutral concept - the programmed Method (Procedure) within an imperative language. We will distinguish between the Method Signature (its name plus parameters passed), the Method Body of the method (the logic that can resolve the goal), and an Executing Method. An Executing Method represents a task underway. In ShaMAN a method signature is the equivalent to a Goal, where the terms can equate to parameters. As mentioned earlier, in Section 2.3 this predicate format for goals is not only an acceptable way to specify method signatures capable of achieving goals in imperative languages, it is equally acceptable for expressing RPC web services (WS), certain database queries and other languages.

HTA does not attempt to represent cognitive systems (as BDI, ShaMAN and other MAS architectures do), but it does allow a functional analysis of goals, sub-goals, tasks, sub-tasks and plans. As with the ShaMAN Goal the HTA Goal is analogous to a Method Signature, while the HTA Plan is analogous to a Method Body – the specific logical recipe for achieving the goal. The Method Body may call upon other Methods

Table 1. ShaMAN meta-model comparison against selected Task Meta-models

ShaMAN	Hierarchical Task Analysis (HTA)	Task Knowledge Structure (TKS)	GOMS - Goals, Operators, Methods, Selection	Task World Ontology (TWO)	DIANE+
Goal (tree)	Goal (tree)	Goal (tree)	Goals(tree), Methods	Goal (tree)	Goal, Procedure
Role (tree)		Role		Role (tree)	
Responsibility		Responsibility (task) [2]		Is-responsible [2]	
Agent (tree)	Plan (tree)	Agent, Plan	Methods; Selection rules	Agent	Actor; Logical relationships
AgentRole		Playing [2]		Plays [2]	
Percept					
Event				Event	
SocialWorld(tree)					
SocialRole					
Member					
Item					
AgentRoleGoal			Operators	Performed-by [2]	
Task	Task (tree)	Task (tree)		Task (tree)	Temporal Relationships; Iteration
SpeechAct					Procedure
ActionType					
SpeechFlow					
Term					Data
Concept					
Association					
Resource (tree)		Object		Object (tree)	Object, Widget
AgentResource		Manipulate [2]			
Ontology (tree)					
List					
Locale (tree)					
Attendee					
Inhabitant					
OnSiteResource					
HotSpot					
LinkCondition					
R,A,D,I,T,Rt [1]	R,A	R,A,D	A,D,T[1]	R,A,D	R,A,D,I[2]

Note 1: R,A,D,I,T,Rt: Requirements, Analysis, Design, Implementation, Testing, Runtime.
Note 2: In the Task Meta-model, this is represented as a relationship rather than an entity.

(by Method Signature). I.e. The logic in a plan hierarchy can reference goals. So, a goal hierarchy can be specified without any procedural logic, although logical AND, ORs and XORs, are commonly used between predicates, as is the case in ShaMAN goal hierarchies. In application, HTA relies heavily on the feedback loop to: monitor progress of goals; to detect errors and reactive events, to call upon alternative plans in the event of errors and reactive events, In fact, the HTA feedback loop is very similar in principle to the functional event loop in a BDI agent.

The TWO version of a Task is two-fold: a unit task is the lowest level task that people want to consider in their work, while a basic task is system-oriented such as a single command in an applicaion. Tasks may be further subdivided into actions. The TWO Role is similar to that in ShaMAN, although it is seen as a collection of Tasks for which it is Responsible. Both have Agents playing/fulfilling Roles. TWO Objects are not OO-like, but are very similar to ShaMAN Resources in that they can be real objects or abstract objects that exist in the knowledge context of an agent. What can be done with a TWO Object is specified by a list of actions. TWO Objects are strongly related to TWO Tasks, via the uses relationship.

The TKS Goal is very agent-like, in that it represents the goals in a human's head. Agents are synthetic intelligence with meta-models often mimicking a human psychology in the quest to achieve some level of intelligence. The concept of Role and Responsibility are directly equivalent to that used in several agent meta-models, including ShaMAN. However, in ShaMAN, Responsibility can be constructed at the analysis and design, as it is an associative entity between Role and Goal, rather than between Role and Task. Where the TKS Task manipulates TKS Objects, the ShaMAN Agent (which performs Tasks via AgentRoleGoal) has access to ShaMAN Resources (stored in a Knowledge tree), via the AgentResource associative entity, and so on. In the full study we do examine each twin comparison of each concept in detail.

4   Some Challenges for Task Analysis and Modelling

In Chapter 30, the final chapter of the Task Analysis handbook [6] editors Diaper and Stanton consider the future of Task Analysis. They make a case for the removal of two substantial concepts within Task Analysis, namely: Functionality and Goals:

"It (functionality) is a concept only applied to computer systems and not to the other main type of agents in HCI and task analysis, people (i.e., we do not usually discuss the functionality of a person, although we might discuss the functionality of an abstract role). The concept of functionality as what application software is capable of doing to transform its inputs into its outputs may well have been a reasonable one in computing's infancy, when programs were small and did very little, but today computer systems, particularly when networked and/or involving some artificial intelligence (AI), have outgrown the utility of the functionality concept. We believe that future computer systems will become further empowered as agents and that either we should happily apply the functionality concept to both human and nonhuman agents or drop it completely and use the same concepts we use for people when addressing the behavior of complex computer systems." (Note: the bolding is added).

They discuss the use of goal in TA: "What are goals for in task analysis? Chapter 1 identifies two roles for goals in task analysis: to motivate behavior and to facilitate abstraction away from specific tasks and thus promote device independence." Then outline ways to achieve those two things without the use of goals at all (using of attentional mechanisms), and conclude that goals ought to be dropped from TA.

"On this view, people, including task analysts, merely use goals as a post hoc explanation of system performance. Furthermore, attention, both selective and divided (see chaps. 14 and 15), is an existing cognitive psychological mechanism that controls the allocation of the massive, but still ultimately limited, mental information-processing resources, and we think that attentional mechanisms can entirely replace the motivational role of goals ... we suspect that goals in task analysis are similarly post hoc, whether elicited from task performers or inferred in some other way by task analysts. That is, we believe that goals are not part of the psychology that causes behavior but are used to explain it."

Both of these calls upon TA - to recede from the current inclusion of motivational Goals, and from the modelling of the ever growing functionality of complex modern computer applications - are one response to growing complexity and to interdisciplinary influences upon a discipline. Another response is to embrace and expand the field, inspired by the incursions of and into other disciplines and domains.

5   Enriching Task Modelling with Some AO Concepts

Today's users are multi-tasking much of the time and often have their computer systems running 24/7. The use of inputs and outputs in the earlier quotation highlights a different view of computational systems within the AO paradigm: Agents have percepts rather than inputs, and they act rather than just having an output - this underlines their perpetual operation in a task world or environment. They are designed to run 24/7, as are many current day mainstream applications, for example, an email client.

If AO concepts could influence TA with regard to the first recommended change to TA by Diaper and Stanton, it would advocate modelling of both users and agents – TKS and TWO have gone down this path to some degree. The AO approach is compliant with the idea of applying functionality concepts to both humans and agents – particularly within mixed-initiative systems. E.g. In ShaMAN an individual human is modelled as a hierarchy of sub-agents – a ShadowBoard agent - together representing the myriad of roles an individual user has [10]. Also note, that sub-agents in a multi-agent system are often much less than fully autonomous entities [2,5,7,10,11,13,14,22,24], and so functionality can and does get broken down into small definable units in these outwardly complex AI systems.

In response to the call to remove motivational goals, an Agent analyst would point out, that to restrict an agent to react to events only, in an attentional manner, would render it a simple reactive agent - the earliest form of agent architectures. Reactive agents were superseded by deliberative architectures, which, in addition to being reactive, are also proactive in pursuing their own goals, including motivational goals.

If, for example, you take either the TWO or the TKS task meta-model in figures 4 and 5, replace the agent entity with the SocialWorld sub-model in figure 10 above, replace the Object entity with the Knowledge Tree sub-model in figure 11, replace the Event entity with the MessageFlow sub-model in figure 8 – the result is a much expanded meta-model, which is as much an Agent meta-model as it is a Task meta-model. While it is large, it is also now capable of representing multiple users together with multiple agents, complex memberships and complex messaging, rich knowledge representations and complex goal, role and responsibility interrelationships.

The futures of Task Analysis and Task Modelling and the AO paradigm have much in common. AO researchers are predominantly intent on putting intelligence into artefacts (e.g. trading systems, robots, simulations, etc.), with only a small percentage of their number currently concerned with mixed-initiative human-agent systems. Task analysts and modellers are focused on people more than artefacts, and are therefore well-positioned and more inclined to embrace the modelling of people in mixed initiative human-agent systems, of which computer games are but demonstrative of the possibilities such systems hold for people in all walks of life.

References

1. Annet, J.: Hierarchical Task Analysis. In: Diaper, D., Stanton, N. (eds.) The Handbook of Task Analysis for Human-Computer Interaction. Lawrence Erlbaum Associates, Mahwah (2004)
2. Bresciani, P., Perini, A., Giorgini, P., Guinchiglia, F., Mylopoulos, J.: Tropos: An Agent-Oriented Software Development Methodology. In: AAMAS 2004, pp. 203–236 (2004)
3. Chen, P.: The Entity-Relationship Model - Toward a Unified View of Data. ACM Transactions on Database Systems 1, 9–36 (1976)
4. Cossentino, M.: Different perspectives in designing multi-agent systems. In: AgeS 2002, workshop at NodE 2002, Erfurt, Germany (2002)
5. Da Silva, V.T., De Lucena, C.J.P.: From a Conceptual Framework for Agents and Objects to a Multi-Agent System Modeling Language. In: Autonomous Agents and Multi-Agent Systems, vol. 9, pp. 145–189. Kluwer, The Netherlands (2004)
6. Diaper, D., Stanton, N. (eds.): The Handbook of Task Analysis for Human-Computer Interaction. Lawrence Erlbaum Associates, Mahwah (2004)
7. Fischer, K., Hahn, C., Madrigal-Mora, C.: Agent-oriented software engineering: a model-driven approach. International Journal of Agent-Oriented Software Engineering 1(3/4), 334–369 (2007)
8. Fitzpatrick, G.: The Locales Framework: Understanding and Designing for Wicked Problems. Kluwer Academic Publications, London (2003)
9. Fleming, M., Cohen, R.A.: User Modeling Approach to Determining System Initiative in Mixed Initiative AI Systems. In: 6th International Conference on User Modeling (1997)
10. Goschnick, S.B.: ShadowBoard: an Agent Architecture for enabling a sophisticated Digital Self. Thesis, Dept. of Computer Science, University of Melbourne, Australia (2001)
11. Goschnick, S.B.: The DigitalFriend: the First End-User Oriented Multi-Agent System. In: OSDC 2006, Open Source Developers Conference, Melbourne, Australia (2006)
12. Goschnick, S.B., Sterling, L.: Enacting and Interacting with an Agent-based Digital Self in a 24x7 Web Services World. In: Workshop on Humans and Multi-Agent Systems, at the AAMAS 2003 International Conference, Melbourne, Australia (2003)
13. Guinchiglia, F., Mylopoulos, J., Perini, A.: The Tropos Software Development Methodology: Processes, Models and Diagrams. In: Autonomous Agents and Multi-Agent Systems (AAMAS 2002) International Conference. ACM, New York (2002)
14. Hahn, C., Madrigal-Mora, C., Fischer, K., Elvesaeter, B., Berre, A., Zinnikus, I.: Meta-models, Models, and Model Transformations: Towards Interoperable Agents. In: Fischer, K., Timm, I.J., André, E., Zhong, N. (eds.) MATES 2006. LNCS (LNAI), vol. 4196, pp. 123–134. Springer, Heidelberg (2006)
15. Johnson, P., Johnson, H.: Knowledge Analysis of Tasks: Task analysis and specification for human-computer systems. In: Downton, A. (ed.) Engineering the Human-Computer Interface, pp. 119–144. McGraw-Hill, London (1991)
16. Juan, T., Sterling, L.: The ROADMAP Meta-model for Intelligent Adaptive Multi-Agent Systems in Open Environments. In: 4th International Workshop on Agent Oriented Software Engineering, AAMAS 2003 International Conference, Melbourne (2003)
17. Kent, W.: A Simple Guide to Five Normal Forms in Relational Database Theory. Communications of the ACM 26(2), 120–125 (1983)
18. Kieras, D.: GOMS Models for Task Analysis. In: Diaper, D., Stanton, N. (eds.) Hand-book of Task Analysis for Human-Computer Interaction. Lawrence Erlbaum Inc., Mahwah (2004)

19. Kinny, D., Georgeff, M., Rao, A.: A Methodology and Modelling Technique for Systems of BDI Agents. In: Van de Velde, W., Perram, J.W. (eds.) Seventh European Workshop on Modelling Autonomous Agents in a Multi-Agent World. Springer, Berlin (1996)
20. OMG: MDA Guide V1.0.1 (2003), http://www.omg.org/docs/omg/03-06-01.pdf
21. Padgham, L., Winikoff, M.: Prometheus: A Methodology for Developing Intelligent Agents. In: AOSE Workshop, AAMAS 2002, Bologna, Italy (2002)
22. Shen, Z., Li, D., Miao, C., Gay, R.: Goal-oriented Methodology for Agent System Development. In: International Conference on Intelligent Agent Technology, IAT (2005)
23. Strauss, A.: A Social World Perspective. Studies in Symbolic Interaction 1, 119–128 (1978)
24. Sun, R.: Duality of the Mind - A Bottom Up Approach toward Cognition. Lawrence Erlbaum Associates Inc, Mahwah (2002)
25. Tarby, J.C., Barthet, M.C.: The Diane+ Method. In: Second International Workshop on Computer-Aided Design of User Interfaces, University of Namur, Belgium (1996)
26. Van der Veer, G., Van Welie, M.: Groupware Task Analysis. In: Hollnagel, E. (ed.) Handbook of Cognitive Task Analysis Design, Lawrence Erlbaum Inc., Maywah (2003)
27. Van Welie, M., Van der Veer, G.: An Ontology for Task World Models. In: DVS-IS 1998, Adington, UK. Springer, Wein (1998)
28. Wooldridge, M., Jennings, N.R., Kinny, D.: The Gaia Methodology for Agent-Oriented Analysis and Design. Autonomous Agents and Multi-Agent Systems 3, 285–312 (2000)
29. Zambonelli, F., Jennings, N.R., Wooldridge, M.J.: Developing Multi-Agent Systems: The Gaia Methodology. ACM Transactions on Software Eng. and Methodology 12, 417–470 (2003)

Steps in Identifying Interaction Design Patterns for Multimodal Systems

Andreas Ratzka

IMIK, Universität Regensburg
93040 Regensburg
Andreas.Ratzka@sprachlit.uni-regensburg.de

Abstract. The context of this work is usability engineering for multimodal interaction. In contrast to other work that concentrates on prototyping toolkits or abstract guidelines, this research focuses on user interface patterns for multimodal interaction. Designing multimodal applications requires several skills ranging from design and implementation. Thus, different kinds of patterns (from architecture patterns to user interface patterns) can be applied to this field. This work focuses on user-task near user interface patterns. At first, a traditional approach of modality selection based on task- and context-based rules is presented. Next, a twofold process of pattern mining is presented. In the first phase, pattern candidates are derived top-down from proven knowledge about how multimodality enhances usability. In the second phase, literature is mined for real solutions to underpin these pattern candidates and find new ones. Along with this, relationships between patterns are depicted.

1 Introduction

The context of this work is usability engineering for multimodal interaction. Traditional approaches in this field focus on prototyping [15, 16, 30] or decision support for requirements analysis and work reengineering [6, 9, 32]. The later stages in the usability engineering lifecycle, i.e. design standards and detailed design, are only marginally covered by those decision support systems.

The idea of this work is to apply the concept of design patterns to the field of multi-modal interaction. A design pattern is a rule connecting a common design problem with a proven solution and a description of the contexts and conditions in which this pattern is applicable [8, 17].

The idea of patterns originates from architecture [1, 2] but has gained popularity mainly in different fields of computing such as object orient programming [18], software architecture [10] and user interface design [7, 40, 41, 42].

A good pattern provides a solution which cannot be derived from general guidelines using trivial mapping rules. A pattern is a context-specific design rule that discusses why other apparent solutions are not applicable in this context. This is done in pattern sections titled *forces* – to discuss the goal conflicts impeding simple and obvious solutions – and *consequences* – to discuss how the goal conflicts are resolved by the proposed solution and which new problems might arise.

P. Forbrig and F. Paternò (Eds.): HCSE/TAMODIA 2008, LNCS 5247, pp. 58–71, 2008.
© IFIP International Federation for Information Processing 2008

Multimodal interaction has not yet reached wide-spread market penetration. Nevertheless, after almost thirty years of research, several demonstration systems have been designed. Recurring problems have lead to solutions which were reused successfully in subsequent projects so that these solutions can be identified as interaction design patterns [34].

Designing multimodal systems requires a lot of skills comprising among others software architecture, implementation techniques, speech and screen design, and task modelling. Each of these fields can be supported by different kinds of patterns such as the (implementation-near) architecture patterns PAC, MVC and Blackboard [10] or (user-task-oriented) user interface patterns such as those described in [40, 41].

This work focuses on patterns of the latter (user-task-near) category. Even within this group, one can distinguish different levels of granularity. This paper describes on the one hand higher level patterns that are based on the general principles of the multimodal design space (patterns of multimodal combination and multimodal adaptation), as well as more concrete use case specific patterns on the other hand [36, 37].

Similar approaches for multimodal interaction are rare. Only the work described in [19] goes in the same direction and identifies patterns for multimodal interaction. However, that work emphasises formalisation and avoids direct links to already existing "traditional" user interface patterns. This work, by contrast, identifies specific multimodal interface patterns and attempts to put them in relation to traditional, more general user interface patterns.

This paper illustrates first a simplified approach of modality selection which is based on design rules that are derived from modality theory and interaction constraints. The designer selects appropriate modalities according to the requirements of the target application. This approach results in propositions such as "use modality A", which are helpful during the first phases of usability engineering. But it lacks more detailed speech and screen design recommendations. This work assumes that patterns can complement this gap and provide decision support across all design phases.

The following sections describe the process of mining user interface patterns which consists of two temporally overlapping phases.

In the first (top down) phase, user interface patterns are derived from general properties of the multimodal interaction design space. In the second (bottom up) phase concrete use cases are discussed. This paper focuses on mobile applications, discusses, how traditional user interface patterns [40, 41, 42, 43] can be applied, and identifies new user interface patterns that build specifically on multimodal interaction techniques.

Patters are not standing alone but are mutually interrelated and form a pattern language [25]. Relationships cover typically usage (pattern A makes use of pattern B) and refinement (pattern A is refined by pattern B). Beyond relationships among specifically multimodal user interface patterns, this paper illustrates relationships between multimodal and traditional user interface patterns such as those found in [40, 41, 42, 43].

2   Traditional Approach of Design Support: Modality Selection Based on Task Properties and Context of Use

Traditional approaches such as modality theory and modality properties [6], interaction constraint models [9, 32] and other guidelines for multimodal interaction provide solutions for design problems. This section exemplifies modality selection according to task properties and context-based constraints.

2.1 Modality Selection According to Task Properties

The first step in designing multimodal interactive systems is to elicit interaction modalities that are appropriate for the current task. One starting point are the modality properties described in [6], which tackle following issues:

- **Required interaction channels.** (Spoken language is conveyed auditively, written text visually)
- **Salience.** (Auditive signals are more attention catching than visual ones)
- **Local selectivity.** (visual data are perceived only if they are paid attention to)
- **Degree of user control.** (static modalities like written text allow more user control over pacing than dynamic modalities such as videos or spoken text)
- **Learning requirements.** (arbitrary modalities such as newly defined symbols require more learning efforts than those building upon existing conventions)
- **Expressiveness.** (analogous modalities such as graphics are preferred for conveying spatial relationships whereas linguistic modalities like text convey conceptual information such as detailed descriptions better).

Rules taken from modality theory and modality properties [6] are universally valid and expected to be stable even for novel interaction techniques. Nevertheless a concretisation for each individual project, for currently available modality combination is needed. Figure 1 shows an exemplary task-modality matrix, which gives the user advice on modality selection.

Input	Speech Input	Typing	Handwriting	Pointing	Free Gestures	Eye movements	Output	Auditive Output	Visual Output	Haptic Output	Motor Input	Speech Input
Sketching	−	−	−	+	?	?	Urgent Information	+	?	?		
Graphic manipulation	?	?	?	+	?	?	Highly current information	+	?	?		
Selecting (small sets)	+	?	?	+	+	?	Status information	−	+	?		
Selecting (large sets)	+	+	?	?	?	?	Private information	−	+	+	+	−
Text input	?	+	+	?	?	?	Security relevant visual primary task	+	−		−	+

Fig. 1. Exemplary Modality Selection Criteria based on Task Characteristics

2.2 Interaction Constraints Based on Context of Use

After selecting (several alternative) task appropriate modalities, the designer has to check further interaction constraints imposed by user characteristics, device characteristics and the environment [9, 32]. These additional constraints can be cast into similar problem-solution matrices such as the one for task characteristics. However, it is difficult for the designer to keep track of a bunch of several constraint matrices all at once.

Instead, these additional interaction constraints are presented in an (exemplary) contradiction matrix. The columns of this matrix contain cases that encourage the use of an individual interaction modality whereas the rows are listing those cases that discourage the respective modality. The designer first checks which interaction modalities are most appropriate for the tasks to be supported by the system. Then he checks whether for each individual candidate modality the factors listed in the columns outweigh the factors listed in the rows and contrasts these results for each interaction modality. Roughly speaking, the fields near the matrix diagonal (crossed out in our examples) mark cases of conflicting usability goals.

Output Constraints

	Speech output preferred						Audio tones preferred					Visual text preferred			Graphics preferred		
	Illiterate people	Visually impaired people	Car user interfaces	Phone user interfaces	Smartphones, PDAs	Bad lighting conditions	Visually impaired people	Car user interfaces	Phone user interfaces	Smartphones, PDAs	Bad lighting conditions	Hearing impaired people	Noisy environments	Public, crowded environments	Hearing impaired people	Noisy environments	Public, crowded environments
Speech output — discouraged — Hearing impaired people	X	X	X	X	X	X											
Speech output — discouraged — Noisy environments	X	X	X	X	X	X											
Speech output — discouraged — Public / crowded environments	X	X	X	X	X	X											
audio tones — discouraged — Hearing impaired people							X	X	X	X	X						
audio tones — discouraged — Noisy environments							X	X	X	X	X						
audio tones — discouraged — Public / crowded environments							X	X	X	X	X						
Visual text — impossible — Illiterate People												X	X	X			
Visual text — impossible — Car user interfaces												X	X	X			
Visual text — discouraged — Visually impaired people												X	X	X			
Visual text — discouraged — Bad lighting conditions												X	X	X			
Graphics — discouraged — Visually impaired people															X	X	X
Graphics — discouraged — Car user interfaces															X	X	X
Graphics — discouraged — Bad lighting conditions															X	X	X

Fig. 2. Exemplary Output Constraints

2.3 Shortcomings of This Approach

This traditional approach is valuable for the first steps of user interface design. Nevertheless it lacks detailed design recommendations on how several modalities have to be combined and coordinated, which requires more detailed guidelines.

This work assumes that patterns are a valid approach to provide design support across all phases of user interface design. The next sections outline the twofold process of identifying user interface patterns for multimodal interaction. This process is both top-down – based on general principles of multimodal interaction – and bottom-up – based on real world examples of multimodal interactive systems.

3 Deriving Patterns from Generic Principles of Multimodal Interaction

According to [31] multimodal interaction can be classified along several orthogonal dimensions. The main dimensions of fusion (content related vs. unrelated) and parallelism (temporally overlapping vs. sequential) lead to four major classes of exclusive, alternating, concurrent and synergistic multimodality.

Input Constraints

			Speech input preferred							Typing preferred			Hand-writing preferred		Pointing preferred					
			Illiterate people	Visually impaired people	Motor impaired people	Car user interfaces	Phone user interfaces	Smartphones, PDAs	Bad lighting conditions	People with speech disorders	Noisy environments	Public and crowded environments	People with speech disorders	Smartphones, PDA, Tablets	People with speech disorders	Public information Kiosk	Phone user interfaces	Smartphones, PDAs	Noisy Environments	Public environments
Speech input	discouraged	Hearing impaired people	X	X	X	X	X	X	X											
		People with speech disorders	X	X	X	X	X	X	X											
		Noisy environments	X	X	X	X	X	X	X											
		Public / crowded environments	X	X	X	X	X	X	X											
Typing	impossible	Illiterate people								X	X	X								
		Car user interfaces								X	X	X								
	discouraged	Visually impaired								X	X	X								
		Motor impaired								X	X	X								
		Smartphones, PDAs								X	X	X								
		Glaring environments								X	X	X								
Handwriting	impossible	Illiterate People											X	X						
		Motor impaired People											X	X						
	discouraged	Visually impaired people											X	X						
		Car user interfaces											X	X						
Pointing	discouraged	Visually impaired people													X	X	X	X	X	X
		Motor impaired people													X	X	X	X	X	X
		Car user interfaces													X	X	X	X	X	X
		Bad lighting conditions													X	X	X	X	X	X

Fig. 3. Exemplary Input Constraints

The potential of multi-modal interaction lies in enhanced flexibility, naturalness, robustness and interaction performance. This can be achieved via suitable modality combinations as well as via selection of appropriate interaction modalities, that is via adaptation during runtime.

The CARE properties [14] define classes of modality combination in multimodal interactive systems:

- **Equivalence:** One piece of information can be exchanged via several modalities alternatively
- **Specialization:** One piece of information can only be exchanged via one interaction modality
- **Redundancy:** One piece of information is conveyed via several interaction modalities in a redundant way.
- **Complementarity:** Several connected pieces of information are conveyed via several mutually complementing modalities

3.1 Patterns for Modality Combination

Modalities are combined to minimise task interference, maximise information throughput, disambiguate distorted input (and output) signals, optimise saliency and assure usability across diverse and varying contexts of use.

Patterns identified in the context of modality combination are:

- Audio-visual Workspace (makes use of complementarity)
- Audio-visual Presentation (makes use of complementarity)
- Redundant Input (makes use of redundancy)
- Redundant Output (makes use of redundancy)

Following section outlines the pattern *Redundant Input* in some more detail.

Redundant Input

Context

Communication channels might be unpredictably distorted due to bad lighting conditions, background noise, technical (network) problems or disabilities such as speech, motor or perception disorders.

Problem

How to assure input when communication channels are distorted in an unforeseeable way?

Forces

- The system can be configured to use interaction modalities that are less affected by channel disorders but in some cases all available interaction channels are distorted to some degree. Consider following scenarios:
    - How to support hands free tasks in noisy environments?
    - How to interact with motor-impaired users in loud environments?
    - How to interact with people with speech disorders in a hands-free scenario?

Solution

Combine several interaction channels in order to make use of redundancy. Input coming from several channels (visual: e.g. lip movements, auditive: e.g. speech signal) should be interpreted in combination in order to reduce liability to errors.

Consequences

- Even if several channels are distorted the distortion rarely affects exactly the same pieces of information. Combining sound pieces of information from several channels some distorted parts can be reconstructed:
    - In loud environments, speech recognition performance increases significantly when audio-signals are combined with visual signals (from lip movements).
    - Multimodal speech recognition can increase recognition performance for accent, exhausted and disordered speakers.

Rationale

Independent disturbances of different channels rarely affect the same aspects of the content. That's why for instance audio-visual speech recognition which combines acoustic signals and lip movement analysis leads to better recognition performance than unimodal speech recognition [5, p. 24 f.]:

Plosives ([p], [t], [k], [b], [d], [g]) sound similar and are likely to be confused when sound quality is low. At the same time these phones have distinctive lip shapes such as open lips (in the case of [g] and [k]) vs. initially closed lips (in the case of [b] and [p]). Lip shapes may differ for some similar sounding vowels, too.

Distortions rarely affect both the recognition of (acoustic) phonemes and corresponding "visemes" in the same way. Fusion algorithms allow to combine sound pieces of information from several channels to reconstruct distorted parts.

Known Uses

This variant is manifested in very different application areas including among others data input (audio-visual speech recognition), person identification [39], emotion recognition [44].

3.2 Patterns for Modality Adaptation

Systems that are used by different users subsequently (changing users), by individual users extensively (growing user expertise), in different or changing environments, or with changing degrees of service availability (changing network bandwidth) have to be adapted to these unforeseeable context factors. Adaptation can be done automatically (channel analysis, user modelling, etc.) or initiated by the user (changed behaviour or explicit configuration). Based on these aspects, following patterns, which require the presence of *equivalent* modalities, were identified (for a detailed description cf. [37]):

☐ Multiple Ways of Input
☐ Global Channel Configuration
☐ Context Adaptation

4 Identification of Multimodal User Interface Patterns Based on Real World Examples – Illustrated by Mobile Systems

Patterns are never inventions by their authors but always relate to – at least three – successful examples of system design [8]. Among several use-cases such as mobile interaction, interactive maps, graphic design applications and systems for augmented dual-task environments, mobile systems are selected for detailed discussion, underpinning of pattern candidates and pattern identification.

Examples for multimodal mobile interaction are personal assistants for e-mail and web access such as *MiPad* [22], *Personal Speech Assistant* [13], tourist guides and city information systems such as *SmartKom mobile* [26], *MATCH* [21, 24], *MUST* [3] or *COMPASS* [4].

4.1 Pattern Discussion Based on Use-Case Aspects

Multimodal mobile systems and smartphones make use of spoken commands to avoid the necessity of deep menu navigation for starting programs, placing phone calls etc.

This new user interface pattern is called *Voice-based Interaction Shortcut* [36] and can be used in diverse interaction scenarios.

Starting an Application

The pattern *Hub and Spoke* [41] is an appropriate approach for organising applications on mobile devices. Each one of the most important applications is easily reachable from the main page. At the same time, when leaving an application, you return to the main page as well. This way, orientation can be granted despite the lack of space.

Additionally, mobile devices usually provide so called *quick launch buttons* to start the four or five most common applications with one press. This can be seen as an extension of *Hub and Spoke*.

The above mentioned pattern *Voice-based Interaction Shortcut* can be applied for launching applications in one interaction step. This way, the desired program can be started without the need for the current display to include a direct link to this application.

List Selection

List selection is another application area for the pattern *Voice-based Interaction Shortcut*. Instead of scrolling through lists or poking on a screen keypad the user can simply speak the desired list item.

Structured Text Input

Text input can be facilitated using the pattern *Autocompletion* [41]. The user only has to input some letters until the list proposed by the system includes the desired entry. Similarly list selection in very large lists can be alleviated by applying the pattern *Continuous Filter* [42] allowing the user to enter the first letters of an entry until no scrolling is necessary any more.

In some cases structured input is necessary. Think of web *forms* [40] or e-mail messages. The user has to select an input field and then enter textual information. Some input fields can be enriched with a *Dropdown Chooser* [41] to offer list selection instead of text input. If this *Dropdown Chooser* is enriched with the pattern *Voice-based Interaction Shortcut* in the context of structured input forms we receive as a result the new multimodal user interface pattern *Speech-enabled Form* [36].

The mobile multimodal organiser MiPad makes use of this pattern as it allows the user among others to create e-mails via combining pen input and spoken language the following way: When the user selects the receiver field, a recognition vocabulary consisting of contact items is selected and speech recognition is activated. When the user selects the subject or message field, a free-text recognition vocabulary is selected instead.

The user's tapping with the pen onto the input field is used to activate the speech recogniser. This is important because speech recognition must not be active all time, otherwise background noise, private speech, respiration and harrumphing could lead to undesired results. Instead, activating the recogniser via tapping and deactivating it after input or a certain period of time can avoid this problem. Thus, *Speech-enabled Form* makes use of Tidwell's [41] pattern *One-off Mode*.

Implementation techniques supported by XHTML+VoiceXML [23] enforce this *Speech-enabled Form* paradigma.

Avoiding Recognition Errors

Mobile messaging systems [27] and car navigation systems [29] deal with large vocabularies that can lead to poor speech recognition performance. To improve dialogue quality some systems offer the user not only to re-speak the misrecognised word or phrase but to select it from a list – via pointing, speaking the line number or re-speaking with additional attributes. This change of input technique is important as it avoids endless error-correction loops. The presentation of the n-best list in a *Dropdown Chooser* [41] which allows the user to correct initially spoken words via pointing is a new multimodal user interface pattern called *Multi-modal N-best Selection* [37].

Other systems propose the user to spell or type the first character(s) of the item/name to be input. This way the size of speech recognition vocabulary can be reduced which results in more robust recognition performance. This combination of *Continuous Filter* and *Voice-based Interaction Shortcut* results in the new pattern *Spelling-based Hypothesis Reduction* [37].

Both *Multi-modal N-best Selection* and *Spelling-based Hypothesis Reduction* are specialisations of the above mentioned pattern *Redundant Input*.

4.2 Summary of Identified Patterns

Following patterns were identified for mobile multimodal interaction:

☐ Voice-based Interaction Shortcut
☐ Speech-enabled Form
☐ Multimodal N-best Selection
☐ Spelling-based Hypothesis Reduction

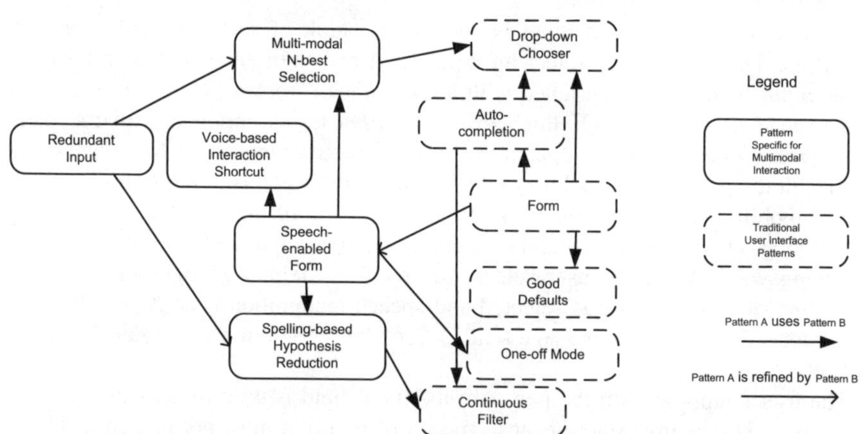

Fig. 4. Patterns for Multimodal Mobile Interaction

Pattern Relationships

The four main patterns identified in this paper are in close relationship to one another: The pattern *Voice-based Interaction Shortcut* is used by *Multi-modal N-best Selection* as well as by *Speech-enabled Form*. Speech-enabled Form, a refinement of Tidwell's

[40] *Form*, makes use of *Spelling-based Hypothesis Reduction* and *Multi-modal N-best Selection* as well as of Tidwell's [41] *One-off Mode*. *Multi-modal N-best Selection* makes use of Tidwell's [41] *Drop-down Chooser*. *Spelling-based Hypothesis Reduction* uses the pattern *Continuous Filter* [42]. Following figure illustrates these relationships visually.

Following section describes the pattern *Speech-enabled Form* in some more detail. The remaining patterns can be found [36, 37].

Speech-Enabled Form

Context

The user has to input structured data which can be mapped to some kind of form consisting of a set of atomic fields.

Devices such as PDAs do not provide a keyboard for comfortable string input. In other situations the device may support keyboard input but the user has only one hand available for interacting with the system.

This pattern is frequently used together with the patterns *Dropdown Chooser* [41] and *Autocompletion* [41]. For error handling and avoiding *Multi-modal N-best Selection* and *Spelling-based Hypothesis Reduction* can be used.

Problem

How to simplify string input in form filling applications?

Forces

- Selecting areas in 2D-space is accomplished comfortably with a pointing device but string input via pointing (with on-screen keyboards) is awkward.
- Values for some form items (academic degree, nationality etc.) are restricted and can be input using drop down choosers (combo boxes). But this may lead to screen clutter and additional navigation and scrolling.
- Speech recognition is very comfortable for selecting invisible items but the input of unconstrained text suffers from recognition errors.

Solution

Wherever possible determine acceptable values for each form field. Support value selection via *Dropdown Choosers* and, alternatively, via voice commands.

Let the user select the desired form field via pointing and input values via speech. The speech input complexity can be reduced, as only the vocabulary of the selected form item needs to be activated at the time.

In order to avoid that the speech recogniser interprets background noise as input, the recogniser should be activated only when the user is using speech input. One possibility is to activate the speech recogniser only while the user is holding down the pointing device over the desired entry field (cf. Tidwell's [41] pattern *Spring-loaded Mode*). Another possibility is to activate the speech recogniser for a certain time window after entry field selection (cf. Tidwell's [41] *One-off Mode*).

Consequences

- The user can comfortably combine pen input for selecting input fields with speech for value specification.
- Navigation and scrolling in drop down lists can be avoided.

☐ Constraining the voice recognition vocabulary according to the selected text field helps to avoid speech recognition errors.

☐ Speech recognition errors might occur anyway. In case of poor recognition performance all speed advantages might be lost due to the need of error corroboration.

Rationale

Users prefer speech to input descriptive data, or to select objects among large or invisible sets [20, 33].

In QuickSet, standard direct-manipulation was compared with the pen/voice multi-modal interface. Multi-modal interaction was significantly faster [12].

Known Uses

Mobile Systems such as Microsoft's MiPad [22] and IBM's Personal Speech Assistant [13] are good examples.

With MiPad the user can create e-mail messages via *Tap And Talk*. The user can select the addressee field and the speech recognition vocabulary is constrained to address book entries. If the user selects the subject or message field an unconstrained vocabulary is selected so that the user can input unconstrained text.

As a further example one could cite the QuickSet System [11].

The multi-modal facilities offered by X+V (XHTML and VoiceXML) and supported by the Opera Browser are heavily focussed on this *Speech-enabled Form* paradigm [23].

Related Patterns

This pattern is a multi-modal extension of *Form* as found in [40] and [38]. It is implemented using the pattern *Voice-based Interaction Shortcut* in the same way as *Forms* are implemented using patterns such as *Dropdown Chooser* and *Autocompletion*.

Tidwell's [41] patterns *Spring-loaded Mode* and *One-off Mode* can be used to control recogniser activation.

For error handling consider to use *Multi-modal N-Best-Selection* and *Spelling-based Hypothesis Reduction*.

5 Conclusion

This paper revealed the activities for mining patterns and creating a pattern language in emerging interaction paradigms of multimodal interaction. Modality properties and interaction constraints seem to give helpful advice in deciding which interaction technique should be used in which context. But for deeper design support more detailed guidelines or patterns are needed.

Patterns are identified both during top-down phases (based on multimodal interaction principles) and during bottom-up phases (based on pertinent use cases).

Recently, case studies involving empirical user tests on a multimodal email organiser both for desktop and mobile systems have been performed [35]. The results support the plausibility of this approach. In particular, the patterns *Voice-based Interaction Shortcut* and *Speech-enabled Form* were met with high user acceptance. This holds also for traditional interface patterns such as Tidwell's [41] *Autocompletion*. Tidwell's [41] *Spring-loaded Mode* or *One-off Mode* seem to be crucial for controlling recogniser activation.

References

1. Alexander, C., Ishikawa, S., Silverstein, M., Jacobson, M., Fiksdahl-King, I., Angel, S.: A Pattern Language. Oxford University Press, Oxford (1977)
2. Alexander, C.: The Timeless Way of Building. Oxford University Press, Oxford (1979)
3. Almeida, L., Amdal, I., Beires, N., Boualem, M., Boves, L., den Os, E., Filoche, P., Gomes, R., Knudsen, J.E., Kvale, K., Rugelbak, J., Tallec, C., Warakagoda, N.: Implementing and evaluating a multimodal and multilingual tourist guide. In: Proceedings of the International CLASS Workshop on Natural, Intelligent and Effective Interaction in Multimodal Dialogue Systems (2002)
4. Aslan, I., Xu, F., Uszkoreit, H., Krüger, A., Steffen, J.: COMPASS2008: Multimodal, Multilingual and Crosslingual Interaction for Mobile Tourist Guide Applications. In: Maybury, M., Stock, O., Wahlster, W. (eds.) INTETAIN 2005. LNCS (LNAI), vol. 3814, pp. 3–12. Springer, Heidelberg (2005)
5. Benoît, C., Martin, J.C., Pelachaud, C., Schomaker, L., Suhm, B.: Audio-Visual and Multimodal Speech Systems. In: Gibbon, D. (ed.) Handbook of Standards and Resources for Spoken Language Systems - Supplement Volume (1998)
6. Bernsen, N.O.: Multimodality in Language and Speech Systems – from theory to design support tool. In: Lectures at the 7th European Summer School on Language and Speech Communication (ESSLSC) (1999)
7. Borchers, J.: A Pattern Approach to Interaction Design. John Wiley & Sons, Inc., Chichester (2001)
8. Brown, W., Malveau, R., McCormick, H., Mowbray, T., Thomas, S.W.: The Software Patterns Criteria (1998), http://www.antipatterns.com/whatisapattern/
9. Bürgy, C.: An Interaction Constraints Model for Mobile and Wearable Computer-Aided Engineering Systems in Industrial Applications. Department of Civil and Environmental Engineering, Carnegie Mellon University, Pittsburgh, Pennsylvania, USA (2002)
10. Buschmann, F., Meunier, R., Rohnert, H., Sommerlad, P., Stal, M.: Pattern-orientierte Softwarearchitektur. Addison-Wesley, Reading (1998)
11. Cohen, P.R., Johnston, M., McGee, D., Oviatt, S., Pittman, J., Smith, I., Chen, L., Clow, J.: QuickSet: multimodal interaction for distributed applications. In: MULTIMEDIA 1997: Proceedings of the fifth ACM international conference on Multimedia, pp. 31–40. ACM Press, New York (1997)
12. Cohen, P., McGee, D., Clow, J.: The efficiency of multimodal interaction for a map-based task. In: Proceedings of the sixth conference on Applied natural language processing, pp. 331–338. Morgan Kaufmann, San Francisco (2000)
13. Comerford, L., Frank, D., Gopalakrishnan, P., Gopinath, R., Sedivy, J.: The IBM Personal Speech Assistant. In: Proc. of IEEE ICASSP 2001, pp. 319–321 (2001)
14. Coutaz, J.I., Nigay, L., Salber, D., Blandford, A., May, J., Young, R.M.: Four Easy Pieces for Assessing the Usability of Multimodal Interaction: the CARE Properties. In: Proceedings of INTERACT 1995 (1995)
15. Dragičević, P.: Un modèle d'interaction en entrée pour des systèmes interactifs multi-dispositifs hautement configurables. Université de Nantes, école doctorale sciences et technologies de l'information et des matériaux. Diss. (2004)
16. Duarte, C., Carriço, L.: A conceptual framework for developing adaptive multimodal applications. In: IUI 2006: Proceedings of the 11th international conference on Intelligent user interfaces. ACM Press, New York (2006)
17. Gabriel, D.: A Pattern Definition. web ressource (2007), http://hillside.net/patterns/definition.html

18. Gamma, E., Helm, R., Johnson, R., Vlissides, J.: Design Patterns: Elements of Reusable Object-Oriented Software. Addison-Wesley, Reading (1995)
19. Godet-Bar, G., Dupuy-Chessa, S., Nigay, L.: Towards a System of Patterns for the Design of Multimodal Interfaces. In: Proceedings of 6th International Conference on Computer-Aided Design of User Interfaces CADUI 2006, pp. 27–40. Springer, Heidelberg (2006)
20. Grasso, M.A., Ebert, D.S., Finin, T.W.: The integrality of speech in multimodal interfaces. ACM Transactions on Computer-Human Interaction 5(4), 303–325 (1998)
21. Hastie, H.W., Johnston, M., Ehlen, P.: Context-Sensitive Help For Multimodal Dialogue. In: ICMI 2002: Proceedings of the 4th IEEE International Conference on Multimodal Interfaces. IEEE Computer Society, Los Alamitos (2002)
22. Huang, X., Acero, A., Chelba, C., Deng, L., Duchene, D., Goodman, J., Hon, H., Jacoby, D., Jiang, L., Loynd, R., Mahajan, M., Mau, P., Meredith, S., Mughal, S., Neto, S., Plumpe, M., Wang, K., Wang, Y.: MiPad: A Next Generation PDA Prototype. In: ICSLP 2000 (2000)
23. IBM: Developing X+V Applications Using the Multimodal Toolkit and Browser. Manual (2002)
24. Johnston, M., Bangalore, S., Vasireddy, G., Stent, A., Ehlen, P., Walker, M., Whittaker, S., Maloor, P.: MATCH: an architecture for multimodal dialogue systems. In: Proc. of the 40th Annual Meeting on Association for Computational Linguistics, ACL 2002, pp. 376–383 (2002)
25. Mahemoff, M.J., Johnston, L.J.: Usability Pattern Languages: the "Language" Aspect. In: Hirose, M. (ed.) Human-Computer Interaction: Interact 2001, pp. 350–358. IOS Press, Amsterdam (2001)
26. Malaka, R., Haeussler, J., Aras, H.: SmartKom mobile: intelligent ubiquitous user interaction. In: IUI 2004: Proceedings of the 9th international conference on Intelligent user interface, pp. 310–312. ACM Press, New York (2004)
27. Marx, M., Schmandt, C.: Putting people first: specifying proper names in speech interfaces. In: UIST 1994: Proceedings of the 7th annual ACM symposium on User interface software and technology, pp. 29–37. ACM Press, New York (1994)
28. Milota, A.D.: Modality fusion for graphic design applications. In: ICMI 2004: Proceedings of the 6th international conference on Multimodal interfaces, pp. 167–174. ACM Press, New York (2004)
29. Neuss, R.: Usability Engineering als Ansatz zum Multimodalen Mensch-Maschine-Dialog. Fakultät für Elektrotechnik und Informationstechnik, Technische Universität München, Diss. (2001)
30. Niedermaier, F.B.: Entwicklung und Bewertung eines Rapid-Prototyping Ansatzes zur multimodalen Mensch-Maschine-Interaktion im Kraftfahrzeug. Fakultät für Elektrotechnik und Informationstechnik, Technische Universität München, Diss. (2003)
31. Nigay, L., Coutaz, J.: A design space for multimodal systems: concurrent processing and data fusion. In: Proceedings of Human Factors in Computing Systems, INTERCHI 1993 Conference, pp. 172–178. ACM Press, New York (1993)
32. Obrenović, Ž., Abascal, J., Starčević, D.: Universal accessibility as a multimodal design issue. In: Commun. ACM, vol. 50, pp. 83–88. ACM Press, New York (2007)
33. Oviatt, S., Cohen, P., Wu, L., Vergo, J., Duncan, L., Suhm, B., Bers, J., Holzman, T., Winograd, T., Landay, J., Larson, J., Ferro, D.: Designing the User Interface for Multimodal Speech and Pen-based Gesture Applications: State-of-the-Art Systems and Future Research Directions. Human Computer Interaction 15(4), 263–322 (2000)

34. Ratzka, A., Wolff, C.: A Pattern-based Methodology for Multimodal Interaction Design. In: Sojka, P., Kopeček, I., Pala, K. (eds.) TSD 2006. LNCS (LNAI), vol. 4188, pp. 677–686. Springer, Heidelberg (2006)
35. Ratzka, A.: A Wizard-of-Oz Setting for Multimodal Interaction. An Approach to User-Based Elicitation of Design Patterns. In: Osswald, A., Stempfhuber, M., Wolff, C. (eds.) Open Innovation. Proc. 10th International Symposium for Information Science, Universitätsverlag Konstanz, pp. 159–170 (2007a)
36. Ratzka, A.: Design Patterns in the Context of Multi-modal Interaction. In: Proceedings of the 6th Nordic Conference on Pattern Languages of Programs 2007 VikingPLoP 2007 (to appear, 2007b)
37. Ratzka, A.: Design Patterns for Robust and Accessible Multimodal Interaction. In: Proceedings of EuroPLoP 2008 (to appear, 2008)
38. Sinnig, D., Gaffar, A., Reichart, D., Seffah, A., Forbrig, P.: Patterns in Model-Based Engineering. In: CADUI 2004, pp. 195–208 (2004)
39. Snelick, R., Indovina, M., Yen, J., Mink, A.: Multimodal biometrics: issues in design and testing. In: ICMI 2003: Proceedings of the 5th international conference on Multimodal interfaces, pp. 68–72. ACM Press, New York (2003)
40. Tidwell, J.: COMMON GROUND: A Pattern Language for Human-Computer Interface Design (1999), `http://www.mit.edu/~jtidwell/interaction_patterns.html`
41. Tidwell, J.: Designing Interfaces: Patterns for Effective Interaction Design. O'Reilly, Sebastopol (2005)
42. van Welie, M., Trætteberg, H.: Interaction Patterns in User Interfaces. In: Proceedings of the Seventh Pattern Languages of Programs Conference (2000)
43. van Welie, M.: Task-based User Interface Design. Dutch Graduate School for Information and Knowledge Systems, Vrije Universiteit Amsterdam, Diss. (2001)
44. Zeng, Z., Tu, J., Liu, M., Zhang, T., Rizzolo, N., Zhang, Z., Huang, T.S., Roth, D., Levinson, S.: Bimodal HCI-related affect recognition. In: ICMI 2004: Proceedings of the 6th international conference on Multimodal interfaces, pp. 137–143. ACM Press, New York (2004)

Information Supply Mechanisms in Ubiquitous Computing, Crisis Management and Workflow Modelling

Jurriaan van Diggelen, Robbert-Jan Beun, Rogier M. van Eijk,
and Peter J. Werkhoven

Institute of Information and Computing Sciences
Utrecht University, the Netherlands
{jurriaan,rj,rogier}@cs.uu.nl, peter.werkhoven@tno.nl

Abstract. The successful application of ubiquitous computing in crisis management requires a thorough understanding of the mechanisms that extract information from sensors and communicate it via PDA's to crisis workers. Whereas
query and subscribe protocols are well studied mechanisms for information exchange between different computers, it is not straightforward how to apply them
for communication between a computer and a human crisis worker, with limited
cognitive resources. To examine the imposed cognitive load, we focus on the relation of the information supply mechanism with the workflow, or task model, of
the crisis worker. We formalize workflows and interaction mechanisms in colored
Petri nets, specify various ways to relate them and discuss their pros and cons.

Keywords: Ubiquitous Computing, Notification Systems, Human-machine Interaction, Workflow Modelling, Petri Nets.

1   Introduction

Ubiquitous computing [20] is a model of human-computer interaction which offers specific application possibilities and which requires specific design methodologies. In this
paper, we will study the use of Workflow Modelling (WM) for designing Ubiquitous
Computing (UC) systems, in the domain of Crisis Management (CM). We shall briefly
explain these three disciplines and their relations below.

CM involves identifying an incident or a disaster, such as fire or a traffic accident,
and subsequently confronting and resolving it in order to minimize the damage. Information transfer plays a crucial role in these activities. Lack of information (*information
underload* [11]) is often identified as a potential cause of mistakes as it leads to decisions based on incomplete information. Also, too much information (*cognitive overload*
[10]) may cause errors, as it distracts the crisis worker from his or her primary tasks.

Ubiquitous computing provides an adequate way to bridge the information gap in
CM. UC aims at making hundreds of networked computing devices and sensors work
together to get the *right* information to the *right* person at the *right* time [4]. What
qualifies as *right* information then depends on the work that is performed by the crisis
team member.

P. Forbrig and F. Paternò (Eds.): HCSE/TAMODIA 2008, LNCS 5247, pp. 72–83, 2008.

This is how Workflow Modelling fits in. WM has proven itself as a successful method to precisely describe a business process and optimize various aspects such as efficiency, average completion time, and utilization of resources. In our opinion, WM is also a promising approach to model work processes in the CM domain. In general, we believe that WM yields valuable insights in the design phase of *any* UC system. The reason for this is simple. If we expect a system to pro-actively present valuable information to its user (as in UC), the system must know something about the user's *task*. In this paper, we will use the term workflow interchangeably with the term task, although in the literature the two terms are sometimes used to denote slightly different things (we will come back to this issue in Section 5). Therefore, WM can be regarded as a necessary part of the design phase of the system.

Whereas UC, CM and WM are all well-developed research areas, the combination of the three disciplines raises several issues that have not yet been addressed in the literature. In this paper, we tackle two of these issues, which are briefly described below.

The first issue concerns the application of WM to CM. Current workflow management techniques are typically tailored to business processes. Likewise, current workflow analysis techniques are typically concerned with business goals, e.g. minimizing production costs. To apply WM to the CM domain, the important aspects of CM should be well-representable, such as ignorance, information underload, cognitive overload and distraction. In this paper we will apply a WM technique which uses Petri Nets [16]. We will show how the knowledge of the crisis worker can be modelled in this approach. Furthermore, we will show how notions such as information underload and cognitive overload can be mapped to well-known theoretical properties of Petri Nets.

The second issue concerns the application of WM to UC, i.e. the modelling of the interaction mechanisms that are responsible for providing the crisis worker with the right information. Two well-known interaction mechanisms in UC (and multi-agent systems in general) are the Query protocol and the Publish/Subscribe protocol [3]. Both of these protocols have been specified using various formal methods, among which Petri Nets. Nevertheless, these specifications focus on the low level properties of the interaction mechanisms, such as possible network failures, input buffer overloads and so forth. Because UC and CM require us to consider the cognitive aspects of information exchange, these specifications do not suffice. We will show that, by modelling various interaction mechanisms directly in the workflow model, we can examine the effects of these interaction mechanisms in terms of cognitive aspects. In fact, it appears that, next to the query protocol, at least four different types of subscription mechanisms exist. For each of the interaction mechanisms, we will give a Petri net specification and give template design procedures to join these with the workflow model. Furthermore, we will compare the different interaction mechanisms by evaluating their effects on resolving information underload and preventing cognitive overload.

Section 2 presents workflow modelling. Section 3 discusses how information supply mechanisms can be formalized in relation to a workflow. Analysis techniques are discussed in Section 4. Related work is discussed in Section 5, followed by a conclusion and directions for future work in Section 6.

2 Workflow Modelling

Standard workflow modelling techniques distinguish between tasks, conditions and cases. A *task* refers to an indivisible piece of work that needs to be done. The order of these tasks is determined by *conditions*. The thing that is produced or modified as a result of the work carried out, is called the *case*.

In crisis management, the case is the incident or crisis that is being handled, e.g. a *fire* reported at the fire station. A condition represents the current state of the incident, for example whether the *fire* is being fought by firemen or not. The tasks in this example are the pieces of work carried out by the firemen, such as moving to the disaster area, or extinguishing the fire. In the CM-workflows discussed in this paper, all tasks are carried out by the same resource. We refer to this resource as the *actor*.

Workflows can be specified using Petri nets. Figure 1 specifies the workflow of the fire example.

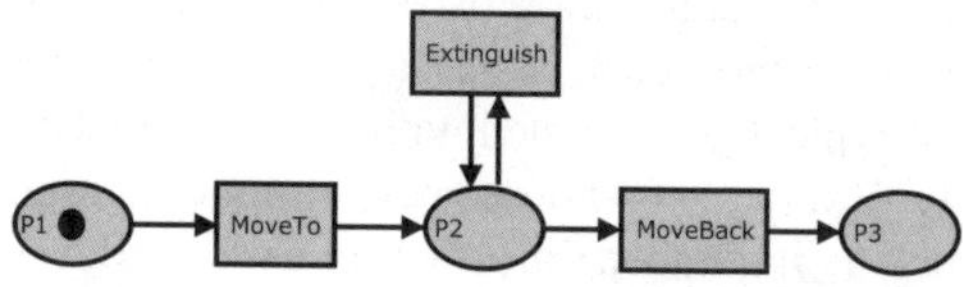

Fig. 1. The CM Workflow

A Petri net consist of places, transitions and tokens. Places are represented by ovals and correspond to the conditions of the workflow. Transitions are represented by rectangles and correspond to tasks. Tokens are represented by black dots and correspond to the cases being handled.

In Petri nets, transitions are the active components, i.e. they can move tokens from input places (places connected by incoming arrows) to output places (places connected by outgoing arrows). A transition can fire if a token resides at all of its input places. After a transition has fired, it consumes a token at each of its input places and produces a token at each of its output places.

In Figure 1, the transition *MoveTo* can fire, because place *p1* contains a token. After the transition has fired, place *p1* is empty, and place *p2* contains one token. In this configuration, the transitions *Extinguish* and *MoveBack* can fire (it is undefined which one of the two will actually fire). The process ends when the token arrives at place *p3*.

To model the characteristics of a case, known as case attributes, we extend the classical Petri net with *color*. In colored Petri nets, tokens have a value which can be used in conditional statements at transitions and which can be altered by the firing of transitions. For example, suppose that the token in Figure 1 contains the value ⟨*fire:on* , *location:townhall*⟩[1]. The transition *MoveTo* contains a conditional statement that only tokens with value *fire:on* can be consumed. This establishes that the firemen only move to locations where a fire is burning. The transition *MoveBack* states that the token must have the value *fire:out*. This prevents that the firemen leave the disaster area too quickly.

---

[1] For readability, we have not included color information in the Petri net diagrams.

Contrary to most WM techniques, token values do not represent what the characteristics of the case actually *are*, but what the actor *knows* about the case. For example, the transition *Extinguish* states that after the transition has fired the token has the value *fire:unknown*. This represents that the firemen do not know whether their extinguishing efforts have resulted in the fire going out. It may be that there are still flames inside the building which are not visible from outside. For the fireman to continue with the task *Extinguish* or *MoveBack*, he must know whether the fire is still burning or not. In a ubiquitous computing environment, the fireman obtains this information via his PDA which establishes a wireless connection with the fire sensors in the building. For a technical analysis on the interaction between the PDA and the sensors in the environment, the reader is referred to [19].

In this paper, we are mainly concerned with the interaction between the PDA and the crisis worker. In the next section, we discuss different ways in which the PDA can present information to its user and how this can be modeled in the workflow.

3   Information Supply Mechanisms

To model an information supply mechanism, two additional Petri nets must be introduced. For modularity, we have separated these Petri nets from the main workflow. Additionally, the relations between these Petri nets and the main workflow are specified.

One Petri net model concerns the world, which is the ultimate source from which information is obtained. Figure 2 shows a model of a dynamically changing world. This Petri net simply replaces the value of the token in place *p15* with a random value, following either transition *Update1* or *Update2*. This simple model is sufficient for our purposes, but can be easily replaced by a more sophisticated world model, if required.

Fig. 2. World model

Another Petri net is used to model how information is obtained from the world and how the interaction protocol provides access to this information. Throughout the rest of this section, we will describe several simple models of well-known interaction mechanisms, such as query and subscribe.

Most insight into the information supply mechanisms is provided by the way in which the three individual Petri nets are combined into a whole. This aspect forms the most important part of the remainder of this section. For the query mechanism, this is described in Section 3.1. Three different kinds of subscribe mechanisms are described in Section 3.2, and a conditional subscribe mechanism is presented in Section 3.3.

3.1   Query

The first interaction mechanism we will discuss is Query. The left-hand side of Figure 3 shows the workflow plus one additional transition to establish the coupling with the query protocol. The places and transitions belonging to the workflow are colored grey.

The right-hand side of the figure shows the query protocol. The two Petri nets are coupled by a so-called hierarchical transition (indicated by a double-lined box). The hierarchical query transition in the WF-net achieves that place p2 (i.e. the place with which the hierarchical transition is connected), becomes identical with the input/output place of the query Petri net (place *p4* which is labelled with "I/O").

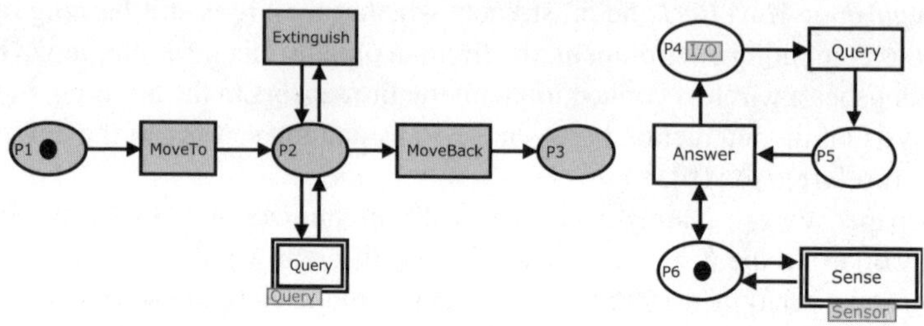

Fig. 3. Query

The mechanism works as follows. If the token arrives at place *p2*, both the transition *Query* and the transition *Extinguish* are enabled. If the transition *Query* fires, the token leaves the workflow net and arrives at place *p5*. The token stays there until the transition *Answer* fires. This transition produces a token at place *p4* (or equally well *p2*) with some of the token attributes replaced by the attributes of the token in *p6*. The token in *p6* represents the current sensor reading, which is occasionally updated by the hierarchical transition *Sense*. The Petri net behind this transition is the world model depicted in Figure 2. In this way, the token in *p6* is regularly updated with up-to-date world information. Note that the token in *p6* is not removed when the *Answer* transition fires, as it is connected with a double-headed arrow (it is both an input and an output place).

We will characterize this information supply mechanism by discussing interruption and optionality.

As appears from the Petri net specification, the mechanism causes a major interruption of the main workflow process. Firstly, the task *Query* must be performed, which is not a part of the workflow process. After that, the token arrives at place *p5*, which is also not part of the workflow process. It must wait until the transition *Answer* fires to return to the main workflow.

The other issue is that the obtaining of information is optional. This is because in place *p2*, two transitions may be enabled at the same time, i.e. *Extinguish* and *Query*. Hence, the fireman may choose not to ask for an information update and carry out the *Extinguish* immediately. The benefit may be time savings. The drawback may be ignorance.

3.2 Subscribe

Besides querying, a common interaction mechanism in ubiquitous computing and peer-to-peer systems is the Publish-Subscribe protocol [15]. By subscribing to a piece of information, a continuous flow of information is initiated. There are three ways in which this information may actually be absorbed by the actor: non-interruptive,non-optional; interruptive,optional or interruptive,non-optional.

Figure 4 specifies the non-interruptive, non-optional subscribe mechanism. One can think of this subscribe mechanism as the low fuel light on the dashboard of a car. It guarantees that information is delivered to the driver (it is non-optional) and does not require any effort (its is non-interruptive).

In the Petri net specification, the workflow model (on the left) is coupled with the subscribe model (on the right) using a fusion set.[2] (called *Fusion 1*). Multiple places that occur in the same fusion set become identical. The mechanism works as follows. The subscribe protocol contains a token in place *p6* which represents the content of the subscription, for example *fire:on*. If this content matches the current sensor reading (represented by the token in *p7*), the transition *Notify* fires. Otherwise, the transition *Remain Silent* fires. The token in place *p5* (and likewise *p3*) is provided with up-to-date token attributes as a result of this firing. The information arrives at the actor during the execution of his tasks, i.e. the information in the token of *p3* is blended with the information in the token of the workflow.

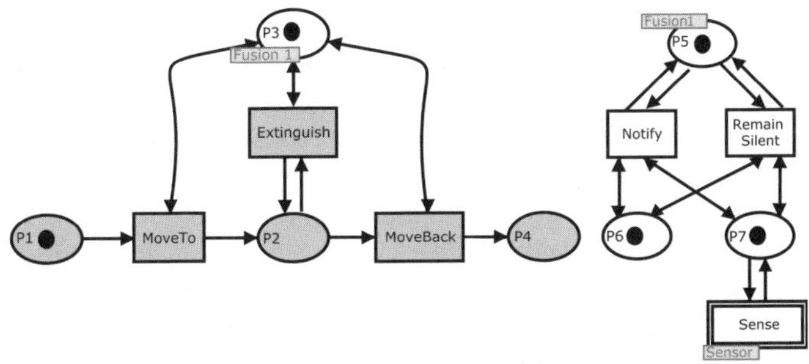

Fig. 4. Subscribe 1 (non-interruptive, non-optional)

Contrary to the Query mechanism, this communication mechanism does not cause any interruption. This is expressed in the Petri net specification by the fact that the case token can never leave the workflow model. Furthermore, the obtaining of up-to-date information is not optional but is enforced by the model.

Some information is too complex to be conveyed without interruption as it requires some mental processing by the receiver. For these cases, an interruptive subscribe mechanism can be used. Figure 5 shows an interruptive, optional subscription mechanism. One can think of this subscribe mechanism as the clock on a mobile phone. The phone maintains up-to-date information which the owner can choose to consult by investing a little effort, namely getting it out of his pocket.

In the specification *p4,p5,p6* and *p7* are identical, and contain a token which represents up-to-date information about the world. When the transition *Consult* fires, the token attributes of this token are passed to the token in the workflow model.

---

[2] The difference of assembling Petri nets with a fusion set instead of with a hierarchical transition, is that when the hierarchical transition occurs multiple times in the main Petri net, multiple instances of the sub-Petri net are created. This is not the case when places from the same fusion set occur multiple times in the main Petri net.

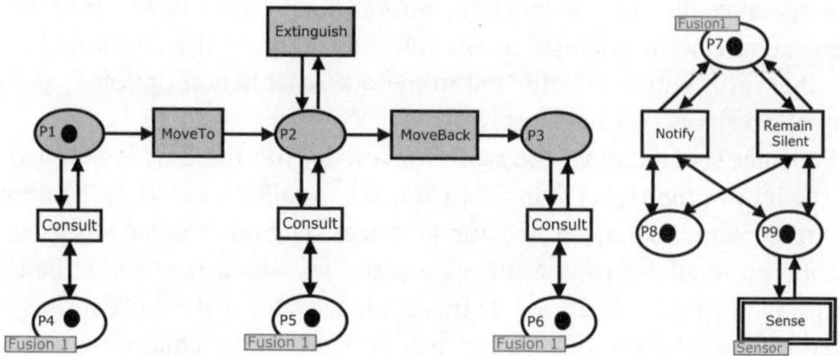

Fig. 5. Subscribe 2 (interruptive, optional)

This interaction mechanism causes a little interruption. This appears from the fact that the *Consult* task (which is not part of the workflow model) must be carried out. As with the Query mechanism, the obtaining of information is optional.

Yet another type of subscribe mechanism is the interruptive, non-optional subscription, as depicted in Figure 6. This mechanism can be thought of as a mobile phone, i.e. when it rings, the owner is forced to consult it before he can continue with the task at hand.

This specification uses two fusion sets. *Fusion 1* consists of *p4,p6,p8* and represents that there is currently a notification to be processed. *Fusion 2* consists of *p5,p7* and *p9* and represents that there is currently no notification to be processed. The notification protocol (shown on the right of the figure) ensures that a token cannot be in the groups *Fusion 1* and *Fusion 2* at the same time. This is because, when *Notify* fires, the token is removed from *Fusion 2* and added to *Fusion 1*. The only way that the token can return to *Fusion 2* is via *Consult*, which removes a token from *Fusion 1* and adds a token to *Fusion 2*. Therefore, when a token resides in *Fusion 1* the tasks in the workflow are blocked (because all tasks require a token to be present in *Fusion 2*). This means that the actor has no choice but to consult the notification. After the transition *Consult* has fired the token is moved from *Fusion 1* to *Fusion 2*, and the workflow tasks are enabled again.

Like the previous subscribe protocol we discussed, this mechanism causes a little interruption due to the *Consult* task. However, this subscribe mechanism is not optional, i.e. when a notification is sent, the actor has no choice but to turn his attention to it.

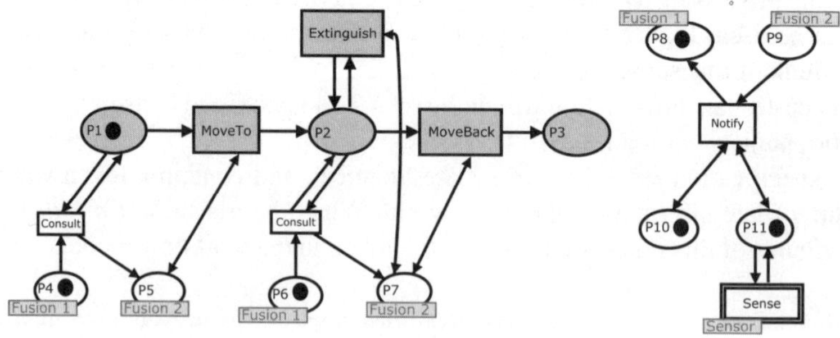

Fig. 6. Subscribe 3 (interruptive, non-optional)

3.3 Conditional Subscribe

By using a conditional subscription, a user requests to receive notifications of something only if some condition holds. For example, the fireman may request to receive notifications about *fire:out* only when he is at the disaster area, and not when he is at the office. In order to realize such a notification system, the system must be *context-aware* [1], i.e. it must know the user's location and adapt its behavior to it. Although for every communication mechanism discussed so far, a context-aware variant can be specified, we focus on a variant of the interruptive, non-optional subscribe mechanism (Subscribe 3 in Figure 6). As an example of this conditional subscribe mechanism, one can think of a context-aware mobile phone, which automatically shuts off when the user enters a lecture hall.

The specification of the conditional subscribe is depicted in Figure 7. This specification uses a third fusion set *Fusion 3*, consisting of *p13*, *p14* and *p15* (see the world model in Figure 2). The purpose of this fusion set is to model the effect of task execution on the world (place *p15*). For example, the transition *MoveTo* updates the token in place *p13* (and *p15*) to represent the information that the fireman is no longer at the office but at the disaster area. The *Sense* transition is specified such that it also obtains information about the location of the fireman (for example, using GPS). An extra place is added (*p12*), which represents the condition when the subscription applies (in our example, that the fireman is not at the office). Like the protocols discussed before, place *p10* represents the information to which the actor is subscribed (in our example *fire:out*).

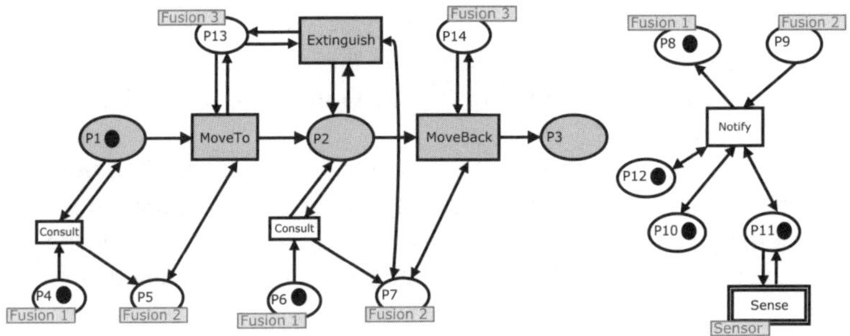

Fig. 7. Conditional Subscribe (interruptive, non-optional)

With respect to interruption and choice, this protocol has the same properties as the third subscribe protocol (Figure 6). It causes a little interruption when a notification is received and the owner of the device has no choice but to process the incoming notifications.

3.4 Comparison

The differences between the five information supply mechanisms discussed in this section are summarized below. We have used three degrees to indicate interruption. High interruption (+) means that a transition and a place are visited which are not part of the workflow model. Medium interruption (+/-) means that only a transition is executed which is not part of the workflow model. No interruption (-) means that no states and transitions are executed which are not part of the workflow. Optionality can be positive (+), when the actor has a choice to obtain information, or negative (-) when there is no such choice. Context aware (+) means that the information supply mechanism behaves differently depending on at which place the actor resides at that moment. Otherwise, the system is not context aware (-).

	Query	Subscr1	Subscr2	Subscr3	CondSubscr3
Interruption	$+$	$-$	$+/-$	$+/-$	$+/-$
Optionality	$+$	$-$	$+$	$-$	$-$
Context aware	$-$	$-$	$-$	$-$	$+$

As we have argued before, a context aware variant can be made also for the other information supply mechanisms. This would yield three more protocols. With respect to the properties of Interruption and Optionality, there are six possible combinations. We believe that the four combinations we have covered are the only sensible ones. A protocol with optionality and no interruption is impossible because a choice can only be modeled by introducing a transition which is not part of the workflow, which would cause interruption again. A protocol with high interruption but no optionality would be possible, but not very useful, because the second subscribe mechanism can be used for the same purpose, causing only medium interruption.

4   Analysis Techniques

We have implemented the Petri nets described in this paper in CPN-tools [5], a tool for modelling and validating colored Petri nets. Using this tool, several kinds of errors in the model can be detected.

Firstly, there are the trivial structural errors in the design model. The transitions and tokens may be wrongly connected, the transitions may be configured in a way which conflicts with the token values, or the data structures may contain syntactic errors. In these cases, the CPN-tool will simply generate a syntax error stating that the Petri net is incorrect.

More interesting are the errors in the crisis management model which the Petri net represents. For the workflow part of the model, all analysis techniques can be used which have been developed for workflow analysis [17]. For example, it can be checked whether the workflow terminates, i.e. whether the token eventually arrives at a place which is the final destination (in our example, this is place $p3$). Another important property for workflow Petri nets is the boundedness property. This property states that every place will never contain more than a certain number of tokens. This is important because otherwise the relation between the token and the case that it represents becomes unclear.

In the remainder of this section, we describe some validation criteria that are specific to the combination of workflow models and information supply mechanisms.

The first issue we discuss is information underload. In our workflow model, we have represented the information needs of the actor [18] as the *preconditions* of a task. For example, the transition *MoveBack* in Figure 1 can only fire if *fire* has the value *out*. Because the precondition of the task *Extinguish* is *fire:on*, a token with value *fire:*

unknown in *p2* can go nowhere. In Petri net theory, such a situation is called *deadlock*. Many algorithms exist to compute deadlock situations efficiently. In our crisis management models, deadlock indicates information underload of the actor, which should be resolved by adding information supply mechanisms. For example, the workflow model in Figure 1 suffers from information underload. This is because after the transition *Extinguish* has fired the value of *fire* is *unknown* and the net is in a deadlock situation. The other models (in Figure 3, 4, 5, 6, 7), do not lead to a deadlock situation and thus do not suffer from information underload.

As mentioned before, another important problem in crisis management is cognitive overload, i.e. when the actor receives too much information to be able to stay focussed on his main tasks. In our framework, we can measure the expected cognitive load of the information supply mechanisms by performing a simulation analysis. Using CPN-tools, the execution of a Petri net can be simulated to analyze how the token moves through the transitions and places. By applying a counter to some of the transitions and places that do not belong to the main workflow (such as *consult* in our example), an indicator is obtained on the expected cognitive load.

We have applied this simulation analysis to the Petri-nets described in this paper. Because the workflow and world model are very simple, this analysis merely confirmed the properties which we had already theoretically determined in Section 3.4. In a more realistic scenario, however, the workflow is much larger and the actor might obtain his information from multiple sources which makes it impossible to theoretically foresee all possible behaviors of the model. In these cases, a simulation analysis provides a valuable contribution to what can be theoretically assessed.

5   Related Work

We will divide our discussion on related work into three categories, corresponding to the different purposes for which our approach can be used.

Firstly, our approach can be viewed as a formalization of an interaction protocol. Petri-net formalizations of computer-computer interaction have a long tradition in computer science (e.g. [9], [2]). However, theories on human-computer interaction are usually not mathematically formalized. For example, [8] identifies an *attention-utility trade-off* in notification systems. The costs of notification are defined as the amount of attention removed from the user's primary task. The benefits of a notification system are characterized along three dimensions, i.e. comprehension, reaction and interruption. Another approach addressing this trade-off focusses on peripheral information displays [7]. This work presents experimental results on what we would call a non-interruptive, non-optional subscribe mechanism (Subscribe 1). Whereas these approaches nicely identify the different aspects that are important in human-computer communication, they do not provide a formal underpinning. We believe that our Petri-net formalization of human-computer communication is useful to make the attention-utility trade-off more precise, resulting in a better understanding of the different aspects involved.

A second way to view our approach is as a method for analysing and evaluating interactive systems. For this purpose, task models are frequently applied, e.g. Concur-TaskTrees [14]. Whereas task models and workflows are tightly related [6], there are also some differences. We will discuss some relevant correspondences and differences between ConcurTaskTree models and Petri-net workflow models below. Both models allow the representation of concurrency, have an intuitive graphical syntax, and can be automatically verified. A difference is that task models are usually hierarchically structured whereas workflows are not. Because for our purposes, it suffices to view the work process at one level of abstraction, this restriction of workflow models is not problematic. Another difference is that Petri-nets are suitable for modelling information flows at a high level of detail (as proven by the popularity of Petri-net based communication protocols), whereas it is not clear how this can be done in a task model. Because modelling information flows is crucial to our approach, we have chosen for Petri-net workflows instead of ConcurTaskTree models.

A third way to apply the results described in this paper is as a model to be used by the computer at runtime (as is proposed in [13]). For example, it can be used by a PDA to adjust its notification style by estimating the cognitive load it imposes on its user. Because our model is computational, it can be applied to this purpose.

6   Conclusion and Future Research

In this paper, we have characterized different information supply mechanisms by specifying their relation with a workflow. This allows us to precisely capture those aspects of query and subscribe mechanisms that are important for human crisis workers. In general, we believe the techniques proposed in this paper provide valuable insights for modelling the interaction between humans and multi-agent systems.

We have identified two promising directions for future research. Firstly, we plan to apply more advanced workflow modelling techniques to enable a more thorough analysis of crisis management. One option would be to extend the Petri nets with time. This would allow us to estimate the average completion time of the process, and to study the influence of different information supply mechanisms on this. Another option would be to use *adaptive workflows*, which is the area of workflow management concerned with modelling exceptions on the normal course of action. Particularly for crisis management, this aspect is highly relevant.

Another direction for future research is concerned with agent-organizational aspects of workflow modelling [12]. It is typically unknown at design time which sensors will be available at the time and place a crisis takes place. Therefore, it should be possible to discover and invoke sensors that provide valuable information at runtime. In workflow modelling, this is called resource allocation, i.e. assigning a resource to a task in an efficient way. In our case, the resource is a sensor and the task is making a measurement. We plan to investigate how results from resource allocation can be used to enhance efficiency in ubiquitous computing, for example to decide which sensor can best be queried for which type of information.

References

1. Abowd, G.D., Dey, A.K., Brown, P.J., Davies, N., Smith, M., Steggles, P.: Towards a better understanding of context and context-awareness, pp. 304–307 (1999)
2. Cost, R.S., Chen, Y., Finin, T., Labrou, Y., Peng, Y.: Using colored petri nets for conversation modeling. In: Dignum, F., Greaves, M. (eds.) Issues in Agent Communication, pp. 178–192. Springer, Heidelberg (2000)

3. Finin, T., Fritzson, R., McKay, D., McEntire, R.: KQML as an agent communication language. In: Proceedings of CIKM, pp. 456–463. ACM Press, New York (1994)
4. Fischer, G.: User modeling in human-computer interaction. In: User Modeling and User-Adapted Interaction, vol. 11. Springer, Heidelberg (2001)
5. Jensen, K., Kristensen, L., Wells, L.: Coloured petri nets and CPN tools for modelling and validation of concurrent systems. International Journal on Software Tools for Technology Transfer 9(3), 213–254 (2007)
6. Kristiansen, R., Traetteberg, H.: Model-based user interface design in the context of workflow models. In: Winckler, M., Johnson, H., Palanque, P. (eds.) TAMODIA 2007. LNCS, vol. 4849, pp. 227–239. Springer, Heidelberg (2007)
7. Maglio, P.P., Campbell, C.S.: Tradeoffs in displaying peripheral information. In: CHI 2000: Proceedings of the SIGCHI conference on Human factors in computing systems, pp. 241–248. ACM Press, New York (2000)
8. McCrickard, D.S., Chewar, C.M.: Attuning notification design to user goals and attention costs. Commununications of the ACM 46(3), 67–72 (2003)
9. Mikkilineni, K., Chow, Y.-C., Su, S.: Petri-net-based modeling and evaluation of pipelined processing of concurrent database queries. IEEE Transactions on Software Engineering 14(11), 1656–1667 (1988)
10. Neerincx, M., Griffioen, E.: Cognitive task analysis: harmonizing tasks to human capacities. Ergonomics 39(4), 543–561 (1996)
11. Netten, N., Bruinsma, G., van Someren, M., de Hoog, R.: Task-adaptive information distribution for dynamic collaborative response. Special Issue on Emergency Management Systems of the International Journal of Intelligent Control and Systems (IJICS) 11(4), 237–246 (2006)
12. Oliveira, M.D., Cranefield, S., Purvis, M.: Normative spaces in institutional environments by the means of commitments, reputation and colored petri nets. In: Proceedings of the 8th International Workshop on Agent Oriented Software Engineering (AOSE) (2007)
13. Pangoli, S., Paternó, F.: Automatic generation of task-oriented help. In: UIST 1995: Proceedings of the 8th annual ACM symposium on User interface and software technology, pp. 181–187. ACM Press, New York (1995)
14. Paternò, F., Mancini, C., Meniconi, S.: Concurtasktrees: A diagrammatic notation for specifying task models. In: INTERACT 1997: Proceedings of the IFIP TC13 Interantional Conference on Human-Computer Interaction, pp. 362–369. Chapman and Hall, Boca Raton (1997)
15. Ranganathan, A., Campbell, R.H.: An infrastructure for context-awareness based on first order logic. Personal Ubiquitous Computing 7(6), 353–364 (2003)
16. van der Aalst, W., van Hee, K.: Workflow management: models, methods, and systems. MIT Press, Cambridge (2002)
17. van der Aalst, W.M.P.: Verification of workflow nets. In: Azéma, P., Balbo, G. (eds.) ICATPN 1997. LNCS, vol. 1248, pp. 407–426. Springer, Heidelberg (1997)
18. van Diggelen, J., Beun, R.J., van Eijk, R.M., Werkhoven, P.J.: Modeling decentralized information flow in ambient environments. In: Proceedings of ambient intelligence developments (AmI.D 2007) (2007)
19. van Diggelen, J., Beun, R.J., van Eijk, R.M., Werkhoven, P.J.: Agent communication in ubiquitous computing: the ubismart approach. In: Proceedings of the Seventh International Conference on Autonomous Agents and Multi-agent Systems (AAMAS 2008), pp. 813–820. ACM Press, New York (2008)
20. Weiser, M.: The computer for the 21st century. Scientific American 265(3), 66–75 (1991)

A Method for Modeling Interactions on Task Representations in Business Task Management Systems

Todor Stoitsev and Stefan Scheidl

SAP AG, SAP Research, Germany
{todor.stoitsev,stefan.scheidl}@sap.com

Abstract. Task modeling approaches facilitate the design of interactive systems by bridging the gap from understanding human tasks to designing interfaces to support these tasks. Business Task Management (BTM) systems provide explicit task representations for managing and coordinating work items, by further requiring definition of how such task representations can be created, distributed and monitored throughout an organization. This paper presents a method for modeling interactions on task representations in BTM systems. It introduces generic task-centric roles as useful abstractions, encapsulating different perspectives on tasks and related interactions. This allows generic, domain-independent views on tasks resulting in enhanced adaptability of BTM systems in different application contexts. The method is implemented in the Collaborative Task Manager (CTM) tool.

Keywords: Task management, interactions modeling, end user development.

1 Introduction

The need to develop adaptable software applications which can be swiftly tailored to specific end user needs and application domains has resulted in flexible, model-driven software engineering approaches. Task modelling approaches have proven highly efficient for designing interactive applications. CTT [16] enable system designers to describe the logical activities that an interactive application should support and facilitate model-driven software engineering from requirements analysis to user interface design. Further approaches like GOMS [8] take a goal-oriented view and provide comprehensive description of activity sequences and tasks' interrelations. GTA [21] combines task analysis methods from human computer interaction with ethnographic methods as used in computer supported cooperative work and provides comprehensive methodology for the design of groupware systems. While the above approaches focus on describing user activities and the interactions needed to support them, they do not consider interactions on explicit task representations in formal systems. Such representations are used in Business Task Management (BTM) systems to manage and coordinate work items, and can be e.g. to-do items in personal task lists or in a central work list of a company department. Modelling of interactions on task representations can bring flexibility to BTM systems and make them adaptable to different business domains and application contexts. This requires abstractions of the possible

P. Forbrig and F. Paternò (Eds.): HCSE/TAMODIA 2008, LNCS 5247, pp. 84–97, 2008.

interactions from personal and from organizational point of view, which can allow clustering of requirements and detection of generic interaction patterns on task representations.

Molina et al. consider deficiencies in known approaches for modelling collaborative aspects of human work and propose pattern-based techniques for designing groupware applications [13]. However, their methodological framework starts with modelling of the given organizational structure, which binds the approach to a given enterprise and business domain. Organizational patterns for early requirements analysis are discussed in [9]. These patterns are however elicited based on case studies in concrete enterprises and do not provide a high-level generalization of organizational roles and basic interactions, needed to support collaborative work.

This paper presents a generic modelling approach, which is not confined to a given business domain or concrete organizational structure. The approach provides abstractions for defining high level interactions on explicit task representations in BTM systems based on generic, task-centric roles. This enables flexible adaptation of the BTM system in different usage contexts. Domain-specific extensions are enabled through mapping of the task-centric roles to organizational roles. The presented approach is implemented through the Collaborative Task Management (CTM) prototype.

The remainder of the paper is organized as follows. In section 2 we discuss the background of the presented modelling method. The method is described in section 3. In section 4 we present the implementation of the method in the CTM prototype. In section 5 we give conclusions and future research directions.

2 Background

The presented work founds on empirical research based on site visits and interviews at three companies from different industries: textile (120 employees), software (ca. 500 employees), automotive (ca. 150 employees) and is consolidated with extensive literature research. As part of our activities we investigated end user interactions with software systems within the context of day-to-day work. Our purpose was to reveal basic user demands and pain-points in the area of task management and software support for agile business processes.

There is plenty evidence that some aspects of human work are similar in different business domains, organizational or individual day-to-day activities. Reappearing interaction schemes are discussed in related literature in the field of interactive systems design, i.e. as task patterns, providing reusable structures for task models [6, 14, 15]. The idea for reappearing interactions is in the background of the presented work. We suggest that as a first step towards user-centric task management observations it is essential to determine basic user segmentation. It should provide high level abstractions for different user activity types and thereby also basic directions for the detection of significantly different interaction schemes on task representations.

There is a common notion of basic user activity types. These are divided into strategic, tactical and operational and are especially used in decision-making and planning studies [5, 17]. Further studies use this segmentation to reduce the complexity for system observations from significantly different perspectives [23]. An extended view, focusing on intellectual capital governance is presented in [22], where additionally

'Global/Societal' and 'Implementation/Application' perspectives are introduced. We suggest that this segmentation can be considered also in task management context. For our studies we used the following basic activity types:

- **Strategic:** Refers to activities with high degree of unpredictability and strong innovation character, further involving extended collaboration and people management. Example activity – strategy planning.
- **Tactical:** Refers to activities with higher need for flexibility and rapid adaptation. Such activities often imply 'on demand' innovation and creativity to increase efficiency, avoid bottlenecks and workaround unanticipated problems. Example activities – supply chain management, production planning.
- **Operational:** Refers to activities with higher degree of predictability and repeatability. Such activities mostly consist of routine tasks. Example activities – support center activities, sales order processing.
- **Implementation/Application:** Refers to activities, where existing abstract knowledge is transformed to tangible implementations and processes. It is different from operational as there is a noticeable creative element. There is also a significant difference to the tactical level as the focus is set on the actual implementation and not on the overall planning. Example activity – software implementation, non-automated production/crafting.
- **Societal/Educational:** Refers to activities with strong societal character, where new knowledge is created, systematized and transferred. Example activity – teaching/training course preparation.

The presented activity types provide abstract categories for tasks of significantly different nature. Nevertheless, it should be considered that it is not always possible to match all day-to-day activities of a system user to only one activity type. For example a project manager, who is usually executing tactical activities, may have also operational tasks, deriving from common organizational practices like e.g. performance feedback or quarterly reports.

An overview of the background information that we collected for the elaboration of the presented method is shown in Figure 1. The three top level layers build the foundation for a business centric top-down view on a task management system. We examined the different activity types described above based on identified example users from different business domains. These were 10 employees from the textile production company, 9 employees from the software company and 7 from the automotive company. In the given overview on Figure 1 a possibly wide activity type scoping is presented for completeness. We however did not explore the societal/educational level as our focus was on business users which were not involved in any educational activities. The involved users in each company covered all other activity types. The users' organizational roles in the textile company ranged for example from brand manager (strategic/tactical) and chief sales officer (tactical) to sales officers (tactical/operational) and IT employees (implementation/application). The users were put in the context of scenarios and use cases, which revealed their work practices and helped to identify their demands and pain-points regarding task management. We elaborated 3 mainstream scenarios in each company, detailed through 2 to 3 further supportive scenarios, i.e. for special case handling or peripheral activities. For the textile company mainstream scenarios were the initiation of special sales procedures, e.g. consignment and annual discount sales, and the binding of new partner enterprises for electronic data interchange. For the software company these were the preparation of new product package, new software release and support center scenarios. In the automotive company we explored prototype development and mature prototypes' transfers from prototyping to manufacturing. The user studies were conducted using contextual enquiry techniques [2] at the site of the respective company in the familiar work place surrounding of the interviewees to preserve their context as far as possible. The interviews were recorded using a digital voice recorder and transcribed for analysis. A thorough examination of the elaborated scenarios and use cases led to the identification of reappearing interaction patterns with a software system related to task management. Such were e.g. the creation of calendar entries with reminders, the sending of meeting requests or the management of to-do items in Microsoft Outlook task lists. These patterns reappeared in cross-functional areas or sometimes repeated in different scenarios for the same user type.

The two low level layers on Figure 1 constitute the bottom-up view towards a task management system. They provide task management concepts and features which can support a system implementation. As the concepts provide lower granularity, a concept can be relevant for more than one of the reappearing interaction patterns. In some cases concrete features could be mapped to the detected concepts. For example, a concept 'Awareness', referring to the ability to keep the user informed of possibly approaching bottlenecks or escalations, can be supported by a feature, displaying warning dialogs for approaching task deadlines.

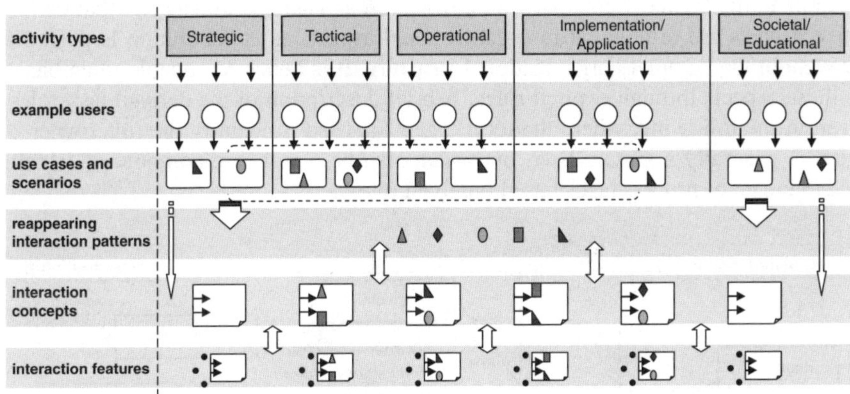

Fig. 1. Example users (circles on second layer from top) with different activity types (top layer) are examined in concrete use cases and scenarios. End-to-end scenarios (dotted line on use cases and scenarios level), comprising the activities of various users with different activity types reveal, how the system should mediate between users with different business roles. Various reappearing interaction patterns (triangles, circles, diamonds and squares) are detected and extracted from the different use cases and scenarios. The patterns are linked to generic interaction concepts (rectangles containing arrows and interaction pattern symbols). Some concepts are directly extracted from the use cases and scenarios (arrows on the right and on the left and nearest empty concept rectangles containing only arrows). Concrete interaction features (black dots beside interaction concepts' symbols on lowest level) for supporting given interaction concepts are identified where possible.

We ordered the elaborated content in a semantic mediawiki which provided a highly interlinked structure with certain evaluation mechanisms like e.g. querying the (number of) occurrences of interaction patterns and related concepts in the various scenarios and use cases. This helped to evaluate the resulting requirements towards the interactions in real-life context. Based on these observations we were able to clearly identify several common perspectives on task representations. These were associated with the attitude of the persona towards a task which was always noticeable in the background of the interactions. These perspectives were able to describe the complete end user interaction landscape on explicit task representations in all scenarios. We extracted them as generic task roles.

3 Task Roles

Task roles aim at providing generalizations that group certain interactions with an explicit task representation and basically state the question: What interactions should be supported, when a user is acting in a given task role? Task roles hence provide task-centric perspectives that reveal different aspects of task management and enable domain-independent abstractions of the necessary interactions on task representations. The task roles are shown in Figure 2. The dotted line areas mark different aspects, which influenced the derivation of the roles. The Requester and the Recipient roles are related to the collaborative handling of a task. The right hand side area contains roles, for which relationships to the organizational structures and hence closer connections to the business context can be discovered. Thereby we suggest that collaborative aspects are orthogonal to organizational aspects as collaboration is performed throughout the complete organizational structure. It is hence reasonable to emphasize on these aspects through explicit roles. A brief description of the derived task roles is given in the following, where the term 'agent' is used to identify the role owner. An agent is generally a system user, but it can also be a software component, which is able to create or process tasks based on given rules.

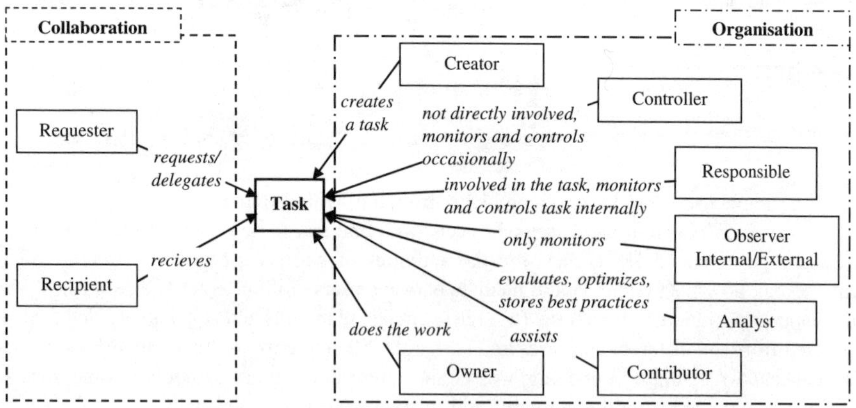

Fig. 2. Task roles

- **Creator** – An agent which creates a task. We here only refer to the action of creating a task, excluding its further processing.
- **Owner** – An agent which is executing on a task and should deliver the results.
- **Controller** – An agent which is able to monitor and interfere in the task activities, and which is not being directly involved in the task. Such could be e.g. a senior manager, not directly contributing or performing on the task but who is able to occasionally view the task and eventually trigger escalations.
- **Responsible** – An agent which is in charge of the successful completion and coordination of a task. Such can be e.g. a project manager responsible for sub tasks distributed in the project team. Thereby a responsible has lower level expertise on a task than a controller.
- **Observer**
    - **Internal** – An agent which can view the evolution of others' tasks without interfering. Such would be e.g. team members, who can view each other's tasks or various shared tasks.
    - **External** – An agent which does not belong to a company or team but is able to view given company's or team's tasks externally. Such is e.g. a customer, who is able to track the processing of his order.
- **Analyst** – An agent which evaluates the outcomes of a task, considers optimizations, and saves reusable data as best-practices or recommendations. This role is clearly related to knowledge management functions.
- **Contributor** – An agent which is informally connected to a task, without being involved in it. The contributor is occasionally delivering information or resources to a task, without being responsible for it, executing on it or even having access to the complete task contextual information.
- **Requester** – An agent which delegates a task to another party.
- **Recipient** – An agent which receives a task from another party.

A similar representation of the task roles is given also in [7]. The Owner and Recipient roles are discussed also in [19]. The next section presents how task roles are used for interactions modeling in the CTM system.

4 Modeling Interactions with Task Roles

We have realized the task roles as extensions to the task model used in the Collaborative Task Manager (CTM) in order to enable enhanced adaptability of the system in different application contexts. CTM is a process-enhanced groupware system which provides advanced End User Development (EUD) capabilities and aims at enabling users with different IT and business background to efficiently participate in business process composition and management. EUD is defined as "a set of methods, techniques, and tools that allow users of software systems, who are acting as non-professional software developers, at some point to create, modify, or extend a software artefact" [11]. In CTM, a process model is considered as a software artifact, which can be adapted and enacted to support human-centric business processes.

4.1 The CTM Prototype

This section gives a general overview of the CTM functionalities with respect to the presented method for interactions modeling. A more comprehensive description of the CTM prototype is given in [20]. CTM generally involves end users in process composition by providing added value on personal task management and leveraging their experience with standard tools for task management (to-do lists) and collaboration (email) towards definition of process models. The solution provides a "gentle slope of complexity" [12] for process tailoring by closely integrating the process definition in the actual user working environment and unfolding emergent processes behind the scenes in an unobtrusive manner. For achieving this it uses enterprise-wide "programming by example" [10] by implicitly reconciling data on personal task management of multiple process participants to end-to-end process execution examples.

In order to ensure integrated support in a common user working environment, the CTM front-end is designed as a Microsoft Outlook (OL) add-in. CTM extends OL mail and task items and enables "programming by example" by capturing OL events and using web services to replicate task data in a tracking repository, residing in a Database (DB) on the CTM server. The CTM To-Do List (TDL) is shown in Figure 3. Extensions to the standard OL tasks enable end users to create hierarchical to-do lists. When the end user is creating or editing a CTM task they work with the familiar OL task fields. Files can be added to CTM tasks as common OL attachments. An email can be as well saved as a CTM task, whereby the email subject, text and attachments are transferred to the resulting task.

Tasks can be delegated over email, whereby the recipients can further break down the received tasks and delegate resulting (sub)tasks to other end-users. A CTM task is delegated through a preformatted "Request" message, which recipients can "Accept", "Decline" (similarly to meeting requests in OL) or "Negotiate". The latter action

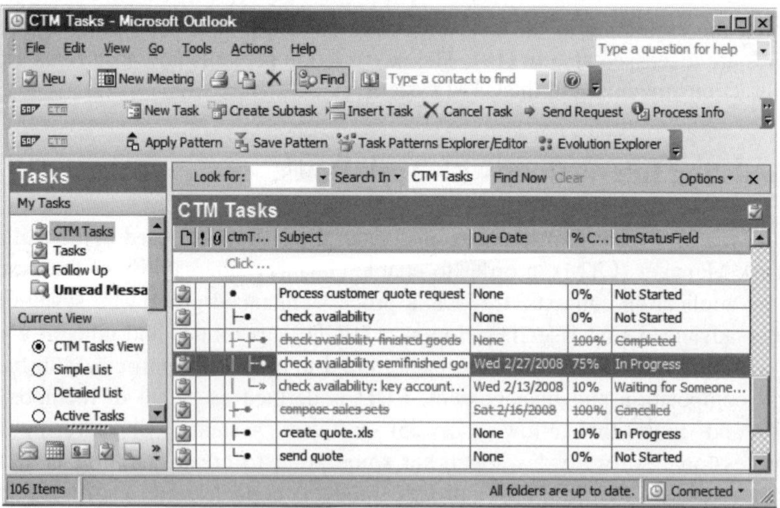

Fig. 3. CTM To-Do List (TDL)

enables iterative negotiations for additional clarifications on tasks. When a request is accepted, and later on completed by a recipient, the latter issues a "Declare Complete" message. Hereupon the requester can respond with "Approve Completion" or "Decline Completion" message. These actions allow negotiation of deliverables before the final completion of a delegated task. The actual discourse takes place in the email text, independently from the given message type. This allows open-ended collaboration and prevents from submitting user behavior to strict speech-act rules, which is a known limitation in speech-acts adoption [3].

Tracking of email exchange for task delegation integrates the personal to-do lists of different process participants to overall Task Delegation Graphs (TDG) [19] on the server. TDGs can be inspected through a web front-end as shown on Figure 4. They represent weakly-structured process models which are captured as actual process execution examples and contain all task data including artifacts (attachments) and stakeholders' information. Tasks of different users are contained in different user containers. TDGs provide a workflow-like overview of evolving user activities, aiming to facilitate "the creation of a shared understanding leading to new insights, new ideas, and new artifacts as a result of collaboration" [4]. In a TDG users can view status of related tasks, identify potential bottlenecks and evaluate work distribution, which is not possible by using common email and to-do items. Currently, due date, task processing status and percent complete indications are provided. Attachments, added in OL tasks, are replicated in a central DB-based Artefacts Repository (AR) on the CTM server, and are accessible in the task nodes.

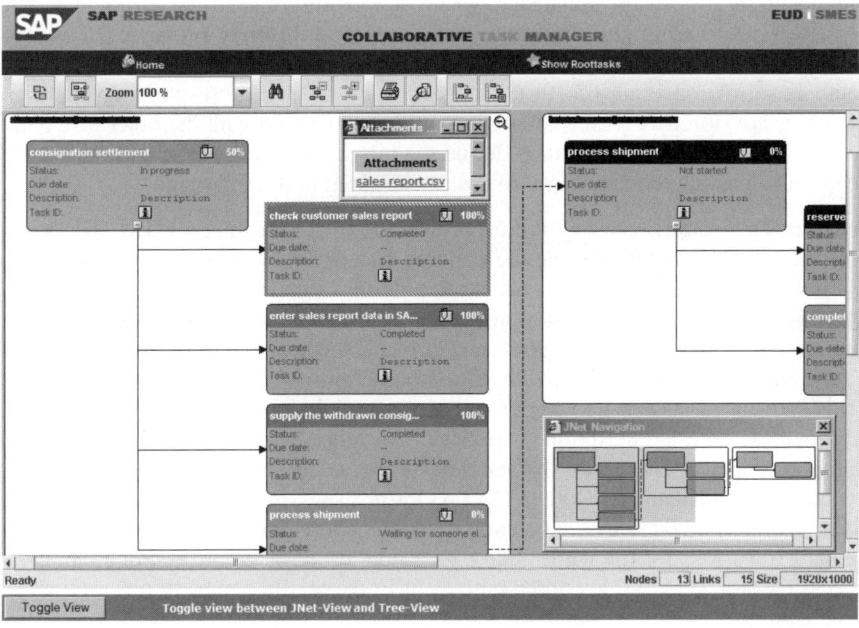

Fig. 4. Task Delegation Graph (TDG)

As end users have different levels of technical expertise and attitudes towards maintaining process data, we suggest that it is important to consider possibilities for "seeding, evolutionary growth, and reseeding (SER)" [4] of user-defined process models for their iterative refinement and complementation. CTM enables SER of weakly-structured process models through extraction, adaptation and reuse of Task Patterns (TP) [19]. We consider a TP as a reusable task structure, comprising one task with its sub task hierarchy and the complete context information of the contained tasks like e.g. description, used resources, involved persons etc. A TP hence represents a high level task as a step in an ad-hoc business process and corresponds to the notion introduced in [18]. In the literature 'task patterns' are discussed also regarding reusable structures for task models in the field of interactive systems design [6, 14, 15]. However, such observations focus on low-level interactive activities, like e.g. searching, browsing or providing generic system input, and deviate from the notion of TP that we use. In CTM, TPs can be enacted to create a new process instance and execute it along the provided example flow. This flow can be altered by changing suggested task recipients or reusing referenced TP hierarchies. Task evolution through TPs' adaptation and reuse is traced through task instance-based ancestor/descendant relationships [19]. These enable end users to establish best-practices and to trace best-practice deviations in different application cases.

4.2   Modeling Interactions on CTM Tasks

CTM enables end users to implicitly develop end-to-end process execution examples as TDGs, which provide a shared context between all involved process participants. This results in a need for enhanced system adaptability due to the different requirements towards sharing and managing task content in different processes. Task roles are applied to the task model defined in [19] as optional XML elements in 'task' elements as shown on Figure 5. In CTM, task roles and the corresponding interaction properties are stored as OL task item properties and tracked with the other task data to the CTM server. Through this they define the interactions with CTM tasks throughout the system. The implemented task roles are discussed in the following.

Creator: This role is taken by the users while they are creating a CTM task and defines the interactions for entering the required task input. We suggest that modeling of task item creation is important as users often define tasks in an underspecified manner [1], which may lead to omission of important information and defer the task processing later on. For example, if the *needsDescription* element (see Figure 5) is omitted or set to false in the task model, this means that no description for the task may be specified. If this element exists and its value is true, the OL dialog for creating a new CTM task will not close until a description is specified. All other 'needs' elements function in an analogous manner. The needsArtifact element can occur multiple times and accepts a text command in Character Data (CDATA) form, specifying the artifacts (attachments) which need to be added to a task upon creation. These commands represent standard regular expressions for file names like e.g. '*.doc' or 'sales report.*'. For example, the processing of a weekly sales order settlement in the textile company (cf. section 2) is based completely on a customer sales report which is sent by the customer as a file in Comma Separated Values (CSV) format. It is necessary to ensure that the report will be attached in the initial process (root) task. This can be accomplished by adding a needsArtifact element with '*.csv' command text in the task model.

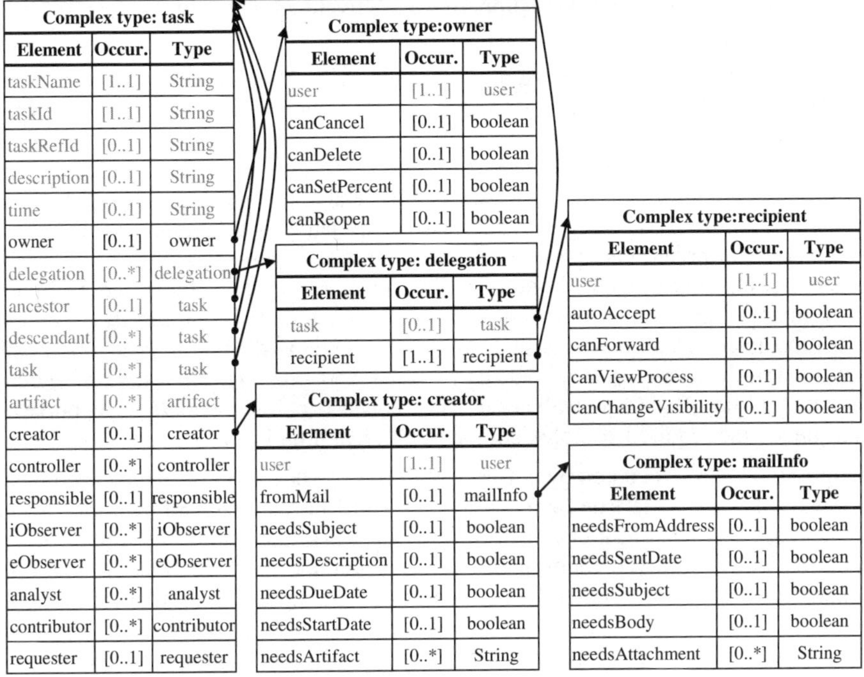

Complex type: task

Element	Occur.	Type
taskName	[1..1]	String
taskId	[1..1]	String
taskRefId	[0..1]	String
description	[0..1]	String
time	[0..1]	String
owner	[0..1]	owner
delegation	[0..*]	delegation
ancestor	[0..1]	task
descendant	[0..*]	task
task	[0..*]	task
artifact	[0..*]	artifact
creator	[0..1]	creator
controller	[0..*]	controller
responsible	[0..1]	responsible
iObserver	[0..*]	iObserver
eObserver	[0..*]	eObserver
analyst	[0..*]	analyst
contributor	[0..*]	contributor
requester	[0..1]	requester

Complex type: owner

Element	Occur.	Type
user	[1..1]	user
canCancel	[0..1]	boolean
canDelete	[0..1]	boolean
canSetPercent	[0..1]	boolean
canReopen	[0..1]	boolean

Complex type: delegation

Element	Occur.	Type
task	[0..1]	task
recipient	[1..1]	recipient

Complex type: creator

Element	Occur.	Type
user	[1..1]	user
fromMail	[0..1]	mailInfo
needsSubject	[0..1]	boolean
needsDescription	[0..1]	boolean
needsDueDate	[0..1]	boolean
needsStartDate	[0..1]	boolean
needsArtifact	[0..*]	String

Complex type: recipient

Element	Occur.	Type
user	[1..1]	user
autoAccept	[0..1]	boolean
canForward	[0..1]	boolean
canViewProcess	[0..1]	boolean
canChangeVisibility	[0..1]	boolean

Complex type: mailInfo

Element	Occur.	Type
needsFromAddress	[0..1]	boolean
needsSentDate	[0..1]	boolean
needsSubject	[0..1]	boolean
needsBody	[0..1]	boolean
needsAttachment	[0..*]	String

Fig. 5. Task model extensions with task roles - only the owner, recipient and creator roles are given for simplicity. The task role extensions embody the user information where each role is defined as a complex type, additionally allowing embedding of XML elements for specifying concrete interactions. Grayed-out elements are discussed in the original task model [19].

The *fromMail* element defines the applying of email contents to a CTM task. Several employees in the sales department of the textile company required to be able to create a CTM task from an email over a mouse click. CTM hence enables creation of a new (root) task from an email and application of email content to existing CTM tasks. The latter operation is especially relevant for tasks, resulting from TP reuse. When this operation is performed, all available tasks from the TDL are given in a tree view with check boxes where the user can select target task(s) for the email content. During this operation, the *mailInfo* properties take effect and define which data should be transferred from the email. If for example the *needsBody* element exists and is set to true, the email body will be transferred to the CTM task(s) as task description. The *needsAttachment* element functions analogously to the *needsArtifact* element, discussed above, and accepts a text command in CDATA form. This allows filtering of artifacts while transferring them from an email to a CTM task. For example, if a user has applied a TP for weekly settlement of a customer sales order, the CSV sales report file from the original execution (previous settlement) will be available in the CTM root task. By applying the contents of a new customer email with attached CSV sales report file to the reused root task and using the appropriate '*.csv' filtering command, the task content will be updated with the new sales report from the customer email, excluding any email attachments with other file extensions. The *needsFromAddress* and *needsSentDate* are true by default. They transfer the corresponding sender and sent-date information as OL task properties to activate a control for searching for the original email in the common OL mail folders.

Owner: This role is generally taken by the users when they have created (or, in case of delegation, received and accepted) a CTM task in the CTM TDL and have to process it. This role comprises all necessary interactions for processing a task in a BTM system. CTM supports modeling of several interactions on active task representations. It can be specified for example, if a user should be able to cancel an active task, to set the percent complete of tasks with sub tasks (alternative is to automatically increase percentage of a parent task based on sum of sub tasks' percentage), delete a task or reopen a completed task (cf. Figure 5). The set of supported actions can be limited due to limited functionality of a system or due to intentional limitations. For example, we set the delete capability to false during a case study at the textile production company to deactivate any delete controls on tasks and preserve the whole amount of generated ad-hoc tasks for evaluation. The reopen capability is still unsupported in CTM due to the required complex compensation handling in TDGs.

Recipient: This role is taken by a user, which receives a CTM task. If the *autoAccept* option (cf. Figure 5) is true, a requested task will be automatically inserted in the recipient's TDL. This option is helpful e.g. for work distribution in support center scenarios as we observed them at the software company (cf. section 2), where the number of error reports handled by each employee and in the whole support center are monitored and tasks are automatically delegated according to the work load. The *canForward* option is also applicable in such scenarios and specifies, if the recipient is allowed to forward a requested task to another person. The *canViewProcess* element defines if a task recipient should be able to view the overall TDG of a process, to which the received task belongs. Such viewing can be deactivated, e.g. if a person from a given department is asked to accomplish a task in the context of a confidential process, managed in another department and containing sensitive customer data. The *canChangeVisibility* option enables administration of the visibility of recipients' tasks in the TDG. If this option is true, the recipient will be allowed to specify if their user container will appear blank in the TDG (cf. Figure 4) or it will show their personal task hierarchy.

Requester: A user is taking this role, while they are delegating a task. An element *canSuggestPattern* enables a requester to add (attach) suggested TPs as recommendations for the further task processing in a CTM request message. A *canSetRecipient-Properties* element defines if a requester should be able to customize the recipients' properties described above, i.e. to specify if the recipients are allowed to view the process tree and to change the visibility of the resulting accepted tasks' hierarchies. This is accomplished in a CTM property dialog, which can be displayed if the above property is set to 'true'.

Controller: In CTM controllers can be explicitly set in an additional dialog, which can be shown on CTM tasks in the TDL or during TP editing (explicit task modeling). Controllers are specified based on their user email address. When a user opens a TDG for an active process, they log in with their email address and the system determines the tasks, for which the user is specified as controller. These tasks receive further buttons in the web form, which allow controllers to add comments, increase priority or trigger task escalations (enabled/disabled accordingly through *canAddComment*, *canIncreasePriority* and *canTriggerEscalations* elements in the model).

Contributor: Contributors are explicitly set in tasks through additional property dialogs accessible from the TDL and during TP editing, and are as well specified through a user email address. When a user logs in to view a given TDG, the task nodes for which they are specified as contributors contain additional controls, which allow them to upload attachments in the artifacts list and to set comments on tasks (enabled through *canAddAttachments* and *canAddComments* elements in the model). Controls in task nodes for changing due dates, priority and triggering escalations will not be active as these are only relevant for Controllers.

Responsible: This role results from the task owner role after a task is delegated, and contains properties for automated notifications on task changes, like e.g. percent complete changes, structure changes (sub task creation), content changes (subject or description), due date changes, delegations. The relevant elements in the task model are respectively: *notifyOnPercentComplete*, *notifyOnSubjectChange*, *notifyOn-DueDateChange*, *notifyOnBrakedown*. Further properties define if the responsible should be able to cancel, complete or delete a task (*canCancelFromAbove*, *canCom-pleteFromAbove*, *canDeleteFromAbove*), which results in cancellation, deletion or completion of a delegated task and the underlying task hierarchy.

Internal & External Observer (i/eObserver): These roles are set explicitly on tasks based on the user email address in the TDL or during TP editing. When the users log in for viewing a TDG, CTM determines their role and shows different view of tasks for the different roles. Internal observers may be allowed to view task descriptions, attachments or task delegation dialogs, i.e. through properties respectively *canViewDe-scription, canViewAttachments, canViewDialog*. External observers may be allowed to view only high level description of the processes where user containers are substituted with generalized containers for departments, which are for example processing the customer (external observer) order (if property *canViewPersonalizedTaskList* is false).

Analyst: This role comprises interactions for extracting reusable task and process knowledge. This includes e.g. interactions for viewing the task execution history (changes) and task evolution (ancestors/descendants), for extracting TPs and publishing them to central TP repositories. The relevant properties in the task model are: *canViewDialog, canViewExecutionHistory, canViewEvolutionHistory, canExtractTDG, canSaveGlobalTP*. The controls for the latter two operations are not enabled for other users, to avoid generation of multiple, concurrent best-practice definitions. This role basically targets at consolidation of the captured process experience.

4.3 Summary

In CTM some task roles (controller, contributor, internal and external observer) can be explicitly defined during task execution, while work is managed and user-defined task hierarchies evolve. This can be accomplished in property dialogs, where users can select the appropriate roles on tasks, assign them to different users based on email addresses and set the appropriate options for interactions in CTM in the scope of a given task role. This results in runtime task modeling of the interactions on the evolving weakly-structured processes. Other task roles are implicitly taken over by the system users, while they are creating CTM tasks (creator), managing them in their TDL (owner), delegating tasks (requester), receiving tasks (recipient), managing delegated tasks (responsible) or extracting best-practice definitions (analyst). The interactions, necessary to act in these roles and in the previously mentioned explicit roles, can be predefined in the task model of a TP. When this TP is applied (enacted), the pre-modeled interactive behavior is activated for the tasks in the resulting ad-hoc process instance.

Task roles enable enhanced flexibility of BTM systems, as they provide an additional abstraction layer. While the interactions are defined and modeled on a generic level through the task roles, these roles can be mapped to organizational roles to enable domain-specific adaptations of the BTM system. For example, an organizational role 'manager' can be mapped to the task role controller in the DB on the CTM server. This will provide the corresponding interactions on a task in the TDG when a user with manager permissions logs in. If the 'manager' role is further mapped to the analyst task role, additional interactions will be enabled, through which a manager will be able to extract TPs from the task tracking repository and to store them as global best-practice prescriptions.

5 Conclusions

In the presented paper we describe a method for modeling interactions on task representations in BTM systems, which uses generic task-centric roles to enable domain-independent, flexible adaptation of the user interface and the available interactions on task representations. We have shown how task roles can be enriched with a set of application-specific interaction descriptions, supporting various aspects of task management – from task creation to delegation, controlling, contributing to tasks and analyzing user-defined task hierarchies. The study reveals how task roles can provide an abstracted, high-level view for modeling interactions from significantly different perspectives of BTM system usage and can result in enhanced system flexibility.

As further research topics we consider the adding of runtime-dependent interaction properties in the scope of task roles and the cascading of (parent) task properties to emerging (sub)tasks during process execution.

Acknowledgments

The reported work was supported financially by the German "Federal Ministry of Education and Research" (BMBF, project EUDISMES, number 01 IS E03 C). We thank to all participants in our user studies for their time and cooperation.

References

1. Bellotti, V., Dalal, B., Good, N., Flynn, P., Bobrow, D.G., Ducheneaut, N.: What a To-Do: Studies of Task Management towards the Design of a Personal Task List Manager. In: CHI 2004, pp. 735–742. ACM Press, New York (2004)
2. Beyer, H., Holtzblatt, K.: Contextual Design: Defining Customer-Centered Systems. Morgan Kaufmann, San Francisco (1998)
3. Button, G.: What's Wrong With Speech-Act Theory. Computer Supported Cooperative Work 3(1), 39–42 (1994)
4. Fischer, G., Giaccardi, E., Ye, Y., Sutcliffe, A., Mehanjiev, N.: Meta-Design: A Manifesto for End-User Development. Communication of the ACM 47(9) (September 2004)

5. Flynn, P., Curran, K., Lunney, T.: A decision support system for telecommunications. International Journal of Network Management 12(2), 69–80 (2002)
6. Gaffar, A., Sinnig, D., Seffah, A., Forbig, P.: Modeling patterns for task models. In: Proceedings of the 3rd annual Conference on Task Models and Diagrams, pp. 99–104. ACM Press, New York (2004)
7. Grebner, O., Ong, E., Riss, U., Brunzel, M., Bernardi, A., Roth-Berghofer, T.: Task Management Model,
   `http://nepomuk.semanticdesktop.org/xwiki/bin/view/Main1/D3-1`
8. John, B., Kieras, D.: The GOMS family of analysis techniques: Comparison and contrast. ACM Transactions on Computer-Human Interaction 3(4), 320–351 (1996)
9. Kolp, M., Giorgini, P., Mylopoulos, J.: Organizational Patterns for Early Requirements Analysis. In: Eder, J., Missikoff, M. (eds.) CAiSE 2003. LNCS, vol. 2681. Springer, Heidelberg (2003)
10. Lieberman, H.: Your Wish is My Command: Programming by Example. Morgan Kaufmann, San Francisco (2001)
11. Lieberman, H., Paterno, F., Wulf, V.: End-User Development. Springer, Heidelberg (2006)
12. MacLean, A., Carter, K., Lövstrand, L., Moran, T.: User-tailorable systems: pressing the issues with buttons. In: Proc. CHI 1990, pp. 175–182. ACM Press, New York (1990)
13. Molina, A., Redondo, M., Ortega, M.: Applying Pattern-Based Techniques to Design Groupware Applications. In: Luo, Y. (ed.) CDVE 2006. LNCS, vol. 4101, pp. 225–233. Springer, Heidelberg (2006)
14. Palanque, P., Basnyat, S.: Task Patterns for Taking into Account in an Efficient and Systematic Way Both Standard and Abnormal User Behaviour. In: IFIP 13.5 Working Conference on Human Error, Safety and Systems Development, Toulouse, France, pp. 109–130 (2004)
15. Paternó, F.: Model-Based Design and Evaluation of Interactive Applications. Springer, Heidelberg (2000)
16. Paterno, F., Mancini, S., Meniconi, S.: ConcurTaskTree: a diagrammatic notation for specifying Task Models. In: Proceedings Interact 1997, pp. 362–369. Chapman & Hall, Boca Raton (1997)
17. Rabelo, L., Eskandari, H., Shalan, T., Helal, M.: Supporting simulation-based decision making with the use of AHP analysis. In: Proceedings of the 37th conference on Winter simulation, pp. 2042–2051 (2005)
18. Riss, U., Rickayzen, A., Maus, H., v. d. Aalst, W.: Challenges for Business Process and Task Managemen. Journal of Universal Knowledge Management 0(2), 77–100 (2005)
19. Stoitsev, T., Scheidl, S., Spahn, M.: A Framework for Light-Weight Composition and Management of Ad-Hoc Business Processes. In: Winckler, M., Johnson, H., Palanque, P. (eds.) TAMODIA 2007. LNCS, vol. 4849. Springer, Heidelberg (2007)
20. Stoitsev, T., Scheidl, S., Flentge, F., Mühlhäuser, M.: Enabling End Users to Proactively Tailor Underspecified, Human-Centric Business Processes. In: Proceedings of the 10th International Conference on Enterprise Information Systems, Barcelona, Spain (2008)
21. Veer, G., v. d. Lenting, B., Bergevoet, B.: GTA: Groupware task analysis - modeling complexity. Acta Psychologica 91, 297–322 (1996)
22. Wiig, K.M.: People-focused knowledge management: how effective decision making leads to corporate success. Elsevier Butterworth–Heinemann (2004)
23. Winter, A.F., Ammenwerth, E., Bott, O.J., Brigl, B., Buchauer, A., Gräber, S., Grant, A., Häber, A., Hasselbring, W., Haux, R., Heinrich, A., Janssen, H., Kock, I., Penger, O.-S., Prokosch, H.-U., Terstappen, A., Winter, A.: Strategic information management plans: the basis for systematic information management in hospitals. International Journal of Medical Informatics 64(2), 99–109 (2001)

AMBOSS: A Task Modeling Approach
for Safety-Critical Systems

Matthias Giese[1], Tomasz Mistrzyk[2], Andreas Pfau[1], Gerd Szwillus[1],
and Michael von Detten[1]

[1] University Paderborn, Institute for Computer Science, 33102 Paderborn, Germany
[2] OFFIS e. V., 26121 Oldenburg, Germany
{flipsi,andypf,szwillus,austin}@upb.de, Tomasz.Mistrzyk@offis.de

Abstract. In a recent project we created AMBOSS, a task modeling environment taking into account the special needs for safety-critical socio-technical systems. An AMBOSS task model allows the specification of relevant information concerning safety aspects. To achieve this we complemented task models with additional information elements and appropriate structures. These refer primarily to aspects of timing, spatial information, and communication. In this paper we give an introductory overview about AMBOSS and its contribution to modeling safety-critical systems. In addition, we present AmbossA, the visual pattern language for detecting particular constellations of interest within a task model.

Keywords: task modeling, safety-critical systems, socio-technical systems, task editor, simulation, task patterns.

1 Introduction

Task modeling approaches such as ([12], [9], [17], [2], and [5]) primarily concentrate on the hierarchical decomposition of tasks into subtasks and their relative ordering with temporal relations. Task models are typically used in the early phases of system design or as documentation method for the result of task analyses. The models are semi-formal in nature in the sense that they formally structure (hierarchy, temporal relations) informal elements (task descriptions). They have been used in system design ([10], [8]) or user interface design ([14], [6], [18]), but are also used increasingly for the design and analysis of workplace situations [17].

An important concept in most task modeling approaches concerns the actors performing the tasks. In CTTE [12], for example, explicitly identified roles co-operate in the concurrent performance of a highly structured task. An appropriate role or user model is included in all approaches mentioned above. Using these models, it is possible to describe task execution in complex socio-technical systems. These systems on one hand include technical components, such as computers, transport devices, telecommunication devices and production machines, and on the other hand they incorporate human actors, who are performing manual tasks and interactive tasks, i.e. are using machines to support their work. Typical examples are, for instance, execution of

P. Forbrig and F. Paternò (Eds.): HCSE/TAMODIA 2008, LNCS 5247, pp. 98–109, 2008.

routine maintenance procedures in a hydro power plant, or blood sample processing in a hospital. Both examples are performed by a group of co-operating human actors who are working both with technical systems and without them.

Specifying a task model for such a system documents the order of and the rationale behind the planning and structuring of the tasks to be performed. This is useful for analyzing an existing socio-technical system, or to start the design of a new not yet existing process. If in addition the socio-technical system is a safety-critical system the task model can be helpful in detecting potential problems created by, for example, inadequate task order, disproportionate distribution of workloads between actors, or lack of time in critical phases of task execution.

In a recent project we created AMBOSS [1], a task modeling environment taking into account the special needs for safety-critical socio-technical systems. An AM-BOSS task model allows the specification of risk assessment factors, barriers protecting human beings and material value from harm [7], and the information flow between tasks. AMBOSS allows the specification of relevant information concerning these and additional issues. In this paper, however, we want to focus on some aspects which have not yet been integrated with task modeling to that extent before and which are especially relevant for socio-technical safety-critical systems: timing, topology, and communication.

A correct timing of co-operative actions is frequently vital for the correct and safe execution of safety-critical processes. We deal with this aspect within the simulation component of AMBOSS, which takes into account preconditions for tasks and their explicit link with barriers sheltering man and material. An example from health care would be to make sure that the x-ray device is only switched on after the operator has left the room. In addition, AMBOSS allows the specification of the spatial behavior of a process, i.e. to say where some task is performed, which objects are available at this position, and whether objects are transferred from one room to another during task execution. As an example consider the fact that it has a crucial influence on the end result whether a patient is in the neighboring room or far away from all nurses. While both time and space may be irrelevant for a large number of task models, as they are either trivial or self-evident, there are important cases of safety-critical processes depending on this type of information.

This applies even more so to the aspect of communication between the actors in a task model. Special emphasis has been given within AMBOSS to model possible variants of the properties of communication as needed for task execution. In co-operative processes it is often the case that an actor (man or machine) performing a subtask needs information from another actor performing another subtask. This implies task dependencies, with respect to task ordering, task triggering, and the quality of the communication between tasks. As an example, we analyzed a medication dosage process based on a blood sample, which included communication via hand-written notes, database queries, and casually uttered oral remarks between the actors.

Enriching a task-model with more detail burdens the designer or analyzer of a system, i.e. the AMBOSS user, with an increasingly complicated model which is hard to master. Task models tend to grow a lot when applied to real-world cases, and there is no use in specifying to great detail, when the user loses control over an outgrowing model. This is why we created a possibility to specify patterns of task model elements, and to automatically check their existence within a large task model. The

"AmbossA" language is a visual language which can be used to define "critical" or "interesting" patterns within task models and then apply a search function to detect or negate their existence in a model.

We will deal with the aspects mentioned in the subsequent chapters and conclude with a statement on the current state of the development. The features described here are all implemented in the current version, with the exception of the procedure for communication analysis, as sketched out in chapter 5. The current version of AMBOSS is freely available for non-commercial use for download on the AMBOSS website [1].

2 The Task Modeling Environment AMBOSS

AMBOSS is a task modeling environment following the traditional approach of hierarchical task structures with temporary relations between subtasks. Hence, AMBOSS provides the typical tree-based editing functions, such as adding a child node or a sister node; apart from that, however, we allow direct manipulation of nodes and connections for easy structure manipulation tasks. A task node, for instance, can be placed into the drawing area without being connected at all, and it can later on be linked to other nodes. Although liberal in the interaction style, structure constraints are ensured by checks in the background, inhibiting for instance the creation of cycles. The order of subtasks is defined by the relative placement around the parent node; hence the order can be modified by simply shifting the child nodes into the correct order. This concept has been implemented in K-MADe [3] as well, while CTT [12] and VTMB [5] are restricted to tree operations. A similar freedom of interaction is available in Tamot [9] without underlying checks being performed.

AMBOSS goes far beyond the traditional task modeling approach. Based on its implementation with plug-ins to the Eclipse framework, the editor provides flexible views on additional information necessary for modeling safety-critical systems. The elements included deal with roles, barriers, task objects, risk factors, and messages. As the Eclipse framework enables a flexible customized arrangement of views, the user is able to open, maximize, minimize, or close whatever view is needed for a specific analysis task.

AMBOSS allows the user to implement hierarchical role specifications in order to appoint the performing actor to a task and to stress its duties and abilities. Similar approaches were already mentioned in other environments ([12], [5], and [3]).

There are three basic types of actors in a socio-technical system: human, system, and abstract – the last describing tasks performed in co-operation between man and machine. In addition, we can specify subtypes of actors (such as physician or nurse) and instances of actors (such as the nurse Ms. Smith) as refinements of the roles human and system. When defining a role for a task this is consequently inherited by the subtasks and propagates up to the parent nodes in the task tree. In addition to being an actor within a task, a role can also be specified as being the person responsible for the task (such as for the correct treatment of a blood sample). A screenshot of the AMBOSS environment is shown in Fig. 1.

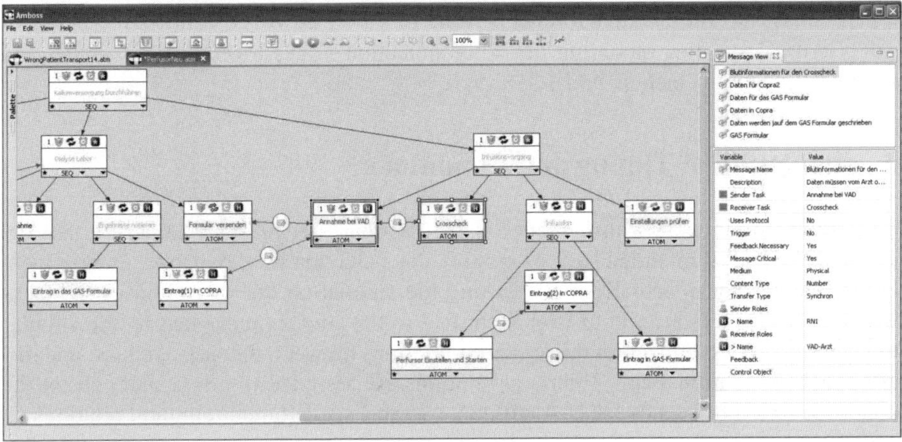

Fig. 1. The AMBOSS Environment

A concept showing up in several approaches for modeling safety-critical systems is the concept of barriers [7]. Barriers are means to prevent harm from human beings and material while operating a system; examples are the lead apron sheltering the patient and the operator from X-ray radiation, or the law against crossing a red traffic light. Barriers are linked in different ways to task performance: barriers can ensure that safety-critical tasks do not harm life or material; tasks can activate a barrier (such as putting on the lead apron), or deactivate it (e.g. by switching of a traffic light for maintenance). Hence, AMBOSS allows the specification of relations like these between barriers and tasks, and they are evaluated an can be "observed" during the simulation included in the environment (see chapter 3 below).

In addition, tasks can be rated as being critical. A numerical risk factor is assigned, based on estimations of probability, severity of consequences, and detectability on a scale from 1 to 10 [16]. By multiplying the numbers the overall factor is computed, which enables a summative evaluation of the risk involved. Another important influential factor when executing safety-critical tasks is timing. Hence, we allow the assignment of timing information to tasks, specifying minimal, maximal, or average task durations. This timing information is also used during the simulation of the models. In addition, AMBOSS incorporates a task object concept, which means that the user can specify which objects are modified by a task.

Once the model is defined, the user can start a simulation which takes into account the task hierarchy, temporal relations, conditions, barriers, message flow, and triggering through communication. The user can observe, which task (and actor) is sending what kind of information to whom, and whether or not triggering information has been sent or not. As the simulation also reflects the activation and deactivation of barriers, the user in every situation of the simulation can tell whether a necessary barrier is in place while a safety-critical task is executed. To compare and analyze different threads of execution one can save scenarios and watch their simulation repeatedly. Task model simulation has been done before ([9], [5], [3]) in part including the scenario feature mentioned as well, with the special case of K-MADe [3] which is a particularly detailed and rich model. None of these, however, reflects the needs of safety-critical systems including the communication issues together with timing and spatial behavior as much as AMBOSS does.

3   Simulation of Timing and Conditions

The ability to simulate a task model is an essential tool in order to assure that the model behaves as intended and to control the behavior in a dynamic environment before the system is actually built. During the simulation the user chooses the tasks which he wants to start and to stop according to the choices presented by the simulator. These choices depend on the temporal relations between the tasks and are updated after each simulation step. Temporal relations are assigned to a task and control the course of action of its subtasks. AMBOSS contains six different temporal relations:

- SEQ: The subtasks are performed in a fixed sequence from left to right
- SER: The subtasks are performed in an arbitrary sequence
- PAR: The subtasks can start and stop in an inordinate way.
- SIM: All subtasks have to start before any subtask may stop.
- ALT: Exactly one subtask is performed.
- ATOM: This task has no subtasks.

In addition, the simulator of AMBOSS focuses on the integration of safety relevant aspects of the task model by controlling the state of the barriers and considering the flow of communication. Fig. 2 shows an AMBOSS simulator screen-shot. The system allows the user to view all parameters which influence the current task without switching back to AMBOSS task modeling view. As shown on the bottom left of Fig. 2 the user is informed about the objects being manipulated by the task, the rooms in which the task occurs (see chapter 4), the roles performing the task, the communication flow of the task and the barriers protecting the task from hazards. Furthermore the user is able to recognize at a glance which tasks are executed concurrently as shown in the middle area of Fig. 2. Task execution is symbolized by rectangles, where the ordering from left to right coincides with the order of performance. The user operates the simulator by starting and stopping tasks. This is done by double clicking the name of a task in the lists at the top left.

In order to guide the user's attention to the safety critical elements of a system it is possible to define certain preconditions for a task. If a task's precondition is not met the user will not be able to start it during the simulation. There are two different types of preconditions.

Message preconditions denote the concept that a message containing certain information is necessary to trigger a task, and allow its correct performance. The simulator keeps track of communication that has already taken place and enables the start of tasks accordingly. The user is kept informed about the progression of the simulation including the communication textually (see bottom right of Fig. 2). The simulator also checks for some mistakes being made during the modeling phase, such as if a message requires feedback but the feedback has not been defined yet.

The second type of preconditions refers to dynamical, "enactable" barriers. An enactable barrier is a barrier which does not achieve its protective impact all the time but has to be activated to do its service. This activation is being accomplished during the performance of a task. An example for this is X-ray protective clothing which has to be put on before it can render its service. During the simulation the user can check whether the simulated chain of action led to a situation in which the task can be performed safely.

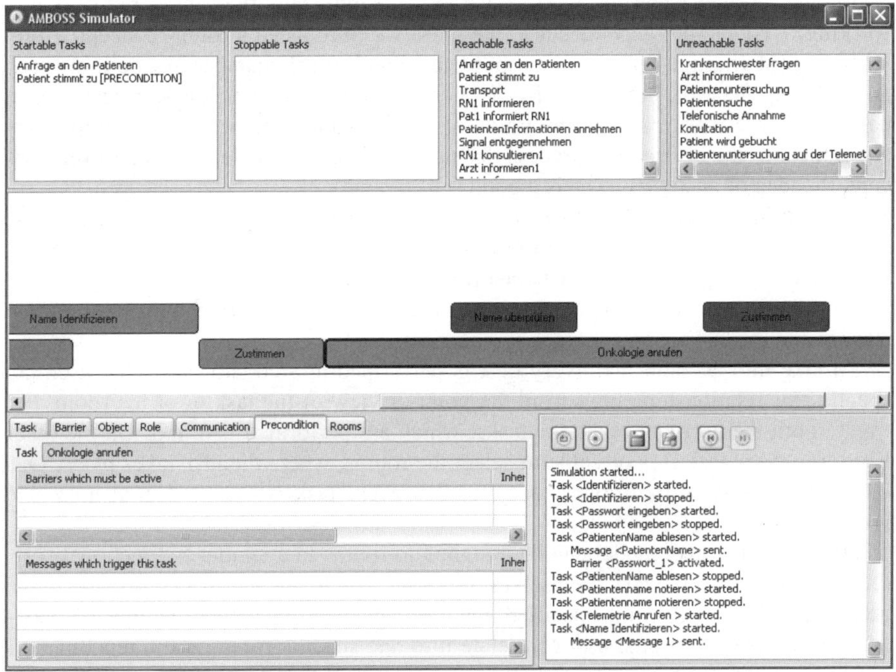

Fig. 2. AMBOSS Simulator Overview

Another feature of the AMBOSS simulator is the inclusion of scenarios. A scenario is an instance of the task model, i.e. one concrete task execution sequence to perform the complete task described. The user is able to save these scenarios and to compare the different effects of his decisions during the simulation.

With these possibilities it is possible to check safety relevant aspects of a task before a system is even built or to inspect the work flow of an existing system. The user can experiment with the different possible chains of events and compare the different effects of the chosen scenarios on the execution of the whole task. The simulator stresses the need to provide security for the performance of the tasks and incites the user to deal with potential hazards. This ultimately leads to an improvement of the way a task is performed and the elimination of the weak points of a system.

4 Spatial Behavior

In most of all considered models which represent safety critical systems or scenarios one of the important aspects is topology, i.e. a specification of the spatial relations between different task execution steps. This deals with the "positions" of both actors and material or objects, needed for the task. Frequently, there are situations where tasks are performed in a certain position of the work space (e.g. directly aside an x-ray device) which are harmless as long as the work space is "clean" (e.g. the x-ray device is off) and critical when the work space is "contaminated" (e.g. the x-ray device is working). To capture dependencies like these we introduced a rooms concept within AMBOSS. A room in this abstract sense can be a physical chamber in a building (e.g. an operating theatre), but it can also be a complete floor in a hospital, or an airplane hangar on an aircraft carrier. The limits of a room cannot be defined generally; they are subject to the abstraction process during modeling. For understanding of the concept, the idea of an actual room is a good start though.

A room in AMBOSS has different static properties, a unique name to identify the element, an informal textual description, a maximum number of persons that fit into a room, and a flag that indicates, whether this room is lockable or not.

More important are the dynamic properties, which specify the relationship between a room and the tasks, objects, roles and barriers.

To take into account that every task is performed at a certain place, the user can specify this relationship either from the point of view of the task or of the room. For every room the user can relate the tasks, which are performed within it. On the other hand, for every task it is possible to select the rooms, where the task takes place. One inherent property of the room concept is that every task is executed in at most one room.

Objects of the task model can be assigned to rooms in a similar bidirectional way. Objects, other than the task themselves, however, can be moved from one room to the other. So, when an object is specified, the user can specify whether the object is movable or not. If it is not, the user can relate it to one specific room, where this object is located (such as the x-ray device in the x-ray room). If the object is movable, the user has to specify, in which rooms the object can be located, and in which ones the object is not allowed because of procedural or factual restrictions (such as a free-to-move perfusor device, which is allowed in the patients' rooms but not in the operating room).

In some cases, it is important to express that not every person has access to a room. This is represented with the room-role-relationship. For every room the user can select the roles, which have either the permission to enter the room, a restricted kind of permission or no permission to enter.

During the modeling process, AMBOSS checks whether the user is about to create an invalid situation. For instance, when an object has already a fix assignment to one room, it cannot have an assignment to other rooms as well. Other validation checks are performed dynamically during the simulation. If there are any conflicts in dependent relationships, the simulator will indicate this. For instance, if some roles are performing a certain task in a certain room, and some of the roles do not have the permission to enter the room, the simulator will indicate that conflict.

Using this concept AMBOSS is able to handle topological aspects and relationships that may be important in safety critical systems. We see this approach as a first step in this direction, which has to be developed further. We could, however, successfully model the safety-critical process of the take-off process of airplanes from an aircraft carrier, where the location of material and human actors is of vital importance.

5 Analyzing Communication

Deficiencies in the communication between the actors of a socio-technical system are recognized as a major cause for critical incidents and accidents [4]. Therefore the integration of this aspect into the task model represents an important expansion for our approach. A lot of problems in safety-critical socio-technical systems have their roots in communication problems. An improper sequence of task performance, for instance, could be caused by missing communication (too early, too late); a task could be mal-performed by lack of feedback (misunderstanding vital information), which could also be the case when problematic situations are unobservable (wrong display). On a higher level of abstraction, tasks could put an unbalanced strain on actors, because they do not communicate enough.

Some approaches like CTTE [12] or TaskArchitect [17] integrate communication to some degree as a part of the model. However, they do not take into account relevant parameters of the communication, such as triggering mechanisms, criticality, necessity of feedback, kind of medium or content. Within AMBOSS we included the possibility to specify communication and its parameters and developed an appropriate method of analysis.

As a fundamental theoretical model, we choose the information-communication model of Shannon and Weaver. In this model communication is seen as exchange of information (signals) between transmitter and receiver. This excludes a priori a large part of aspects otherwise coming under the term of communication, such as psychological, social, or ethical issues. Basing our concept on information theory restricts communication in our model to the flow of information. In this context, every task and its associated role in a model can be sender and recipient of information. The most important circumstances for good communication (especially important when taking into account safety critical systems) are, that the information is correct, that the information is complete and its transmission cannot be changed by external factors, and that the information is correctly interpreted by the recipient.

The examination of success or failure of communication necessitates considering the following aspects of information flow: the actors (transmitter, receiver), the information itself, the transmission medium, supervising control structures, timing, and the environmental situation. Most of these parameters can be captured in an AMBOSS model, with the exception of the last, which is a very open property. Communication in AMBOSS is dealt with during the modeling phase, and taken into account by the simulator, as mentioned before. Apart from that, however, we developed an analysis process of the communication in socio-technical systems which will be integrated into our approach of the extended task modeling. This process goes beyond the evaluation of single communication paths but provides an overall assessment of the communication situation in the given task model and hints directly at weak points.

The analysis consists of four steps, which we sketch out only roughly here, details can be found in [11]. In the first step, all communication sequences are classified into one of three groups of criticality. This is done based on the critical status of the sender and the receiver which provides a basis for the priority of the fact-finding. Second, we look closer on particular message sequence. This exploration contains a binary evaluation of each sequence from the point of view of both partners. This part of the analysis already shows the most important weaknesses of the communication flow. After identifying the communication weaknesses in the system we start with the qualitative judgment. Based on this judgment we can give a more informative statement about each parameter within the different sequences of the communication flow. Third, the aggregation of the identified weak spots in the system takes place. The analyst is able to recognize which parameters are affected and therefore should be modified to improve the safety of the whole communication flow. Finally, the analyst can specify at which position of the communication flow the system shows deviations from the expected procedure. Finally, it is possible to derive suggestions that are classified along the single communication parameters for a proposed improvement.

By applying this analysis method to real-world case studies, we found out that it is especially valuable for detecting latent errors in a system. These are errors which have been "done" much earlier and in general by completely different people than the ones that suffer from the consequences when actually performing a task. An example is the erroneous adjustment of a perfusor which happened due to a blurred communication protocol between the responsible actors. The definition of the protocol was identified as a latent error during the communication analysis.

Currently the method is based on AMBOSS but is not yet formally integrated. The emphasis up to now was to define the single steps. We will work on a tool, however, to help the analyst to perform the analysis on AMBOSS models.

6 Defining and Finding Patterns

The enhancements of task modeling approaches within AMBOSS presented so far, add more information and detail to a potentially already complex model. The analyst needs to master the complexity of this model and while entering more detail information, he might lose the overview. In situations, where the detail information specified in different places in its combination creates a critical situation the following approach referred to as AmbossA helps to detect these constellations.

AmbossA is a visual query language which enables the user to define certain relationship structures between AMBOSS elements and to search for them within a task model. In AMBOSS all elements have or do not have a connection with one another. For example, a message has a sender and a receiver, a role executes or does not execute a task etc. Hence, a task model can be seen as a complex structure of connections between the single elements. AmbossA allows the user to visually create patterns connecting AMBOSS elements such as tasks, roles, object, messages etc. and thus characterizing relationship structures. Given such a pattern, the system localizes the pattern in the task model. If the pattern represents a pathological or dangerous constellation, or some other type of "weak spot", the analyst is directly guided to these problem areas.

To specify a pattern, AmbossA provides certain visual elements (shown in Fig. 3 on the left), corresponding to the elements which can be used within AMBOSS to specify a task model. These can be linked visually with relations of objects, denoting certain semantic relations, such as a role executing a task, or a message triggering a task (see Fig. 3 on the top right).

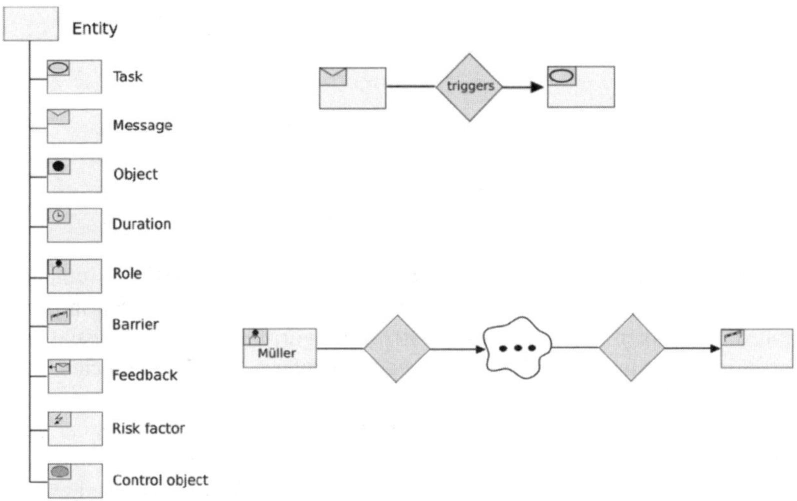

Fig. 3. Visual elements (left) and example relations (right) in AmbossA

Using these elements, the user can find all tasks executed by a certain role, or all messages triggering a certain task etc. In addition to abstract representatives for concrete elements in the task model, the cloud element provides a powerful mechanism for finding certain constellations. If two elements are connected with the cloud, then they are connected "somehow", and all possible paths between the two elements are considered. Hence, the cloud plays the role of a wild card symbol in the diagram language. For example, it is possible to search for any relationship between a specific role ("Müller") and any barrier, as depicted in Fig. 3 on the bottom right.

In combination with the logical operators AND, OR and NOT, the user can express complex constellations of AMBOSS elements and search for them. In the diagram shown in Fig. 4, all situations are found where a message is sent from either two tasks or a role to a target task.

The result of such a query is a table of elements matching the given diagram. In its current version the user can skip through this list and is directly shown the position of the situation in the task model. In addition, the match currently selected in this list is shown as a highlighted substructure in the AMBOSS editor.

The speed of the parser process directly depends on the abstraction level of the relationship pattern. The more abstract the pattern is, the more time the search algorithm needs. The most challenging situation for the algorithm arises if the relationship pattern contains several „clouds". However, for practical purposes we found the runtime behavior perfectly acceptable. More work will have to be done to develop this idea further towards a tool to administer a library of "good" or "bad" patterns, which could then automatically be applied to task models of safety-critical socio-technical systems.

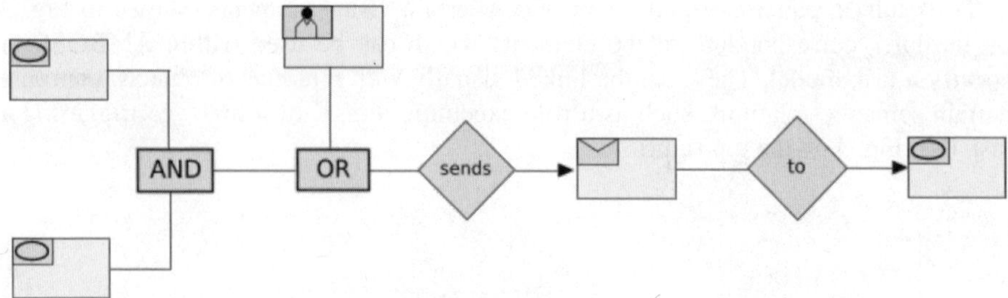

Fig. 4. A visual query in AmbossA

7   Conclusions

The current state of AMBOSS is that the editing component and the simulator comprise all elements mentioned in chapters 3 and 4, and the communication parameters mentioned in chapter 5. The pattern matching algorithm, resp. the visual language AmbossA is fully functional. As mentioned in chapter 5, the communication analysis algorithm is a recent development; the integration with AMBOSS is under way.

Overall, the approach provides a rich set of enhancements over classical task models which are especially useful for safety-critical socio-technical systems. As single concepts they exist in the rich literature on safety-critical systems but they have not been integrated with the concepts of task modeling before. The inclusion of a powerful simulator taking all these elements into account enables the analyst to get an overview of effects such as information flow, barrier dynamics, role distribution, and spatial relations during task execution.

AMBOSS invites enhancements, based on its underlying model structures, as we implemented a programming interface to link new analysis tools to the environment. We exploit this in a first co-operation with the developers of PetShop ([2], [13], and [15]), to link task model simulation and user interface prototyping during runtime.

In our view, the combination of task modeling and safety-critical analysis concepts, as instantiated in AMBOSS, is a promising approach. It takes procedural knowledge of a work process into account and links it to the otherwise unrelated safety aspects. The task model contains knowledge about timing, dependencies of tasks, modified objects, sent messages, etc. – hence it can provide valuable information where targeted safety improvements for those concerned can be implemented.

References

1. Amboss: Homepage of the AMBOSS project, Universität Paderborn, Institut für Informatik (accessed April 2008), http://wwwcs.upb.de/cs/ag-szwillus/lehre/ws05_06/PG/PGAMBOSS/index.php
2. Barboni, E., Navarre, D., Palanque, P., et al.: A Model-Based Tool for the Formal Modelling and Simulation of Interactive Safety Critical Embedded Systems. In: Proceedings of HCI aero conference (Demonstration) (HCI Aero 2006), Seattle, USA (September 2006)

3. Baron, M., Lucquiaud, V., Autard, D., et al.: K-MADe: un environement pour le noyau du modèle de description de l'activité. In: Proceedings of the 18th French-speaking conference on Human-computer interaction, Montreal, Canada, April 18-21 (2006)
4. Bellamy, L.J., Geyer, T.A.W.: Development of a working model of how human factors, safety management systems and wider organisational issues fit together. Health and Safety Executive Report, RR543 (2007), `http://www.hse.gov.uk/research/rrpdf/rr543.pdf` (accessed, June 2007)
5. Biere, M., Bomsdorf, B., Szwillus, G.: Specification and simulation of task models with VTMB. In: CHI 1999 Extended Abstracts on Human Factors in Computing Systems, Pittsburgh, Pennsylvania, May 15 - 20, 1999. ACM Press, New York (1999)
6. Guitare: GUITARE Homepage (Last access: April 2008), `http://giove.cnuce.cnr.it/Guitare/`
7. Hollnagel, E.: Barrier analysis and accident prevention. Aldershot, UK, Ashgate (2004)
8. Isolde, Isolde Homepage (Last Access: April 2008), `http://www.ict.csiro.au/staff/Cecile.Paris/from-cmis/projects/Isolde/scientificProgress.htm`
9. Lu, S., Paris, C., Vander Linden, K.: Tamot: Towards a Flexible Task Modeling Tool. In: Proceedings of Human Factors, Melbourne, Australia, November 25-27 (2002)
10. Mefisto: Mefisto Homepage (Last Access: April 2008), `http://giove.cnuce.cnr.it/mefisto.html`
11. Mistrzyk, T.: Analysis of Communication in Hierarchical Task Models focused on Safety Critical Systems. Dissertation, University of Paderborn, Institute of Computer Science (in print) (2008)
12. Mori, G., Paternò, F., Santoro, C.: CTTE: support for developing and analyzing task models for interactive system design. IEEE Trans. Softw. Eng. 28(8), 797–813 (2002)
13. Navarre, D., Palanque, P., Barboni, E., et al.: On the Benefit of Synergistic Model-Based Approach for Safety Critical Interactive System Testing. In: Winckler, M., Johnson, H., Palanque, P. (eds.) TAMODIA 2007. LNCS, vol. 4849, pp. 140–154. Springer, Heidelberg (2007)
14. Puerta, A.R.: The Mecano Project: Enabling User-Task Automation During Interface Development. In: AAAI 1996: Spring Symposium on Acquisition. Learning and Demonstration: Automating Tasks For Users, pp. 117–121 (1996)
15. Petshop: Petshop Homepage (Last access: April 2008), `http://liihs.irit.fr/petshop/`; Shannon, C., Weaver, M.: The Mathematical Theory of Communication, University of Illinois (1949)
16. Storey, N.: Safety-Critical Computer Systems. Addison-Wesley, London (1996)
17. Stuart, J., Penn, R.: TaskArchitect: taking the work out of task analysis. In: Proceedings of the 3rd Annual Conference on Task Models and Diagrams, TAMODIA 2004, Prague, Czech Republic, November 15 - 16, 2004, vol. 86, pp. 145–154. ACM Press, New York (2004)
18. Szekely, P., Luo, P., Neches, R.: Facilitating the Exploration of Interface Design Alternatives: The HUMANOID Model of Interface Design. In: CHI 1992 Conference Proc. (1992)

UI Design without a Task Modeling Language – Using BPMN and Diamodl for Task Modeling and Dialog Design

Hallvard Trætteberg

Associate Professor
Dept. of Computer and Information Sciences
Norwegian University of Science and Technology
`hal@idi.ntnu.no`

Abstract. In the field of model-based user interface design (MB-UID) task modeling is established as a necessary activity. However, in many (industrial) contexts, it is not realistic to introduce yet another modeling notation, particularly when user interface design is considered less important than overall process logic and system architecture. Therefore, it may make more sense to adapt existing process-oriented notations to task modeling, than vice versa (adapting task modeling languages to process modeling). This paper describes our experiences with using BPMN and Diamodl for process and task modeling and dialog design, respectively.

Keywords: User interface design, dialog modeling, business process management notation.

1 Introduction

Within the field of model-based user interface design (MB-UID), the standard design process includes task modeling, dialog modeling and concrete design 2. . Specialized modeling task and dialog modeling languages/notations have been developed for supporting the first two of these, while the latter involves mapping from dialog to either a concrete model or specific toolkit or runtime platform. Specialized languages are important, for at least two reasons: 1) they put focus on the specific information that an activity should result in, and 2) they enable better tool support by formalizing the relevant information. There is however a cost associated with introducing new notations in software development, as it adds to the already high complexity of modern development methods and tools.

An alternative approach is taking established (within the target industry) modeling languages as a starting point and augmenting the methods built around them, so the desired information still is captured, although in a different form. The advantage lies in lowering the cost of adopting the methods (hopefully below the threshold of adoption). In addition, we see a potential for coupling information in different models, i.e. there may be a synergy between the main usage of the notation and the new, augmented usage. In our work we have looked at how the Business Process Modeling Notation (BPMN) may be extended to cover tasks and augmented with extra

P. Forbrig and F. Paternò (Eds.): HCSE/TAMODIA 2008, LNCS 5247, pp. 110–117, 2008.

information concerning object life-cycle. The basic idea is that business processes and tasks are similar concepts at different levels of abstraction, and that the essential information from task analysis may captured by using BPMN in a different way, augmented with some extra information. As a bonus, the relation between the high-level processes and lower-level task structures becomes clearer and the gap between system logic and architectural and dialog structure and behavior, becomes smaller.

In the following sections we will review related work, describe the overall approach and outline a practical method for modeling and deployment of applications using BPMN 8. , Diamodl 10. and Eclipse-based tools.

2 Related Work

In 6. several task and process modeling languages are compared, to see how they may support model-based design of eServices in eGovernment applications. We have previously discussed the relation between process modeling and task modeling in 3. and more recently in 4. . Our focus on this paper is on a lean method based on a the standard process modeling language BPMN and Diamodl and deployment using standard, open-source tools and modern architecture. 7. also take a business process model (BPM) as a starting point, but uses a less formal UI model with a weaker coupling to the BPM. The goal of 5. is similar to ours, that of supporting server-side workflow with model-based UI client, but they do not use a standard workflow modeling notation.

3 Overall Approach

In the prototypical MB-UID process, a task model is the starting point for developing a dialog model and subsequent concrete user interface design. The task model may be seen as capturing human behavior, the dialog model describes software behavior. The deployment of the UI will be a combination of concrete user interface elements and the software and models necessary for implementing the dialog behavior, like state machinery, data binding, etc. and the concrete interface describes what is actually deployed.

This is actually fairly similar to the standard approach of business process modeling using BPMN and execution and deployment using the Business Process Execution Language (BPEL) 9. . First, the behavior of the process, or rather the roles and systems taking part in the process, is described as communicating processes, activities and tasks in a BPMN diagram. This model is transformed to a BPEL model, which describes the software part of the (future) process, i.e. the (automation of) coordination (also called choreography and orchestration) aspects of the process and relies on web services for linking all the participants (people, processes and external services). The BPEL model is then deployed, together with other supporting software like business objects, web services, persistence etc.

As can be seen, the and overall approach and role of the models is similar, although they have the (group) system perspective instead of the (individual) UI perspective. This more than suggests that the models can be related across the domains of business process management and user interface design, as illustrated in 0. According to this figure, process models (in BPMN) may be related to task models since they both capture the behavior of people, BPEL models may be related to dialog models, since they both model software for supporting people and BPEL and a deployed BPEL model executed by a server-side engine may interact with the client-side UI runtime. We are currently investigating how this may be more than analogy, i.e. we propose method whereby BPMN is used for both business process and task modeling and BPEL and diamodl are used for modeling software support and deployment on a SOA-based platform.

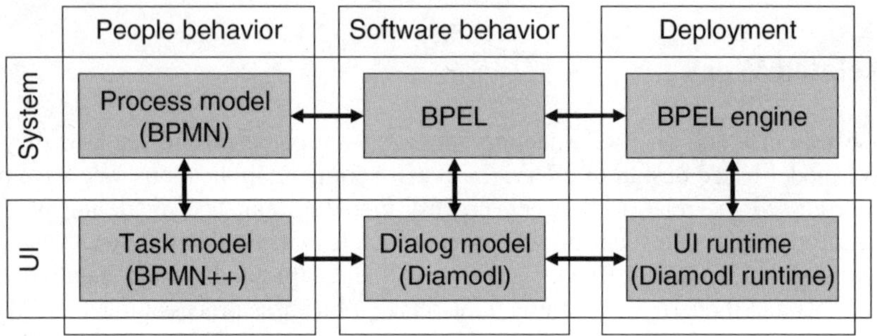

Fig. 1. Relationship between system and user interface domains

4   Using BPMN for Task Modeling

According to www.bpmn.org "… Business Process Modeling Notation (BPMN) will provide businesses with the capability of understanding their internal business procedures in a graphical notation…". Such a business procedure is a set of coordinated tasks performed by a set of roles and structured in hierarchy (called activity). Tasks in *different* processes communicate and implicitly coordinate by means of message connections. Tasks in the *same* process use flow connections for controlling sequencing and variables for storing XML data as process state. A task may repeat and be conditional. Web services are used for communicating with external systems, including business objects and UI clients.

A task modeling language typically structures tasks in a hierarchy. *Operators* are used for controlling the enablement and sequencing of tasks, e.g. tasks may be performed in sequence, in parallel, one of several tasks may be conditionally selected, a task (structure) may repeat, etc. Events from the environment, including objects representing the domain, may trigger or enable tasks, and operations may be performed on the environment.

The main difference between BPMN and task modeling languages is more a matter of style than expressive power and both essentially model a task hierarchy. Similarly, the control flow connections of BPMN and operators in task modeling languages are visually different, but have essentially the same expressive power. Finally, messages may take the role of events, to model tasks that are triggered by changes in the environment.

The weakest point of BPMN is domain modeling and data. Due to its focus on process message exchange and integration of web services, XML schemas and XML data has been chosen as the data model. Fortunately, many tools for object-oriented modeling, e.g. EMF 1. , can generate XML schemas, serialize models as XML and in general interoperate with XML, so this is more a practical obstacle than a conceptual problem. E.g. although a variable cannot be declared to reference an object of a particular class, is can be declared to refer to an XML fragment that *represents* an object of a particular class.

What is still missing is a way of declaring pre-conditions and post-conditions in terms of objects and their life-cycle (creation and destruction) and state. E.g. a pre-condition for performing a review of an application is of course the application, and the post-condition is that the review has been created. Hence, we augment the BMPN "task" model with annotations on each task that makes these conditions explicit, not very different from how Use case diagrams are elaborated be means of structured text.

5   Step-by-Step Modeling Method

Fig 1 shows the relationship between system and UI perspectives on the process of going from a process/task model to a deployed system which combines a BPEL engine and the Diamodl runtime. In this section we detail the practical method we propose for this process. The process is illustrated by a simple example, that of reviewing a request (for something) and returning the answer. As shown in fig 2, the Customer sends in an application that is received by our User role. The User performs a shallow review and may decide to either let the Expert role perform a deep review or do it himself. The resulting review is sent back to the Customer.

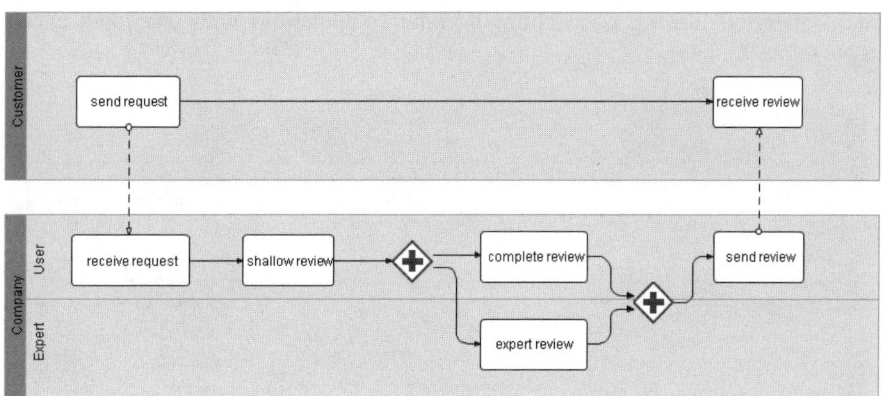

Fig. 2. Business process

Creating this BPMN model is the first step in our method, combined with domain modeling, where concepts in the domain are formalized in a class diagram. In practice, the domain model may already exist, either from previous projects or as a reference model for a well-established domain, e.g. order management. Since BPMN is XML-centered, we need to be able to convert the domain model to an XML Schema, before annotating the connections between processes (and possibly internal variables) with XML types. We use Ecore, the Eclipse Modeling Framework's modeling language for domain modeling, and export the XML Schema from the Ecore editor. The Intalio Designer Eclipse application, which we use for BPMN modeling, allows us to open the XML Schema in the Process navigator and drag XML types into the connections in the diagram.

This model is system centric, in that it does not focus on any particular user or distinguish between the user and the system. The next step in the method is disentangling the users' task from the system, as a kind of process *refactoring*. The general idea is to model the User role in a process of its own and make the connection (interface) to other roles and processes explicit. The refactored process model is shown in fig 3. As can be seen, this process interacts with both the Executable process, i.e. the system, and the Expert role.

This refactored process model is similar to a task model, in that it makes explicit what each uses does (task structure) and how it interacts with its environment (events and data). It may require further decomposition to be detailed enough, and in addition we annotate it with pre- and post-conditions that make explicit how domain data is operated on (life-cycle and states). E.g. the pre-condition for the User task "shallow review" is that there exist an unhandled request and the post-condition is that a review has been created and is in progress. This step may result in a refined domain model, to better capture the objects' possible states.

The connections flowing into and out of the User process, defines the necessary input and output of the user interface, and hence the dialog model, which is the next step. Our dialog modeling language Diamodl fits well with the dataflow nature of process models and web services. The connections are modeled as computations in Diamodl, the in-flowing connections become computations without input (sources of data), while out-flowing connections become computations with one input and no output (sinks of data).

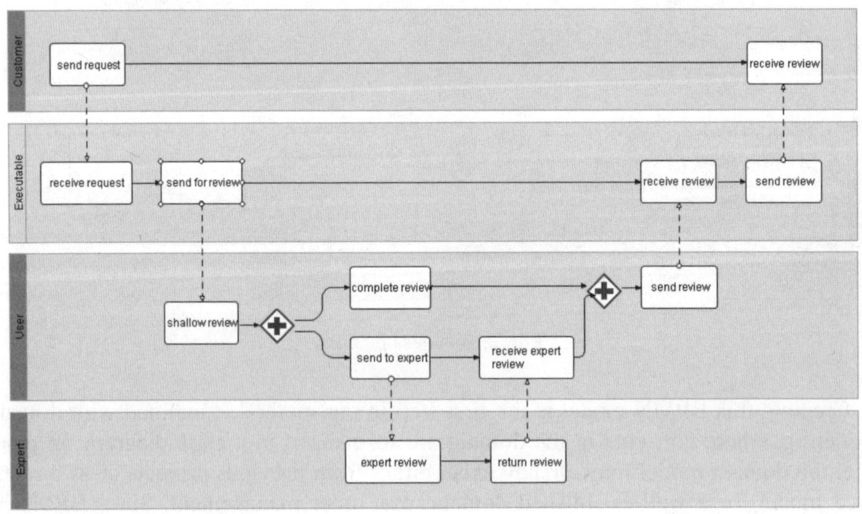

Fig. 3. Refactored process

Although the BPMN diagram is a model of how the user works, it is not a model of how the user works with the to-be-designed UI. In our experience, one of the main decisions to be made is how the user manages multiple and possibly parallel instances of the process. This possibility is implicit in the process model and if not considered in the design process, we may end up with a user interface that forces the user to work with each process instance independently. E.g. in this case, we should consider if the user should be able to see the finished review of one request while performing the shallow review of another, and perhaps support copying the former review.

Part of the dialog model and corresponding GUI prototype is shown in fig 4. The two large, shaded triangles are computations that represent connections from the process model, receiving a request and sending a review to the expert, respectively. This models lets the user see the list of unhandled requests, select and view one and choose to review the selected one. There is also a list of reviews in-progress, from which the user may select one and send to the expert. The GUI prototype has mostly been generated from the model, with only the layout and labels added by hand. The sample data that populates the GUI has been created with standard EMF tools, based on and validated against the domain model.

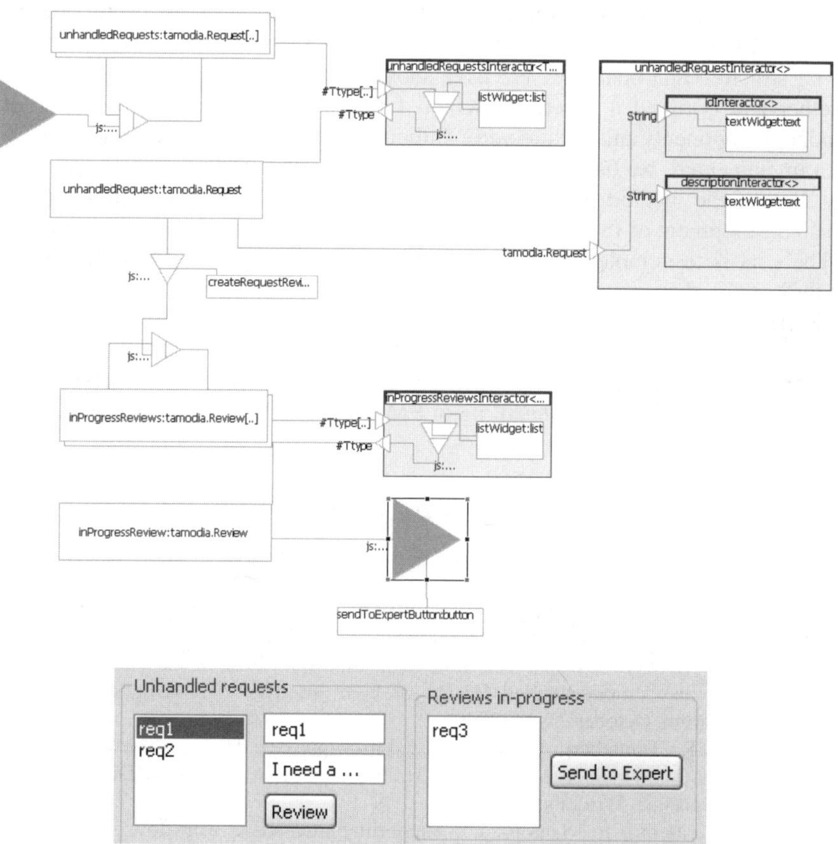

Fig. 4. Dialog model fragment and GUI prototype

The last step is deployment, which in general will include the part of the BPMN process marked as executable, the GUI and dialog and supporting services like task and data management. As work in-progress, this is the weak part of the current tool chain. A valid (and executable) BPMN process fragment may be translated to BPEL code and deploying it on one of several open source BPEL engines, and Intalio Designer is able to generate and deploy to a standards-compliant server in a few clicks.

The GUI and dialog model is executable, but the Diamodl runtime currently lacks general support for web services, so the final link between GUI and the BPEL engine is missing. We have, however, validated that we can initiate tasks from the Diamodl runtime and receive data from the BPEL engine, using the existing support for Javascript and XML. Similarly, although EMF-based data hasn't been integrated into the BPEL engine, EMF supports serializing and de-serializing Ecore instances as XML, so in principle any BPEL engine can store and communicate EMF-based data to and from the Diamodl runtime and web services.

6 Conclusion and Further Work

We have presented an approach for modeling business applications using BPMN and Diamodl, where BPMN is used for both process and task modeling and Diamodl for the UI structure and behavior. We have shown how these two modeling methods fit together and outlined a practical method for modeling and deployment, based on standard components and architecture. Although some technical components have not been implemented, we have validated the feasibility of both the method and technology. Part of the method is currently being taught in an advanced course on model-driven development of IS at our department.

The goal is to complete the missing parts, by improving the connection between the three main elements of our approach, domain, process and dialog modeling using EMF, BPMN and diamodl. More specifically, we need to 1) add support for modeling web services in the domain model using EMF, to enable deployment of domain-specific web services, 2) add two-way support for invoking web services in the diamodl runtime and 3) improve handling of EMF-based data in a BPEL engine.

References

1. The Eclipse Modeling Framework home page, `http://www.eclipse.org/modeling/emf/`
2. Paternò, F.: Model-based Design and Evaluation of Interactive Applications. Series of Applied Computing. Springer, London (2000)
3. Trætteberg, H.: Workflow and task modelling. In: Proceedings of the Fourth International Conference on Computer-Aided Design of User Interfaces CADUI 1999, Louvain-la-Neuve, Belgium, October 21-23 (1999)
4. Kristiansen, R., Trætteberg, H.: Model-based user interface design in the context of workflow models. In: Winckler, M., Johnson, H., Palanque, P. (eds.) TAMODIA 2007. LNCS, vol. 4849. Springer, Heidelberg (2007)
5. Bruno, A., Paternò, F., Santoro, C.: Supporting interactive workflow systems through graphical web interfaces and interactive simulators. In: Proceedings of Tamodia 2005, Gdansk, Poland. ACM International Conference Proceeding Series, vol. 127 (2005)

6. Pontico, F., Farenc, C., Winckler, M.: Model-based support for specifying eService eGovernment Applications. In: 5th International Workshop on TAsk MOdels and DIAgrams, Hasselt, Belgium, October 23-24 (2006)
7. Sukaviriya, N., Sinha, V., Ramachandra, T., Mani, S., Stolze, M.: User-Centered Design and Business Process Modeling: Cross Road in Rapid Prototyping Tools. In: Baranauskas, C., Palanque, P., Abascal, J., Barbosa, S.D.J. (eds.) INTERACT 2007. LNCS, vol. 4662. Springer, Heidelberg (2007)
8. Object Management Group. Business process modeling notation specification, final adopted specification dtc/06-02-01 (2006)
9. Havey, M.: Essential Business Process modeling. O'Reilly, Sebastopol (2005)
10. Trætteberg, H.: Dialog modelling with interactors and UML Statecharts - a hybrid approach. Design, Specification and Verification of Interactive Systems. Funcall, Madeira (June 2003)

Task-Based Development Methodology for Collaborative Environments

Maik Wurdel[1,*], Daniel Sinnig[2], and Peter Forbrig[1]

[1] University of Rostock, Department of Computer Science, Rostock, Germany
{maik.wurdel,peter.forbrig}@uni-rostock.de
[2] Concordia University, Faculty of Engineering and Computer Science, Montreal, Canada
d_sinnig@encs.concordia.ca

Abstract. The paper presents a task-based development methodology for collaborative applications. According to our methodology a collaborative task model may be used during analysis, requirements and design. In order to ensure that analysis information is correctly translated into subsequent development phases a refinement relation is proposed supporting the incremental development of task specifications. The development methodology is exemplified by a case study in which interactive support for a conference session is developed.

Keywords: Collaborative Task Models, Development Methodology, Refinement, Tool Support.

1 Introduction and Background Information

In modern software engineering, the development lifecycle is divided into a series of iterations. With each iteration a set of disciplines and associated activities are performed while the resulting artifacts are incrementally perfected and refined. The development of cooperative applications is no exception to this rule. Analysis level models are further refined into requirements- and/or design level models, finally resulting in a complete specification of the envisioned collaborative application.

In this paper we define a development methodology for collaborative systems covering the phases from analysis to design. Such an integrated development methodology will serve as a blueprint for practitioners to derive an iterative development process according to which collaborative task models are stepwise refined. For this purpose we analyze the various roles that collaborative task models may play in software development. Moreover, we define a refinement relation for collaborative task models. The practical applicability of our development methodology is demonstrated by a case study in which we develop interactive support for a conference session.

Within the domain of human-computer interaction collaborative task models are widely used for the specification of collaborative (multi-user) interactive systems. Among the most popular ones is Collaborative ConcurTaskTrees (CCTT) [1]. In

---

* Supported by a grant of the German National Research Foundation (DFG), Graduate School 1424, Multimodal Smart Appliance Ensembles for Mobile Applications (MuSAMA).

P. Forbrig and F. Paternò (Eds.): HCSE/TAMODIA 2008, LNCS 5247, pp. 118–125, 2008.

CCTT modeling starts with the creation of a task model for each involved role in the cooperation. Additionally, a so called "coordinator model" is developed to specify the temporal dependencies of tasks involved in the cooperation. CCTT is suitable for situations where only one actor is fulfilling one role simultaneously. Often, however, this is a too rigid constraint. In order to overcome this shortcoming, we have developed the collaborative task modeling language (CTML) [2]. It is based on the idea that the behavior of an actor can be approximated through her role. CTML incorporates concepts for the specification of interrelation between different actors based on roles, where the behavior of a role is defined by collaborative task expressions. Collaborations of actors are specified by means of an OCL-like notation used to specify preconditions based on the state of the tasks of the involved actors.

The remainder of the paper is structured as follows: in Section 2 we review key principles of CTML, which will serve as foundation for the presented approach. Additionally a refinement relation, based on meta-operators for CTML specifications is proposed. Section 3, the core part of this paper, presents a methodology for the incremental and iterative development of CTML models which is guided by a refinement relation for CTML specifications. In Section 4 we exemplify our methodology by elaborating a small case study. Finally we conclude and give an outlook to future research avenues.

2 The Collaborative Task Modeling Language

Similar to [1], CTML is based on a role-based approach for modeling cooperative task models. Formally, a CTML model is a tuple consisting of a *set of actors*, a *set of roles* and a *set of collaborative task expressions* (one for each role) where each actor belongs to one or more role(s). Each collaborative task expression has the form of a task tree, where nodes are either tasks or temporal operators. Each task is attributed with an *effect* and a *precondition*. An *effect* denotes a state change of the system or environment as a result of task execution. A *precondition* adds an additional execution constraint to a task. In particular a task may be performed only if its precondition is satisfied. Conditions can be either defined over the system state or the state of other tasks (a task life cycle is defined in terms of a state chart [2]), which potentially may be part of another task definition. Both, preconditions and effects are needed to model collaboration and synchronization across collaborative task expressions. The development and simulation of CTML specifications is supported by the tool CTML Editor and Simulator, first introduced in [2].

2.1 Refinement of CTML Specifications

Refinement is a formal process which transforms one specification into another such that required properties of the original specification are preserved [3]. In support of an iterative development methodology we propose, in this section, a refinement relation for CTML models. In [4] we presented a formal approach to define and check refinement between (non-collaborative) task model specifications. In what follows, we extend the approach to CTML specifications in a straightforward manner. Refining collaborative task models can be achieved using two different instruments: Structural and behavioral refinement.

Structural Refinement. The refined CTML model may contain more detailed information than its base model. This is achieved by further refining the atomic units (i.e. the leaf tasks) of the superordinate model. It is, however, important to retain type consistency. Refined tasks need to revise their task type if necessary according to the added subordinate tasks. An exception to this rule are tasks that have been marked with the *deep binding* meta-operator (will be explained in the context of behavioral refinement). These tasks cannot change their task type and the respective subtasks need to be chosen such that type consistency is ensured.

Behavioral Refinement. Whether a behavioral refinement is valid or not depends on the usage of meta-operators in the respective CTML models. Unlike temporal operators, meta-operators do not determine the execution order of tasks, but define which tasks must be retained or may be omitted in the refining CTML model. We distinguish between three different meta-operators: *shallow binding* ($\odot$), *deep binding* ($\otimes$), and *exempted binding* ($\ominus$). All three operators denote tasks which need to be preserved in all subsequent refining CTML models. While in the case of *shallow binding* subtasks may be omitted during refinement, in the case of *deep binding* all subtasks need to be preserved. Tasks attributed with the *exempt binding* operator have been newly introduced during design and should be preserved in all subsequent refinements.

Details of the algorithm implemented to check refinement can be found in [4].

3   Development Methodology

Current software engineering processes advocate iterative development lifecycles during which artifacts are incrementally perfected and refined [5]. The development of collaborative task models is no exception to this rule. We believe a CTML model is best developed in five steps:

1. Definition of roles and corresponding collaborative task expressions
2. Animation and validation of these sub-specifications
3. Specification of the environment including actors, associated roles and devices
4. Annotation of tasks with precondition and effects
5. Animation and validation of the entire specification

Instead of creating the entire model at once, which can be quite overwhelming, we suggest to first define (1) and test (2) the involved roles and their individual collaborative task expressions. Both steps can be performed iteratively. In case of an unsatisfying animation the developer typically adapts the underlying specification and restarts the simulation. Next (3) the designer defines the environment and involved actors. Additionally (4) task specifications are completed by adding preconditions and effects based on the analysis of the dependencies between actors and roles. Finally (5) the entire specification consisting of several "concurrently" executing task expressions can be tested and animated. This sequence is to be repeated until the simulation exhibits the expected behavior. Please note that in each stage it is possible to return to any previous step to revise made design decisions, based on evaluation results. Each of the above steps is fully supported by our tool CTML Editor and Simulator.

Fig. 1 indicates that throughout the development lifecycle of a collaborative application different "versions" of a CTML model are used. As will be detailed next, the usage and role of the CTML model vary, depending on the development stage within which it is utilized.

Analysis. The purpose of analysis is to understand the user's behaviors, their collaborations and interactions. Consequently, the analysis CTML model captures the current work situation and highlights elementary domain processes as well as exposes bottlenecks and weaknesses of the problem domain. As portrayed in Fig. 1, the focus is on the actual users while the envisioned interactive system is not yet taken into account.

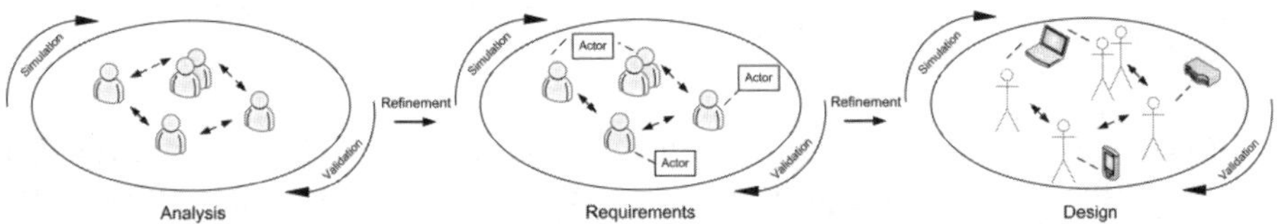

Fig. 1. CTML in the Development Lifecycle

Requirements. When moving to the requirement stage the analysis information is further refined by taking into account the support of the envisioned interactive application. Correspondingly requirements level CTML models specify the envisioned way tasks are performed using the system under development. That is, tasks that were formerly performed by the user may now be taken over by the envisioned interactive system. Generally, the artifacts gathered during requirements specification are part of the contract between stakeholders about the future application.

Design. During design, the various tasks of the requirements model are "instantiated" to a particular target device by taking into account its interaction capabilities. Typically, new design specific, tasks are also introduced. An example of such a design specific task for a conference session management system (will be introduced in Section 4) is "Register Presenter". This task was not part of the analysis or requirements model, but is needed during design such that the session management system is able to keep track of the participating presenters.

When moving from analysis to requirements to design, the collaborative task model is further refined since application and design specific information is added. With each refinement step it is important to verify that the refining model is a valid refinement of its base specification. The interpretation of what constitutes a valid refinement depends on the artifacts involved, as well as on their purpose in the software lifecycle.

4 Case Study

In this section we showcase the application of the presented development methodology by elaborating a small case study which has as its goal the development of interactive tool support for a conference session. For this purpose let us consider the following scenario:

Before starting the session Peter, the chairman, connects his notebook to the projector installed in the conference room and switches to presentation mode. Afterwards he starts the session by introducing himself and giving a short introduction about the presentations to be given during the session. Then, Peter gives the floor to the first speakers, Daniel and Maik, who give a joined presentation. Daniel connects his notebook to the projector and starts the presentation by briefly introducing the general approach. The technical details are explained by Maik. His slides are stored on his own notebook, which has to be connected to the projector before he presents his ideas. Afterwards, Daniel resumes the talk by giving the conclusion and an outlook for future research which results in an additional reconfiguration of the notebook and the projector. After finishing the talk the chairman asks for questions from the plenum which are answered by the speakers. The subsequent talks are given in ordinary manner until Peter closes the session.

Based on our experiences such a scenario is quite common. The technical burden of state of the art computing devices leads to a tedious and error prone configuration process. But pure automation does not solve this problem. From our point of view a thorough analysis of the collaboration of the actors involved in this process is able to expose where automation is really helpful. The question to be addressed is: "What is the appropriate assistance in the current situation for the actual actor?"

Clearly the scenario shows that actors involved in a joint presentation have to synchronize and agree on who is taking the control of the presentation. Daniel and Maik must not perform the task "Present" concurrently. This is a key collaboration constraint and hence should be taken into account in any corresponding collaborative task model. In Fig. 2 the analysis level CTML model for the joint presentation is given. It is role-based and represents how involved presenters perform their joint presentation. As already hinted by the afore-mentioned scenario, a presenter has to gain control and set up the equipment before presenting his slides. After finishing her/his part the presenter surrenders the control and hence enables other actors to present their parts.

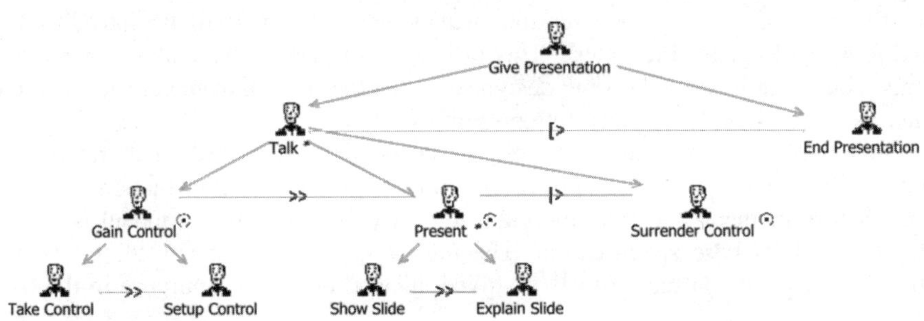

Fig. 2. Analysis Task Model for the Role "Presenter"

The interplay between gaining and surrendering control is modeled using the effects given in Table 1. The effect of an actor performing the task "Gain Control" is that for all other presenters the "Gain Control" task becomes disabled. Conversely, the execution of the task "Surrender Control" enables the "Gain Control" task to all participating presenters among which, one presenter will be able to "Gain Control" of the presentation.

Table 1. Effects of Analysis Task Model for "Presenter"

#	Task	Effect
(1.)	*Gain Control*	*Presenter.allInstances.Gain Control.disable*
(2.)	*Surrender Control*	*Presenter.allInstances.Gain Control.enable*

Before moving to the requirements stage, we have to ensure that pivotal domain specific tasks are preserved in all subsequent refining models. This is done by the use of meta-operators which have been introduced in the previous section. In the context of this case study, the important tasks to be retained are "Gain Control", "Present" and "Surrender Control" and therefore are marked with the shallow *binding operator*.

During the requirement stage new aspects come into play. Compared to the analysis model, the envisioned work situation is enriched by taking into account the support of interactive devices. In our case the interactive support consists of a remote presenter device and a steerable projector. The former can be used to navigate through the slides but also to surrender and gain control of the presentation. The latter can soft-switch between multiple input sources and projection surfaces and hence, can relieve the presenters from manually setting up the equipment (e.g. connecting the laptop to the projector).

As depicted in Fig. 3 the requirements level task model refines the analysis model in terms of structure and behavior. The task "Gain Control" has been structurally refined into interaction and application subtasks denoting how the control of the presentation is gained using the envisioned software system. In particular the execution of the subtask "Assign Control" assigns the control of the remote presenter device and thus to its user. The "Present" task is now regarded as an interaction task since presentations given with the new system are requiring the interaction with the newly introduced remote presenter device. The execution of the "Setup Equipment" task has the effect that the input source of the steerable projector is set to the current actor's laptop. Note that for the sake of simplicity the necessary preconditions and effects are not shown.

In order to ensure that the requirements are preserved in subsequent design models the tasks "Gain Control" and "Present" are marked with the *deep binding* meta-operator. This guarantees that each of these tasks including the subtasks is carried on to the design stage. Additionally "Surrender Control" keeps being marked with the shallow binding operator.

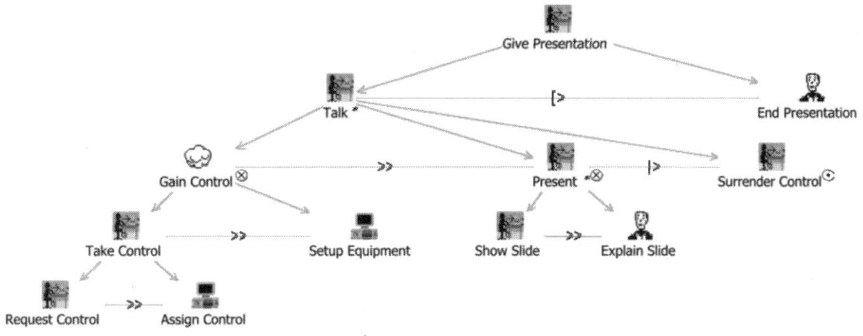

Fig. 3. Requirement Task Model for the Role "Presenter"

During design, the focus is put on tasks related to the specific interaction with the newly introduced system. Fig. 4 portrays the corresponding task model for our case study. In particular the task "Request Control" has been further refined with subtasks which take into account concrete interactions with the remote presenter (e.g. "Press Request Button"). The same applies for "Surrender Control". Additionally, technology related tasks are introduced. In the context of the case study the presenter has to register her/his remote presenter device to the system ("Register Presenter") before it can be used. The "Register Presenter" task has been attributed with the *exempted binding* operator, denoting that it should be preserved in all subsequent refinements.

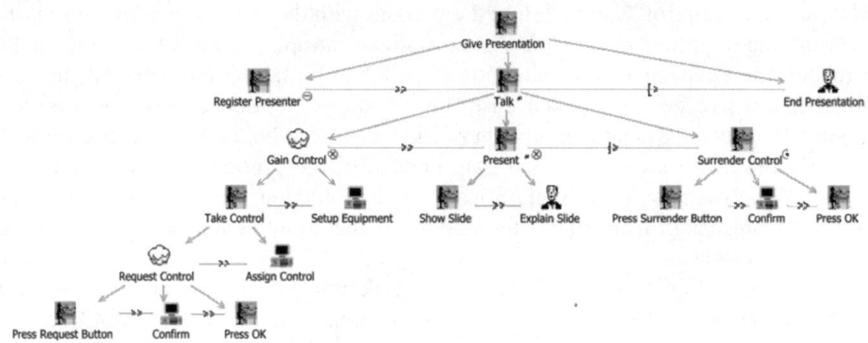

Fig. 4. Design Task Model for the Role "Presenter"

We conclude this section by noting that for each phase (i.e. analysis, requirements and design) we interactively animated the developed CTML models using the tool CTML Editor and Simulator. This was particularly helpful in gradually refining the model until the envisioned behavior was achieved. A snapshot of the interactive animation of the requirements level task model is depicted on the right hand side of Fig. 5. On the left hand side a snapshot of the tool in specification mode is given.

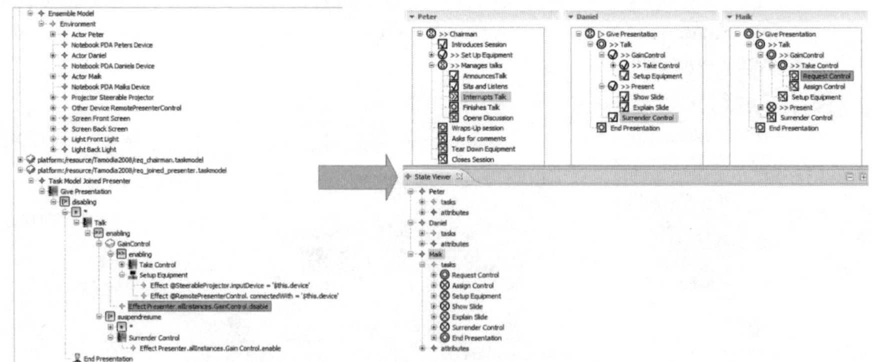

Fig. 5. CTML Editor and Simulator in Specification and Animation Mode

5   Conclusion and Future Work

In this paper we presented a development methodology for collaborative task models. In particular, we proposed a set of steps for the incremental development of CTML models. Each step is supported by our tool the CTML Editor and Simulator. We explored the different roles of a CTML model within the development lifecycle of a collaborative application. In particular we proposed a development methodology according to which an analysis level CTML model is further refined to a requirements and design level model. Finally we validated and illustrated our proposed development methodology by elaborating a small case study, which had as its goal the development of interactive support for a conference session.

As future work we are currently investigating how CTML can be integrated into state of the art model-based UI development processes for collaborative environments. Another future avenue deals with the enhancement of the CTML Editor and Simulator with model checking capabilities such that the tool will be able to prove certain properties of a CTML model (e.g. livelock and deadlock freedom) and mechanizes the verification of refinement between CTML specifications.

References

1. Mori, G., Paternò, F., Santoro, C.: CTTE: Support for Developing and Analyzing Task Models for Interactive System Design. IEEE Trans. Softw. Eng. 28(8), 797–813 (2002)
2. Wurdel, M., Sinnig, D., Forbrig, P.: Towards a Formal Task-based Specification Framework for Collaborative Environments. In: CADUI 2008, Albacete, Spain (2008)
3. Bowen, J., Reeves, S.: Refinement for User Interface Designs. In: FMIS 2007, Lancaster, UK (2007)
4. Wurdel, M., Sinnig, D., Forbrig, P.: Task Model Refinement with Meta Operators. In: DSV-IS 2007, Kingston, Canada (2008)
5. Larman, C.: Applying UML and Patterns: An Introduction to Object-Oriented Analysis and Design and Iterative Development, 3rd edn. Prentice Hall PTR (2004)

An Event-Condition-Action Approach for Contextual Interaction in Virtual Environments

Lode Vanacken, Joan De Boeck, Chris Raymaekers, and Karin Coninx

Hasselt University - tUL - IBBT, Expertise Centre for Digital Media (EDM),
Wetenschapspark 2, B-3590 Diepenbeek, Belgium
{lode.vanacken,joan.deboeck,chris.raymaekers,
karin.coninx}@uhasselt.be

Abstract. In order to support context-dependency in model-based development, three components need to be realised: Context Detection, Context Switching and Context Handling. Context detection is the process for detecting changes in context, while context switching brings the system in the new state that needs to be supported. Finally, context handling adapts the interaction possibilities to the current context. In this paper we discuss an approach for context detection and switching for virtual environments that is based on the Event-Condition-Action paradigm. Both context detection and switching are split-up and supported by our graphical notation for the design of multimodal interaction techniques. The main advantage of this approach is that we provide the designer with a flexible context system, supported by scalable diagrams.

Keywords: Multimodal Interaction Techniques, Model-Based User Interface Design, Context-Awareness.

1 Introduction and Related Work

The development of interactive computer applications takes much time, especially for the design and implementation of the user interface. This is in particular true for 3D multimodal interfaces for Virtual Environments (VEs). The process of creating or selecting interaction techniques for such interfaces is not straightforward. A large amount of possibilities exist with regard to input and output devices and the combination of these with respect to the interaction techniques being designed. One possible approach that can be applied in order to simplify the development process is using model-based user interface design as described in [4, 10].

In model-based user interface design (MBUID) different models are used through gradual progression. Typically, such a process starts at the level of a task model, moves over several other models, such as the dialog model up to the final user interface. Models can be transformed from one model into another or can be combined. Specifically for the design of a VE, it is necessary to model the multimodal interaction techniques, such as 'object manipulation'. Several high level notations exist, which can be used for this purpose [5, 7, 10]. In our research we use NiMMiT (Notation for Multimodal Interaction Techniques) [5] for describing the interaction.

P. Forbrig and F. Paternò (Eds.): HCSE/TAMODIA 2008, LNCS 5247, pp. 126–133, 2008.

The use of context information in a MBUID process when developing mobile or hand-held interfaces, already has been studied thoroughly [2, 8]. Indeed, a mobile application can have different locations, platforms or services which allow other features or actions to be available, resulting in interfaces that must adapt to each context. The same can be true in a VE application where the context is often defined by the available devices (and input/output modalities), external parameters such as the experience level of the user, or whether the user is seated or standing. All those parameters may have their influence on the interaction with the system.

Without special facilities for context in the diagrams, these features have to be supported in an ad-hoc manner. Clerckx [3] distinguishes several levels at which context may have its influence. A context system can be represented at the task or the dialog level, but in this work we focus on the dialog level. Such a context system consists of three components. Firstly, changes in context need to be sensed through a context detection system. Next, the system needs to react upon this change. The context switching makes sure that only parts of the system that react on the new context are active, while interaction techniques can act upon the current context through the context handling system.

We will first briefly discuss our approach to handle contextual knowledge at the dialog level as earlier proposed in [9]. In section 3 we elaborate on how this approach can be improved to dynamically support context switches using the *Event-Condition-Action* (ECA) [1, 6] paradigm. Using this paradigm we achieve a scalable approach which can be supported by (semi-)automatic generation. As we will be using NiM-MiT as a high level notation for interaction techniques, we can reuse the existing run time system, and as we can assume that designers may already know this notation from the design of their user interaction, they do not need to learn a new notation to model context information.

2 Runtime Context

In earlier work [9], we introduced handling context knowledge using NiMMiT. The graphical notation NiMMiT, inherits the formalism of a state-chart in order to describe the (multimodal) interaction within the virtual environment. Furthermore, it also supports data flow which occurs during the interaction, as well. A more detailed description of NiMMiT can be found in [5].

Our approach to integrate contextual information was inspired from earlier results of research in the area of model-based design [3]: (1) incorporating context in task and dialog modelling and (2) adding modality constraints to tasks. We discuss a combination of these two approaches, enabling context-aware selection of modalities.

Consider for instance a VE application that has two setups (external contexts), which differ in devices/modalities to be used. An application, that can be used in either an immersive setup using stereo vision and gloves or in a desktop setup with a keyboard and a mouse, illustrates this idea.

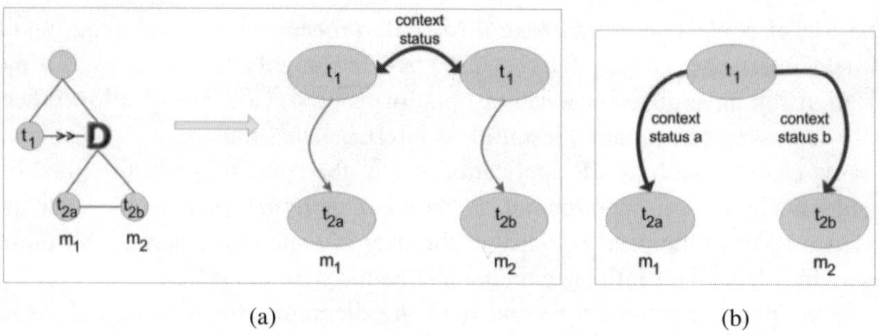

(a)   (b)

Fig. 1. (a) Combining modality constraints with the decision task notation (task model and dialog model). (b) Merged dialog models.

One way to incorporate this, is to introduce the contexts at the task level [3], this means that according to the contextual constraint (m_1 and m_2), a different task is selected, as is illustrated in figure 1(a). Task t_2 is divided into two distinct tasks t_{2a} and t_{2b}. This approach expands into two different dialog models, one for each context. Both models contain two states, containing one task each, in this example. According to the context m_1 or m_2, the appropriate dialog model is selected.

This solution is suitable when a context switch enables other tasks or requires other interaction techniques and thus affects the task model. The drawback is the duplication of the dialog model for each context. Alternatively, in a typical VE situation as in our example, the tasks may remain the same for each context. In this situation defining 'context' at the dialog level is considered as a more efficient approach.

Moreover, to overcome the problem of duplication both approaches may be combined: instead of having two distinct dialog models, we simply merge them together and make a distinction only where a difference is made by a context status. This is illustrated in figure 1(b). The two states containing t_1 are merged into one state in one and the same dialog model, but a choice is made to the appropriate state transition depending on the context. In this way the decision at the task level is modelled at the dialog level.

In our former work [9], we implemented this approach at the dialog level using our interaction description model: NiMMiT. In figure 2 an example of our approach is depicted. In figure 2(a) we can see that in the 'Start'-state several different events (modalities) could trigger the execution of the task chains. Using 'context' information, we are able to attach a certain context to a certain event or modality, such that, depending on this context, only those events belonging to that context are active. If for example 'GLOVE.MOVE' is intended to be used in the immersive setup, one can attach the 'immersive'-context to the event-arrow 'GLOVE.MOVE'. Similarly the event 'KEYBOARD.MOVE' can be used in the 'desktop'-context. Note that if there was no support to couple events to a context the same diagram should be created twice with different events (as in figure 2(a)) which would make maintenance much harder.

Adding this contextual knowledge to events transforms the view of the diagram depending onto which context of the diagram we are viewing. A part of the resulting diagram containing context arrows is shown in figure 2(b).

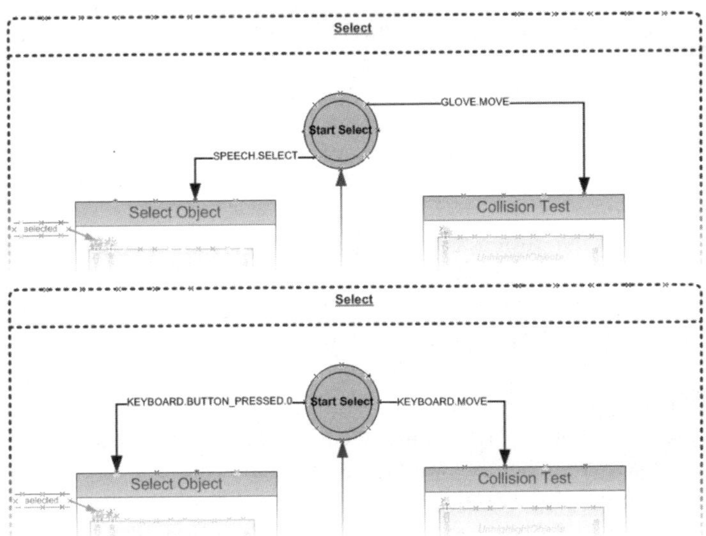

(a) Events active in two different contexts

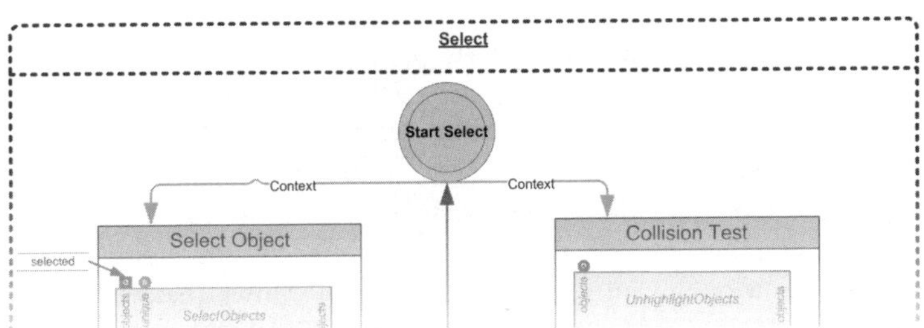

(b) Events were attached to context arrows

Fig. 2. Our approach to contextual knowledge at the dialog level

3 Defining a Context System

3.1 Context Detection and Switching

Our previous work concentrated on context handling. The detection and switching was handled through explicit user interaction. In order to realise a context-dependent interaction, it is also necessary to automate this detection and handling of the context. The following section therefore discusses how this has been integrated into our existing system.

The process of context detection and switching can be seen as an Event-Condition-Action process. A certain *event* or combination of events can signal a change in context, possibly depending on certain *conditions*. Finally if the conditions are met, it might be necessary to perform an *action* such that the context switch is finalised. For instance, a user may stand up from his chair (*event*). Before executing a context switch, we must ensure that he wears tracked gloves (*condition*). If the condition is met, we disable the toolbars that are needed in the desktop setup and connect the cursor to make the glove visible (*action*). Note that we assume that 'standing up' can be recognised as an event. If this would not be possible, it is also possible to listen to a more general event, e.g. the movement of a tracker mounted to the user's head *event*, and assert for the tracker's position in order to decide whether the user is seated or standing (*condition*).

In order to keep the design as modular as possible, this Event-Condition-Action process is split up in two parts. One part is the context detection, the other handles the context switch. According to Event-Condition-Action, the context detection should identify what events to listen for, checks whether or not the conditions are fulfilled and it eventually triggers a 'context switch' event. This event is recognised by the Context Switching part.

The Context Switching part captures the 'context switch' event and executes the actions that are necessary before switching to the target context.

Dividing the process in two distinct parts, connected through the 'context switch' event, has the advantage that the code necessary for checking the conditions is separated from the action code. In the next section we will explain why this will lead to smaller and well-organised diagrams.

3.2 Implementation through NiMMiT Diagrams

In our research, interaction techniques are defined using NiMMiT diagrams. As NiMMiT offers a convenient way to describe systems in which events fire a set of tasks, we propose that both the context detection and switch can be implemented using NiMMiT diagrams, as well. Besides this reason, designers already know NiMMiT from the design of the interaction itself, which allows them to model context without having to learn a new modelling notation. Finally, the run time system to execute NiMMiT diagrams is already realised.

The Context Detection NiMMiT diagram defines a state for each 'context' where the relevant events that can evoke a context switch are available. The events activate a task chain, which checks the condition by a more complex set of tasks. When the condition is not met, nothing happens. Otherwise, before moving on to a new state, reflecting the new context, the task chain has to fire a 'context switch' event. A template of such a diagram can be seen in figure 3. Two contexts, SITTING and STANDING are represented using the two states 'Context-SITTING' and 'Context-STANDING'.

A second NiMMiT diagram, responsible for the action, contains a state for each context. In each state, the respective 'context events' are awaited. Upon occurrence of such an event a task chain is fired, containing the code that has to be executed before the context switch. This code might be enabling or disabling certain devices, showing or hiding objects or controls in the world, etc. The last action in this task chain, before moving to the new context state, is explicitly setting the context, so that the running NiMMiT diagrams that define the user interaction can adapt to the context switch, and handle the new context.

The NiMMiT diagrams defining the context system, will share a similar pattern among different projects. Independent of the nature or the number of contexts, each context will be represented as a state in both diagrams. Each context transition will then be represented by an *event* arrow in the context detection diagram and a 'context event' arrow in the context switching diagram, invoking a task chain.

The similar patterns of these 'context' diagrams open the opportunity for an editor to generate a template diagram that can be completed by the designer. Obviously, for specific purposes the designer is free to alter the generated diagrams, e.g. if he wants to restrict possible context switches.

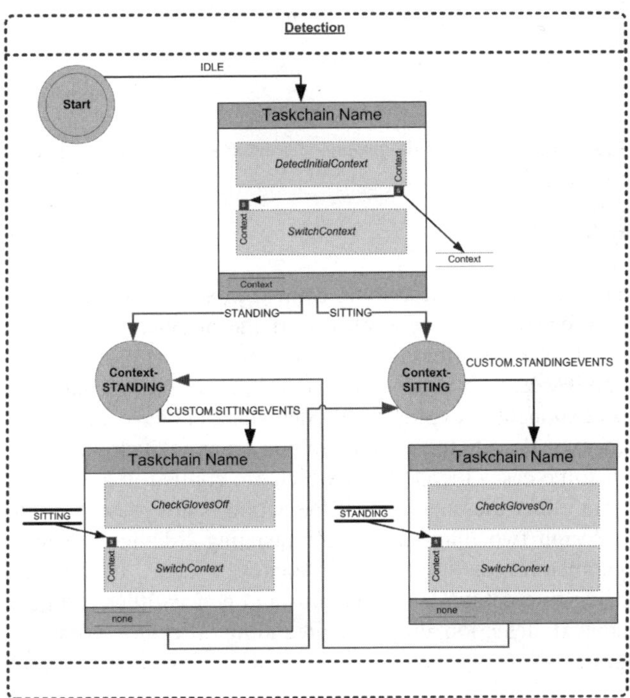

Fig. 3. Implication of the proposed context system at the task level

3.3 Implications at the Dialog Level and Task Level

The proposed context detection and switching system is a process which is active during the entire execution of the application. This obviously has its implications on the task level and dialog level of the model-based process. For the dialog model, every state contains two new tasks which are performed concurrently with the normal tasks, these tasks include the context detection and the context switching diagrams.

Considering the task level, this means that a new subtree concurrent with all other subtrees is part of the task hierarchy, as can be seen in figure 4. The ContextSystem tasks perform the detection and switching of the context, while the VE tasks may change their execution based upon this context switch, as discussed in figure 2.

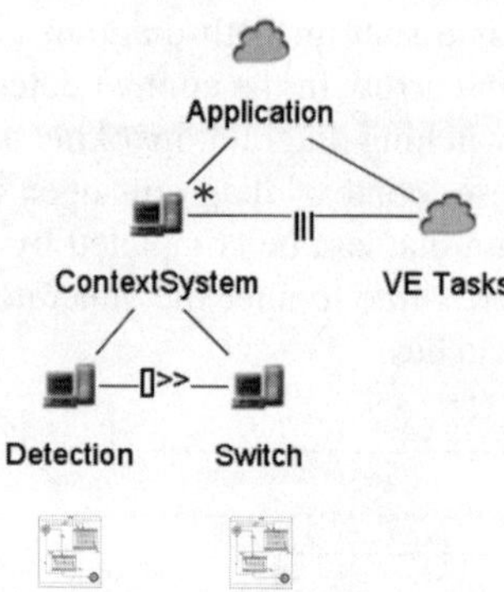

Fig. 4. Implication of the proposed context system at the task level

4 Discussion

A possible problem related to describing context in a state chart, is the fact that these diagrams can suffer from a state explosion if the number of different contexts becomes too high. This especially is true if we consider a context as an n-dimensional vector of observed values. If these observed values are orthogonal to each other, this will result in an exponential explosion of contexts, and hence will make the diagrams hard to manage, even despite the division in two separate diagrams.

However, in some cases the contexts which are applied in a VE are rather simple, which means that either the condition or the action is not present. In that case it may be overkill to design two diagrams: one translating '(device) events' into 'context events', and another responding to those 'context events'. In this situation, the designer may decide to combine both diagrams and hence either add context switching code to the context detection diagram, or adding '(device) events' to the context switching diagram.

5 Conclusion

Context detection and context switching are necessary components of an overall approach for context-dependency in model-based development. In this paper, we presented our approach for context detection and switching.

Event-Condition-Action rules are used as a basis for the context system. Both context detection and switching are split up and supported by NiMMiT diagrams, this results in a scalable approach. The run time system for NiMMiT is already present and the designer also uses NiMMiT to design interaction techniques, therefore the usage of NiMMiT eliminates the overload of having to learn a new notation for context modelling or adding a new module to the run time system. As the general pattern of the context detection and switching diagrams is similar among different projects, the approach also opens the opportunity for a (semi-)automatic generation of the diagrams by an editor. In the future, we would like to further investigate how our approach compares to other approaches and validate it using case studies.

Acknowledgments. Part of the research at EDM is funded by the ERDF (European Regional Development Fund) and the Flemish government. The VR-DeMo project (IWT 030248) is directly funded by the IWT, a Flemish subsidy organisation.

References

1. Beer, W., Christian, V., Ferscha, A., Mehrmann, L.: Modeling Context-aware Behavior by Interpreted ECA Rules. In: Kosch, H., Böszörményi, L., Hellwagner, H. (eds.) Euro-Par 2003. LNCS, vol. 2790, pp. 1064–1073. Springer, Heidelberg (2003)
2. Capra, L., Emmerich, W., Mascolo, C.: Carisma: Context-aware reflective middleware system for mobile applications. IEEE Trans. Software Eng. 29(10), 929–945 (2003)
3. Clerckx, T.: Model-based development of context-aware interactive applications in ambient intelligence environments. Ph.D. thesis, transnationale Universiteit Limburg (2007)
4. De Boeck, J., Gonzalez Calleros, J.M., Coninx, K., Vanderdonckt, J.: Open issues for the development of 3d multimodal applications from an MDE perspective. In: MDDAUI (2006)
5. De Boeck, J., Vanacken, D., Raymaekers, C., Coninx, K.: High-level modeling of multimodal interaction techniques using nimmit. Journal of Virtual Reality and Broadcasting 4(2) (2007)
6. Etter, R., Costa, P., Broens, T.: A Rule-Based Approach Towards Context-Aware User Notification Services. In: Proceedings of the IEEE ICPS 2006, pp. 281–284 (2006)
7. Figueroa, P., Green, M., Hoover, H.J.: InTml: A description language for VR applications. In: Proceedings of Web3D 2002, Arizona, USA, pp. 53–58 (2002)
8. Sohn, T., Dey, A.K.: icap: an informal tool for interactive prototyping of context-aware applications.In: CHI Extended Abstracts, pp. 974–975 (2003)
9. Vanacken, L., Cuppens, E., Clerckx, T., Coninx, K.: Extending a dialog model with contextual knowledge. In: Winckler, M., Johnson, H., Palanque, P. (eds.) TAMODIA 2007. LNCS, vol. 4849, pp. 28–41. Springer, Heidelberg (2007)
10. Willans, J., Harrison, M.: A toolset supported approach for designing and testing virtual environment interaction techniques. International Journal of HCS 55(2), 145–165 (2001)

Automated Usability Evaluation during Model-Based Interactive System Development

Sebastian Feuerstack[1], Marco Blumendorf[1], Maximilian Kern[1], Michael Kruppa[2], Michael Quade[1], Mathias Runge[1], and Sahin Albayrak[1]

[1] DAI-Labor
Technische Universität Berlin
Ernst-Reuter-Platz 7,10587 Berlin
Firstname.Lastname@DAI-Labor.de
[2] Deutsches Forschungszentrum für Kuenstliche Intelligenz GmbH
Trippstadter Str.122, 67663 Kaiserslautern
Firstname.Lastname@dfki.de

Abstract. In this paper we describe an approach to efficiently evaluate the usability of an interactive application that has been realized to support various platforms and modalities. Therefore we combine our Multi-Access Service Platform (MASP), a model-based runtime environment to offer multimodal user interfaces with the MeMo workbench which is a tool supporting an automated usability analysis. Instead of deriving a system model by reverse-engineering or annotating screenshots for the automated usability analysis, we use the semantics of the runtime models of the MASP. This allows us to reduce the evaluation effort by automating parts of the testing process for various combinations of platforms and user groups that should be addressed by the application. Furthermore, by testing the application at runtime, the usability evaluation can also consider system dynamics and information that are unavailable at design time.

Keywords: model-based user interface development, automated usability evaluation.

1 Introduction

User interfaces (UI) are more and more required to support several contexts-of-use. They need to be able to be run on several platforms, consider different types of users and adapt to various usage situations. This poses new challenges when it comes to the development of interactive applications as well as their evaluation. In this work we present our approach combining a model-based runtime system with an Automated Usability Evaluation (AUE) tool to provide the ability to evaluate UIs that adapt at runtime. In order to attend to these issues we combined two approaches: The Mental Models (MeMo) workbench, a workbench for AUE and the Multi-Access Service Platform (MASP), a model-based framework for UI generation. Model-based UI development approaches [1, 2, 3, 4] already support the generation of multi-platform user-interfaces as well as context-of-use adaptation. They contain semantics stored in

P. Forbrig and F. Paternò (Eds.): HCSE/TAMODIA 2008, LNCS 5247, pp. 134–141, 2008.

a well-structured form of declarative design models. This allows tools to assist developers at design-time by detecting questionable features and by offering the help of automated advisors. However, most of these approaches do not consider ad-hoc adaptation to the context-of-use which can only be calculated at runtime. The MASP allows the derivation of a UI from a set of executable models [5], defining the user interface state. Besides having the possibility to describe adaptive UIs, the models and the state information can also be utilized to support the AUE of the UI. By working with abstract UI models, which ideally contain all required concepts, the UIs could be generated for any platform and thus usability evaluation could be done by considering any platform without being forced to redefine the concepts of the evaluation target.

After we give an overview of related work in the research field of automated usability evaluation in the next section, we elaborate on the combination of the two approaches. We illustrate the results of the evaluation using the interactive Cooking Assistant we developed based on the MASP (the Cooking Assistant has also been deployed as a demo application in our Ambient Assisted Living Testbed [6]) and we conclude with a summary and outlook in section 5.

2 Related Work

AUE methods can support the evaluation process, whereas they differ significantly in their degree of automation and the effort for evaluators [7]. The majority of AUE methods is usually applied on already existing systems or prototypes and therefore requires re-constructing a system interaction model by reverse-engineering or manually annotating the semantics of already existing applications [8, 9, 10]. The Cog-Tool [11] is a tool to predict execution times for certain tasks. The max model [12] is considering cognitive aspects via user simulation for measuring accessibility of information within web sites and the PROSKIN project [13] is tracking user data in order to aggregate it to higher-level profiles to gain personalized UI designs. The AIDE [14] tool focuses on organizing the controls of an interface by incorporating five metrics (efficiency, alignment, horizontal balance, vertical balance and constraints) into the design process, while initial automated assistance has been proposed by USAGE [15]. Furthermore, tests have been developed for certain aspects of completeness, consistency and command-reach ability [16]. Model-based interface development environments, such as TADEUS's [17], support simulation and model-checking by translating the dialog model into a Petri net.

In contrary to these approaches we are moving the AUE from design-time to runtime in order to enable the evaluation of ad-hoc context-of-use adaptations as well as considering system dynamics that are unknown at design-time, such as data queries. We use the MeMo workbench [18] to simulate different user profiles that perform certain tasks and benefit in the way that usability issues are uncovered for a wide range of possible users. Further on, we can simulate users performing more errors as usual to diagnose the system's behavior which is difficult to predict by real persons within complex systems. The evaluation process of the MeMo workbench is based on a cognitive walkthrough (CWT) carried out by a usability expert and includes a rule engine which contains a set of modifier rules extracted from the CWT methodology.

Compared to the related work, our approach offers the following benefits:

- No need for a manual re-creation of the specification of an application which is fragile for introducing misunderstandings and incompleteness.
- All combinations of platforms and users that are addressed by the interactive application can be efficiently targeted to an automated user interface evaluation.
- By utilizing the model-based run-time system, the evaluation can consider system dynamics and parameters, and context-of-use variations.

3   Model-Based Automated Usability Evaluation

In order to automate the usability evaluation for several context-of-use scenarios, each specifying a combination of a specific platform, a certain group of users and conditions of the environment, we replaced the system interaction model (SIM) of the MeMo workbench with the runtime models of the MASP. The simulation starts with the MASP generating the initial representation of the user interface for a certain context-of-use. This representation is sent to the MeMo workbench by delivering a system interaction state (SI state) which consists of the current enabled set of interaction input and output tasks. Based on this information and the current user profile, the MeMo workbench chooses an interaction which is related to an input task of the MASP. The correlated user action will be performed and a new SI state is generated until the user's goal has been accomplished.

3.1   System Interaction State Generation

In the MASP we are interpreting task trees that define the temporal relations as the basic interaction flow for the interactive system. A domain model completes the task model by providing content for the tasks. The model defines the data structures and holds instances of these structures which are objects that become accessible at runtime. The life-time of these objects is determined by the task model, which also references the objects in the designated tasks as we described in detail in [19]. Modifying objects of the domain model happens either through the service model (1), connecting backend services to application tasks (2) or by user interaction (3) while entering and changing information. User interaction is mediated by the interaction model, detailing the interaction tasks (4). Here we distinguish input interaction tasks (IIT) and output interaction tasks (OIT), which identify the interaction on the highest level of abstraction. While OITs require no human intervention but present information to the user until they become disabled by another task, IITs require human intervention such as data input. The tasks are also annotated with the objects that are read, modified, created or declared and refer to the related classes of the domain model. A reification of the interaction in terms of details is provided by the interaction model. It encloses an abstract interaction description that is modality independent and a concrete interaction description that adds the modality dependent information. Additionally, by mappings between the interaction and the layouting model (5) presented in [20], absolute positions and element sizes of the concrete interaction objects are calculated based on the context model (6) and filled with information delivered by various sensors at runtime. Thus, each SI state will be composed of encapsulated sets of enabled tasks. Each atomic task is linked to the concrete domain object class and the relevant class attributes which are presented in the interface together with the expected user operation (read, create or modify) (3). Further, the relevant interaction model elements and the calculated layouting information are added for each enabled task of the SI state (5). Finally a cascading style sheet defining the style for the graphic elements of the concrete model is attached to the SI state.

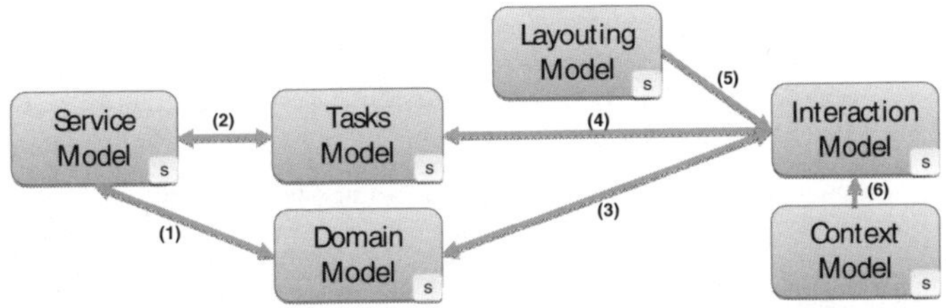

Fig. 1. Overview of the involved runtime MASP models, separating multiple levels of abstraction. Each model comprises (part of) the runtime state(s).

The relation between the models is formalized by mappings which support the exchange of information between the models and keep the models synchronized. Figure 1 shows the different models and how they are related. At runtime each model contains additional state information, allowing the derivation of the final UI according to the state of the application. Through the utilization of mappings between the models, we support an information flow at runtime, which allows identifying active elements of the models based on the enabled task set. The derived SI state allows the creation of a final UI which can be evaluated by an AUE tool as described in the next section.

From the AUE perspective, the runtime interpretation of the UI models creates a SIM containing SI states, which describe the interface and interaction capabilities of the evaluation target. The UI elements contained in a SI state are communication elements with different interactions, e.g. a button can be used with left click or right click as input interaction, whereas the information of the caption is carried through an output interaction from the system to the user. Every input interaction and the successive SI state, which is enabled after the interaction, are encapsulated in a transition to the subsequent SI state. In the simulation phase the SIM is mapped to a dynamic SIM representation which is handed over to the simulator for interaction with the user interaction model (UIM). The simulator continuously presents SI states to the UIM and maps the input interactions, chosen by the UIM depending on the current user task, to the corresponding transitions of the SIM.

3.2 User Action Generation

After the MASP presents the SI state to MeMo, the information processing unit (IPU) of the UIM evaluates all input and output interactions and manipulates the data storage which is used by the planning unit for the final interaction selection process. Both modules are influenced by two types of user attributes (UA). Static UA express the characteristics of a user group and cannot be influenced by the simulation process, whereas dynamic UA (DUA) are flexible properties of a user.

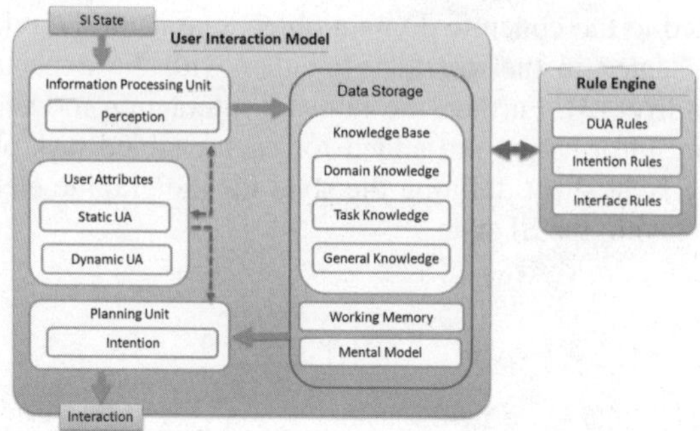

Fig. 2. The components of the user interaction model and the interaction selection process

As shown in figure 2 the knowledge of the UIM is divided into three categories. While the task knowledge describes the knowledge which has to be exchanged to successfully accomplish a task, general knowledge describes knowledge all user groups have in common and domain knowledge depends on the system to be evaluated, e.g. experts know where to look for required information in the system.

During the analysis process, the UIM has to handle four different situations: receiving new information (1), already known information (2), known information with differing values (3), or a request for information (4). Situations 1 and 2 are easy to handle. Either the UIM already knows what the system is presenting or the UIM stores the presented information in its data storage. Situation 3 is a mismatch between the knowledge of the UIM and the presented information by the system. The UIM can react in different ways. If the mismatch refers to the task knowledge, the UIM stores the wish for correction in its working memory, otherwise its domain or general knowledge will be corrected. If the requested information in situation 4 is contained in its knowledge, the UIM is able to respond to the request.

After analyzing the output interactions, the rule engine is called to modify the dynamic user attributes according to DUA rules. The DUA influence the intention of the UIM, e.g. high frustration or irritation level increase the probability of a task abortion, time pressure reduces the probability for requesting help. Four intentions are implemented so far: *forward*, *cancel*, *help* and *abort*. If the UIM has the intention *forward*, it tries to transfer its task knowledge to the system and therefore prefers interactions which support the transfer. In case that no interaction is preferred the UIM tries to navigate in order to analyze further states. If the UIM is navigating and believes further navigation is not possible or reasonable the intention turns to *cancel* and the UIM tries to navigate back. In case it could find neither interactions for knowledge transfer nor meaningful interactions for navigation, the intention becomes *help*. The intention *abort* leads to an abort of the current task.

After the intention alteration the UIM starts to evaluate the available input interactions. Assuming the intention is *forward*, the UIM tries to transfer its task knowledge to the system and therefore prefers interactions which support the transfer. These interactions are set up with a higher probability of selection. In case that no interaction was preferred by the IPU, the planning unit systematically evaluates the UI objects for navigational functionalities (navigation objects) in correlation with its knowledge and increases their interaction selection probability. If the intention is not *forward*, the UIM tries to find navigation objects related to its intention, e.g. the intention is *help* it prefers buttons labelled with "?", "i" or "Help". In case that no interaction related to *help* or *cancel* can be identified, the intention will be set to *abort* and the UIM gives up. Finally each interaction is set up with a probability of selection, whereas the preferred interactions have higher probabilities than alternative interactions. In order to modify these probabilities, the rule engine analyzes the complete SI state and generates facts for numerous attributes of the UI objects. A dice throw selects the interaction according to the probabilities. The selected interaction is given back to the MASP which generates a new SI state. The interaction selection process will be started again until the task is finished or the UIM aborts the process.

4 Evaluation Process and Results

All data collected during the simulation is captured with the help of a logging module and stored in log files. With the help of an internal view the designer gains access to simulation details for each task, user group and iteration of the simulation. This way, the designer can retrace every interaction the UIM has chosen. This information consists of the interaction element, the list of triggered rules, the probability distribution of the available interactions and further statistics, e.g. execution time. A portion of these data is visualized within an interactive graph (compare figure 3). Each node of this graph represents a SI state which has been passed by the UIM and each transition represents the chosen interaction. Deviations from the shortest goal driven path are highlighted in different colors This helps the designer to easily uncover problematic SI states and to find reasons for the deviations, because in the current state of implementation the workbench is not offering this level of critique by itself. As described in section 1 the MeMo workbench evaluated the interactive Cooking Assistant (CA) which is presented to the workbench by the MASP. In the following, evaluation results of several simulation runs are described.

With the help of the rule engine, several limitations of the CA regarding its usability were exposed. Figure 3 illustrates a problematic iteration in which the UIM accidently chose a different meal from a list of presented meals and did not discover this fact immediately in the state *RecipeDetails*. In fact the probability of this interaction is low, but the consequences might cause costs for the user, e.g. buying ingredients for a different recipe as intended. In the subsequent state a dialog in which the number of persons to whom the meal should be prepared for was presented to the UIM. In this state the name of the meal is not displayed and therefore the UIM did not discover its wrong meal choice. The same problem occurs in the state *ShoppingList*, where the UIM can decide whether to continue with the CA or prepare a shopping list with the necessary ingredients. Finally the UIM is able to discover its wrong meal choice in the last state of figure 3.

In this dialog the information of the chosen meal is displayed and returned to the user as output interaction. The only input interaction to undo the selection is via a link

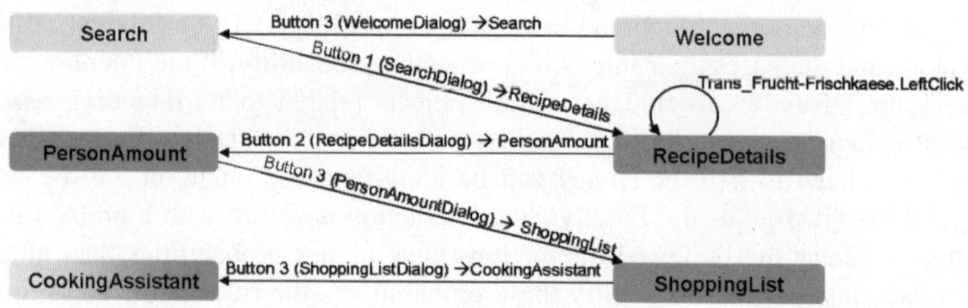

Fig. 3. An interactive graph which displays user interactions and presented SI states

to the start page in the upper left corner of the screen. As a result of its non-conform coding as a link it might not be recognized as an interaction element and the rule engine therefore reduces its interaction probability. Within a couple of iterations the UIM did not choose this interaction which has the consequence that the user finds no proper interaction to correct the meal selection and therefore aborts the task.

Another result of the evaluation was the low contrast of the font compared to the underlying interaction elements and furthermore the low contrast of some buttons compared to the background, e.g. a small white font was used on light blue buttons. The rule engine discovered this fact and reduced the interaction probabilities for user groups representing elderly people with poor vision. These user groups had a higher probability of not finding the appropriate interaction element and therefore choosing an alternative interaction that deviated from the shortest goal driven path.

Finally, using standard labels for some interaction elements (e.g. "Next") to achieve higher coherences could improve the usability as well, which was confirmed by further simulations done with the help of the workbench.

5 Conclusion and Outlook

In this paper we presented our approach to utilize user interface design and runtime models to support an AUE of the modeled system. Utilizing the models allows skipping the usually required manual annotation of the final UI with the underlying design concepts. The approach also makes the evaluation of multi-platform and context adaptive user interfaces much more straightforward because the automated system is able to make assumptions about context parameters or used platforms. Thus it can evaluate multiple variants of the UI much easier. We have also shown the evaluation of one of our applications which revealed several usability problems.

For the near future we plan to extend the approach to consider more details of the UI descriptions as well as to consider multimodal aspects of the UI and extended context information (e.g. voice-based feedback could help noticing the selection of a wrong recipe earlier). We would like to support the evaluation of different context situations, e.g. simulating migrated or distributed UIs. Along with the challenge, we would also like to enrich the perception of the UIM by concerning further mental aspects. Finally our goal is to automatically make constructive suggestions (beyond critique) for improving the usability.

References

1. Calvary, G., Coutaz, J., Thevenin, D., Limbourg, Q., Bouillon, L., Vanderdonckt, J.: A unifying reference framework for multi-target user interfaces. Interacting with Computers 15(3) (2003)
2. Coninx, K., Luyten, K., Vandervelpen, C., Van den Bergh, J., Creemers, B.: Dygimes: Dynamically generating interfaces for mobile computing devices and embedded systems. In: Mobile HCI (2003)
3. Mori, G., Paternò, F., Santoro, C.: Design and development of multidevice user interfaces through multiple logical descriptions. IEEE Trans. Softw. Eng. 30(8) (2004)
4. Reichard, D., Forbrig, P., Dittmar, A.: Task models as basis for requirements engineering and software execution. In: Proceedings of TAMODIA (2004)
5. Blumendorf, M., Lehmann, G., Feuerstack, S., Albayrak, S.: Executable Models for Human-Computer Interaction. In: Proc. of DSV-IS (2008)
6. Blumendorf, M., Feuerstack, S., Albayrak, S.: Multimodal smart home user interfaces. In: Proc. of IUI4AAL Workshop on IUI 2008 (2008)
7. Ivory, M.Y., Hearst, M.A.: The state of the art in automating usability evaluation of user interfaces. ACM Comput. Surv. 33(4) (2001)
8. Tarta, A., Moldovan, G.: Automatic Usability Evaluation Using AOP. In: IEEE International Conference on Automation, Quality and Testing, Robotics, vol. 2, pp. 84–89. IEEE Computer Society, Los Alamitos (2006)
9. Ritter, F.E., et al.: High-level behavior representation languages revisited. In: ICCM (2006)
10. Paternò, F., Piruzza, A., Santoro, C.: Remote web usability evaluation exploiting multimodal information on user behaviour, pp. 287–298. Springer, Heidelberg (2006)
11. Teo, L., John, B.E.: Comparisons of keystroke-level model predictions to observed data CHI 2006: CHI 2006 extended abstracts on Human factors in computing systems, pp. 1421–1426. ACM Press, New York (2006)
12. Lynch, G., Plamiter, S., Tilt, C.: The max model: A standard web site user model. In: 5th Conference of Human factory & the Web (1999)
13. Fine, N., Brinkman, W.: EUSAI 2004, pp. 15–18. ACM, New York (2004)
14. Sears, A.: Aide: a step towards metric-based interface development tools. In: UIST (1995)
15. Byrne, M.D., Wood, D., Sukaviriya, P.N., Foley, J.D., Kieras, D.E.: Automating interface evaluation. In: CHI Conference Companion (1994)
16. Braudes, R.E., Sibert, J.L.: Conmod: a system for conceptual consistency verification and communication. SIGCHI Bull. 23(1) (1991)
17. Elwert, T., Schlungbaum, E.: Modelling and generation of graphical user interfaces in the tadeus approach. In: DSV-IS (1995)
18. Jameson, A., Mahr, A., Kruppa, M., Rieger, A., Schleicher, R.: Looking for unexpected consequences of interface design decisions: The memo workbench. In: Winckler, M., Johnson, H., Palanque, P. (eds.) TAMODIA 2007. LNCS, vol. 4849, Springer, Heidelberg (2007)
19. Feuerstack, S., Blumendorf, M., Albayrak, S.: Prototyping of multimodal interactions for smart environments based on task models. In: European Conference on Ambient Intelligence: Workshop on Model Driven Software Engineering for Ambient Intelligence Applications (2007)
20. Feuerstack, S., Blumendorf, M., Schwartze, V., Albayrak, S.: Model-based layout generation. In: Proc. of Advanced Visual Interfaces (2008)

Integrating Groupware Notations with UML

William J. Giraldo[1], Ana I. Molina[2], Manuel Ortega[2], and Cesar A. Collazos[3]

[1] Systems and Computer Engineering, University of Quindío, Quindío, Colombia
wjgiraldo@uniquindio.edu.co
[2] Department of Information Technologies and Systems. Castilla – La Mancha University
{AnaIsabel.Molina,Manuel.Ortega,Miguel.Redondo}@uclm.es
[3] IDIS Research Group, University of Cauca, Popayán, Colombia
ccollazo@unicauca.edu.co

Abstract. In this paper we introduce a notation integration proposal. This proposal supports the user interface design of groupware applications enabling integration with software processes through UML notation. We introduce our methodological approach to deal with the conceptual design of applications for supporting group work, called CIAM. A study case (the design of a *Conference Resiew System*) is presented to describe our proposal. The integration process proposed is supported by a software tool called CIAT.

Keywords: GUI development, groupware design, interaction design.

1 Introduction

The groupware system design integrates disciplines such as Software Engineering (SE), CSCW, and Usability Engineering (UE), therefore, it requires the interaction of multiple *stakeholders* by using their own specific *workspaces* [1, 2]. Typically, these workspaces support modelling diagrams using different notations. It is necessary that the specified information on each workspace could serve as a complement for the modelling on other workspaces. The *integration* of approaches of model-based design and development with UML notation is conceptually possible to relate main concepts of Human Computer Interaction (HCI) to the classic ones in SE [3]. The approach of the fields of the HCI and the SE are taking a great importance and attention in the last years [4, 5]. On the one hand, the SE begins to consider *usability* like a quality attribute that must be measured and promoted [6]. On the other hand, if the proposed techniques in HCI want to gain solidity within the SE field they should clearly indicate how to integrate their techniques and activities within the process of software development. Nowadays, there is a growing number of proposals for the development of collaborative systems, however, there is still a gap between the development process of the functionality of these systems and the development of their user interface, particularly, proposals that combine group work applications and interactive aspects. CIAM (*Collaborative Interactive Applications Methodology*) is a proposal to assist designer with methodological support for modelling systems for group work [7]. CIAM proposes a specific notation called CIAN [8], which promotes modelling collaboration, communication and coordination. CIAN adequately supports modelling

P. Forbrig and F. Paternò (Eds.): HCSE/TAMODIA 2008, LNCS 5247, pp. 142–149, 2008.

collaboration, but does not allow modelling the system functionality. In this sense we need UML. Similarly, neither UML nor RUP are intended for the design of interactive system considering usability features. In order to complete the development process of groupware systems, modelling the interaction and collaboration, supported by CIAN, this process must be supplemented adequately to improve the modelling of the functionality, which is based on the use of standard UML notation. Our aim is to integrate the information specified with CIAN with the information gathered in the UML models, and so, try to reduce the gap between the development of the interface and the software development process, as well as the mapping between the two types of notations. This purpose is achieved by specifying a *taxonomy* to define methods, rules, principles and terms for classifying and organizing all necessary information for the specification of groupware systems.

This paper is organized in the following way: section 2 introduces our methodological approach for designing interactive groupware applications, presenting a brief explanation of its stages and the aspects that can be specified in each one. Also, some aspects of the CIAN notation are described in this section. Section 3 introduces the integration proposal, especially the taxonomy. Section 4 presents an example which a case study is used. Finally, the conclusions and further work is presented.

2   CIAM: A Methodological Approach for User Interface Development of Collaborative Applications

In this section we present the stages in our methodological approach. CIAM is an approach based on Model Driven Development (MDD), which promotes the use of models to simplify the complexity of groupware design. CIAM is supported for a notation called CIAN [8] (*Collaborative Interactive Applications Notation*). CIAM considers the interactive groupware modelling in two ways: the group-centred modelling and the process-centred modelling. Initially, the social relations are studied and an organizational scheme is specified. Next, the group work is modelled. The modelling process is more user-centred when we go deeper into the abstraction level, in which interactive tasks are modelled, that is, the dialog between an individual user and the application is modelled. In this way, collaborative aspects (groups, process) and interactive (individual) modelling problems are tackled jointly. The stages on this proposal (Figure 1) and their objective are enumerated as follows:

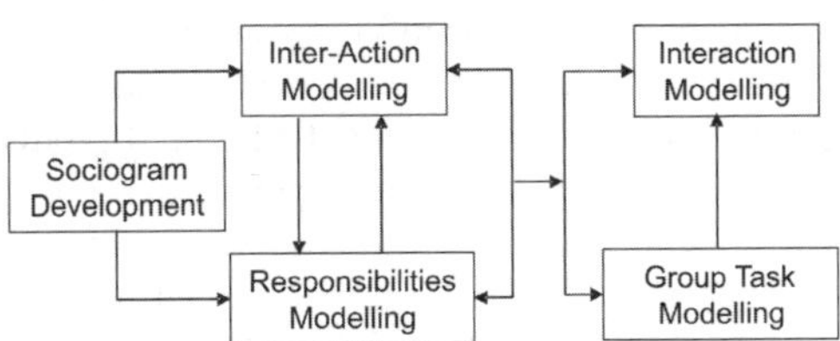

Fig. 1. CIAM methodological proposal stages

The **Sociogram Development** is the fist stage of the methodological approach. In this stage, the organization structure is modelled, as well as the relationship between its members. Organization Members belong to these categories: *roles, actors, software agents*; or in associations of them, forming *groups* or *work teams*. The elements in those diagrams can be interconnected by means of three kinds of basic relationships (*inheritance, acting* and *association*). In the **Inter-Action Modelling** stage, the main tasks that define group work performed in the previously defined organization are described. For each task, the roles involved, the data manipulated and the products generated are specified. Each task must be classified in one of the following categories: *group* or *individual tasks*. Tasks will be interconnected by means of several kinds of relationships (temporal or data relationships). In **Responsibilities Modelling** stage, the individual and shared responsibilities of each role are modelled. In **Group Tasks Modelling** stage the group tasks identified in the previous stage are described in a more detailed way. There are two different kinds of tasks, which must be modelled in a differentiated way: *cooperative* and *collaborative tasks*. *Collaborative Tasks* modelling includes specification of the roles involved, as well as the data model objects manipulated by the work team (that is, the *shared context* specification). Once the objects that make up the *shared context* have been decided, it is necessary to fragment this information into three different parts: the objects and/or attributes manipulated in the *collaborative visualization area*, the ones which appear in the *individual visualization area* and the ones that make up the *exclusive edition segment* (a subset in the data model that is accessed in an exclusive way for only one application user at the same time). Finally, in the **Interaction Modelling** stage, interactive aspects of the application are modelled using the notation. An *interaction model* for each individual task detected in the diverse stages of the gradual refinement process is created. An *interactive tasks decomposition tree* in CTT [9] is developed. In the case of collaborative tasks, the interactive model is directly derived from the shared context definition. Our methodological approach includes the way of obtaining this model from the shared context modelling [8].

3   The Integration Proposal

Our integration proposal is based on the assumption that an interactive groupware system can be classified and, therefore, modelled through one or more abstraction layers and using several families or sets of specifications. This idea, expressed graphically in Figure 2, leads to the definition of our proposal. Each layer could be a stand alone software component. A *layer* is a set of diagrams organized according to a particular criterion, for example: diagrams modelled with the same notation, diagrams representing a particular abstraction, diagrams representing a quality indicator, etc. In this paper our interest is centered in the integration of some models in CIAN and UML; however, our integration proposal can be applied to a large number of notations, each one appropriate to specify different aspects of the system.

The integration layer we propose is based on the Zachman Framework [10]. This Framework proposes a systematic ***taxonomy*** that allows us associating concepts that describe the real world with those who describe their information system and its subsequent implementation. This taxonomy is defined in two dimensions organized in **perspectives** and **views**. We use only the *business* model, *system* model and *technology* model perspectives and the *data*, *function*, *network* and *people* views. The intersection of views and perspectives leads to 12 Modelling cells, (Figure 2). Each cell provides a container for models that address a particular perspective and view. The Framework provides a representation from different points of view, different levels of granularity, generality and abstraction.

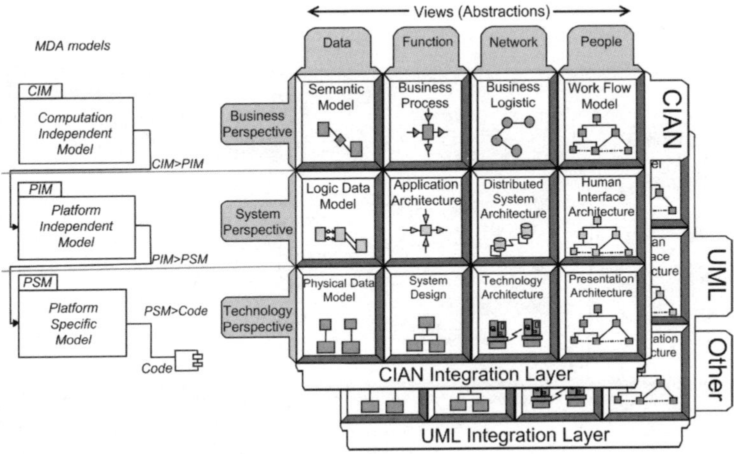

Fig. 2. Integration layer structure and MDA mapping

A **perspective** is an architectural representation at a specific abstraction level and represents a set of logical or physical constraints that may affect the development of a system at that level. This classification by using perspectives enable designers to establish independence between different levels of abstraction, however, it is necessary to have a solid architecture that allows its subsequent integration. MDA (*Model Driven Architecture*) [11] is an architecture that promotes design guided by models and, as can be seen in Figure 2, there is a relationship between the perspectives and levels of MDA. The concept of **view**, or abstraction, is a mechanism used by designers to understand a specific system aspect. A key issue in software architectures (perspective) is the support to handle different levels of abstraction. The abstraction is the tool that enables software developers to manage the complexity of their developments. During development we focus, first, on abstractions, and later on implementations that are derived from these abstractions. With the aim at obtaining *integrity, uniqueness, consistency* and *recursion* of the information specified, taxonomy defines a series of rules. Therefore, the seven rules of the Zachman Framework has been adopted and refined [12]. Examples of these rules are: (R2) All of the cells in each column-view-is guided by a single metamodel. (R5) The composition or integration of all models of the cells in a row is a complete model from this perspective. (R7) The logic is recursive.

4 Case Study: A Conference Review System

In this section a brief example of the application of this method for integrating CIAN and UML is presented. This proposal is supported by a tool, called CIAT (*Collaborative Interactive Applications Tool*). CIAT [13] is an Eclipse-based tool that helps developers to specify models using CIAN. Eclipse Framework provides tools for guiding the software modelling by using metamodel concepts [14]. By using the EMF (*Eclipse Modelling Framework*) and GMF (*Graphical Editing Framework*), we design the CIAT tool as an Eclipse Plug-in. We have chosen a *Conference Review System* as a case study, extracted from [15].

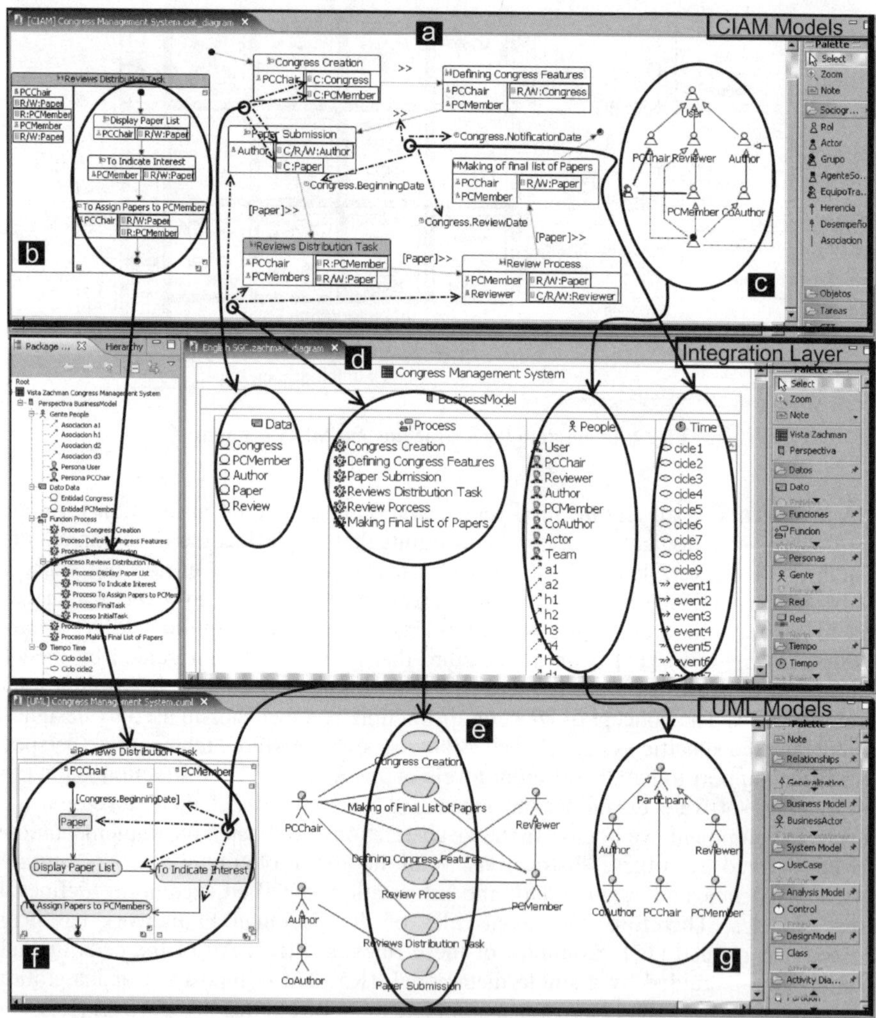

Fig. 3. Integration example between CIAN and UML by using the CIAT tool

In this section we are going to present the transformation from CIAN to UML of the information specified in the *Sociogram Development,* the *Group Task Modelling* and the *Inter-Action Modelling* stages. As it has been indicated previously, the **Sociogram** is a diagram that allows representing the organizational structure, as well as the relationships that can exist among its members. In our case study we have the following roles: *PCChair, PCMember, Reviewer, Author* and *CoAuthor.*

The Figure 3(c) shows the structure of the organization in CIAN notation. In particular, the mapping process from the diagram called Sociogram of CIAN and its corresponding representation in UML notation is shown (Figure 3 (c) to Figure 3 (g) and Figure 4). The information regarding the roles and relationships among organization members, as it is shown in the Sociogram, is processed through the transformations to generate partial information of *Business Model* and *System Model* perspectives. This information is classified into these two perspectives for the *People* view mainly. Each actor in CIAN can represent both a *Business Actor* as a *System Actor* in UML. The first transformation generates an UML Business Actor diagram -Figure 4(c) - from the Sociogram in CIAM -Figure 4(a). The People column -Figure 4(b) - contains information that relates these two models. The h4 relationship -Figure 4(d) - establishes the inheritance relationship on Author and CoAuthor. The relationships dependency and association do not have direct representation in UML; however, information must be stored to generate other artifacts.

The **Inter-Action** diagram, see Figure 3(a), illustrates the system macro activities and their interdependencies. This model is essential, because certain temporal information (precedence and coordination information) is represented. This information can be enriched through using information related with the domain (that is extracted from the models of the ES process). This diagram provides information about the preconditions, post conditions, messages and data that are required or generated by the activities. UML lacks a diagram of this type.

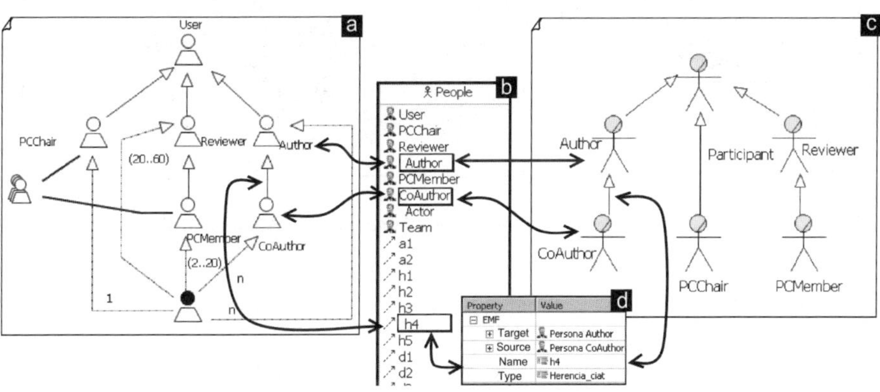

Fig. 4. Transformation process by using CIAT

The Inter-Action diagrams are very rich in information to populate the integration layer. The Figure 3(d) illustrates the information extracted from this diagram. The transformations separate information as follows: (1) The Inter-Action activities are associated with business use cases. The cooperative activities are transformed into diagrams activity. (2) The interdependencies are associated with preconditions, post conditions and events among various activity diagrams. (3) The domain objects are associated with business entities. A business object diagram is derived from the information in each activity, which is related with roles and objects.

Figure 5 shows in a more detailed way the mapping between the Inter-Action model (Figure 5(b)) and UML diagrams that specifies the same information (business uses cases, Figure 5(c), and the activity diagram, Figure 5(g)). The integration is based on information from the *Process* column (function) -Figure 5(a)- and the *Time* column -Figure 5(d)- into the integration layer. The variables cicle4, event4 and event5 have the information needed to build the activity diagram in UML. See Figure 5(e,f,h), respectively. The variables of type event become preconditions or postconditions of business use cases. In Figure 5(g) is observed as the event4 and event5 are transformed into the guard [Congress.Beginning.Date] and the object node "Paper". Similarly, the variable "Reviews Distribution task" stores the information required to relate the business use case with their respective Actors - Figure 5(i).

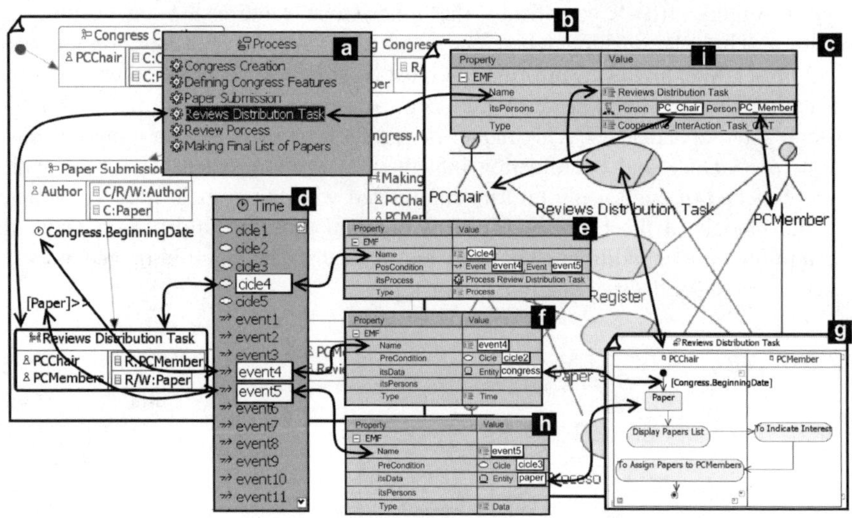

Fig. 5. Detailed integration example between CIAN and UML

5 Conclusions

In this paper we have shown a brief picture of our methodological proposal for modelling interactive groupware applications and an integration proposal of the notation used in this approach (called CIAN) into the Unified Development Process (supported by the UML notation). This integration proposal is based on the definition of a integration layer (*taxonomy*) and it is supported by a tool called CIAT. We have used a case study in order to explain the integration method by using our integration layer.

The integration proposal presented can be extended to support the integration of a large number of notations. The implemented tool allows the stakeholders involved in the development of a groupware system to construct models, supported by a suitable workspace and using specific notations in their specific domains. Besides, thanks to the use of GMF, CIAT can be integrated with other tools and services available in Eclipse project.

Acknowledgements. This work has been supported by the Universidad del Quindío, Castilla–La Mancha University and Junta de Comunidades de Castilla–La Mancha in the projects AULA-T (PBI08-0069), mGUIDE (PBC08-0006-512) and M-CUIDE (TC20080552).

References

1. Molina, A.I., Redondo, M.A., Ortega, M.: A conceptual and methodological framework for modeling interactive groupware applications. In: Dimitriadis, Y.A., Zigurs, I., Gómez-Sánchez, E. (eds.) CRIWG 2006. LNCS, vol. 4154, Springer, Heidelberg (2006)
2. Gutwin, C., Greenberg, S.: Design for Individuals, Design for Groups: Tradeoffs between power and workspace awareness. In: ACM CSCW 1998. ACM Press, Seattle (1998)
3. Artim, J., et al.: Incorporating work, process and task analysis into industrial object-oriented systems development. SIGCHI Bulletin, 30(4) (1998)
4. Granollers, T., et al.: Integración de la IPO y la ingeniería del software: MPIu+a. In: III Taller en Sistemas Hipermedia Colaborativos y Adaptativos, Granada España (2005)
5. Ferré, X., Moreno, A.M.: Integración de la IPO en el Proceso de Desarrollo de la Ingeniería del Software: Propuestas Existentes y Temas a Resolver. In: V Congreso Interacción Persona-Ordenador (Interacción, 2004. Lleida, España (2004)
6. Ferre, X., Juristo, N., Moreno, A.M.: Improving Software Engineering Practice with HCI Aspects. In: SERA. Springer, Heidelberg (2004)
7. Molina, A.I., et al.: CIAM: A methodology for the development of groupware user interfaces. Journal of Universal Computer Science(JUCS) (2007)
8. Molina, A.I., Redondo, M.A., Ortega, M.: A conceptual and methodological framework for modeling interactive groupware applications. In: Dimitriadis, Y.A., Zigurs, I., Gómez-Sánchez, E. (eds.) CRIWG 2006. LNCS, vol. 4154. Springer, Heidelberg (2006)
9. Paternò, F., Mancini, C., Meniconi.: ConcurTaskTree: A diagrammatic notation for specifying task models. In: IFIP TC 13 International Conference on Human-Computer Interaction Interact 1997. Kluwer Academic Publishers, Sydney (1997)
10. Zachman, J.A.: A Framework For Information Systems Architecture. IBM Ssystems Journal 26(3) (1987)
11. Miller, J. and J. Mukerji. MDA Guide Version 1.0.1. (2003) [cited 08-07-2007], `http://www.appdevadvisor.co.uk/express/vendor/domain.html`
12. Sowa, J.F., Zachman, J.A.: Extending and formalizing the framework for information systems architecture. IBM Syst. J., 590–616 (1992)
13. Giraldo, W.J., et al.: CIAT, A Model-Based Tool for designing Groupware User Interfaces using CIAM. In: Computer-Aided Design of User Interfaces VI, CADUI 2007, España: Springer, Heidelberg (2008)
14. Moore, B., et al.: Eclipse Development using the Graphical Editing Framework and the Eclipse Modeling Framework. Redbooks: ibm.com/redbooks (2004)
15. Schwabe, D., Rossi, G.: Conference Review System in OOHDM. International Workshop on Web Oriented Software Technology Volume (2001)

MuiCSer: A Process Framework for Multi-disciplinary User-Centred Software Engineering Processes

Mieke Haesen, Karin Coninx, Jan Van den Bergh, and Kris Luyten

Hasselt University -tUL -IBBT, Expertise Centre for Digital Media,
Wetenschapspark 2, 3590 Diepenbeek, Belgium
{mieke.haesen,karin.coninx,jan.vandenbergh,
kris.luyten}@uhasselt.be

Abstract. In this paper we introduce MuiCSer, a conceptual process framework for Multi-disciplinary User-centred Software Engineering (UCSE) processes. UCSE processes strive for the combination of basic principles and practices from software engineering and user-centred design approaches in order to increase the overall user experience with the resulting product. The MuiCSer framework aims to provide a common understanding of important components and associated activities of UCSE processes. As such, the conceptual framework acts as a frame of reference for future research regarding various aspects and concepts related to this kind of processes, including models, development artefacts and tools. We present the MuiCSer process framework and illustrate its instantiation in customized processes for the (re)design of a system. The conceptual framework has been helpful to investigate the role of members of a multi-disciplinary team when realizing artefacts in a model-based approach. In particular process coverage of existing artefact transformation tools has been studied.

Keywords: User-Centred Software Engineering, User-Centred Design, Process Framework.

1 Introduction

The perceived quality of the user experience of an interactive application is well emphasized nowadays. It has raised attention from the HCI community for user-centred design (UCD) approaches. Key issues in UCD processes that contribute to the overall user experience with the resulting product are continuous attention for the end-user needs, iterative (and possibly incremental) design and development, and a dominant presence of evaluation with respect to external quality attributes such as usability, accessibility and apparent performance [9]. UCD approaches have proven their value for interactive systems development for new as well as for legacy systems. We have the impression, however, that redesign of legacy systems places higher demands on the process being used due to the need to capture existing knowledge and reuse requirements from existing documentation. Besides analysis and design artefacts such

P. Forbrig and F. Paternò (Eds.): HCSE/TAMODIA 2008, LNCS 5247, pp. 150–165, 2008.

as diagrams and models related to the application back end, the running system itself and manuals are valuable sources. Because diagrams and models related to the application back end (e.g. UML diagrams) often result from a software engineering (SE) process, there is a search to combine basic principles and practices from the SE domain and UCD approaches in order to define an overall process that fulfils the needs of a multi-disciplinary design team. We coin the processes that unite both HCI and SE perspectives as "User-Centred Software Engineering Processes" (UCSE processes).

Based on former research results, we explore extensions of model-based user interface development approaches to bridge the gap with SE approaches such as model-driven development. A model-based approach typically employs different types of models, thereby conveying enough information to generate the skeletons for concrete user interfaces. Models still tend to emphasize facilitating the more technical phases in application development over the creative design phase and overall development cycle. Overcoming these shortcomings in a unified HCI and SE approach, and paying attention to multi-disciplinary teams are a necessity to allow for a pragmatic approach and applicability of model-based techniques in real-world projects.

To accommodate for both flexibility in selecting the techniques for one particular UCSE process and consistency in models in consecutive developments, we prefer starting from a conceptual process framework rather than a single, exhaustively defined UCSE process. The conceptual process framework can be considered as a generic process that can be customized or instantiated for the specific design task at hand. Though UCD research in the HCI community is focused on processes, process frameworks are gaining importance in the software engineering community (e.g. The Eclipse Process Framework[1]). Therefore, we believe this approach is helpful to strive at the same time for practical processes for applied research and for a comparison and evaluation framework, driving research activities regarding models, development artefacts and tools.

In this paper, we present our proposal for a UCSE process framework and detail the tools, models and artefacts that support the approach. This process framework has been the basis for two process instances employed during case studies, which are also used to summarize some lessons we learned. A discussion of our current and future work, as well as conclusions are presented.

2 The MuiCSer Process Framework

Comparable to several UCD approaches, our process framework for Multi-disciplinary user-Centred Software engineering processes, MuiCSer, focuses on the end-user needs during the entire SE cycle in order to optimize the user experience provided by the software that is delivered. The user experience is typically determined by measuring the usability, accessibility, availability of required functionality etc. of the delivered application.

Based on our experiences and observations when working with multi-disciplinary teams, we are gradually introducing model-based processes in applied research embodies UCD with a structured Agile Software Engineering (ASE, [11]) approach

---

[1] http://www.eclipse.org/epf/

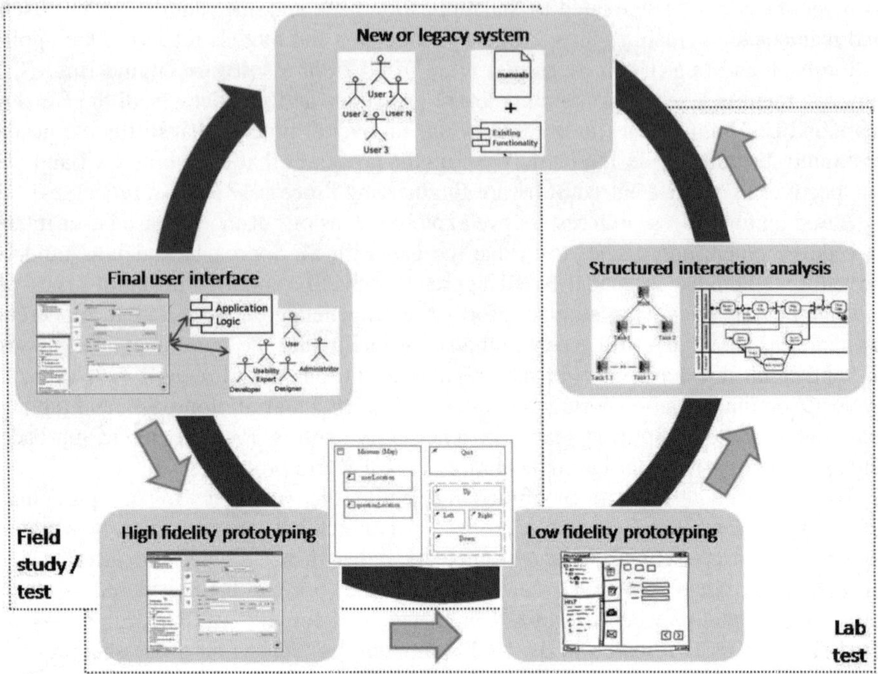

Fig. 1. Our MuiCSer process framework. The dark arrow indicates the overall design and development direction. The light arrows indicate feedback from evaluation, verification and validation efforts.

and organizes the creation of interactive software systems by a multi-disciplinary team. We will support different models throughout processes that are derived from the framework, where each model describes a specific aspect of an interactive system and represents the viewpoint of one or more specific roles in the multi-disciplinary team. The need for communication with end-users or customers results in additional models or artefacts (e.g. low-fidelity and high-fidelity prototypes) on top of the commonly used models in a model-driven approach. This has also a positive effect on the visibility and traceability of the processes that are based on our process framework, in particular when artefacts are stored in a central repository: the models and artefacts describe the status of the system being designed at various stages, support the design decisions made during these processes and are ready for use in the next iteration.

Fig. 1 gives an overview of the proposed process framework. Existing UCD approaches such as GUIDE [23], Effective Prototyping [1] and Rapid Contextual Design [8] can be represented using this framework. Likewise, when projects are carried out following a UCSE approach, the approach that is used, can be seen as a process that is created according to the MuiCSer process framework. Both functional and non-functional requirements are tackled by the process framework and unlike traditional software engineering processes, it supports processes with a continuous and smooth integration between user interface design and software development. The next paragraphs discuss the properties of the process framework we propose in more detail.

MuiCSer processes typically start with an analysis phase in an initial iteration where the users tasks, goals and the related objects or resources that are important to perform these tasks are specified. If the user experience of a legacy system needs to be optimized, the functionality of such a system can be often found in existing manuals and also contributes to the analysis. Several notations are used to express the results of the analysis phase: HCI experts take a user-centred approach and commonly use domain-specific notations to express the task model and use personas to identify the user characteristics that are important. The software engineer specifies the required behaviour of the system with use cases and behaviour diagrams. Although the relationship between both is clear, linking them in an engineering process remains a difficult issue. However, when a process framework helps to define what artefacts are important in which stages and how progress from abstract to concrete models can be realized, this helps to identify, create and relate the required models in each stage.

During the structured interaction analysis, the results of the analysis are used to proceed towards system interaction models and presentation models. These models are often expressed using the UML notation, thus keeping in pace with the traditional SE models.

Since both user needs and functional information are specified, they can both serve as input for the low-fidelity prototyping stage, as is shown in Fig. 1. User interface designers create mockups of the user interface, based on the information contained in the task and interaction models, while using design guidelines and their experience. In subsequent phases, low-fidelity prototypes are transformed into high-fidelity prototypes, which on their turn evolve into the final user interface while each stage is related to the artefacts created in a previous stage.

By evaluating the result of each stage, the support for user needs and goals and the presence of required functionality is verified. If possible, an evaluation with target users can be very useful to get feedback from the end-user directly. Because most of the artefacts do not present a fully functional system, part of the testing takes place in a usability lab. To evaluate some advanced prototypes, field tests can examine the user interface in more realistic situations. If the results of a phase are not suited (e.g. too complex) to involve an end-user during evaluation, it is still necessary to evaluate, verify or validate the models or prototypes, e.g. in meetings with domain experts or by performing an expert evaluation.

3 Tools and Models

In this section we discuss to what extent MuiCSer can be covered by existing tools for the creation and transformation of artefacts and in what stages tool-support should be improved. The current use of tools also reveals how the collaboration within multi-disciplinary teams is supported. Besides the discussion of tools, this section gives an overview of models that can be used in processes based on MuiCSer.

3.1 Artefact Transformation Tools

The process framework described in the previous section has been used in practice to support several real-life cases. During the execution of the MuiCSer processes to

Table 1. An association of tools that can be used to support MuiCSer and their accessibility for different roles in a multi-disciplinary team

Tools / Roles in a multi-disciplinary team:

Roles in a multi-disciplinary team	Word processor [1]	Presentation [1]	Spreadsheet [1]	Drawing [1]	Paper [1]	PDF viewer [1]	Paint program [1]	Simple programming [1]	HTML (site) editor [1]	Animation tool [1]	Advance programming [1]	CTTE [17]	TaskSketch [3]	Vista Environment [2]	CanonSketch [3]	Teresa [18]	SketchiXML [7]	Damask [12]	GrafiXML [16]	Gummy [14]	IntuiKit [4]
End-user					✓												✓				
Purchaser, manager of user	✓	✓	✓	✓	✓	✓															
Application domain specialist	✓	✓	✓	✓	✓	✓															
Systems analyst, systems engineer, programmer	✓	✓	✓	✓	✓	✓		✓	✓		✓	✓	✓	✓	✓	✓	✓	✓	✓	✓	✓
Marketer, salesperson	✓	✓	✓	✓	✓	✓															
UI designer, visual designer	✓	✓	✓	✓	✓	✓	✓		✓	✓		✓	✓	✓	✓	✓	✓	✓	✓	✓	✓
Human factors and ergonomics expert, HCI specialist	✓	✓	✓	✓	✓	✓															
Technical author, trainer and support personnel	✓	✓	✓	✓	✓	✓	✓														

develop these cases, some of which will be explained more into detail further in this paper, we observed what tools members of the project team used to contribute in the different stages of these processes. This information in combination with literature that describes tools that fit in this process gave rise to Table 1. This table presents different roles which can be part of a multi-disciplinary team [1, 8, 9] and the tools associated with the role. The table shows that the leftmost tools are widespread and accessible for different roles of the multi-disciplinary team, which is confirmed by Campos and Nunes in [3].

Table 2 provides an overview of a selection of these tools and their applicability for creating artefacts that are used in the HCI engineering process. We use the term

Table 2. Overview of artefacts supported by artefact transformation tools

		Artefacts										
		Scenario	Use case	Task model	Task Oriented Specification	Task Flow	Domain model	Activity Diagrams	User Interface Architecture	System Architecture	Abstract UI	Concrete UI
Artefact transformation tools	CTTE [17]	✓	✓	✓								
	TaskSketch [3]		✓			✓		✓		✓		
	Vista [2]			✓	✓		✓		✓			
	CanonSketch [3]						✓				✓	✓
	Teresa [18]			✓							✓	✓
	SketchiXML [7]			✓			✓				✓	✓
	Damask [12]											✓
	Gummy [14]											✓
	GrafiXML [16]											✓
	IntuiKit [4]											✓

artefact transformation tool to describe a tool that can be used by two or more different roles and supports relating two artefacts or models. Such a tool allows to progress the design and development of an interactive system involving different roles, often by providing different views on the same artefact or model. The ways in which a tool can manipulate, create relations or transform between artefacts and models are summarized in [5].

Mapping these tools on the stages of MuiCSer (Fig. 1) results in the time-line shown in Fig. 2. Most tools that are suitable for interactive, incremental and multi-disciplinary user-centred processes are artefact transformation tools which comes as no surprise. Fig. 2 also shows that it is possible to combine two or three tools to cover most stages of MuiCSer. While Teresa [18] can be used to model tasks of a multi-platform application and generate a system task model, an abstract user interface and a concrete user interface, Gummy [14] can be used by designers to add creative aspects to the medium-to high-fidelity prototypes for multi-platform user interfaces.

The overview of tools in Fig. 2 also reveals that there is little tool support for the transformation of the results of user studies into structured models. Furthermore, when a new iteration takes place after a final user interface is deployed, there is no single tool that completely covers MuiCSer. The main drawbacks of most of these tools are their inaccessibility for non-experts and their relative immaturity for

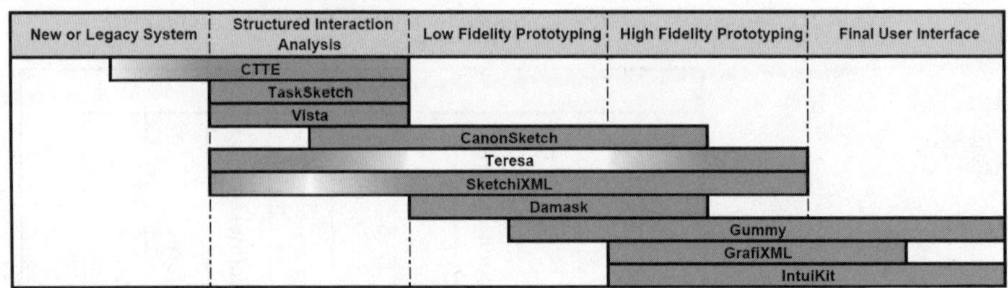

Fig. 2. A timeline presenting the stages of MuiCSer and how artefact transformation tools can be mapped on it

real-world software development processes. Several of the aforementioned tools are being increasingly used in industrial projects, so we expect this situation will improve rapidly. SketchiXML for instance is already suitable to be used by a wider range of roles including designers and end-users [7]. Gummy supports the roles of software developers and designers but this tool is gradually being extended to be used by application domain specialists [13].

The following describes different models being created, changed and transformed during the execution of MuiCSer processes in order to support a smooth transfer towards the final user interface. The models and tools discussed in the remainder of this section are not required. They provide a clear idea of how MuiCSer processes can be instantiated with concrete models, notations and tools.

3.2 Structured Interaction Analysis

Task models are frequently used to specify requirements for an application from a user's point of view. Most task models have an hierarchical structure, allowing a gradual refinement of the high-level tasks and goals into fine-grained actions and activities. A task specification for a system can be found by transforming the requirements text and the scenarios of the personas into a hierarchical task model with temporal operators, such as the ConcurTaskTrees notation. Although this step is not automated, the expert performing this step uses a set of (informal) rules and is supported by a tool such as CTTE [17].

This task model can be related to other user interface and software engineering models expressed using e.g. UML diagrams, which are widely known by software analysts and programmers. These user interface models can provide an alternative view on the information captured in the task model [20, 24] or additional information [21, 24].

3.3 Low-Fidelity Prototyping

Since the creativity of designers and other members of a multi-disciplinary team may influence the user experience in positive way, MuiCSer does not imply the use of specific tools or technologies to create low-fidelity prototypes. The first prototypes can be created using pencil and paper or using a tool. Tools such as SketchiXML [7] or CanonSketch [3] have the advantage that they provide support for the transition to high-fidelity prototypes. This ability to make the transition from low-fidelity to high-fidelity using these tools and notations is illustrated by the drawing between the low-fidelity and the high-fidelity stage in Fig. 1.

3.4 High-Fidelity Prototyping

For the high-fidelity prototyping stage, design and development tools that support serialisation of the user interface design to (high-level) XML-based languages are preferred. This allows more rapid prototyping of user interfaces that support a common set of tasks. Tools such as Gummy [14] or GrafiXML [16] even have specific support for adapting the designs to different platforms, screen sizes or in general different contexts of use. A loose coupling with the application logic is preferred to enable reuse.

3.5 Final User Interface

To speed up development of the final user interface and to make it as flexible as possible, we preferably reuse as much as possible of the developed artefacts, such as the XML-based high-fidelity prototypes and even selected models. A flexible user interface management system allows the use of these models at runtime. Coupling for example the task model to the user interface descriptions allows to check for task coverage of the user interface and even selection of a subset of features for certain users while ensuring that all remaining tasks are still valid. Using these artefacts in the final user interface also ensures that they are still available and up-to-date for the development of future increments.

4 Case Studies

We explain how MuiCSer can be used by describing two MuiCSer processes that are customized for two cases, carried out within the VIP-lab project [6] The first case study concerns the redesign of a legacy system while the second case study presents the approach that has been used for the design of a new system. The project team was not limited to computer scientists but also psychologists and social scientists were involved and in some cases a graphic designer. Fig. 3 shows an overview of the MuiCSer processes that are employed for these cases. For sake of clarity of the presentation and to allow comparison, both processes are shown as a linear path without emphasis on the intra-and inter-stage iterations.

4.1 NewsWizard

When a reporter is on location, he or she not only has to write an article. The biggest challenge is often to configure a network connection to send the article to the editorial staff. The NewsWizard prototype, developed in this case study, should ease the job of a journalist on location by guiding him / her while making the appropriate network connection and sending the article(s).

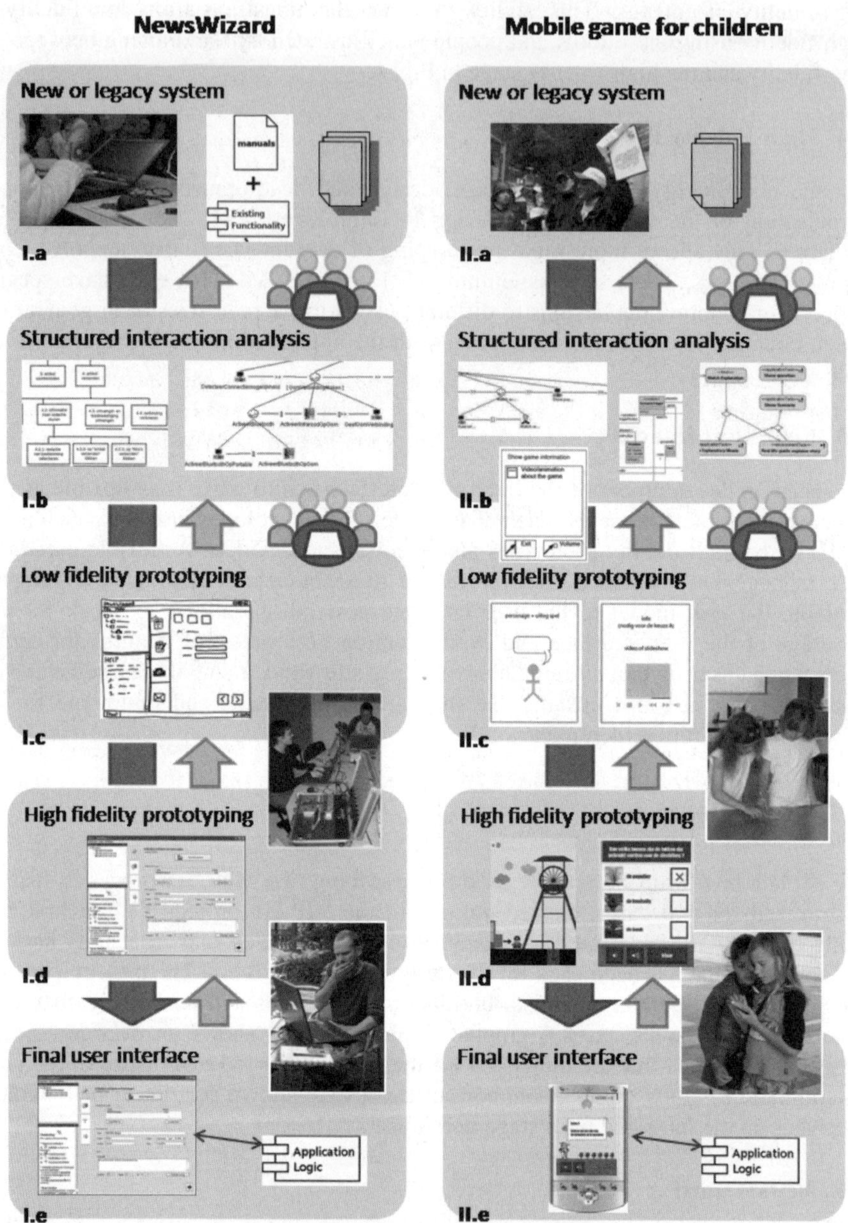

Fig. 3. MuiCSer process instances of the NewsWizard and the mobile game for children. In both processes the verification between steps a and b, and steps b and c was done during brainstorm meetings within the multi-disciplinary team, while the evaluation in later stages involved end-users during lab and field tests.

As recommended by MuiCSer, first the legacy system has been explored. Manuals of the existing editor to write and send articles have been studied and the system was demonstrated to the project team. Next journalists and photographers were observed and interviewed by social scientists while they were collecting information and sending it to the editorial office. Besides the comparison of the job of a contemporary journalist and a photographer, this contextual inquiry resulted in primary and secondary personas [22] and scenarios (Fig. 3 I.a, tool: word processor and PDF viewer).

At the second stage of this process which concerned the structured interaction analysis, some task models were created by developers using the Hierarchical Task Analysis (HTA) and CTT notation (Fig. 3 I.b, tool: drawing tool and CTTE). The verification of these task models was carried out during meetings with the project team. The social scientists checked consistency with the observations, the personas and the scenarios while the computer scientists examined the technical possibilities and representatives of the news publishing agency verified the design according to the needs of the journalists and their own expectations. The task models were refined within two iterations. The threshold for progression is the agreement of the domain experts and stakeholders on structure and content of the task model, scenarios and personas.

By putting together the results of the user and task analysis and the structured interaction analysis, it became clear that journalists mainly experience problems when they need to send an article on location. Consequently a user interface in wizard-style was designed to collect articles and pictures (in case the journalist is not accompanied by a photographer), followed by sending the data successfully. The relations between the task model and the low-fidelity prototype on paper were determined manually and the prototype was checked for completeness with respect to the task model during meetings, similar to the meetings held during the structured interaction analysis stage.

In order to have a prototype that could be evaluated by journalists in a usability lab, soon the low-fidelity prototype of NewsWizard evolved into a high-fidelity prototype (Fig. 4, tool: advance programming tool). Although this was done manually, there is a clear one-to-one mapping from each component in the low-fidelity prototype to each component in the high-fidelity prototype. By consequence, the high-fidelity prototype is also complete with respect to the task model. In three iterations and increments the NewsWizard prototype was developed and functionality was added. After each

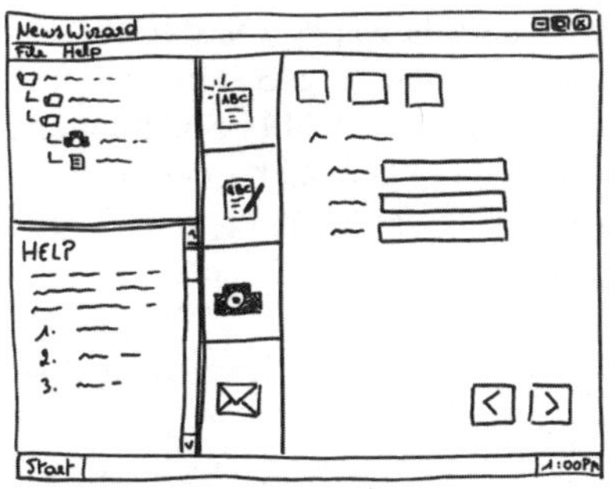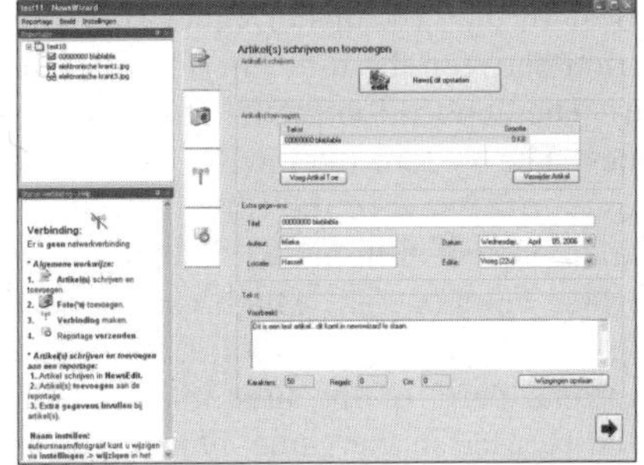

Fig. 4. Low-and high-fidelity prototype of the NewsWizard interface. The main part of the user interface concerns the wizard. The user can navigate between steps using arrow-buttons or tab pages.

iteration and increment the UI was evaluated by journalists in a portable usability lab (Fig. 3 I.d). In order to evaluate the prototype in the natural environment of a reporter, some field tests were carried out (Fig. 3 I.e). During the field tests, the participating journalists were observed and interviewed while accomplishing a realistic assignment on location using NewsWizard. The general observations showed that the use of NewsWizard was much more intuitive than using the existing system. Most of the journalists confirmed that in the future they would rather send articles from location instead of going back to their desk if they could use the NewsWizard application.

4.2 Mobile Game for Children

A second case study concerns the development of a prototype for a mobile game, and was carried out in collaboration with local cultural and tourist organizations. The goal of this game for children is to make educational excursions more interesting and informative.

Since a new system had to be developed in this case study, it was impossible to examine manuals and existing functionality. Mainly results from a user and task analysis could contribute to the structured interaction analysis. During the user and task analysis school groups were observed and interviewed while they were visiting museums and zoos. It turns out that the addressed target users prefer being guided throughout the visit in a narrative style, based on a story they can identify themselves with. After several brainstorm sessions, the multi-disciplinary team including a graphic designer and representatives of cultural and tourist organisations, came up with two game concepts for a PDA application (Fig. 3 II.a, tool: word processor and PDF viewer). The goal of one game is to save the trees in a nature resort, while the other game challenges children visiting a mine museum to help a mine worker to have a safe working day. Scenarios ensured that all team members had the same understanding of the game to be designed (tool: word processor and PDF viewer).

The game scenarios proved to be very useful to structure the user tasks and to create a task model using the CTT notation (Fig. 3 II.b, tool: CTTE). Even though both games are totally different, the same user interface components would be necessary. This resulted in the decision to create a general framework containing the application logic for both games.

Besides the task model, other HCI engineering models were created to present the relation between the user interface and the application logic (Fig. 3 II.b, tool: drawing tool). The application model ensured the application logic would be suitable for both games. The system interaction model, based on the user task and application model gives an overview of the flow of actions carried out by the system and the user. The abstract presentation model, is based on the preceding models and represents the user interface components, which can be used in a Canonical Abstract Prototype (CAP) [10]. This CAP (Fig. 5, tool: CanonSketch) is a first graphical representation of the functional parts of the user interface, independent of the content or the story that would be used in the game. During the verification of the models, the scenarios were used to ensure the models did meet the requirements of the game. After the computer scientists created these models, the task was handed over to the graphic designer. He translated the CAPs into some low-fidelity prototypes, which evolved into a design of

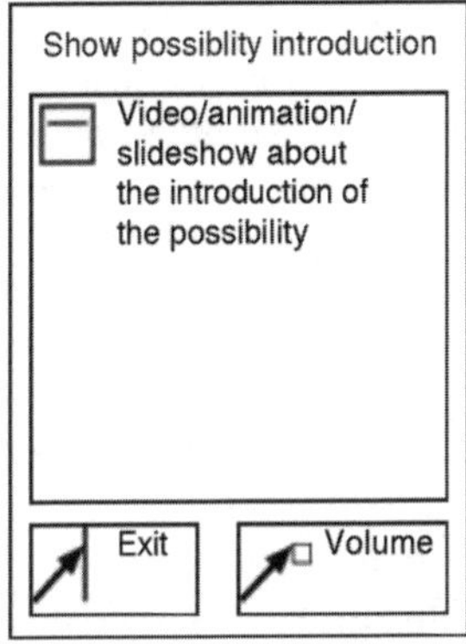

Fig. 5. Three levels of prototypes for one specific screen. From left to right: a Canonical Abstract prototype, a low-fidelity prototype and a high-fidelity prototype.

the prototypes for both games (Fig. 5, tool: paint program) after adding layout and style information.

In order to get some early feedback of the end-users the prototypes were interactively tested in a lab environment with materials similar to what is being used in participatory approaches such as PICTIVE [19] (Fig. 3 II.d). The tests showed children were amused by the game, but revealed problems concerning the size and behaviour of buttons and the content.

Based on the test results, the design of the user interface was adjusted (tool: animation tool), while the models of the structured interaction analysis were used for the development of the application logic of the game (tool: advance programming tool). The resulting high-fidelity prototypes were evaluated by children in a nature resort and a mine museum. During these field tests few user interface problems were detected, so we may conclude that the model-based approach, and the evaluation in early stages influenced the high-fidelity prototype in a beneficial way.

5 Lessons Learned

The case studies presented in section 4 were carried out using MuiCSer processes. In the NewsWizard case a MuiCSer process was used for the redesign of an existing system, while the second case study concerned the design of a new system. In both case studies we experienced that it was hard to structure the information to get a complete overview of the user needs. Since the usage of personas and scenarios implies partially structured narrative information, it was necessary to transform the information into some task models. These task models made it possible to abstract the most important goals of the future prototype. By doing so, some information contained in the personas and scenarios could be overlooked. Therefore, the task models were evaluated during meetings with the computer scientists and team members with other roles.

By carrying out different case studies we had the opportunity to fine-tune the approach in our multi-disciplinary team. In the NewsWizard case study it became clear that task models were understandable for all team members and thus could be evaluated during meetings. On the other hand computer scientists experienced that the information of task models was insufficient for the development of the high-fidelity prototypes. During the structured interaction analysis and prototyping of the mobile game, models presenting the links between the user interface and the application logic were helpful to get more insight into the functional requirements. Furthermore, these models evolved gradually into a first graphical representation, the CAP, which was also presented to the graphic designer.

The low-fidelity prototypes of both case studies were created by putting together the artefacts of earlier stages in MuiCSer. The design of the first prototypes was discussed and evaluated during meetings attended by the multidisciplinary team.

End-users were asked to participate in the evaluation of high-fidelity prototypes. Our experience from other case studies learned us that field tests give more information on the entire user experience. By evaluating a prototype in the natural environment of the end-user, a broader user experience is taken into account and context dependent actions can be observed.

When comparing the processes shown in Fig. 3 we discover that both are in line with the MuiCSer framework from the start where the user studies take place, until the high-fidelity prototyping phase. Several artefacts were created as a result of the process stages. This illustrates the fact that the MuiCSer framework suggests some models and artefacts, but that the design team decides about the particular results for the customized process at hand. All artefacts proved useful to convert artefacts in the next phase. The conversion of these artefacts required some human intervention that is difficult or impossible to automate.

The creation, evaluation, verification and validation of the artefacts, was carried out using several tools. The computer scientists and designers used CTTE, Canon-Sketch, drawing tools, animation tools and advance programming tools for the development of HCI models and coded prototypes. Widespread tools such as pencil and paper, a word processor and a PDF viewer were useful for the other artefacts as the entire project team, including representatives of the participating companies, was familiar with these common tools.

6 Ongoing and Future Work

The process framework introduced in this paper has been tested on software projects of limited complexity and, by consequence, with a development team of limited size. Although our tests did not include any larger software projects, customized processes derived from this framework should be flexible enough to support the increased complexity and team size, partly because parameters such as size of increments, number of iterations, specific models and artefacts are decided about when instantiating the process from the framework. Currently we are investigating how a process instantiated by MuiCSer can be used to model and design adaptable user interfaces for heterogeneous environments [15].

One of the main advantages of the openness of the framework with respect to specific techniques is that different domain experts can use their own notations to create models which can relate to models of other domain experts, in order to obtain a complete and usable interactive system with respect to the requirements. We are testing this conceptual framework for processes supporting multi-disciplinary teams in various application domains, requiring different experts to collaborate. Besides the relationship with existing UCD processes, we will investigate how software engineering processes fit into our framework. These research activities, including application of derived processes and generalization of existing processes for comparison, will give rise to enhancements or extensions of the framework.

Central storage of models and artefacts as well as manual and system-guided transitions between these products turn out to be key factors for the efficiency of the processes and acceptability by the design team. Therefore, the design and creation of a flexible user interface management system (UIMS) that is able to use XML-based user interface descriptions and models is an integral part of our current work [25]. In order to support this UIMS we plan to gradually improve the relation between the different types of artefacts. The combination of HCI models and UML models contributes to a smooth integration of the user interface and application logic. Putting forward the combination of models explicitly also prevents mismatches between the functionality provided by the application logic and the functionality accessible through the user interface.

7 Conclusions

In this paper we introduced MuiCSer, a novel process framework, practicing Multi-disciplinary User-Centred Software engineering in such ways that methodologies used by developers as well as the creativity of developers are included and a positive user experience is more likely to be obtained. Each iteration of a MuiCSer process produces one or more prototypes to enhance the visibility of this process and to allow continuous user involvement and evaluation. Through the case studies, we found the explicit support for multi-disciplinary teams in our process framework one of the strong points of our approach. The definition of the framework stimulates the use of customized processes that pay explicit attention to consistency of design and development artefacts throughout the different cycles of the process. Multi-disciplinarity has been a focus in the current instantiations of the MuiCSer framework and will get additional attention in future research activities in this area. Extending and fine tuning the framework by deriving new and existing processes, will make it a better reference for process comparison and evaluation. Together with the user-interface management system being developed, this will encourage systematic studies of requirements for supporting tools for UCSE processes.

Acknowledgments. Part of the research at EDM is funded by the ERDF (European Regional Development Fund) and the Flemish Government. The VIP-lab project (4-BMG-II-2=37), is financed by the "Interreg Benelux-Middengebied" authorities and co-financed by Province of Limburg (B), Province of Limburg (NL), Ministry of Economic Affairs (NL) and Ministry of Flemish Government/Economic Affairs (B).

The *MuiCSer* Process Framework is also based on our experiences in IWT projects Participate (with Alcatel-Lucent) and AMASS++ (IWT 060051).

References

1 Arnowitz, J., Arent, M., Berger, N.: Effective Prototyping for Software Makers. The Morgan Kaufmann Series in Interactive Technologies. Morgan Kaufmann Publishers Inc., San Francisco (2006)
2 Brown, J., Graham, N., Wright, T.: The vista environment for the coevolutionary design of user interfaces. In: Proc. CHI 1998, pp. 376–383. ACM Press, New York (1998)
3 Campos, P., Nunes, N.J.: Practitioner tools and workstyles for user-interface design. IEEE Software 24(1), 73–80 (2007)
4 Chatty, S., Sire, S., Vinot, J., Lecoanet, P., Lemort, A., Mertz, C.: Revisiting visual interface programming: creating GUI tools for designers and programmers. In: Proc. UIST 2004, pp. 267–276. ACM Press, New York (2004)
5 Clerckx, T., Luyten, K., Coninx, K.: The mapping problem back and forth: customizing dynamic models while preserving consistency. In: Task Models and Diagrams for User Interface Design, pp. 33–42 (2004)
6 Coninx, K., Haesen, M., Bierhoff, J.: VIP-lab: A virtual lab for ICT experience prototyping. In: Proc. Measuring Behavior 2005, pp. 585–586 (2005)
7 Coyette, A., Kieffer, S., Vanderdonckt, J.: Multi-fidelity prototyping of user interfaces. In: Baranauskas, C., Palanque, P., Abascal, J., Barbosa, S.D.J. (eds.) INTERACT 2007. LNCS, vol. 4662, pp. 150–164. Springer, Heidelberg (2007)
8 Holtzblatt, K., Burns Wendell, J., Wood, S.: Rapid Contextual Design. A How-To Guide to Key Techniques for User-Centred Design. Morgan Kaufmann Publishers, San Francisco (2005)
9 International Standards Organization: ISO 13407. Human Centred Design Process for Interactive Systems. Geneva, Swiss (1999)
10 Constantine, L.: Canonical abstract prototypes for abstract visual and interaction design. In: Jorge, J.A., Jardim Nunes, N., Falcão e Cunha, J. (eds.) DSV-IS 2003. LNCS, vol. 2844, pp. 1–15. Springer, Heidelberg (2003)
11 Larman, C.: Agile and Iterative Development: A Manager's Guide. Addison-Wesley, Reading (2003)
12 Lin, J., Landay, J.A.: Employing patterns and layers for early-stage design and prototyping of cross-device user interfaces. In: Proc. CHI 2008 (April 2008)
13 Luyten, K., Meskens, J., Vermeulen, J., Coninx, K.: Meta-GUI-builders: Generating domain-specific interface builders for multi-device user interface creation. In: CHI 2008: extended abstracts on Human factors in computing systems. ACM Press, New York (2008)
14 Meskens, J., Vermeulen, J., Luyten, K., Coninx, K.: Gummy for multi-platform user interface designs: Shape me, multiply me, fix me, use me. In: Proc. AVI 2008 (2008)
15 Meskens, J., Haesen, M., Luyten, K., Coninx, K.: User-Centered Adaptation of User Interfaces for Heterogeneous Environments. In: Advances in Semantic Media Adaptation and Personalisation. CRC Press Edited Book, Boca Raton (2008)
16 Michotte, B., Vanderdonckt, J.: A multi-target user interface builder based on UsiXML. In: Proc. ICAS 2008. IEEE Computer Society Press, Los Alamitos (2008)
17 Mori, G., Paternò, F., Santoro, C.: CTTE: support for developing and analyzing task models for interactive system design. IEEE Transactions on Software Engineering 28(8), 797–813 (2002)

18 Mori, G., Paternò, S.C.: Design and development of multidevice user interfaces through multiple logical descriptions. IEEE Transactions on Software Engineering 30(8), 507–520 (2004)

19 Muller, M.J.: Pictive – an exploration in participatory design. In: Proc. CHI 1991, pp. 225–231. ACM Press, New York (1991)

20 Nobrega, L., Nunes, N.J., Coelho, H.: Mapping ConcurTaskTrees into UML 2. In: Gilroy, S.W., Harrison, M.D. (eds.) DSV-IS 2005. LNCS, vol. 3941, pp. 237–248. Springer, Heidelberg (2006)

21 Nunes, N.J., e Cunha, J.F.: Towards a UML profile for interaction design: the wisdom approach. In: Evans, A., Kent, S., Selic, B. (eds.) UML 2000. LNCS, vol. 1939, pp. 101–116. Springer, Heidelberg (2000)

22 Pruitt, J., Adlin, T.: The Persona Lifecycle: Keeping People in Mind Throughout Product Design. Morgan Kaufmann, San Francisco (2006)

23 Redmond-Pyle, D., Moore, A.: Graphical User Interface Design and Evaluation. Prentice Hall, London (1995)

24 Van den Bergh, J., Coninx, K.: Towards Modeling Context-Sensitive Interactive Applications: the Context-Sensitive User Interface Profile (CUP). In: Proc. SoftVis 2005, pp. 87–94. ACM Press, New York (2005)

25 Van den Bergh, J., Haesen, M., Luyten, K., Coninx, K., Notelaers, S.: Toward Multidisciplinary Model-Based (Re)Design of Sustainable User Interfaces. In: Graham, T.C.N., Palanque, P. (eds.) DSV-IS 2008. LNCS, vol. 5136, pp. 161–166. Springer, Heidelberg (2008)

A Fluid Flow Approach to Usability Analysis of Multi-user Systems

Mieke Massink[1], Diego Latella[1], Maurice H. ter Beek[1],
Michael D. Harrison[2], and Michele Loreti[3]

[1] CNR - ISTI, Pisa, Italy
`{massink,latella,terbeek}@isti.cnr.it`
[2] School of Computing Science, Newcastle University, UK
`Michael.Harrison@ncl.ac.uk`
[3] Universita' di Firenze, Dip. di Sistemi e Informatica, Italy
`loreti@dsi.unifi.it`

Abstract. The analysis of usability aspects of multi-user systems, such as co-operative work systems and pervasive systems, pose particular problems because group behavior of their users may have considerable impact on usability. Model-based analysis of such features leads to state-space explosion because of the sheer number of entities to be modeled when automatic techniques such as model checking are used. In this paper we explore the use of a recently proposed scalable model-based technique based on solving sets of Ordinary Differential Equations (ODEs). Starting from a formal model specified using the Performance Evaluation Process Algebra (PEPA), we show how different groupware usage patterns may be modeled and analyzed using this approach. We illustrate how the approach can explore different design options and their impact on group behavior by comparing file access policies in the context of a groupware application.

Keywords: Formal Methods, Model-based usability analysis, Performance Evaluation Process Algebra, Ordinary Differential Equations, Groupware Systems.

1 Introduction

Tools for usability analysis in relation to one (or at most a few) users are by now relatively mature. However, to date, systematic techniques for analyzing systems, where there are many users and where the collective behavior of these users has an influence on the usability of the system, are currently undeveloped. Such techniques are becoming more necessary as the variety of co-operative work systems, multi-player games, shared virtual spaces and pervasive systems grows.

Collective behavior may have an impact on the usability of a system as it is perceived by an individual. The effect of the behavior of other users may be to change the individual's user interaction. Consider for example a groupware system that offers exclusive access to files by allowing users to get and lock files when files are available. If the lock is already given to another user, and the file is currently in use, then

P. Forbrig and F. Paternò (Eds.): HCSE/TAMODIA 2008, LNCS 5247, pp. 166–180, 2008.

the user will not be able to access the file until the other user has finished with it. In such situations users devise strategies to ensure that they will have the editing rights that they need when they need them. Alternatively they will schedule their work so that there is always something else that they can do in such circumstances. For example, a strategy that might be feasible in this example would be to get hold of the file some time before it is needed. This greedy strategy would be effective for the individual, making it possible for them to carry out their work effectively, but it is not likely to be effective for the whole collaborative activity.

Not only will the individual behavior of a user be affected by changes to the system through its collective use, but the system can also have an effect on the collective behavior of the users. Indeed a system may be designed to achieve precisely this, consider for example a dynamic signage system such as [13] designed to facilitate evacuation of a building. The displays showing where people should go could be designed to change depending on volumes of people within different spaces in the building at any given moment. The displays will together modify the behavior of those in the spaces and thereby, if effective, achieve the most efficient and calm movement of people.

Other factors may affect the usability of these multi-user systems. Usage patterns in relation to technology may also be induced by external factors. For example, in a collaborative design environment it is often the case that the collaboration takes place in a way that reflects project-oriented organization of the work. Projects tend to have different phases: creative phases in which artifacts are developed, which may require longer periods of file creation and modification; fine-tuning phases characterized by frequent but short accesses to a number of critical files. These different phases may lead to a shift between typical usage patterns of the system with a potential impact on its usability characteristics.

Techniques are required that will enable an understanding of both qualitative and quantitative performance aspects of collective usability. In practice few studies have addressed collective behavior. Empirical studies either focus on individual interactions within a system, for example exploring how a group of individuals use flight strips in air traffic management. These studies tend to use ethnographic techniques to provide a rich contextualized account of behavior (see [12] for example) or more anecdotal accounts of social behavior (see [16] in relation to social behavior using the Flickr photo-sharing service). On the other hand detailed statistical analyses of systems have been used to detect biases in their individual use (see for example [21] in relation to a mammography system). These studies are important in exploring patterns of behavior that arise from use of the system. They are time and resource intensive and require a live system. The question of the paper is how to analyze collective behavior of users in relation to a system prior to fielding the system.

While formal models have been developed and explored that are relevant to modeling the interaction between an individual user and device in context (see e.g., [8,9]) and general behavior of users have been captured through normative task models (see e.g. [10,20]) the impact of modeling collective behaviors within interactive systems have not been studied. This issue becomes particularly important in ubiquitous systems, providing smart environments in which many users are immersed and which can have an important impact on the collective behavior of those involved. This paper focuses on the role that modeling approaches can take in enabling the analysis of collective behavior during the early stages of design. The aim is that these techniques should be capable of providing a basis for usability evaluation in the face of different user strategies, when in different phases of collaboration and given different technology designs. A groupware system similar to the one used already for illustration, provides an example of the use of the particular technique.

The fundamental problem with formal modeling in relation to analyses of collective behaviors is how to deal with the state explosion that arises through attempts to model multiple instances of processes required to define the collective behavior. The paper explores a recently proposed *scalable* model-based technique, Fluid Flow Analysis [15]. This technique supports the analysis of many replicated entities with autonomous behavior that collaborate by means of forms of synchronization. It builds upon a process-algebraic approach and adds techniques for quantitative analyses to those for behavioral analysis. The technique has been successfully applied in areas such as large-scale Web Services [11,15], Service-Oriented Computing [23] and Grid applications [5,6], but also in Systems Biology [7].

The technique consists in deriving automatically a set of Ordinary Differential Equations (ODEs) from a specification defined using Performance Evaluation Process Algebra (PEPA) [14]. The solution of the set of ODEs, by means of standard numerical techniques, gives insight into the dynamic change over time of aggregations of components that are in particular states. The approach abstracts away from the identity of the individual components. The derivation of sets of ODEs from PEPA specifications, the algorithms to solve ODE equations and the generation of the numerical results are supported by the PEPA workbench [22].

The problem addressed in the paper is to explore different user strategies and groupware designs for a simplified version of a groupware system called thinkteam. Two different file access policies are analyzed and compared. thinkteam is part of the Product Lifecycle Management system of think3. The Fluid Flow technique can be used in this situation because the system being analyzed involves many replicated components that can be abstracted to relatively few states. The approach can be seen as complementary with model checking in general and stochastic model checking in particular. Stochastic model checking techniques have already been applied to the same example in earlier work [1,2,3,4]. While this approach allows a richer analysis of specific properties of smaller sets of processes, Fluid Flow allows broader analysis of larger aggregations.

The paper introduces PEPA in Section 2 and briefly explains the Fluid Flow interpretation of PEPA models. In Section 3 the thinkteam example is introduced, followed in Section 4 by a specification of the example. Section 5 describes the analysis and section 6 outlines briefly future directions.

2 PEPA: A Process Algebra for Performance Evaluation

In PEPA, systems can be described as interactions of *components* that may engage in *activities* in much the same way as in other process algebras. Components reflect the behavior of relevant parts of the system, while activities capture the actions that the components perform. A component may itself be composed of components. The specification of a PEPA activity consists of a pair *(action type, rate)* in which *action type* denotes the type of the action, while *rate* characterizes the negative *exponential* distribution of the activity duration. A positive real-valued random variable X is exponentially distributed with rate r if the probability of X being at most t, i.e. $Prob(X \le t)$, is $1-e^{-r \times t}$ if $t \ge 0$ and is 0 otherwise, where t is a real number. The expected value of X is $1/r$. Exponentially distributed random variables are more tractable because they have a *memoryless property*, i.e. $Prob((X > t+t')|(X > t)) = Prob(X > t)$ for $t, t' \ge 0$. Exponential distributions are widely used in the modeling of the dependability and performance of real systems where they form the basis for Continuous Time Markov Chains (CTMC), see e.g. [21]. Furthermore, proper compositions of exponential distributions can be used for the approximation of any non-negative distribution. The PEPA expressions used in this article have the following syntax[1]:

$$P ::= (a,\, r).P \mid P + P \mid P \parallel_{\{L\}} P \mid A$$

Behavioral expressions are constructed through prefixing. Component $(a,\, r).P$ carries out activity $(a,\, r)$, with action type a and duration Δt determined by rate r. The average duration is given by $1/r$. It is defined that Δt is an exponentially distributed random variable with rate r. After performing the activity, the component behaves as P. Component $P + Q$ models a system that may behave either as P or as Q, representing a *race condition* between components. The co-operation operator $P \parallel_{\{L\}} Q$ defines the set of action types L on which components P and Q must synchronize (or *co-operate*); both components proceed independently with any activity not occurring in L. The expected duration of a co-operation of activities a belonging to L is a function of the expected durations of the corresponding activities in the components. Typically, it corresponds to the longest one (see [15] for definition of PEPA). An important special case is the situation where one component is passive (a rate T indicates this) in relation to another component. Here the total rate is determined by that of the active component only. The behavior of process variable A is that of P, provided that a defining equation $A=P$ is available for A. We introduce two shorthand notations. If the set L is empty $P \parallel_{\{L\}} Q$ is written as the parallel composition of P and Q: $P|Q$. If there are n copies of P in parallel co-operating with m parallel copies of Q this is written as: $P[n] \parallel_{\{L\}} Q[m]$. We will present PEPA specifications as stochastic state transition diagrams throughout the paper. Full PEPA specifications for the same system can be found in the full version of the paper [19].

One of the advantages of a formal, high-level specification language with a fully formal semantics is that it lends itself to the application of different analysis and evaluation techniques while preserving its semantics. For example, PEPA specifications can be analyzed by means of a stochastic model checker, such as PRISM [18], and it can also be used for simulation. As already mentioned PEPA specifications can be translated into sets of Ordinary Differential Equations (ODEs) [15]. A very brief summary of the approach follows; more details can be found in [19,15]. Suppose a PEPA model $S_1[n_1] \parallel_{L1} S_2[n_2] \parallel_{L2} \ldots \parallel_{Lk-1} S_k[n_k]$ is given, which is composed of $n_1+n_2+ \ldots +n_k$ sequential components. Each component S_j is defined by means of a

---

[1] For technical reasons there are some restrictions on the nesting of parallel processes in the dialect of PEPA suitable for the translation to ODEs. For the sake of simplicity, we refrain from discussing the issue here and refer to [9] for details. The symbol for co-operation in PEPA is different from the one used in the present paper.

PEPA defining equation $S_j = \ldots S_{jr} \ldots S_{jv} \ldots S_{jw}$, where $S_j, S_{jr}, S_{jv} \ldots S_{jw}$ are the relevant states of S_j; all such states are themselves defined by means of equations. The solution of the set of ODEs associated with the PEPA model is a set of *continuous functions*. In particular, there is one function $\underline{S}(t)$ for each state S occurring in the original specification and, for each time instant t, $\underline{S}(t)$ yields a continuous approximation of the total number of components which are in state S at time t, given the initial conditions $\underline{S}_1(0)= n_1, \underline{S}_2(0)= n_2, \ldots ,\underline{S}_k(0)=n_k$. Notice that the fact that the values $n_1, n_2, \ldots, n_k$ of the *number of components* in the system (at the initial configuration) can be very high, e.g. in the order of millions, makes the approach intrinsically scalable. In the experiments described in Section 5, results are compared with those obtained via discrete event simulation and are found to be comparable.

3   The Thinkteam Groupware

Thinkteam (http://www.think3.com/) is think3's Product Data Management (PDM) application. It is designed to deal with the document management needs of design processes in the manufacturing industry. Controlled storage and retrieval of documents in PDM applications is called vaulting, the vault being a file-system-like repository. The system is designed to be a secure and controlled storage environment, in which vaulting prevents inconsistent changes to the document base while still allowing maximal access compatible with business rules. A standard set of operations is supported (see Table 1).

Access to files (via a *checkOut*) is based on *the retrial principle*: no queue or reservation system exists to handle the requests for editing rights. thinkteam typically handles some *100,000* files for *20-100* users. A user rarely checks out more than *10* files a day, but can keep a file checked out for periods from a few minutes to a few days. Log-file analysis of typical use indicated that only a small subset of the files are accessed regularly for editing. Files are typically shared by several users ranging from *2* to *5* with peaks of up to *17*.

Table 1. Thinkteam user operations

Operation	*Effect*
get	extract a read-only copy of a file from the Vault
import	insert an external file into the Vault
checkout	extract a copy of a file from the Vault with the intent of modifying it (exclusive, i.e. only one *checkOut* at a time is possible)
unCheckOut	cancel the effects of the preceding *checkOut*
checkIn	replace an edited file in the Vault (the file must previously have been checked out)
checkInOut	replace an edited file in the Vault, while at the same time retaining it as checked out

To maximize concurrency, a *checkOut* in thinkteam creates an exclusive lock for write access. An automatic solution of the write access conflict is not easy, as it is critically related to the type, nature, and scope of the changes performed on the file.

Moreover, standard but harsh solutions - like maintaining a dependency relation between files and using it to simply lock all files depending on the file being checked out - are out of the question for think3, as they would cause these files to be unavailable for unacceptably long periods. In thinkteam, the solution is to leave it to the users to resolve such conflicts. However, a publish/subscribe notification service would provide the means to supply the Clients with adequate information by (1) informing Clients checking out a file of existing outstanding copies and (2) notifying the copy holders upon *checkOut* and *checkIn* of the file. [3] adds a lightweight and easy-to-use publish/subscribe notification service to thinkteam and verifies several correctness properties such as concurrency control, awareness, and denial of service. Denial-of-service is possible in this system in that one of the users can never get a turn to perform a *checkOut*. This may happen because the system is continuously kept busy by other users. Access to files is based on retrial. The usability aspects of the two file access policies need to be studied under different assumptions about how the group is using the system. In [1] two such usability aspects are studied; (1) how often, on average, users have to express their requests before they are satisfied and (2) under which system conditions (number of users, file editing time, etc.) such a reservation system would really improve usability. In that work a stochastic model-checking approach is used and a limited model with up to ten users competing for one file is analyzed. In this paper we investigate a complementary analysis based on the Fluid Flow approach were we study models with a much larger number of users and files.

4   Modeling File Access Policies

A typical thinkteam user makes requests for edit rights on files using *checkOut* operations. After editing, the file is inserted back into the vault by a *checkIn* operation. Furthermore, a typical file manager is ready to receive a request from a Client and grants this request. It then locks the file for other Clients until it is returned to the vault. Two types of file manager will first be considered. The first supports retrial while the second supports a file reservation system based on a finite queue. It is assumed that the file manager is always able to provide a timely response to the Client on the availability of the file, be it positive or negative. This is modeled using passive rates as explained in Section 2.

4.1   The Retry Policy

Figure 1 describes models of a Client and a FileManager supporting the Retry policy. This particular model will be called the "liberal retrial model" in what follows. PEPA specifications corresponding to all the stochastic state transition diagrams presented in this paper can be found in [19]. The Client initially tries to *checkOut* a file. This can be successful (cos) or fail (cof). The rate a denotes the access rate and characterizes the time that passes between the last *checkIn* of a file and the next access to a file. In other words, it represents the time that a Client is busy with activities other than requesting edit rights for a file and modifying it. If the Client has successfully received edit rights to the file, she works on it for a while and checks the file in. The time involved in this activity is modelled by the rate w. If the edit rights are not granted, the

Client tries again repeatedly with time intervals characterised by rate r, the *retry rate*. The FileManager initially is in a state in which the file is free and can accept a *check-Out* request from a Client. It then moves to a state representing that the file is now locked (FMbusy) in which further Clients' requests result in a failed *checkOut* (cof) until the file is checked in (ci).

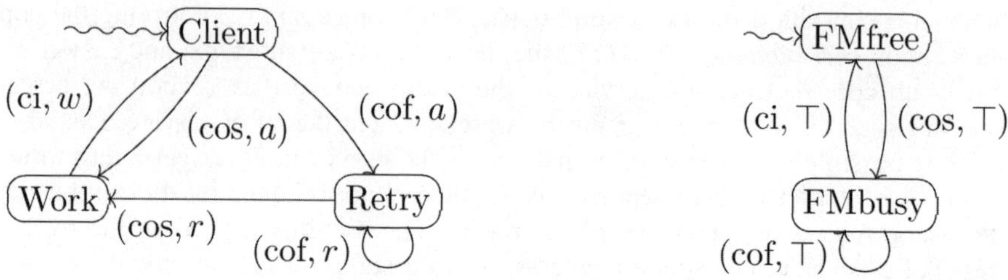

Fig. 1. From left to right: Stochastic Automata of Client and FileManager components

All activities of the FileManager have a passive rate (T), they adapt to any rate induced by the Clients. The model abstracts from the identity of the Clients by not keeping track of which Client exactly is requesting which file. The model of the Client behavior does not require that a Client's retry activity is aiming at obtaining the same file. In fact, it models Clients that try to obtain whatever file they want every time they are making a request. This can be a request for the same file or for any other file, free or occupied. In this sense the model differs from the one we presented in [1], where the fact that there was only one file implied that all three Clients are trying to get the same file. This abstraction can be achieved without loss of generality given the volumes of processes. A composed model with *90* Clients competing for *30* files can now be expressed using the PEPA co-operation operator: Client[90] $\parallel_{\{cos,ci,cof\}}$ FMfree[30].

A modified specification of the Retry model (the waiting retry model) is given in Figure 2. Here when a *checkOut* attempt fails (cof), the Client waits on average an amount of time equal to the length of a typical editing session (*1/w*) before trying again. This is modeled by the pair of states RetryFail and Retry together and related transitions. This model approximates a situation in which Clients keep on trying to obtain a particular file because, on average, they have to wait for such a file at least for the duration of one editing session. It could be argued that a Client may be 'lucky'

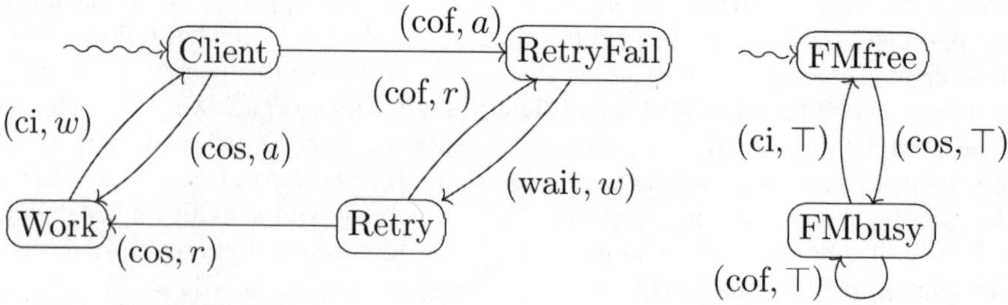

Fig. 2. From left to right: Stochastic Automata of Client and FileManager components

and wait less time when the Client that is currently editing has almost finished. Because the exponential distributions are memoryless the same rate w modeling the working time also models the remaining working time. As in the liberal Retry model we can express the composed model with *90* Clients and *30* FileManagers as Client[90] $\|_{\{cos,ci,cof\}}$ FMfree[30].

4.2   The Waiting-List Policy

Figure 3 models the Waiting-list policy. The model of the FileManager supporting this policy is given in Figure 4. The Client may initially achieve: (1) a successful *checkOut* of the requested file (cos), (2) an unsuccessful *checkOut*, but placement in the waiting list (cof), or (3) a complete failure because the waiting list for the file is full (qf). In the first case, the Client edits the file and checks it in as before. In the second case, the Client waits until a notification arrives saying that it is the Client's turn to edit the file (trn). In the third case the Client has to try again to get the file or to be put on the waiting list. The model of the FileManager that supports the Waiting-list policy includes a queue. In this specific case one Client can be editing the file and at most two other Clients may be in the queue. Initially the file is free and a *checkOut* request is successful (cos). If a further request arrives the request is placed in the waiting list (cof) modeled by state FMbusyW1. If yet a further request arrives before the file is checked in it is placed in the list as well, modeled by state FMfullW2, denoting that the list is now full and two Clients are waiting for write access. Any further requests are answered with a 'queue full' message (qf).

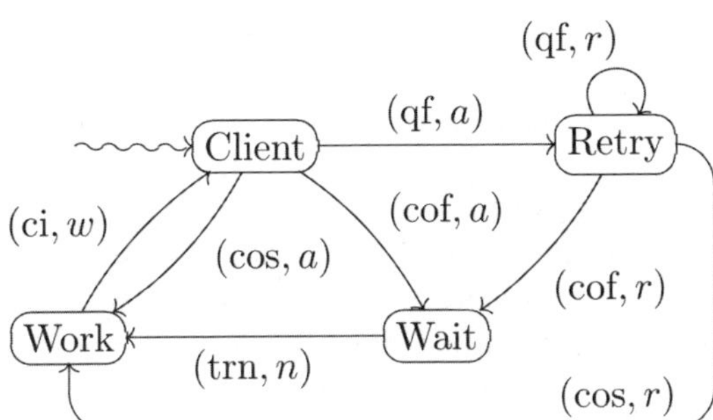

Fig. 3. Client component

When the file is checked in while the FileManager is in state FMfullW2, it moves to state FMfullW2bis from which a notification is sent to the next Client that was waiting for the file (trn). We know that such a Client exists because Clients that receive a (cof) are waiting for such a notification before they can do other things. The model Client[90] $\|_{\{cos,ci,cof,qf,trn\}}$ FMfree[30] now takes the new definitions for Client and FMfree.

This model is not concerned with exactly which Client gets the notification. In fact, when abstracting from identity, any Client that is waiting for a notification will do, because on average for every Client that in theory would have received the notification 'before its turn' there is an equivalent one that receives it later than would be

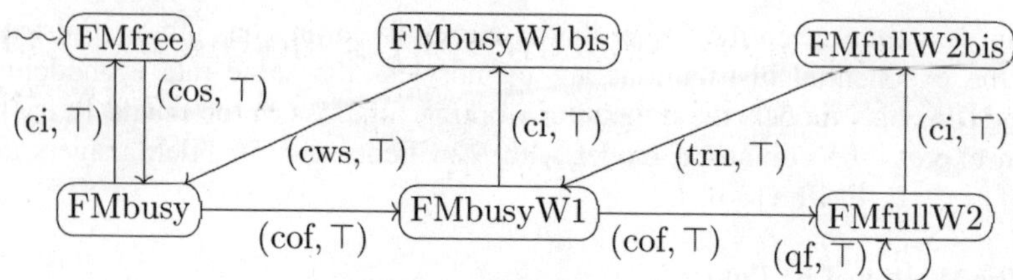

Fig. 4. The FileManager

preferred. In daily life Clients do care about such a random assignment of turns, but note that for the purpose of the analysis we only require that Clients wait until they receive a notification. We can correctly abstract from the identity of the Clients (and files) because we are only interested in the *number* of Clients that are in a certain state. This provides an indication of the performance of the overall system. To make this clearer, consider the following example. If ten people stand in a queue, each with their numbered ticket, the length of the queue is not influenced by two people exchanging their tickets (or their places). If we have two queues, their length is also not influenced by the exchange of two people, one from each queue. In the case of our model therefore we do not need to model in which queue the Client is. In this model it is necessary to synchronize also on the actions denoting queue full (qf) and next turn (trn).

5   Analysis of File Access Policies in Thinkteam

The models in Section 4 can be used to explore the advantages and disadvantages of alternative strategies giving a perspective on the collective usability of these different strategies. Analysis using the PRISM stochastic model checker with a limited number of files and Clients is described in [1]. The specifications are also amenable to discrete event simulation. In this section we present the results of the Fluid Flow analysis. This analysis provides information about how many Clients are editing a file or are waiting in a queue over time. These numbers depend on the typical usage patterns of the system, which in their turn can be characterized by the values of the parameters of the model. The following assumptions are made about usage patterns, that

- The average time between a *checkIn* and the next request is *2* hours (i.e. rate $a = 0.5$)
- The system is used by *90* Clients that compete for *30* files.
- The retry rate r is $5 \times a$
- Editing sessions of different average duration $1/w$
- Each Client has at any moment at most one file checked out.

In addition in the case of the Waiting-list model we assume that there can be at most one Client working on a file and that there can be at most two Clients in the queue before it is full.

5.1 Analysis of the Waiting-List Policy

Results show average durations of editing sessions of *4* hours (Figure 5(a)) and *5* minutes (Figure 5(b)). All other assumptions are invariant. The graphs show how an initial situation of the Waiting-list model with *90* Clients and *30* free files evolves over *20* hours. Each curve shows the evolution of the number of processes in each state described in the specification of section 4. A number of observations can be made about the number of Clients who are editing files, waiting in queues or busy trying to get a file. In all cases stability occurs within an hour or two. We can see in the longer sessions (Figure 5(a)):

1. A steep decrease in the number of Clients involved in other activities, dropping from *90* initially to a stable *6.5*
2. A steep decrease in the number of free files from *30* to almost zero (arising for the fact that so many Clients are competing for files and are involved in relatively long editing sessions)
3. The number of Clients spending their time waiting in some queue is relatively high tending to approximately *52*
4. The queues themselves are quite full, i.e. approximately *26* of the *30* queues are full in the long run.

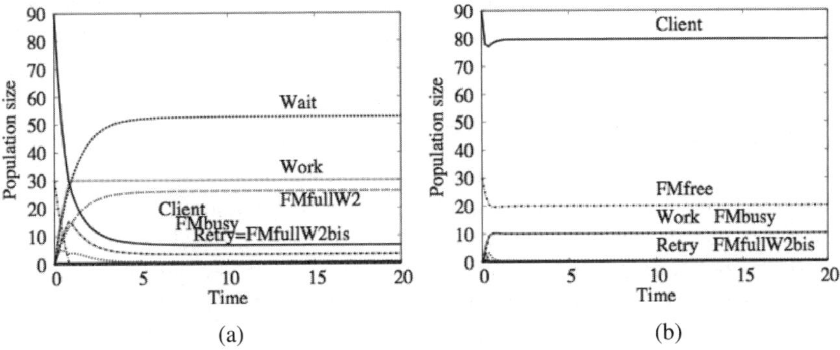

Fig. 5. ODE analysis of Waiting-list model, number of processes in each state with Clients editing files for: (a) *4* hours on average; (b) *5* minutes on average

In the shorter sessions (Figure 5(b)): *10* files are actually being edited at any time and the Clients are hardly wasting any time in the queues obtaining the files they need. This situation may of course change rapidly when shorter editing times are combined with much more frequent requests for files.

5.2 Analysis of the Retry Policy

The liberal Retry policy (Figure 6) shows at first sight a similar pattern to the Waiting-list policy. In the case of long editing sessions of about *4* hours on average we observe:

1. A rapid decrease in the number of users performing other activities than trying to get files and edit them
2. The available files are quickly occupied
3. Approximately *45* Clients are at any time busy (re)trying to obtain files
4. In editing sessions of *5* minutes there remains a considerable number of Clients (about *12*) busy retrying to obtain files, compared with the Waiting-list policy under the same circumstances in that model almost no Clients are waiting in a queue.

5.3   Comparing the Usability of the Two File Access Policies

In summary the liberal Retry model and the Waiting-list model both tend toward a stable situation in relation to the number of processes that are in certain states at any moment. In Figure 7(a) we compare the usability of the liberal Retry model (LRM) and the Waiting-list model (WLM) by showing the number of 'free Clients' (series labelled by FinLRM and FinWLM respectively), the number of working Clients (series labelled by WinLRM and WinWLM respectively) and waiting or retrying Clients (series labelled by RinLRM and WRinWLM respectively) after *20* hours of operation.

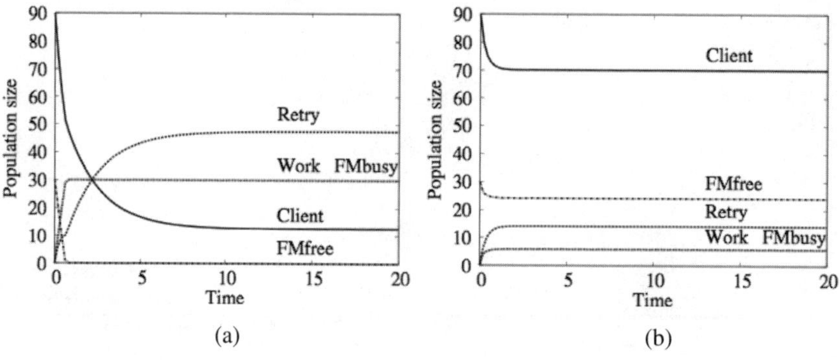

Fig. 6. ODE analyses for the liberal Retry policy for number of processes in each state editing files for (a) *4* hours on average (b) *5* minutes on average

These numbers are shown under different assumptions on the average duration of the edit sessions for both the liberal Retry model and the Waiting-list model. Note that the average edit time ranges from *10* hours on average on the left, to *5* minutes on the right of the figure. The liberal Retry model appears to outperform the Waiting-list model when the duration of the edit time is more than approximately *20* minutes. This is because there are more Clients waiting for a file or involved in retry in the Waiting-list model than in the Retry model. The number of Clients working on a file is the same when the edit time is more than one hour, and the files are in that case all checked out. This result can be explained by the fact that in the liberal Retry model, when many files are checked out, the Client can in every retry attempt have a possibility to obtain a free file when available. In the Waiting-list model the Client is forced to stay in a queue and wait until an occupied file is again available. The Retry model represents a strategy in which a Client is more free to dynamically adapt their work to the situation.

The situation changes considerably, however, for average editing periods shorter than approximately *20* minutes. We can observe then that there are fewer Clients editing a file in the Retry model than in the Waiting-list model. In fact, in the Waiting-list model for edit sessions of less than *20* minutes very few Clients need to wait for a file, whereas a relatively large number of Clients are retrying in the Retry model. This is due to the fact that Clients do not get notified about the fact that a file became available and are wasting time in between consecutive retries. In the Waiting-list model, the waiting Clients are immediately informed about the availability of the file of interest. Figure 7(b) shows the results comparing the Waiting-Retry model (WRM) with the Waiting-list model (WLM).

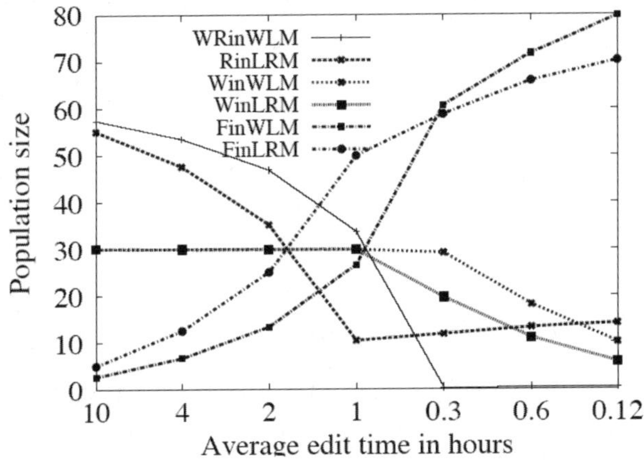

Fig. 7(a). Comparison of policies: liberal Retry vs. Waiting-list

The series shows the number of 'free Clients' (series labelled by FinWRM and FinWLM respectively), the number of working Clients (series labelled by WinWRM and WinWLM respectively) and waiting or retrying Clients (series labelled by WRinWRM and WRinWLM respectively) after *20* hours of operation. We can observe that for edit sessions that last more than one hour the two policies have now a more similar performance. The Waiting-Retry model still gives slightly better performance than the Waiting-list model when looking at the Clients who are free or busy retrying/waiting. This may be explained by the fact that we required that Clients in the Waiting-Retry model wait only for the duration of *one* session whereas when all files are occupied it is much more likely that Clients should wait for two editing sessions. This is the case for the Waiting-list model. For editing sessions of less than one hour, when not all files are continuously occupied, it is clear that the Waiting-Retry model has worse usability performance than the Waiting-list policy in the sense that Clients waste more time in retry activity than they would waiting in a queue in the Waiting-list model. Again, this is due to the fact that Clients do not know how long they should wait before attempting another *checkOut*. So, even if the file of

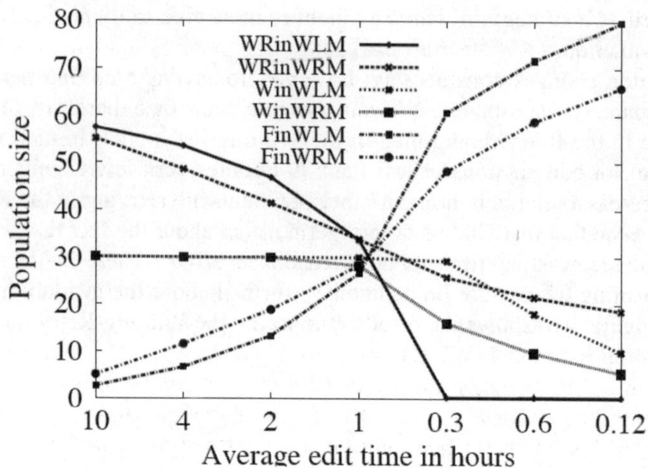

Fig. 7(b). Comparison of policies: Waiting Retry vs. Waiting-list

interest is already available, Clients keep waiting before attempting a next *checkOut* request. In the Waiting list policy instead, Clients are immediately notified about the availability of the desired file, and therefore, on average, they are wasting less time.

6 Conclusions and Further Research

We have used the Performance Evaluation Process Algebra (PEPA) to develop combined user and system models to investigate usability aspects of multi-user systems with a large number of users. This has been achieved by solving sets of Ordinary Differential Equations that are automatically derived from PEPA specifications. This analysis allows for the evaluation of systems with a very high number of replicated, independent components at the cost of abstracting from the identities of these components. We have illustrated how the analysis technique can be used to inform design choices for user interaction in multi-user systems where user behavior may directly affect usability. Different usage patterns may influence performance aspects of groupware systems that are directly relevant to its usability. We have shown how a file access policy based on a retrial principle and one based on waiting lists can be modeled and their effects on usability of the overall system can be compared for different assumptions on usage patterns. The ODE analysis results show that for usage patterns where in the long run not all files are checked out, the Waiting-list policy makes users waste less time in waiting/retry activities than the Retry policy would under the same circumstances. Such a comparison was made by analyzing the number of Clients that are involved in certain activities at any time. These activities correspond to particular states in the respective models.

In this paper we explored some initial ideas for the application of the ODE technique to the analysis of usability aspects of multi-user systems. We think that the results are encouraging and we plan to investigate their use also in more extended case studies. In particular we are interested in using this technique to explore smart spaces, and in particular how a ubiquitous system might affect the collective behavior of users within the smart spaces. First considerations in the context of a dynamic context sensitive guidance system can be found in [13].

Acknowledgments

This work has been partially funded by the Italian MIUR/FIRB project tocai.it, by the EU project Resist/Faerus (IST-2006-026764), by the EU project SENSORIA (IST-2005-016004), and by the Italian CNR/RSTL project XXL. think3, thinkteam and thinkPLM are registered trademarks of think3, Inc.

References

1. ter Beek, M., Massink, M., Latella, D.: Towards Model Checking Stochastic Aspects of the thinkteam User Interface. In: Gilroy, S.W., Harrison, M.D. (eds.) DSV-IS 2005. LNCS, vol. 3941, pp. 39–50. Springer, Heidelberg (2006)
2. ter Beek, M., Massink, M., Latella, D., Gnesi, S.: Model Checking GroupwareProtocols. In: Darses, F., Dieng, R., Simone, C., Zacklad, M. (eds.) Co-operative Systems Design-Scenario-Based Design of Collaborative Systems. Frontiers in Artificial Intelligence and Applications, vol. 107, pp. 79–194. IOS (2004)
3. ter Beek, M., Massink, M., Latella, D., Gnesi, S., Forghieri, A., Sebastianis, M.: Model Checking Publish/Subscribe Notification for thinkteam. In: Arenas, A., Bicarregui, J., Butterfield, A. (eds.) Proceedings of FMICS 2004. Electronic Notes in Theoretical Computer Science, vol. 133, pp. 275–294 (2005)
4. ter Beek, M., Massink, M., Latella, D., Gnesi, S., Forghieri, A., Sebastianis, M.: A Case Study on the Automated Verification of Groupware Protocols. In: Heitmeyer, C., Pohl, K. (eds.) ICSE 2005, pp. 596–603. ACM, New York (2005)
5. Benoit, A., Cole, M., Gilmore, S., Hillston, J.: Scheduling Skeleton-Based Grid Applications Using PEPA and NWS Source. The Computer Journal 48(3), 369–378 (2005)
6. Benoit, A., Cole, M., Gilmore, S., Hillston, J.: Enhancing the effective utilisation of grid clusters by exploiting on-line performability analysis. In: Proceedings of CCGRID 2005, pp. 317–324. IEEE Computer Society Press, Los Alamitos (2005)
7. Calder, M., Gilmore, S., Hillston, J.: Automatically deriving ODEs from process algebra models of signalling pathways. In: Proceedings of CMSB 2005, pp. 204–215 (2005)
8. Campos, J., Harrison, M.: Model checking interactor specifications. Automated Software Engineering 8, 275–310 (2001)
9. Campos, J., Harrison, M.: Considering context and users in interactive systems analysis. In: van de Veer, G., Palanque, P., Wesson, J. (eds.) Proceedings of EIS 2007, Lecture Notes in Computer Science. LNCS. Springer, Heidelberg (to appear, 2007)
10. Fields, R.: Analysis of erroneous actions in the design of critical systems. PhD thesis, Department of Computer Science, University of York (2001)
11. Gilmore, S., Tribastone, M.: Evaluating the Scalability of a Web Service-Based Distributed e-Learning and Course Management System. In: Bravetti, M., Núñez, M., Zavattaro, G. (eds.) WS-FM 2006. LNCS, vol. 4184, pp. 214–226. Springer, Heidelberg (2006)
12. Harper, R.H.R.: The organization in ethnography – a discussion of ethnographic fieldwork programs in CSCW. Computer Supported Co-operative Work 9(2), 239–264 (2000)

13. Harrison, M.D., Kray, C., Campos, J.C.: Exploring an option space to engineer a ubiquitous computing system. Electronic Notes in Theoretical Computer Science, vol. 208C, pp. 41–55 (2008)
14. Hillston, J.: A Compositional Approach to Performance Modelling. Cambridge University Press, Cambridge (1996)
15. Hillston, J.: Fluid flow approximation of PEPA models. In: Proceedings of QEST 2005, pp. 33–43. IEEE Computer Society Press, Los Alamitos (2005)
16. Kindberg, T., Spasojevic, R., Fleck, R., Sellen, A.: The ubiquitous camera: an in-depth study of camera phone use. IEEE Pervasive Computing 4(2), 42–50 (2005)
17. Kulkarni, V.: Modeling and Analysis of Stochastic Systems. Chapman & Hall, Boca Raton (1995)
18. Kwiatkowska, M., Norman, G., Parker, D.: Probabilistic symbolic model checking with PRISM: A hybrid approach. In: Katoen, J.-P., Stevens, P. (eds.) TACAS 2002. LNCS, vol. 2280, pp. 52–66. Springer, Heidelberg (2002)
19. Massink, M., Latella, D., ter Beek, M., Harrison, M., Loreti, M.: A Fluid Flow Approach to Usability Analysis of Multi-user Systems-Full version. ISTI Technical Report (to appear), http://www.isti.cnr.it/People/M.Massink/t3ode.pdf
20. Paterno, F., Mancini, C., Meniconi, S.: ConcurTaskTrees: A Diagrammatic Notation for Specifying Task Models. In: Howard, S., Hammond, J., Lindgaard, G. (eds.) Proceedings of INTERACT 1997, pp. 362–369. Chapman & Hall, Boca Raton (1997)
21. Strigini, L., Povyakalo, A., Alberdi, E.: Human machine diversity in the use of computerized advisory systems: a case study. In: International Conference on Dependable Systems and Networks (DSN 2003), pp. 249–258 (2003)
22. Tribastone, M.: The PEPA Plug-in Project. In: Harchol-Balter, M., Kwiatkowska, M., Telek, M. (eds.) Proceedings of QEST 2007, pp. 53–54. IEEE Computer Society Press, Los Alamitos (2007)
23. Wirsing, M., Clark, A., Gilmore, S., Holzl, M., Knapp, A., Koch, N., Schroeder, A.: Semantic-Based Development of Service-Oriented Systems. In: Najm, E., Pradat-Peyre, J.-F., Donzeau-Gouge, V.V. (eds.) FORTE 2006. LNCS, vol. 4229, pp. 24–45. Springer, Heidelberg (2006)

Task-Driven Plasticity: One Step Forward with UbiDraw

Jean Vanderdonckt and Juan Manuel Gonzalez Calleros

Belgian Laboratory of Computer-Human Interaction (BCHI)
Louvain School of Management (LSM), Université catholique de Louvain
Place des Doyens, 1 – B-1348 Louvain-la-Neuve, Belgium
jean.vanderdonckt@uclouvain.be,
juan.gonzalez@student.uclouvain.be

Abstract. Task-driven plasticity refers to as the capability of a user interface to exhibit plasticity driven by the user's task, i.e. the capability of a user interface to adapt itself to various contexts of use while preserving some predefined usability properties by performing adaptivity based on some task parameters such as complexity, frequency, and criticality. The predefined usability property considered in task-driven plasticity consists of maximizing the observability of user commands in a system-initiated way driven by the ranking of different tasks and sub-tasks. In order to illustrate this concept, we developed UbiDraw, a vectorial hand drawing application that adapts its user interface by displaying, un-displaying, resizing, and relocating tool bars and icons according to the current user's task, the task frequency, or the user's preference for some task. This application is built on top of a context watcher and a set of ubiquitous widgets. The context watchers probes the context of use by monitoring how the user is carrying out her current tasks (e.g., task preference, task frequency) whose definitions are given in a run-time task model. The context watcher sends this information to the ubiquitous widgets so as to support task-driven plasticity.

Keywords: adaptation of user interface, context-aware adaptation, plasticity of user interface, task-based design, task-driven plasticity, user interface description language.

1 Introduction and Motivations

The rise of ubiquitous computing [20] poses significant challenges for designing User Interfaces (UIs) that are adapted to new contexts of use [3,6,20,22]. In conventional interactive systems, the context of use is both limited (e.g., in terms of screen resolution, available input devices) and known (e.g., a person sitting in front of a PC). As computing platforms become more embedded in our daily environment or carried with us, the surrounding world essentially becomes an interface to virtually any type of interactive system. This implies some major changes in the design of these UIs. Porting the UI of specific systems (e.g., a route planning system) or of traditional, popular applications (e.g., a word processing system) to new computing platforms always faces the challenge of designing a UI that is compatible with the constraints imposed by the new computing platform. For instance, porting the UI of a vectorial

P. Forbrig and F. Paternò (Eds.): HCSE/TAMODIA 2008, LNCS 5247, pp. 181–196, 2008.

drawing system from a PC to a PocketPC not only poses constraints of the screen resolution but also introduces alternative modalities of interaction for which the initial UI was not designed initially. For this purpose, many different strategies have been adopted that affect the initial UI design or not.

Techniques that do not affect the initial design include simple porting (when the initial UI is merely reproduced in contents and shapes to the new platform without any change) or zooming (when zoom in/out is applied to the initial UI to increase/decrease the size of a UI portion currently in use according to a focus of interest). While these techniques preserve the consistency between the different versions, the simple porting may dramatically reduce the available screen real estate while the zooming may induce many operations related to the zoom manipulation. Keeping a high number of menu options displayed continuously also maintains a high level of uncertainty on the UI and a high decision time.

The Hick-Hyman Law [16] specifies that this decision time is proportional to the logarithm of equally distributed options. This may suggest that a single screen with more options is more efficient for target selection than a series of screens with less options. But in this case, the screen density may increase, thus impacting the time for searching an item on the screen. For instance, Fig. 1 shows how a traditional UI for a PC-based drawing application is almost entirely reproduced for a PocketPC. Only the bottom left portion of the drawing UI displays some more options depending on the function selected. The rest of the UI remains constant over time.

Fig. 1. Simple drawing application on a Pocket PC (from WinCEPaint - http://www.abisoft.spb.ru/products/cepaint.html)

Techniques that affect the initial design statically may keep the same modality or not when adapting the initial UI. For instance, the UI components can be restructured into tabbed windows gathering functions that are related in principle to the same task. The quality of this gathering highly depends on the quality of the task analysis that has been conducted before. As another example, some Pocket PCs are equipped with physical buttons that can be reassigned to other functions depending on the system running. While this may reduce the functions presented on screen, the assignment may confuse the end user as it is neither systematic nor consistent throughout several interactive systems. In addition, some icons are drawn on these physical buttons, thus making them appropriate for one task (e.g., a particular view for a calendar), but ir-relevant for another (e.g., what does a "Month view" mean for a drawing system?). Similarly, information that was previously assigned to a graphical widget can be sub-mitted to a more general change of modality: sound, voice, or gesture can advanta-geously replace a graphical widget, like in the sound widgets toolkit [2]. In an ultimate example, related functions can also presented in collapsible tool bars (Fig. 2), like the icons belt of MacOSX or like object toolbars in Corel PaintShop that change according to the object currently being drawn.

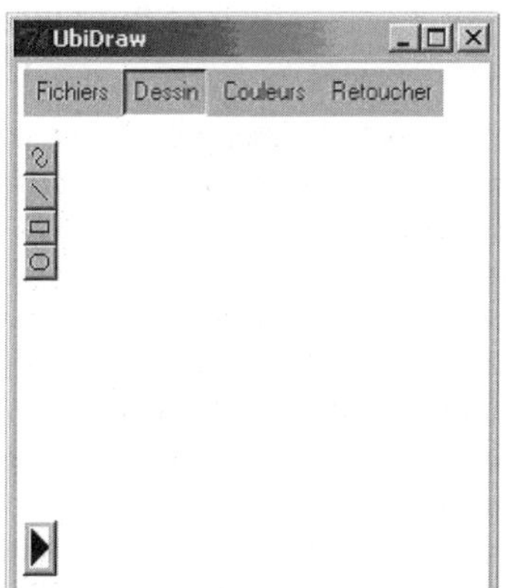

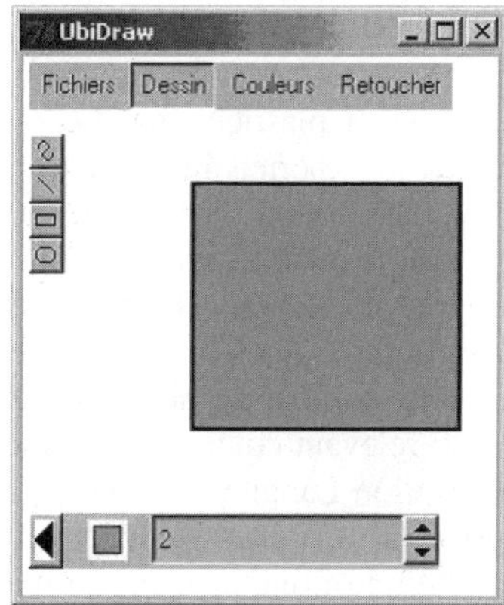

Fig. 2. Collapsible tool bars

Fig. 2 shows how the arrow at the bottom left corner can be expanded to display options related to the object being drawn (one property and its value at a time is dis-played, all properties can be scrolled). When the object is finally drawn, the tool bar is collapsed. If another object is input, the arrow is expanded again with other similar properties. Techniques that affect the initial design dynamically open the door to yet unexplored or unexplored capabilities, including the notion of plastic UIs [3,4,7,24]. The plasticity of UIs concerns the capacity of a multi-context UI to preserve usability properties across the various contexts of use, the context of use being defined here as a triple (user, platform, environment) [3]. To exhibit such a capability, some recon-figuration of the UI is often needed. The reconfiguration of UI widgets such as dialog boxes, controls, menu bars and pull-down menus is an example of a physical adapta-tion. Another possibility is to adapt the very task that the system is to perform. Browne, Totterdell, and Normann [1] present a classification of adaptations in which they observe and regret that most adaptive systems embed hard wired mappings from the set of states to the set of possible adaptations, thus making the adaptivity mecha-nism rather inflexible. To go one step further than this type of adaptivity, while considering the plasticity, we would like to investigate to what extent UI can be "plastified" at a higher level of concern than the physical one.

For this purpose, the remainder of this paper is structured as follows: Section 2 reports on some related work on the different levels of plasticity that have been explored so far. Section 3 describes UbiDraw, a vectorial drawing system whose UI supports task-driven plasticity based on a small toolkit of task-driven plastic widgets, called UbiWidgets. This application has been chosen because it is not a trivial UI: it is not a simple form web-based application, for which multiple adaptation mechanisms have been considered so far. Section 4 investigates the effect of using UbiWidgets on the user preference by conducting some usability testing. Finally, Section 5 concludes the paper by summarizing the advantages and shortcomings of this approach, mainly through properties of interest.

2 Related Work

Since the notion of plasticity has been introduced [24], many different works have been dedicated to experiencing how to implement an interactive system that satisfies this property. The notion of plasticity leaves open the usability or quality properties (e.g., [12]) with respect to which some level of usability should be maintained and leaves open the contextual characteristics with respect to which the UI should be made plastic. In the Cameleon Reference Framework [3], the context of use is defined as a triple (user, computing platform, environment), each of these dimensions being equipped with relevant contextual characteristics. In particular, the UsiXML User Interface Description Language (UIDL) [27] is compliant with this framework and deploys a series of attributes for each of these three dimensions. Consequently, any potential variation of one or many of these attributes may represent a change of context with respect to which the UI should be adapted. Of course, not all such variations should be supported, only those which are really significant.

The mechanism of the *software probe* for sensing the context of use has been explained in [4]: it allows deploying interactive systems that constantly probe the context of use for a significant change and that reflect such a change into a UI adaptation. As far as we know, this adaptation is performed at the level of the *Final UI* [3]. Jabarin demonstrated how to implement efficient software architecture for such a final-UI level plasticity [17]. Schneider *et al.* [21 introduced abstract user interfaces whose implementation is independent of the underlying computing platform and that offers multiple representations of concrete UIs for the same description. Therefore, the plasticity is located at the *Concrete UI* level as defined in the Cameleon Reference Framework [3]. All widgets, although called abstract, belong to a Graphical UI. They should not be confused with a AUI belonging to the Abstract UI level [3]. Crease *et al.* [5] introduced a toolkit of context-aware widgets that embed plasticity at the *Abstract UI* level [3]: in this toolkit, widgets have been abstracted with respect to the underlying physical environment so as to form platform-independent widgets. These widgets can also change their interaction modality.

Hence, the plasticity can be declined at any level of the Cameleon Reference Framework as noticed in [8,17], but so far only the lower levels of this framework have been successfully investigated. The only noticeable exception that we are aware of is the system of Comets [8], that propagates interaction needs from the final UI to the task and domain level through concrete and abstract UIs via a set of logical mappings. The support for plasticity is therefore distributed continuously from the final UI (lowest level) to the task and domain level (topmost level).

Our work differs from the aforementioned initiatives in that it drives the plasticity mechanism from a task model located at the task & domain level. It is then propagated downwards to dedicated widgets. A change of the context of use is firstly interpreted in terms of a task variation that is then reflected into the Concrete UI level and Final UI level, respectively. The difference between Comets [8] and UbiWidgets is that the task definition is embedded in a Comet that is developed fit-to-the purpose, while UbiWidgets is based on a mechanism exploiting a task model dynamically. This makes the system independent of any task. In addition, the concrete UI level is constantly modeled via a CUI as defined in the UsiXML (User Interface eXtensible Markup Language – http://www.usixml.org) [27] and the navigation is specified thanks to a system of screen transitions [26]. Not all attributes used in a UsiXML-compliant CUI are used here though, only a subset of them. On the other hand, the Comets maintain a perpetual correspondence between the Comet type (which is aware of the task it is supporting) and the FUI through AUI and CUI, thus making it more flexible than UbiWidgets supporting only the CUI level.

3 UbiDraw: A Task-Driven Plastic Drawing System

This section is structured as follows: first, a general overview of UbiDraw is provided that shows how the UI is adaptive with respect to the users' task; then, the underlying software architecture is explained, along with its context watcher; finally, Ubi-Widgets, the toolkit of widgets supporting plastic-driven plasticity, is described.

3.1 General Overview of UbiDraw

UbiDraw was developed using Mozart environment [28] and its graphical toolkit Qtk [13]. This environment is by definition multi-platform since it offers an implementation layer where a system is implemented once, and running similarly on Linux, Windows, and Mac platforms. Qtk has been itself implemented on top of the Mozart environment based on the Oz programming language, which is a multi-paradigm programming language. Qtk has been used similarly to implement FlexClock [14].

UbiDraw provides four set of drawing functionalities grouped by similarity in a toolbar attached to an item of the menu bar: File, Draw, Options, and Retouch. Every toolbar can be displayed at different locations of the main application window depending on the size and resolution of the application running on a particular platform. Each group may be displayed in three different ways according to its status (Fig. 3):

1. *Hidden*: all icons of the toolbar attached to the menu item are not visible.
2. *Vertically displayed*: all icons are arranged in a vertically-displayed tool bar.
3. *Horizontally displayed*: all icons are arranged in a horizontally-displayed tool bar.

Fig. 3 graphically depicts these three possible displays: Fig. 3a has the "File" and "Draw" toolbars displayed while the "Options" and "Retouch" toolbars are hidden so as to maximize the screen real estate (here, of a PocketPC running UbiDraw); Fig. 3b has the toolbar "Retouch" in vertical state since it is currently being displayed in a vertical way when activated; Fig. 3c has the "Options" and "Retouch" tool bars in horizontal state since they are displayed horizontally corresponding to the active menu items. Each toolbar does not necessarily displays all icons of the group: its size can range from none (when its status is hidden) to maximum (when all icons are displayed either in vertical or in horizontal status).

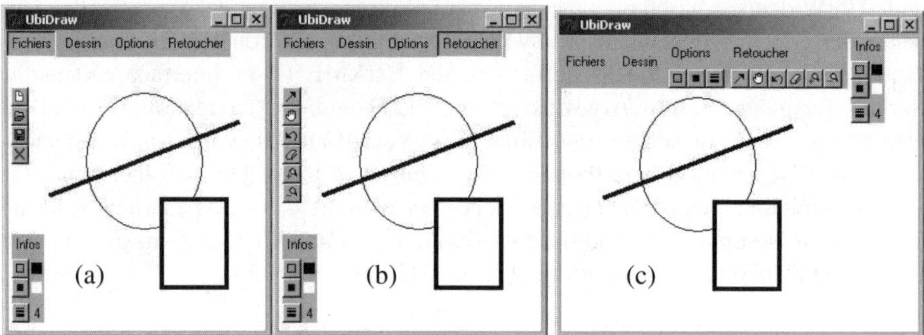

Fig. 3. The three different possible displays of tool bars

In order to determine the size of a non-hidden toolbar and how many icons should be displayed, UbiDraw is relying on a priority scale system where the icons being displayed are regulated by 3 priorities: the last icon being clicked, the rank representing the users' preference/need for this icon, and the amount of clicks on this icon. Therefore, the higher the priority of an icon is, the more likely it will be displayed. In this way, UbiDraw can determine at run-time the UI configuration to be displayed. Fig. 4 reproduces a situation before and after run-time plasticity where the horizontal screen resolution has been increased.

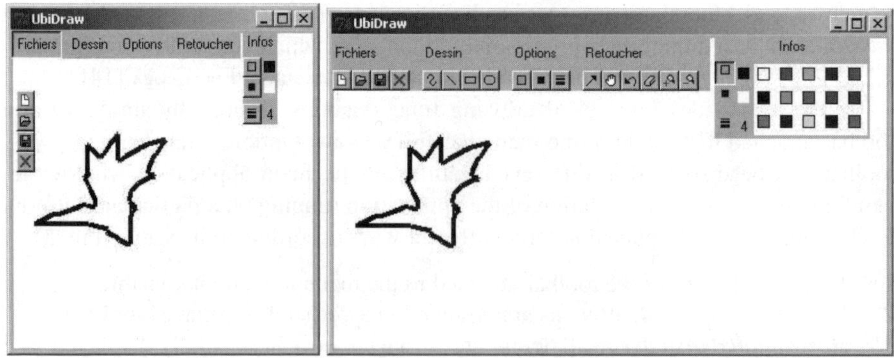

Fig. 4. UbiDraw before and after horizontal resizing of the main window

3.2   Software Architecture of UbiDraw

If we consider the process of plasticity with respect to a view of the software architecture, its processing can be located at different places [12]:

- *At the UI component*: the plasticity is then embedded in the widget level and becomes transparent for the developer;
- *At the UI adaptation component*: the plasticity is embodied in the component so that it can regulated more flexibly through appropriate techniques, such as production rules, inference mechanisms, decision trees, etc.
- *At the UI control component*: the plasticity is regulated at the highest possible level in the metamodel. In this case, only control rules govern the plasticity. We are not aware of ongoing work regarding this level of plasticity apart in Comets [8].

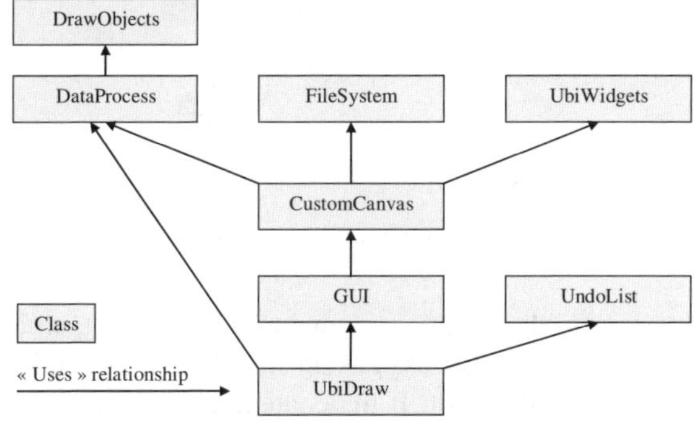

Fig. 5. Software architecture of UbiDraw

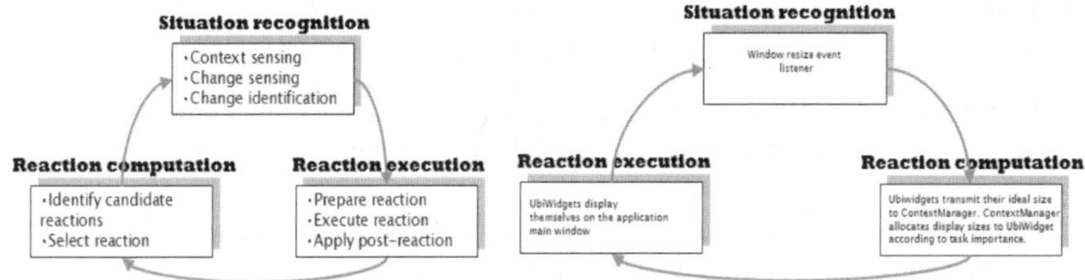

Fig. 6. Steps of run-time plasticity in UbiDraw

For UbiDraw, we chose the last option. UbiDraw is implemented in several classes (Fig. 5): the main class uses respectively a GUI class (implemented as a concrete UI that will be further described later on), an undo list to keep track of action history, and a dataProcess class that uses the various drawing objects and facilities. The GUI mainly consists of a customCanvas that is in turn decomposed of UbiWidgets (the items of the menu bar and their associated tool bars with icons). The customCanvas selects one of the three states for each UbiWidget depending on the ContextWatcher (that is further described in the next sub-section) that is similar to the context probe [4]. The central component for the adaptation mechanism is the UbiWidget component. It contains a class called ContextWatcher, responsible for the placement of the widgets populating the application, and a class UbiWidget, whose instances are plastic widgets.

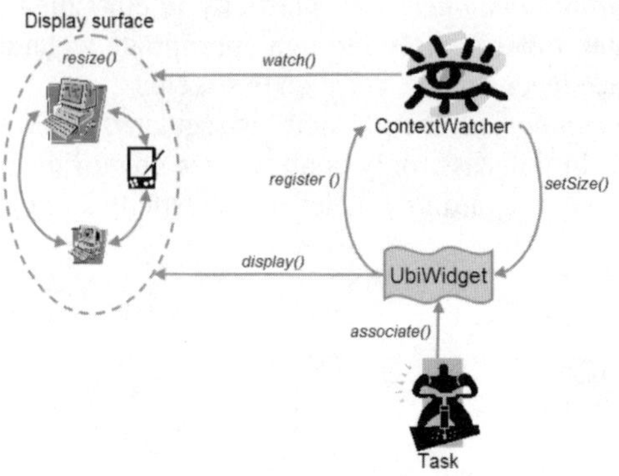

Fig. 7. The run-time mechanism of UbiWidget

Each drawing task of each group is assigned to a UbiWidget, which registers itself to the contextWatcher (Fig. 7) that assigns an initial size. Depending on that status, the UbiWidget displays itself or not. If the context changes, that is if the size of the main application window changes, the contxtWatcher, watching this display surface, is notified and, after calculation, sets a new status and size for each UbiWidget. Ubidraw is composed of a set of components, each assuming a set of functionalities of the application. Fig. 6 shows a general framework identifying several steps for run-time plasticity as it is implemented in UbiDraw. These steps are:

1. **Situation recognition** involves sensing the context, detecting context change and identify context change. In the case of UbiDraw window resize listener triggers the computation of a reaction;
2. **Computation of a reaction** consists in the following: identify candidate reaction, select candidate reactions. UbiDraw has one possible reaction i.e. recalculate layout, its calculation mechanism is explained below
3. **Execute reaction** consists of three steps: prepare the reaction, execute and close the reaction.

UbiDraw applies instantaneously a reaction result. Adaptation with UbiDraw always results from a user initiative (either he/she resizes a window or uses a different platform). Consequently, no particular precaution has to be taken to execute a reaction and there is no need to incorporate an initiative step since it the adaptive UI always triggers adaptivity after a significant change of context occurs. For this purpose, UbiDraw contains a watch method whose main algorithm is explained in pseudo-code below.

```
meth watch()
   Sx={QTk.wInfo width(@canvashandle)}
   Sy={QTk.wInfo height(@canvashandle)}

   % LeftSize provides information on space available
   LeftSizeX={NewCell Sx}
   LeftSizeY={NewCell Sy}

   % ScrollX determines where to locate UbiWidgets
   ScrollX={NewCell 0}

   % StatusList specifies if a UbiWidget should be displayed
   StatusList = {List.make {List.length @ubiwidgets $} $}

   in

   % UbiWidgets are sorted according to their rank of importance
   rankedubiwidgets <- {List.sort @ubiwidgets
                         fun{$ O1 O2}
                            if O1.rank > O2.rank
                            then
                                 false
                            else
                                 true
                            end
                         end}
    % First selection of UbiWidgets to be displayed
   {List.forAllInd @rankedubiwidgets
    proc{$ I UW}

    % If the available size is smaller than the minimal size of
    % the UbiWiget, the nit will be undisplayed. If not, it
    % will be displayed.
    if {Access LeftSizeX $}<{UW getMinSizeX($)}
       then
       % UbiWidget will be undisplayed (hidden)
         {UW hide()}
         {List.nth StatusList I $}='Hide'
       else
       % UbiWidget will be displayed and its minimal size will
       % be removed from pool of available space
         {Assign LeftSizeX {Access LeftSizeX $}
          -{UW getMinSizeX($)}}
         {List.nth StatusList I $}='Show'
       end
    end}

   % Now, we know which UbiWidgets will be displayed. The
   % remaining available space is then shared among them.
   % For this purpose, all UbiWidgets coordinates are computed
   % via the Scroll function and the allocated space is then
   % passed to them.
   {List.forAllInd @rankedubiwidgets
```

```
proc{$ I UW}
  if {List.nth StatusList I $}=='Show'
      then
        % Only the maximum size should be allocated to UbiWidg.
        if {Access LeftSizeX $}<{UW getMaxSizeX($)}
            -{UW getMinSizeX($)}
        then
        % If the space allocated is less than the UbiWidget
        % maximum size, this means that it benefits from
        % remaining available space thanks to the priority
          {UW setCoords({Access ScrollX $} 0)}
          {Assign ScrollX {Access ScrollX $}
           +{UW getMinSizeX($)}+{Access LeftSizeX $}}
          {Assign LeftSizeX 0}
        else
          {UW setCoords({Access ScrollX $} 0)}
          {Assign LeftSizeX {Access LeftSizeX $}
           -({UW getMaxSizeX($)}-{UW getMinSizeX($)})}
          {Assign ScrollX {Access ScrollX $}
           +{UW getMaxSizeX($)}}
        end
    end
  end}
end
```

3.3 The ContextWatcher

The ContextWatcher is equipped with a method called watch which observers any change in the drawing canvas size and applies the appropriate presentation. In order to compute the most appropriate trasformation the ContextWatcher needs three information from every UbiWidgets registered to it: its minimal size, its maximal size, the ranking of the task it supports. The ranking establishes a priority mechanism. The ContextWatcher sorts the UbiWidgets according to their ranking level and, consequently, the widget with the highest ranking will be rendered first. The placement algorithm will always try to place a maximal number of widgets onto the canvas. Consequently UbiWidget minimal sizes are firstly taken into account. If, considering all minimal sizes, all widgets can not be rendered, the space left by unrendered widgets is distributed, on a first rank first serve, among remaining widgets.

The ContextWatcher communicates to each UbiWidget its actual size, and location onto the canvas. UbiWidget can now draw itself. Some tasks are considered as indispensable to the application. In this case, their ranking can be set to 0. Consequently the widgets that support them will be rendered whatever the available size, even if this size in lower than the min size of the widget. Furthermore the registration mechanism allows widgets to register or unregister dynamically. That is to say that from the moment that a widget provides its minimal size, maximal size and the ranking of the task it supports, it can be integrated into the current UI at run-time. The ContextWatcher communicates their position and size constraints to UbiWidgets. Considering this, UbiWidgets have the faculty to choose between different states. The show method assumes the selection of the appropriate presentation.

Table 1 shows different UbiWidget size allocations over time: in the first three rows, 3 UbiWidgets are being allocated a minimum size, a maximum size, and a rank. If the screen resolution is increased to, say, 55 pixels, then the next three rows show the new mimimum size, the increment, and the final allocated size. The last three rows show the same when the screen resolution has been increased of 90 pixels.

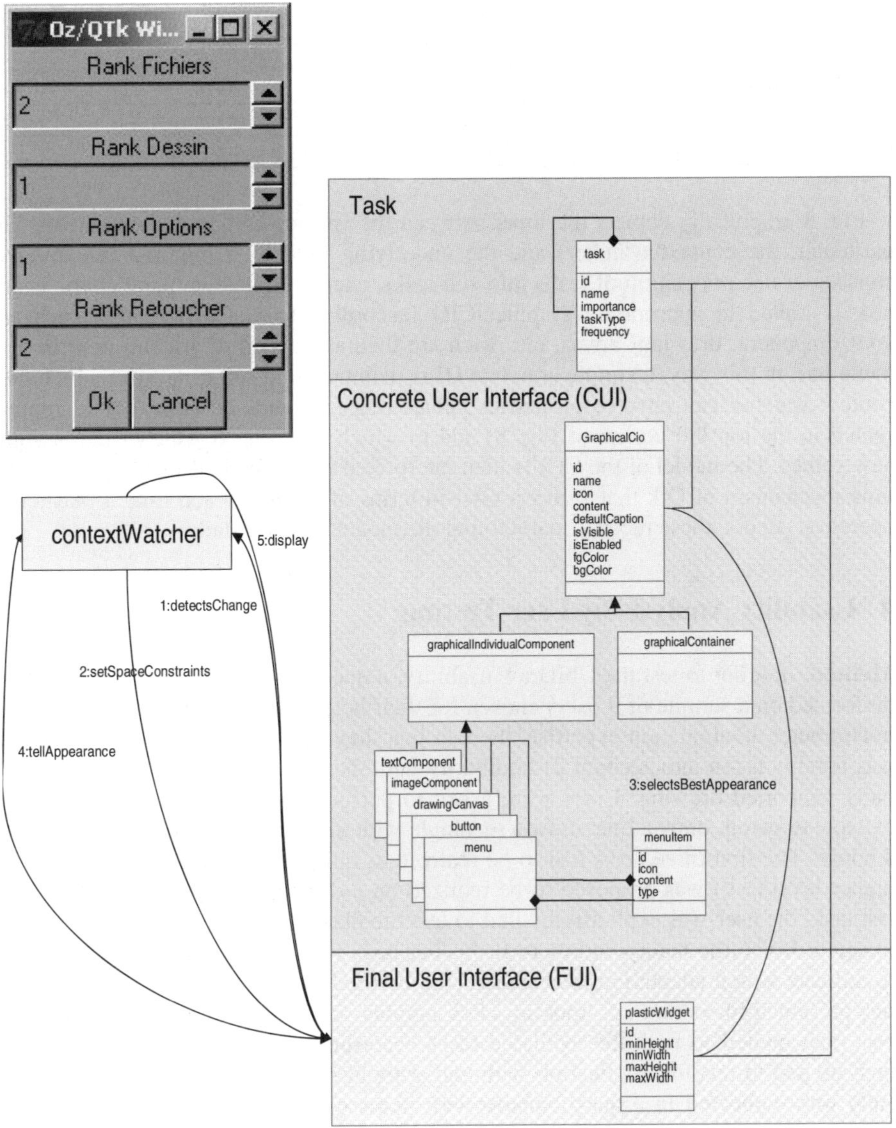

Fig. 8. Links between the context watcher and the underlying models

Table 1. Example of UbiWidget size allocations

	UbiWidget1	UbiWidget2	UbiWidget 3
Minimum size	20	30	10
Maximum size	40	60	20
Rank	1	2	2
Minimum size	20	30	10
Increment	5	0	0
Allocated size	20 + 5 = 25	30	/
Minimum size	20	30	10
Increment	40	60	20
Allocated size	20 + 20 = 40	30 + 10 = 40	10

Fig. 8 graphically depicts the links between the various UbiDraw components (in particular, the context watcher) and the underlying models: a minimal task model consists of decomposition of tasks into sub-tasks, each with its own parameters; each task is linked to appropriate graphicalCIO (according to UsiXML name) such as textComponent, drawingCanvas, etc. wich are then associated to a menu item in the menu bar. In this way, a simple concrete UI is maintained at run-time from which the context watcher can retrieve properties values (e.g., the rank of each task as represented in the top left corner of Fig. 8) and to which the context watcher can assign new values. The model of the CUI is then interpreted into a final UI thanks to the run-time mechanism of Qtk that stores a GUI in terms of records. Each time a plasticity operation occurs, these records maintaining the models are updated.

4 Usability Analysis by User Testing

Method. In order to test the UbiDraw usability, a questionnaire-based evaluation was performed on a sample of 9 users chosen for their heterogeneous level 1) of expertise in computer manipulation expertise, the fact that they already used an iPaq PocketPC was notably taken into account 2) familiarity with the task at hand that is to say computer supported drawing. Users were asked to perform four different tasks: load an existing drawing, draw a line, draw a rectangle with mid-sized lines and, finally, draw a house. The first three tasks had to be realized as quick as possible. The last task (a higher level task) was proposed to be realized on a desktop-based platform. For this last task, the user was explicitly invited to test the plasticity of the application, that is to say to resize the main window to fit his/her task. Furthermore, the user was asked to indicate which adaptation mechanism s/he favored. These choices refer to heuristics presented in section i.e., ranking click number, click number Ranking. The user was then invited to rank the available tasks according to his preferences. S/he was then invited to test the application with and without his customized ranking. The results were collected in a questionnaire with items represented according to 7-point Likert scale. Items were 7-point graphic scales, anchored at the end points with the terms "Strongly agree" for 1, "Strongly disagree" for 7, and a "Not applicable" (N/A) point outside the scale. Some space was left at the end of the questionnaires for positive and negative aspects, and for further comments.

Results and discussion. From the adaptation perspective it seems that most of the users preferred the 'task ranking' heuristic to the 'number of clicks' heuristic. This choice was mainly made by experienced users. This may be explained by the fact that experienced users knew a priori which tasks where more important for them in a drawing application whether inexperienced users wanted to feel the system adapt while using the software. It is also very interesting to note that there was no real consensus between users on the ranking of tasks. This provides us with an unexpected argument foe the need of adaptation mechanisms. Finally, most of the users found that the adaptation mechanism did not disturb them at all in the realization of tasks. Table 2 shows the results collected from this user testing: all participants were able to complete each task in a reasonable amount of time (the last task being of course the longest) and a moderate error rate. Table 3 reports on the final preference for the groups of items. Table 4 gives the average score for each item found in the questionnaire (UbiDraw is easy to use, UbiDraw is more handy than a piece of paper, UbiDraw benefits from a useful context-sensitive help, UbiDraw provides a clear feedback for available functions, UbiDraw enables me to draw what I want, UbiDraw is flexible to use and its adaptation does not disturb task completion, UbiDraw is pleasant to use).

Table 2. Results collected from the user testing

Task	Task completion rate	Speed	Error rate
1	100 %	12 s	0,1
2	100 %	19 s	0,7
3	100 %	18 s	0,7
4	100 %	232 s	1,4

Table 3. Participants' preference for groups of icons

	File	Draw	Options	Retouch
Rank in first configuration	1	2	3	4
Rank in second configuration	2	1	1	2

Table 4. Results from the questionnaire

Item	1	2	3	4	5	6	7
Average	6	4	6	5	5	6	6

5 Conclusion

In this paper, a drawing application called UbiDraw has been presented that benefit from some original properties:

- *A unique form of plasticity*: a mechanism for UI plasticity of both the presentation and the dialogue levels was implemented in order to maximize the observability [12] of UI widgets throughout task completion.

- *A task-driven mechanism*: the display of the four tool boxes is influenced by the respective task frequencies or ranking of these tasks by the user, thus providing some support to plasticity at the task level rather than at the interface level.
- *An instantiation of the general software architecture for plasticity* as introduced in [4]: thanks to the UbiWidget, the UbiMenu, and the ContextWatcher, the plasticity mechanism is supported in a way that leaves room for further inclusion of other functions and tool boxes without affecting the whole architecture. Again, the general software architecture [4] has been proved applicable to an unreached level of flexibility.
- *A distribution of responsibilities*: it is interesting to notice that the control of screen real estate is not concentrated into one single place: rather than having each widget with total local control or totally governed by a higher level controller, the control of screen space in UbiDraw is distributed between the ContextWatcher level, which is responsible for assigning a location and a portion of the screen to a UbiWidget, and the UbiWidget itself, which is responsible for finding out the most usable presentation among the set of alternatives maintained at the widget level. The algorithm used for that has been briefly outlined.
- *A reasonable usability*: although a preliminary user testing conducted to assess the plasticity of UbiDraw revealed that UbiDraw was rather positively adopted by both novice and expert users, it is important to proceed with more empirical studies. Adaptive UIs are well known to induce some sort confusion in the behavior of the end user, whatever the type of adaptation. Indeed, as soon as there is some automatic change in the UI without the prior demand or consent of the end user, some sort of perturbation may arise. We are not aware of any empirical study that proves the positive impact of plasticity on usability, but there are several studies [10,25,29] that prove that for UI adaptivity. Therefore, we reasonable believe that, since plasticity could be considered as a particular case of UI adaptivity, the observation may apply as well to plasticity. Jameson *et al.* [18] argues for the need of empirical basis for adaptation in general and provides a framework for this purpose. Right now, different usability criteria may be considered in evaluating task-driven plastic UIs like the one implemented in UbiDraw to analyse the perturbation type that may be induced by plasticity. For instance, SUPPLE++ demonstrated that it is possible to automatically generate graphical UIs that positively affect predictability and accuracy [10] for general users or motor-impaired [11]. Since today there is no consensus on how to assess the adaptation in general [18,25], we do not know exactly what metric to use for assessing the plasticity, although it has been recognized that it should be a multi-criteria approach.
- *Consistency*: each UI change resulting from changing the context of use (here, the screen resolution changes) should be uniformly applied and perceived as such by the end user. This may turn out hard to achieve as small close changes of window sizes may be perceived as rather different adaptations of the UI.
- *Continuity*: more general than consistency, each UI change resulting from changing the context of use should preserve the three levels of continuity: perceptual, functional, and cognitive [3,9]. Continuity is also a property that can be significant for adaptation to the context of use, as observed in [9].

These criteria, and perhaps other ones, prove that further investigation is required to fully assess the usability properties of interest that are predefined in the plasticity notion. UbiDraw is on the other hand restricted to a simple context change: window resizing and change of platform. We did not investigate further how other changes of contextual properties may significantly or not affect the UI plasticity.

References

1. Brown, D., Totterdell, P., Norman, M.: Adaptive User Interfaces. Academic Press, London (1990)
2. Brewster, S.: The Design of Sonically-Enhanced Widgets. Interacting with Computers 11(2), 211–235 (1998)
3. Calvary, G., Coutaz, J., Thevenin, D.: A Unifying Reference Framework for the Development of Plastic User Interfaces. In: Nigay, L., Little, M.R. (eds.) EHCI 2001. LNCS, vol. 2254, pp. 173–192. Springer, Heidelberg (2001)
4. Calvary, G., Coutaz, J., Thevenin, D.: Supporting Context Changes for Plastic User Interfaces: A Process and a Mechanism. In: Proc. of Joint Conf. on Human-Computer Interaction IHM-HCI 2001, Lille, September 12-14, 2001, pp. 349–363. Springer, London (2001)
5. Crease, M., Brewster, S., Gray, Ph.: Caring, Sharing Widgets: A Toolkit of Sensitive Widgets. In: Proc. of BCS Conf. on Human-Computer Interaction HCI 2000 "People and computers XIV", Sunderland, September 5-8, 2000, pp. 257–270. Springer, London (2000)
6. Coutaz, J., Balme, L., Alvaro, X., Calvary, G., Demeure, A., Sottet, J.-S.: An MDE-SOA Approach to Support Plastic User Interfaces in Ambient Spaces. In: Stephanidis, C. (ed.) UAHCI 2007 (Part II). LNCS, vol. 4555, pp. 63–72. Springer, Heidelberg (2007)
7. Coutaz, J., Calvary, G.: HCI and Software Engineering: Designing for User Interface Plasticity. In: Sears, A., Jacko, J. (eds.) The Human-Computer Interaction Handbook: Fundamentals, Evolving Technologies, and Emerging Applications. Human Factor and Ergonomics series, pp. 1107–1125. Taylor & Francis CRC Press (2008)
8. Demeure, A., Calvary, G., Coutaz, J., Vanderdonckt, J.: The Comets Inspector: Towards Run Time Plasticity Control based on a Semantic Network. In: Coninx, K., Luyten, K., Schneider, K.A. (eds.) TAMODIA 2006. LNCS, vol. 4385, pp. 324–338. Springer, Heidelberg (2007)
9. Florins, M., Trevisan, D., Vanderdonckt, J.: The Continuity Property in Mixed Reality and Multi-platform Systems: a Comparative Study. In: Proc. of 5th Int. Conf. on Computer-Aided Design of User Interfaces CADUI 2004, Funchal, January 14-16, 2004, pp. 321–332. Kluwer Academics Pub., Dordrecht (2004)
10. Gajos, K., Everitt, K., Tan, D.S., Czerwinsky, M., Weld, D.S.: Predictability and Accuracy in adaptive user interfaces. In: Proc. of ACM Conf. on Human Aspects in Computing Systems CHI 2008, Florence, April 5-10, 2008, pp. 1271–1274. ACM Press, New York (2008)
11. Gajos, K., Wobbrock, J.O., Weld, D.: Improving the performance of motor-impaired users with automatically-generated, ability-based interfaces. In: Proc. of ACM Conf. on Human Aspects in Computing Systems CHI 2008, Florence, April 5-10, 2008, pp. 1257–1266. ACM Press, New York (2008)
12. Gram, Ch., Cockton, G.: Design Principles for Interactive Software. Chapman & Hall Publishers, London (1996)

13. Grolaux, D., Van Roy, P., Vanderdonckt, J.: QTk: A Mixed Model-Based Approach to Designing Executable User Interfaces. In: Nigay, L., Little, M.R. (eds.) EHCI 2001. LNCS, vol. 2254, pp. 109–110. Springer, Heidelberg (2001)
14. Grolaux, D., Van Roy, P., Vanderdonckt, J.: FlexClock, a Plastic Clock Written in Oz with the QTk toolkit. In: Proc. of 1st Int. Workshop on Task Models and Diagrams for user interface design TAMODIA 2002, July 18-19, 2002, pp. 135–142. Academy of Economic Studies of Bucharest, INFOREC Printing House, Bucharest (2002)
15. Grolaux, D., Vanderdonckt, J., Van Roy, P.: Attach me, Detach me, Assemble me like You Work. In: Costabile, M.F., Paternó, F. (eds.) INTERACT 2005. LNCS, vol. 3585, pp. 198–212. Springer, Heidelberg (2005)
16. Hick, W.E.: On the rate of gain of information. Quarterly Journal of Experimental Psychology 4, 11–26 (1952)
17. Jabarin, B., Graham, N.T.C.: Architectures for Widget-Level Plasticity. In: Jorge, J.A., Jardim Nunes, N., Falcão e Cunha, J. (eds.) DSV-IS 2003. LNCS, vol. 2844, pp. 124–138. Springer, Heidelberg (2003)
18. Jameson, A., Grossman-Hutter, B., March, L., Rummer, R.: Creating an empirical basis for adaptation techniques. In: Proc. of ACM Conf. on Intelligent User Interfaces IUI 2000, New Orleans, January 9-12, 2000, pp. 149–156. ACM Press, New York (2000)
19. Montero, F., López-Jaquero, V., Molina, J.P., González, P.: An Approach to Develop User Interfaces with Plasticity. In: Jorge, J.A., Jardim Nunes, N., Falcão e Cunha, J. (eds.) DSV-IS 2003. LNCS, vol. 2844, pp. 420–423. Springer, Heidelberg (2003)
20. Rekimoto, J., Masanori, S.: Augmented Surfaces: A Spatially Continuous Work Space for Hybrid Computing Environments. In: Proc. of ACM Conf. on Human Aspects in Computing Systems CHI 1999, Pittsburgh, May 15-20, 1999, pp. 378–385. ACM Press, NY (1999)
21. Schneider, K.A., Cordy, J.R.: Abstract User Interfaces: A Model and Notation to Support Plasticity in Interactive Systems. In: DSV-IS 2002. LNCS, vol. 2545, pp. 28–48. Springer, Heidelberg (2002)
22. Sendin, M., Lores, J., Montero, F., Lopez, V.: Towards a Framework to develop plastic user interfaces. In: Chittaro, L. (ed.) Mobile HCI 2003. LNCS, vol. 2795, pp. 428–433. Springer, Heidelberg (2003)
23. Sottet, J.-S., Calvary, G., Favre, J.-M., Coutaz, J., Demeure, A., Balme, L.: Towards Model-Driven Engineering of Plastic User Interfaces. In: Bruel, J.-M. (ed.) MoDELS 2005. LNCS, vol. 3844, pp. 191–200. Springer, Heidelberg (2006)
24. Thevenin, D., Coutaz, J.: Plasticity of User Interfaces: Framework and Research Agenda. In: Proc. of IFIP Int. Conf. on Human-Computer Interaction Interact 1999, Edinburgh, September 1999, pp. 110–117. IOS Press, Amsterdam (1999)
25. Tsandilas, T., Schraefel, M.C.: An empirical assessment of adaptation techniques. In: Proc. of ACM Conf. on Human Aspects in Computing Systems CHI 2005, Portland, April 2-7, 2008, pp. 2009–2012. ACM Press, New York (2005)
26. Vanderdonckt, J., Limbourg, Q., Florins, M.: Deriving the Navigational Structure of a User Interface. In: Proc. of 9th IFIP TC 13 Int. Conf. on Human-Computer Interaction INTERACT 2003, Zurich, September 1-5, 2003, pp. 455–462. IOS Press, Amsterdam (2003)
27. Vanderdonckt, J.: A MDA-Compliant Environment for Developing User Interfaces of Information Systems. In: Pastor, Ó., Falcão e Cunha, J. (eds.) CAiSE 2005. LNCS, vol. 3520, pp. 16–31. Springer, Heidelberg (2005)
28. Van Roy, P., Haridi, S.: Concepts. MIT Press, New York (2004)
29. Weibelzahl, S.: Evaluation of adaptive systems. In: Bauer, M., Gmytrasiewicz, P.J., Vassileva, J. (eds.) UM 2001. LNCS (LNAI), vol. 2109, pp. 292–294. Springer, Heidelberg (2001)

The Guilet Dialog Model and Dialog Core for Graphical User Interfaces

Jürgen Rückert and Barbara Paech

Institute of Computer Science, University of Heidelberg, Germany
{rueckert,paech}@uni-heidelberg.de
http://www-swe.informatik.uni-heidelberg.de

Abstract. Model-based approaches to graphical user interfaces (GUIs) achieved poor acceptance of software engineers because the offer models, architectures, components, frameworks and libraries that restrict the flexibility of development too much. We propose a dialog model which enables flexible development with no restrictions on presentation and application layer and without any implementation-technology dependence. The dialog model supports GUI designers and developers in understanding the behavior of the GUI. The dialog model controls the dialog core component. The dialog component relieves GUI developers of re-implementing the coordination of presentation and application layer.

Keywords: Model-based user interfaces. Dialog models. Dialog cores. UI engines.

1   Introduction

Model-based approaches to graphical user interfaces (GUIs) achieved poor acceptance of software engineers because they restrict the flexibility of development too much. They rarely offer models, architectures, components, frameworks and libraries that can fully be adapted to customer needs [11]:

P1. GUI designers are not able to describe the presentation that usability engineers defined (in mock-ups). For instance, the approach does not support the modeling of complex graphical components which would be necessary in order to guarantee the usable GUI.

P2. Software architects are not able to integrate existing application layers and their application services into the GUI. For instance, the approach does not consider the different application service technologies and their corresponding different integration mechanisms.

P3. GUI Developers are not able to transfer a GUI to another platform as the behavior is hidden in the platform-specific implementation parts and hardly changeable. In this case it is hardly possible to re-use components that are responsible for controlling the GUI. For instance, the approach does not allow for a desktop application to be transferred to a PDA application by splitting few large screens into many small screens and does not allow adding a wizard-like behavior to walk through the small screens.

P. Forbrig and F. Paternò (Eds.): HCSE/TAMODIA 2008, LNCS 5247, pp. 197–204, 2008.
© IFIP International Federation for Information Processing 2008

P4. GUI Developers use development tools that are not integrated with the modeling tools of the designers which easily results in implementations that no longer reflect the actual design.

We propose an approach to develop GUIs that puts dialog modeling in the center of design and implementation. The *Guilet Dialog Model* (*GDM*) (1.) allows designers to model the behavior of the GUI graphically (P1, P4) and (2.) allows developers to realize the presentation and application layer using any implementation technologies (P2) by identifying abstract behavioural building blocks (P3), namely the *Guilets*. An optional reusable *Guilet Dialog Core* (*GDC*) component that is controlled by the *GDM* (3.) relieves developers of re-implementing the coordination of presentation and application layer without restricting the GUI architecture too much (P2) and (4.) allows developers to transfer (P3) the GUI between applications of a specific platform (e.g. inside the Java platform between Java Swing, Java Web and Eclipse Rich Client applications).

Section 2 defines major functional and non-functional requirements of dialog core models. Section 3 presents an easy to understand example that shows the graphical notation of the *GDM* (3.1). Afterwards, the modeling elements of the *GDM* are explained (3.2). Section 4 presents first experiences gathered in an in-house and in a commercial project. Section 5 summarizes the article and gives an outlook.

2   Requirements of Dialog Core Models

The major functional requirements for dialog cores models can be retrieved from the articles on GUI architectures like the Model-View-Control pattern, the Presentation-Abstraction-Control pattern [5], the Arch model [10] and OpenQuasar [14]. The requirements focus on the coordination of presentation and application layer: A dialog core should be able (F1) to create and destroy graphical components (like views) and their sub-components (like widgets), (F2) to create and maintain the communication channels with application services, and finally (F3) to process events that are created by users in the presentation layer or by application services in the application layer. Processing events encloses (F3.1) sending events to views and widgets in order to change their status, (F3.2) sending data to views or retrieving data from views, and (F3.3) call application services and interpret the results or exceptions. Usually, the event processing is specific to each event source (e.g. graphical component) and each event type (e.g. click, focus).

The major non-functional requirements for dialog cores models are outlined in Figure 1. We detailed the ISO/IEC 9126 quality categories (at the top) by requirements that we elicited from the literature on model-based UI approaches [8] [1] [13] [15] [3] [12] [16] [6] [9] [17] [2] [4]. These requirements are software requirements but not end-user requirements because dialog core models are artefacts that are used hidden inside the GUI.

The quality attribute set *Functionality* describes in how far the DM implements the demanded functionality (see above). The quality attribute set *Reliability* describes in how far the DM is able to model a certain level of performance under defined conditions for a stated period of time. The quality attribute set *Usability* describes the designer's effort of creating and manipulating the DM. The quality attribute set *Maintainability*

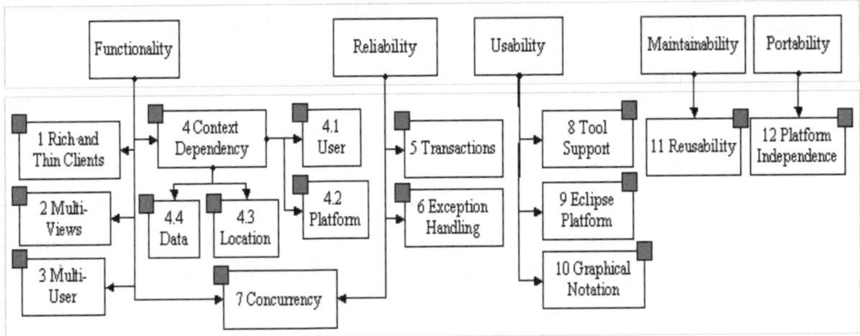

Fig. 1. Non-functional Requirements for Dialog Core Models (gray boxes at the left mark conceptual requirements, gray boxes at the right mark engineering requirements)

describes the effort needed to make necessary changes in the DM. The quality attribute set *Portability* describes the ability of the DM to be transferred from on environment to another.

1. Rich and Thin Clients: The DM should be reusable for stand-alone applications as well as Web applications.
2. Multi-Views: The DM should be able to handle multiple views (e.g. panels), that are visible at the same time and are part of a screen (e.g. a frame or a web page).
3. Multi-User: The DM should be able to model the influence of access rights of users and roles on the GUI behavior.
4. Context Dependency: The DM should be able to model the dependency between page structure, page flow and inserted data, user, computing platform and work environment.
5. Transactions: The DM should support the modeling of two transactions types: transactions during the period of processing multiple events and during processing single events.
6. Exception Handling: The DM should allow modeling expected exceptions during event processing.
7. Concurrency: The DM should support modeling concurrent event processing.
8. Tool Support: The DM should be maintainable with a domain-specific (dialog) modeling tool to shorten design time.
9. Eclipse Platform: The DM should be maintainable on the Eclipse platform because of the high acceptance and usage experience of software developers and the seamless integration of design and implementation.
10. Graphical Notation: The DM should be graphically editable instead of textually (including XML) because this ensures faster understandability.
11. Reusability: The DM should not constrain the usage of implementation technologies for presentation and application layer technologies.
12. Platform Independence: The DM should not contain any presentation and application layer specific information in order to be reusable for a variety of applications in (Web, desktop and mobile) or between platforms (Sun Java, Microsoft .NET).

3   Guilets

3.1   Application Example

In this section we introduce an application example that does not illustrate all of the solution ideas of the *GDM* but instead is easy to understand (transactions are left out e.g.). Figure 2 shows the flow of events between presentation and application layer and the coordination of the flow by the *GDC*. Figure 3 shows a screen shot of the view *Lecture Details* of our in-house application for administrating students and lectures. Figure 4

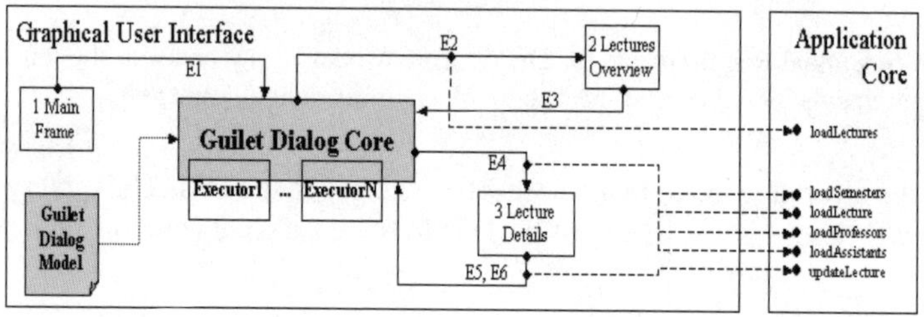

Fig. 2. The *GDC* as central component controlling the behavior of a GUI

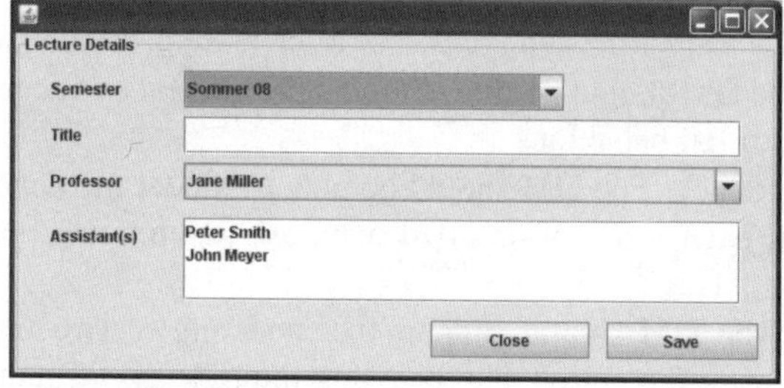

Fig. 3. Screen shot of the view *Lecture Details*

shows the *GDM* of the view *Lecture Details* that describes the view's behavior. The user starts the application (*Main Frame*), retrieves a list of lectures (*Lectures Overview*) and requests the details of a certain lecture by sending event E3 to the *GDC*. The *GDC* reacts on E3 by triggering event E4 (*ShowAndInitialize*). As shown in Figure 4, the *GDC* invokes 4 executors in parallel. 3 executors query lists of business objects from application services and forward the lists into these 3 inner *Guilets* that are able to handle lists of data (e.g. combo boxes or multi line fields). The *LoadLecture* executor reads the variable *LectureId* (circle at the left) that contains the ID of the selected lecture, queries the appropriate lecture data from an application service (a property defines the connection reference) and forwards this data to all 4 inner *Guilets*. The inner *Guilets* are either of type *textfield*, *singleSelection* or *multipleSelection* as the inner *Guilet* type denotes (not shown). The user triggers the update of the modified data by sending event E5 (*Update*) to the *GDC*. The *GDC* invokes the executor *UpdateLecture* that first reads the data of the 4 inner *Guilets*, then calls an application service and finally sends either

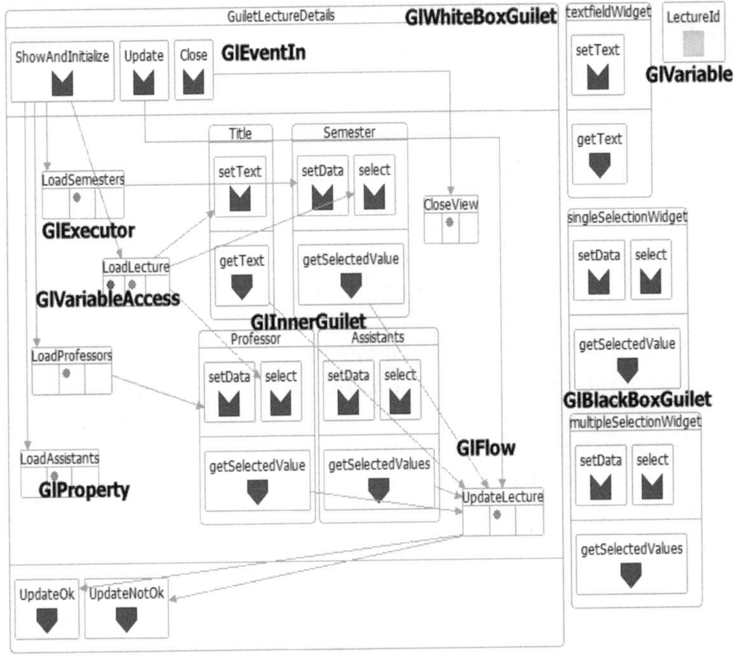

Fig. 4. *GDM* of the view *Lecture Details*

the event *UpdateOk* or *UpdateNotOk* that may be used for refreshing other views that are interested in an update (would be modeled as `GlTransition`). The user closes the view *Lecture Details* by sending event E6 (*Close*) to the *GDC*. The *GDC* invokes the executor *CloseView* that invokes a suitable GUI service.

3.2   Guilet Dialog Model

The *GDM* is based on the major elements `GlWhiteBoxGuilet`, `GlBlackBox-Guilet`, `GlEventIn`, `GlEventOut`, `GlExecutor`, `GlInnerGuilet` and `GlFlow`.

Designers model a `GlWhiteBoxGuilet` whenever they want to model the behavior of a 2d-container like a view, partial view or widget. Widgets are graphical components that receive or provide data and very often allow user input. Partial views are the smallest composition units of logically related widgets, their size is often determined by reuse. Views are a composition of partial views and may contain additional widgets themselves. The hierarchical structure of views needs not to be fixed, the enclosed partial views/widgets and their amount (of recurrence) may depend on the context of usage. The simplest case e.g. is a view that is not shown until a certain data value was inserted/selected in another view. **Designers** model a `GlInnerGuilet` whenever they want to add a view, partial view or widget to a whitebox *Guilet*. An inner *Guilet* enables reuse because it is either of type `GlWhiteBoxGuilet` or `GlBlackBoxGuilet`. It just layouts incoming and outgoing events, but never behavior, in order to avoid redundant information layout. Designers use a `GlBlackBoxGuilet` whenever they want to model a view, partial view or a widget but are not interested in modeling its behavior (of e.g. a complex widget of a fixed graphical library).

Designers model a `GlEventIn` or a `GlEventOut` whenever they want a start- or endpoint for a certain processing logic. They only need to model events when they require a processing logic that needs implementation. They do not need to model events that are processed automatically by the presentation or application layer. For instance, they do not need to model the event *sort rows* if the table widget is already capable of sorting. This decision for the *GDM* was made in order to reduce the amount of modeled elements. Events are created by users or by application cores or by the *GDC*. Typical events are the initialization of a view and the call of semantic functions (e.g. *save data*).

Designers model a `GlExecutor` whenever they require a behavioral component during processing an event. The implemented executors call application services, in order to query data or invoke semantic functions, or they call GUI services in order to change the status of graphical components. **Designers** model a `GlVariableAccess` (referencing a `GlVariable`) whenever they want to store the output of an executor or want to use a stored value as input of an executor. Variables have a scope of validity property.

Designers model a `GlFlow` whenever they want to link an event with an executor or an executor with an event, or an executor with a inner guilet or an inner guilet with an executor. A flow calls several executors always concurrently because sequential executors can be merged into one executor. A flow cannot split into two flows by a condition element because we do not want to overload the model with too much detailed information. The conditional cases have to be implemented in the executor, the documentation property of the executor serves to forward this information from designer to developer. A special case of a flow is a `GlTransition` which is an event-to-event call between two *Guilets*.

Designers add one or more `GlProperty` to any of the modeling elements above whenever they want to enrich the elements with information that they need for processing. Usually, executors use properties for the configuration of application services connections.

4   Experiences

We applied the *GDM* and the *GDC* to develop several desktop applications: (1) an in-house data management application for students and lectures and (2) an application for a pick list creation which is an add-on application for an existing commercial fashion logistic solution. The specifications consist of a task model and a domain data model, virtual windows [7] (task-based mock-ups), system functions and a state chart diagram (page flow). The virtual windows and the state chart diagram are a well-suited starting point to design *Guilets*. The systems were realized as client-server systems. The clients are implemented in Java Swing and include a *GDC* in Java. The *GDC* was reused in both projects. The presentations are loosely coupled with Java Web Services by the *GDC*, more precisely by the executor implementations. The *GDC* is driven by the *GDM* which was modeled using the *GMT*. During these two projects we were able to check the fulfillment of some requirements, as follows. **Functionality:** (+) Multi-views are fully supported. (+) Multi-users can be modeled by using event properties (edited in XML directly). **Reliability** (+) GUI Transactions (useful e.g. for wizards) are supported by tagging the flow elements with transaction IDs (edited in XML directly). (+-) Several exceptions of an executor can be modeled. The reason for an exception cannot be modeled, the reason is only accessible in the executor implementation. (+) The assumption of parallel execution of executors as default is acceptable because sequential executors can be merged into one. **Usability:** (+) The *GDM* definitely should be expressed in a graphical notation and the *GMT* must remain a substantial part of the design because it is very hard to ensure a semantically correct XML using pure text or XML editors. (+-) On the one hand, the *GDM* exempts from too many details because of missing conditional elements. On the other hand, the executor hides the conditional information in its implementation. (-) A graphical modeling support for transaction (e.g. path high-lighting) might be very useful for immediate visualisation of a transaction and its flows. **Maintainability:** (+) The executor elements can be mapped to well maintainable code structures that easily can be understood even weeks later. We expect that executors additionally allow collaborative, parallel implementation by several developers and a transparent tracing of implementation progess. (-) Depending on the level of the modeled presentation details, the *GDM* tends to become very large. We learned that *Guilets* should not be used to model the presentation hierarchy as a whole, but should model instead only these event-sending presentation parts that require an event processing by the *GDM*. (+) The integrated modeling and implementation in Eclipse allowed incremental development of the GUI. (+) *Guilets* made development fast because the hard-to-implement part of coordinating the presentation and application layer is available as the out-of-the-box component *GDC*. (-+) 100% reuse of the modeled elements seems to be rare because usually the properties of same-named *Guilet* sub-elements (e.g. properties of executors) of two *Guilets* differ. Despite, the amount of reuse of executor implementations is high. **Portability:** (+) The blackbox *Guilets* serve as a nice mechanism to model widget libraries and can easily be reused in other *Guilets*.

5   Summary and Outlook

In this article we introduced a design approach to describe the behavior of graphical user interfaces. Designers create a *Guilet Dialog Model* in a graphical notation using the *Guilet Modeling Tool*. Developers apply the *Guilet Dialog Model* as a feed for a reusable *Guilet Dialog Core* component that controls the presentation and application layer using implemented, partially generated *executor components*. In the future, we will, due to encouraging project realizations, continue the evaluation of *Guilets* in order to evaluate the missing requirements in the area of context dependency.

References

1. Barclay, P., Griffiths, T., McKirdy, J., Paton, N., Cooper, R., Kennedy, J.: The Teallach Tool: Using Models for Flexible User Interface Design. In: CADUI, pp. 139–158. Kluwer Academic Publishers, Dordrecht (1999)
2. Brambilla, M., Comai, S., Fraternali, P., Matera, M.: Designing Web Applications with WebML and WebRatio. Springer, Heidelberg (2007)

3. Browne, T., Davila, D., Rugaber, S., Stirewalt, K.: The Mastermind User Interface Generation Project. GVU Technical Report GIT-GVU-96-31, Georgia Institute of Technology (1996)
4. Comai, S., Carughi, G.T.: A behavioral model for rich internet applications. In: ICWE, pp. 364–369 (2007)
5. Coutaz, J.: PAC: An object oriented model for dialog design. In: Bullinger, H.-J., Shakel, B. (eds.) Human-Computer Interaction: INTERACT 1987, pp. 431–436. North-Holland, Amsterdam (1987)
6. ISO. Lotos - a formal description technique based on temporal ordering of observational behaviour (ISO 8807). Technical report, Information Processing Systems - Open Systems Interconnection (1989)
7. Lauesen, S.: User Interface Design. A Software Engineering Perspective. Addison-Wesley, Reading (2004)
8. Lonczewski, F., Schreiber, S.: The FUSE-System: an Integrated User Interface Design Environment. In: CADUI, pp. 37–56 (1996)
9. Martinez-Ruiz, F.J., Arteaga, J.M., Vanderdonckt, J., Gonzalez-Calleros, J.M., Mendoza, R.: A first draft of a model-driven method for designing graphical user interfaces of rich internet applications. In: LA-WEB 2006: Proceedings of the Fourth Latin American Web Congress, pp. 32–38. IEEE Computer Society Press, Washington (2006)
10. Navarre, D., Palanque, P., Dragicevic, P., Bastide, R.: An approach integrating two complementary model-based environments for the construction of multimodal interactive applications. Interact. Comput. 18(5), 910–941 (2006)
11. Paternò, F., Sansone, S.: Model-based Generation of Interactive Digital TV Applications. In: MoDELS 2006, Workshop on Model Driven Development of Advanced User Interfaces. Genova, Italy (2006)
12. Puerta, A.R.: The Mecano Project: Comprehensive and Integrated Support for Model-Based Interface Development. In: CADUI, pp. 19–36 (1996)
13. Rossi, G., Pastor, O., Schwabe, D., Olsina, L.: Web Engineering: Modelling and Implementing Web Applications. Human-Computer Interaction Series, vol. 12, pp. 263–301. Springer, Heidelberg (2008)
14. Siedersleben, J.: Moderne Software-Architektur. Dpunkt (2004)
15. Szekely, P.A., Sukaviriya, P.N., Castells, P., Muthukumarasamy, J., Salcher, E.: Declarative interface models for user interface construction tools: the MASTERMIND approach. In: EHCI, pp. 120–150 (1995)
16. Vanderdonckt, J., et al.: User Interface Extensible Markup Language (UsiXML) 1.8. Université catholique de Louvain (February 2007), http://www.usixml.org
17. Vanderdonckt, J., Grolaux, D., Roy, P.V., Limbourg, Q., Macq, B.M., Michel, B.: A design space for context-sensitive user interfaces. In: IASSE, pp. 207–214 (2005)

An Ontology-Based Adaptation Framework for Multimodal Interactive Systems

Matthias Bezold

Institute of Information Technology, University of Ulm, Germany, and
Elektrobit Automotive GmbH, Erlangen, Germany
`matthias.bezold@uni-ulm.de`

Abstract. One approach for improving the usability of interactive systems is adapting them to user behavior, which can be accomplished by adaptation rules. The advantage of rules is that they are explicit and intuitive, but their expressivity depends on the richness of the underlying data model. In this paper, a framework for the adaptation of interactive systems is presented that relies on a uniform ontology-based information representation, for instance for the system and the user model. Such a description can then be employed by the adaptation rules. By adding semantic information, the scope of the rules is widened. Moreover, special emphasis is put on the dynamic aspects of interactive systems, mainly the interaction of the user with the system and system events. Exemplary rules used in an interactive TV prototype illustrate this framework.

Keywords: Adaptive interactive systems, Knowledge base, Ontology, Interactive systems engineering, Rule-based adaptation.

1 Introduction

User groups of interactive systems become more and more diverse. For instance, home entertainment systems or automotive infotainment systems are operated by old and young, well-educated and uneducated people, who have different capabilities and expectations toward the systems. Therefore, there is a need for approaches to create systems usable by a wide range of different users. Making these systems adaptive to each individual user is a solution that has been a matter of research for many years [1,8]. Adaptive systems observe the user and improve themselves by deriving adaptations from the user's behavior.

There are numerous standards for the definition of interactive systems, such as UIML[1] or XUL[2] for graphical and VoiceXML[3] for speech-based systems, and even more research projects. But not all of them are apt for multimodal systems, which can be controlled by more than one modality at the same time. Statecharts [7], also known from the Unified Modeling Language (UML)[4], offer a sound formalism to describe both

---

[1] User Interface Markup Language (UIML): http://www.uiml.org/

[2] XML User Interface Language (XUL): http://www.mozilla.org/projects/xul/

[3] VoiceXML: http://www.w3.org/TR/voicexml20/

[4] Unified Modeling Language (UML): http://www.uml.org/

P. Forbrig and F. Paternò (Eds.): HCSE/TAMODIA 2008, LNCS 5247, pp. 205–212, 2008.

graphical and speech-based systems. While there are more sophisticated descriptions for instance for speech dialogue systems, such as frame- or agent-based approaches (cf. [9]), these are intended for speech-based systems only and not usable for graphical systems. A statechart model consists of a number of hierarchical states and event-triggered transitions connecting these states. Graphical components, composed of a hierarchy of graphical elements, and speech components, consisting of speech output and grammars for speech input, are attached to states and activated when the respective state is entered. For this work, the statechart-based commercial modeling tool EB GUIDE Studio [5] was extended by an adaptation framework. The tool includes a simulation component, which is used as a dialogue manager.

In order to perform appropriate adaptations in interactive systems, an adaptation framework is required for the development of prototypes and deployed systems. In this work, an adaptation framework is presented that employs rules to define the adaptations. These rules operate on information stored in a knowledge base that describes the system and the user. Special emphasis is put on the dynamic parts of the system, which play a significant role in interactive systems, i.e., the interaction of the user with the system and system events.

This paper is structured as follows. First, Section 2 introduces ontologies and how they are used to create a uniform description of all information relevant for the adaptation. Next, the use of rules on top of the knowledge representation to describe adaptations is discussed in Section 3. Finally, related work is presented in Section 4 and future work is outlined in Section 5.

2   The Semantic Layer

In rule-based adaptive systems, the adaptation rules have to rely on the information provided by the underlying data model. Therefore, the more information is provided by the data model, the more powerful and comprehensive the adaptation rules can be. Moreover, a common representation for all data is needed to make it available to the

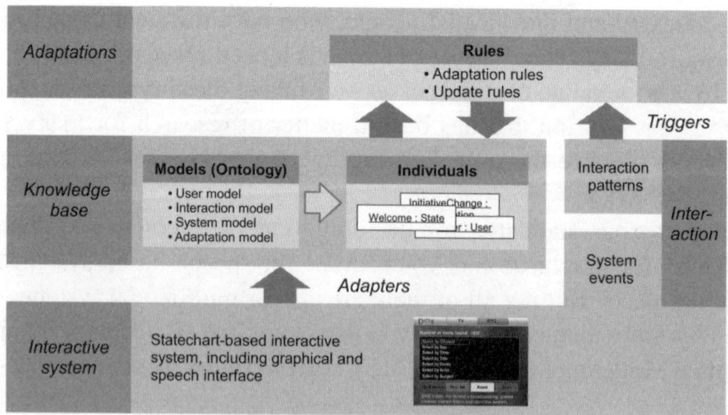

Fig. 1. The architecture of the adaptation framework comprises a knowledge base layer and adaptation rules on top of it. Adaptation rules are triggered by the interaction of the user with the system.

adaptation rules in a uniform way. For this purpose, a semantic layer covering all necessary information was added on top of the interactive system. The different components of the framework architecture shown in Fig. 1 are discussed in the following sections.

Since the information used by the adaptation rules has to be available at runtime of the system, a formalism with extensive instantiation support is required for the knowledge representation. The Web Ontology Language (OWL)[5] provides, in addition to class definition constructs, support for the dynamic instantiation of the models by means of individuals. Hence, OWL is employed in this work by means of the Jena framework[6], a Semantic Web library.

2.1 Ontologies

An ontology is a description of a certain domain, which is expressed as a hierarchy of classes covering all relevant parts of a domain. Classes have a set of properties, which can either be primitive types, such as a string or a number, or references to other individuals. Individuals are stored as so-called triples, which consist of a subject (an individual), a predicate (a property), and an object (a primitive value or another individual). For instance, the name "Welcome" of the state with the ID "State42" is described through the "hasName" property by the following triple:

```
(State42 hasName ''Welcome'')
```

A knowledge base consists of a set of classes and a number of instances of these classes. In the following sections, the different models contributing to the knowledge base are presented and the creation of instances of these models is discussed.

2.2 The Models – System, User, Adaptation, and Interaction Model

As a basis for intuitive and powerful adaptation rules, information about different aspects of the system is required, comprising information about the system, the user and the user's system configuration, the interaction of the user with the system, and information about possible adaptations. Each of these areas is implemented as a model consisting of a set of OWL classes with a number of properties. Most of these classes can be reused for different systems, only application-specific classes, such as annotated information or the interaction, have to be defined for each system.

The *system model* is a technical description of the system, comprising the statechart model and a description of the graphical and speech components. Moreover, to further enhance the scope of the knowledge base, additional semantic information can be annotated to the model. For instance, all elements, e.g. states, buttons, or speech output prompts, have a "type" property that describes their purpose, such as "help".

The *user model* describes the different users of the system. On the one hand, it comprises factual information about the user, such as name or preferences. On the other hand, the user model covers the configuration of the system for the user, e.g. whether certain entities are enabled. Since only the user model can change during the execution of the system, only changes to the user model have to be stored.

---

⁵ Web Ontology Language (OWL): http://www.w3.org/2004/OWL/

⁶ The Jena framework: http://jena.sourceforge.net

The *interaction model* describes the interaction of the user with the system by defining interaction patterns out of low-level system events. These low-level events can be state changes in the statechart model, dialogue manager events, input device events (e.g., remote control or input button), or speech input from the speech recognition system. All events have parameters for additional information, such as the name of the button for input device events, which can be used in the rules.

The interaction patterns are not part of the ontology, but are described by means of a Deterministic Finite Automaton (DFA). Sequences, repetitions, and alternatives combine low-level events or again other patterns into interaction patterns. For instance, a menu entry selection by moving the cursor up and down and pressing the OK button can be described by the pattern "(button up OR button down)* AND button OK", with the "*" denoting a repetition. Context information can be used to refine interaction patterns and to connect them to different parts of the system, e.g. differentiating between selections in different menus of the system.

The *adaptation model* describes the adaptations that can be applied to the system. Adaptations are expressed as rules, which are discussed in the following section.

2.3   Instantiating the Models

In order to use these models at runtime of an interactive system, they have to be populated with instances of the model classes, called individuals. For this purpose, special adapter modules are used to initialize the knowledge base accordingly when the system starts. For instance, the "Statechart Ontology Adapter" creates a knowledge base individual for every state in the system definition and fills the properties accordingly, such as the name, whereas the "User Model Adapter" loads information about the users from the user model.

The dialogue manager consults the knowledge base during the execution of the system. For instance, if a state or a speech output prompt is disabled in the knowledge base, it will be skipped. Therefore, the definitions of the respective elements do not have to be updated and the information needs to be stored only in the knowledge base.

3   Adaptations

This section discusses how adaptations are performed. Adaptation rules can exploit the the information provided by the knowledge base. Contrary to statistical approaches, rules are well-predictable and explicit, which is especially important for graphical systems.

3.1   Adaptation Rules

Rules are used for two different purposes. First, the information in the knowledge base can be inferred from the interaction of the user with the system, e.g. by defining a rule that updates the current state of the dialogue system from (low-level) state change events. Second, adaptations can be performed by rules, e.g. by disabling certain elements of the system. Adaptation rules are connected to entries of the adaptation model in order to make this information part of the knowledge base.

The rules used in this framework consist of three parts. First, the *event* part is used to define a trigger for a rule by connecting the rule to a pattern from the interaction model (e.g. menu selection) or a low-level event (e.g. a state change). If rules have no trigger, they are executed at predefined points, such as system startup or user change. Second, the *condition* part can be used to define additional criteria that have to be fulfilled to execute the body of the rule. Third, the *action* part contains the rule body, usually consisting of knowledge base updates.

Knowledge base updates are composed of two parts, the query part and the update part. Since the Jena rule engine only supports monotonic updates, i.e., does not support modifications of existing triples, and the non-monotonicity is important to allow updates to the user model, a custom rule system is used. The query part of the rule is transformed into a SPARQL[7] query. Parameter values from the event, e.g. the name of the new state for a state change event, are passed to the query as bound variables. The update part is a list of triples that will either be updated in the knowledge base determined by the subject and the predicate, or created if no matching triple exists. Updates can contain functors that perform computations, such as incrementing a value.

The evaluation of rules is carried out within a transaction, performing all updates to the knowledge base only after all triggered rules have been evaluated. This is necessary for consistency reasons. For instance, if rule A updated a value read by rule B, which is evaluated after A, the (implicit) order of execution would be relevant. But making the order explicit would increase the complexity unnecessarily.

3.2 Exemplary Adaptation Rules

Two adaptation rules are shown in this section, updating the knowledge base and performing a simple adaptation respectively. The rules in the actual system use XML as a notation, but for clarity reasons, a simplified notation is used. Variable names start with a "?", properties with a lower case character, and instances with an upper case character. The examples are taken from an adaptive home entertainment model that includes an electronic program guide.

In Fig. 2, an update rule is shown that is triggered when the current state in the statechart model changes. Therefore, a "state change" event trigger is used. In the actions part, a query is defined that retrieves the state element in the knowledge base

```
events: state change: ?name
conditions: none
actions:
    query:
        (?state hasName ?name)
        (?status isAboutEntity ?state)
        (CurrentSession hasUser ?currentUser)
        (?status isAboutUser ?currentUser)
        (?status hasUseCount ?oldUseCount)
    updates:
        (?status hasUseCount addOne(?oldUseCount))
```

Fig. 2. Knowledge base update rule that increments the use counter of a state in the user model

---

[7] SPARQL Query Language: http://www.w3.org/TR/rdf-sparql-query/

```
events: pattern: "UserIsLost"
conditions: none
actions:
    query:
        (CurrentSession hasUser ?currentUser)
        (?element hasType DialogueType_Help)
        (?status isAboutEntity ?element)
        (?status isAboutUser ?currentUser)
    updates:
        (?status isEntityEnabled "true")
```

Fig. 3. An adaptation rule that enables "help" elements (states, speech output prompts, etc.) if a user is lost (defined by the interaction pattern "UserIsLost")

determined by the name of the state ($?name$), selects the current user, her status triple for the state, and the old use count. The "updates" section updates the use count, which is computed from the old value using the "addOne" functor.

A (simplified) adaptation rule is given in Fig. 3. This rule enables help when a user seems to be lost, which is defined by the interaction pattern "UserIsLost", e.g. defined as "random scrolling" (not shown). "Help elements" are defined by annotations to the system model, which are available through the value "DialogueType_Help" of the "hasType" property.

4   Related Work

Ontologies have been used in multimodal systems for other purposes than adapations, such as supporting semantic coherence checking [6] in the SmartKom project or domain reasoning in the dialogue manager [4] in the Talk project. Moreover, ontologies have been used for modeling interactive systems. In [10], an ontology is used in addition to UML in the development process of multimodal interactive systems. The high-level model description is only available at design time to provide development support and for platform mapping, but not at runtime of the system.

Sophisticated adaptation architectures have been presented in the domain of adaptive hypertext systems. A formal definition of an adaptive hypermedia system is presented in [3]. The adaptation component consists of a set of rules expressed as first-order logic statements using a language called TRIPLE. The adaptations rely on a semantic annotation of the document space. Another framework for adaptive systems in presented in [2]. It relies on OWL for describing the system and the domain and the SWRL rule language to express the adaptations. The ODAS domain ontology [11] is used in conjunction with adaptation rules in an adaptive hypertext portal. The authors reason that rules provide a better transparency and controllability for users than statistical adaptation methods. The ontology provides a knowledge foundation for the adaptation rules and contains different models, such as a system model, a task model, and a resource model.

These adaptation architectures have only been applied to hypertext systems, but not to interactive systems in general, which are richer with regard to their interaction possibilities. Hence, this approach is better suited for interactive systems, since interaction patterns and system events can directly be connected to the adaptations rules.

5   Conclusions and Future Work

This work presented a framework for adapting dialogue systems to user behavior that is based on a knowledge base and adaptation rules. The knowledge base, which is defined by a set of OWL models and populated by means of adapter components, covers all aspects that are relevant for the adaptations. The expressivity of adaptation rules benefits from this information. Since the interaction of the user with the system is a vital part of adaptive systems, special emphasis was put on this issue by defining interaction patterns that trigger rules. These interaction patterns are defined out of low-level system events, such as input device or speech input events. Exemplary rules for knowledge base updates and adaptations were given to illustrate the use of this framework.

There are two main directions for future work. First, the description of the user interaction can be improved by adding a task model and connecting it to the interaction model. A task model describes what a user can do with an interactive system on an abstract task level. Thus, the expressivity of adaptation rules can benefit from this additional information. Second, the development of adaptive systems can benefit greatly from defining a list of adaptations and formalizing them as adaptation patterns. Based on existing research on human-computer interaction patterns [12], concrete adaptation patterns can be included in the ontology and connected to the interaction and task models. These patterns can then be added to the model by the system designer or executed automatically.

References

1. Browne, D., Totterdell, P., Norman, M. (eds.): Adaptive User Interfaces. Academic Press Ltd., London (1990)
2. Carmagnola, F., Cena, F., Gena, C., Torre, I.: A Multidimensional Framework for the Representation of Ontologies in Adaptive Hypermedia Systems. In: Bandini, S., Manzoni, S. (eds.) AI*IA 2005. LNCS (LNAI), vol. 3673, pp. 370–380. Springer, Heidelberg (2005)
3. Dolog, P., Henze, N., Nejdl, W., Sintek, M.: Towards the Adaptive Semantic Web. In: Bry, F., Henze, N., Małuszyński, J. (eds.) PPSWR 2003. LNCS, vol. 2901, pp. 51–68. Springer, Heidelberg (2003)
4. Garcia, G.P., de Amores Carredano, J.G., Portillo, P.M., Marin, F.G., Marti, J.G.: Integrating Owl Ontologies With a Dialogue Manager. In: Procesamiento del Lenguaje, pp. 153–160 (2006)
5. Goronzy, S., Mochales, R., Beringer, N.: Developing Speech Dialogs for Multimodal HMIs Using Finite State Machines. In: 9th International Conference on Spoken Language Processing (Interspeech), CD-ROM (2006)
6. Gurevych, I., Porzel, R., Malaka, R.: Modeling Domain Knowledge: Know-How and Know-What. In: Wahlster, W. (ed.) SmartKom - Foundations of Multimodal Dialogue Systems, pp. 71–84. Springer, Heidelberg (2006)
7. Harel, D.: Statecharts: A Visual Formalism for Complex Systems. Sci. Comput. Program. 8(3), 231–274 (1987)
8. Jameson, A.: Adaptive Interfaces and Agents. In: Human-computer Interaction Handbook, 1st edn., pp. 305–330. Erlbaum, Mahwah (2003)
9. McTear, M.F.: Spoken Dialogue Technology: Towards the Conversational User Interface. Springer, London (2004)

10. Obrenovic, Z., Starcevic, D., Devedzic, V.: Using Ontologies in Design of Multimodal User Interfaces. In: Rauterberg, M., Menozzi, M., Wesson, J. (eds.) INTERACT 2003. IOS Press, Amsterdam (2003)
11. Tran, T., Cimiano, P., Ankolekar, A.: A Rule-Based Adaption Model for Ontology-Based Personalization. In: Wallace, M., Angelides, M.C., Mylonas, P. (eds.) Advances in Semantic Media Adaptation and Personalization. Studies in Computational Intelligence, vol. 93, pp. 117–135. Springer, Heidelberg (2008)
12. van Welie, M., van der Veer, G.C.: Pattern Languages in Interaction Design. In: Rauterberg, M., Menozzi, M., Wesson, J. (eds.) INTERACT 2003. IOS Press, Amsterdam (2003)

Some Thoughts about the Horizontal Development of Software Engineers

Anke Dittmar and Peter Forbrig

Rostock University, 18055 Rostock, Germany
`{anke.dittmar,peter.forbrig}@uni-rostock.de`

Abstract. We argue that current patterns of thought and action in software engineering and in HCI will simply be reproduced if we are not able to become more aware of their impact on our own behaviour, attitudes and values. We suggest that a more balanced and intertwined vertical and horizontal development of people can contribute to human-centred design processes. The case study presented describes a modest attempt to demonstrate this with future software engineers and managers. Though not a spectacular example, it shows a small tight network of activities and roles over time with feedback loops to facilitate deep reflection, mutual awareness and respect. The paper supports the idea of design as an ongoing intervention process beyond problem setting and problem solving.

1   Introduction

Diaper points out in [1] that "HCI is most closely related to the computing field of software engineering" and that "no distinction should ever have been made between software engineering and HCI because both are engineering disciplines concerned with the same types of systems and their difference is merely one of emphasis, with software engineering focusing more on software and HCI more on people." However, "integration of software engineering and user-centred design" is the first topic mentioned in the call for papers of this conference. Obviously, there is still a gap between the two approaches. The title HCSE even goes a step further by suggesting not to focus on *users* of technology but on *humans*.

Why is software engineering not inherently human-centred? One explanation is that there is always a lag between the invention of new technologies and the learning of how to use them in a 'reasonable' way. This is also reflected in HCI. According to Cockton, its focus has expanded from being largely system-centred up to the 1970s, then user-centred in the 1980s, context-centred in the 1990s, and now, having a value-centred focus [2]. Appropriate design approaches have been developed since then to improve the design of interactive systems (task-based design, participatory design, design rationale, reflective design, end user development,...). On the other hand, the engineering side of system development is often underestimated today (as stated e.g. in [3]). While ten or twenty years ago users and other stakeholders were often seen as not able to contribute to the design process (and this view might still prevail in software engineering) the HCI field tends to consider now interaction programmers as

P. Forbrig and F. Paternò (Eds.): HCSE/TAMODIA 2008, LNCS 5247, pp. 213–220, 2008.

mere executors of other people's ideas. Maybe this is a kind of counter effect. However, it also shows how difficult it is to really accept contributions from different fields and different people. It is one thing to understand the rationale behind a new approach. It is another thing to internalize those ideas and to bring them into balance with existing habits of thought and action. To give another example, we still struggle to find a balance between so-called formal, semi-formal, and informal approaches and representations, and we are often not even aware that they can share similar assumptions which, perhaps, should be questioned first.

What does it mean to do human-centred software engineering, or maybe value-centred design or sustainable design? Why, for example, does Thimbleby give at the beginning of his book about principles of interaction programming [3] explanations about interests behind short production cycles, about toxic waste, time pressure on programmers and its consequences? Blevis states in [4] that the material effects of current practices of designing and using interactive systems do not reflect a sustainable lifestyle. He proposes several design principles to increase our understanding of the environmental impact of interaction design. However, he also suggests "that faith in technology as usual cannot succeed, and that new thinking is critical to our survival." All this is not new. Einstein is frequently cited (e.g. in [5]): "The world we have created is a product of our thinking, it cannot be changed without changing our thinking".

In this paper, we briefly describe a series of tutorials in requirements engineering with graduate students of software engineering and business informatics (Sec. 2). We will refer to it as a case study though it was not planned as such. However, its specific conditions and its evolution triggered the reflective analysis, and the suggestions for learning practices, which are presented in Sec. 3. We argue that it is not enough to reflect on external products of design activities. Current patterns of thought and action will simply be reproduced if we are not able to become more aware of the impact of actual practices on our own behaviour, on our attitudes and values. We suggest that deep reflection and a more balanced and intertwined vertical and horizontal development of people can contribute to more effective human-centred design processes. Though we do not ground this work in a sound qualitative methodology but rather remain on a descriptive level we think that our reflective analysis can contribute to a more sustainable software engineering culture in which design is understood as an ongoing intervention process beyond problem setting and solving.

2 Case Study

The case study is about tutorials supplementing the requirements engineering lectures (RE) at Rostock in summer 2007. Participants were 15 graduate students of software engineering and business informatics. They were familiar with programming, formal specifications and with software engineering methods. They also had done an internship. The focus of such tutorials is on the early stage in a user-centred design process. Their nature is partly shaped by the following constraints. The participation is optional. The main interest of most students is neither in RE nor in HCI. Even in their industrial training, many had no experience of any deep requirements analysis. Students get no marks or points and their participation is not a prerequisite for other courses or examinations. Hence, the focus of a tutorial is more on the activities in the 11-12 weekly meetings (each about 90 minutes) and less on the production of precise specification documents (though documents are produced). We do not insist on training in particular methods by using specific, independent examples. Instead, a single 'problem' is used throughout the semester. Some of the methods and techniques which were introduced in lectures are chosen to approach the problem. They are mostly applied in a sketchy way. In addition, the meetings are used to reflect personal activities, to see improvements and alternative approaches, and to discuss pros and cons of the artifacts in use.

The reported case study was about analysing the software engineering course (SE) for second-year students at our department in order to find out how to better support student projects. Both authors are involved in the SE course as well. We could ask our colleagues and students to 'act' as participants. We also chose this topic because of the obviously different, and partly conflicting, views of the stakeholders. The following description is based on material created during the tutorials and on the notes of the tutor. Sometimes the first person is used to emphasize that it is the perspective of the tutor (one author).

First Meeting
The students were asked to work in groups and develop initial ideas of how to tackle the analysis. Most participants started by reflecting their own past experiences with the SE course. Some students discussed, for example, whether the goal of a project is to learn about object-oriented software development or to work in a team. One of them said: *I am sure, if you went to one of the teachers right now to ask them about the goals of these projects they would make up a story.* The whole group agreed on conducting semi-structured interviews with the teaching staff involved and with second-year students. Two students were asked to prepare a test interview with the tutor (who also was SE tutor). Eleven students were asked to make appointments with the teachers.

Interviews
The test interview in the second meeting might have helped to make sense of the grading scheme or to understand better the work of tutors. However, it was also obvious that the questions had to be revised to get more insights. The revised list guided the interviews of the other four tutors and the lecturer. Generally, all interviews were recorded. They were transcribed (with differences in detail). We used Stud.IP (a learning management system with wiki support at our university) to store and access audio files and all other documents. In the third meeting, we listened to a 40-minute interview with one of the tutors. In the subsequent meetings only transcriptions were used. We did not perform a thorough analysis. Instead, we rather used the interviews for a kind of 'informed dialogue' between ourselves about the SE course and about project work in particular.

The tutors were asked to help us contacting one or two of their project groups. In another meeting we divided into three groups to prepare a list of questions for students. One group wrote down 'ad hoc' questions. Another group was asked to develop a simple task model from the student's perspective before writing down their questions. The third group created a list of artifacts used in the SE course and developed questions on this basis. Then, all questions were gathered, selected, and grouped.

Finally, four interviews with at least three students of a group (and two interviewers) were conducted. In one case, the whole group was present. The interviews took from 40 to 70 minutes. At that time, I suggested that we should try to organize a 'workshop' at the end of the RE course.

Brainstorming
The following list shows an extract from suggested improvements at the 'brainstorming session' in the 7th meeting. Based on this list, we planned the last four meetings. The group decided to invite teachers but not students for a final workshop "SE 2.0". All invited people were present.

1. Registration: choice of project topic, group formation,
2. More relations between documents of a project,
3. Management tool for teaching staff,
4. Announcement of the SE course, e.g. invitation of the first-year students to the final project presentations,
5. More milestones in the second phase of the project (summer semester),
6. More exchange between project groups, e.g. mutual testing, code reviewing...

Specifying Requirements
In the 8th meeting, we began to explicitly describe requirements. We used different techniques such as use cases and paper prototypes. Prepared material facilitated the meetings. For example, an entity-relationship diagram encouraged consideration of flexible graduation schemes, and helped to find requirements on a management system for tutors. Fig. 1 shows the revised version of the "rough QOC" developed during the discussion about future registration practices for student projects.

3   A Reflective Analysis

Development is often understood as 'vertical' improvement of individuals though supported by social interaction and collaboration [6]. However, vertical development also needs a horizontal movement across social worlds. The T-model (e.g. [7]) is well-known but not necessarily practised in education. The | can stand for the vertical and the ⁻ for the horizontal development. Engeström mentions 'contact zones' as places where people and ideas from different cultures meet, collide and merge. "It is this inability to ever understand another world that has great developmental significance" [6]. Participatory design supports this idea. Authors like Schön initiated a transformation of design by promoting a "reflective practice" with argumentation processes and an intertwined goal shaping and problem solving [8].

Sec. 2 may have already shown that the way we organize the tutorials is rooted in these ideas. They can be seen as complementing 'classrooms' and project work. Students are neither evaluated nor forced to create a 'visible product'. The idea is to support a horizontal development but with a 'starting point' which is familiar to the participants (requirements engineering is part of software development). There are few pre-defined roles and goals. There is no pre-established agenda. The idea is to create a continuous conversation about current and envisioned practices in a certain

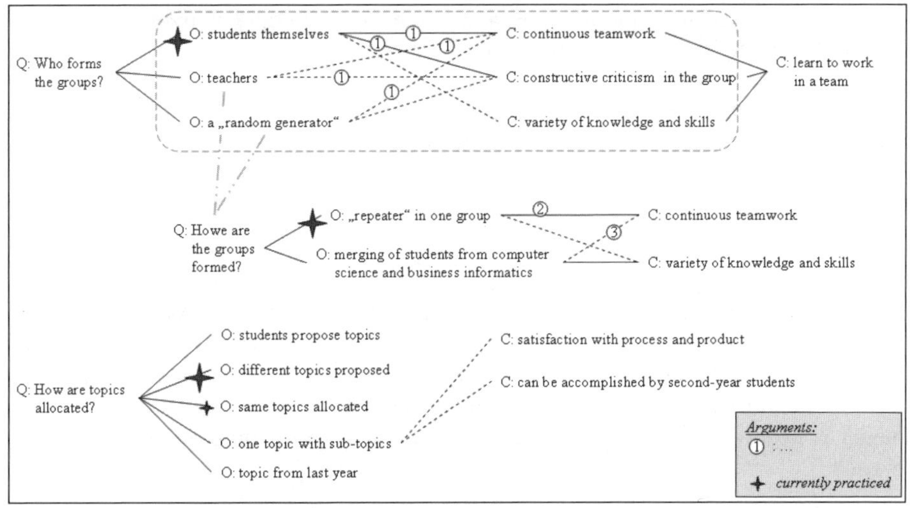

Fig. 1. QOC diagram (8th meeting)

working system. A conversation which is guided by early design techniques, most of them well-known or even developed in the HCI field. The focus is on a continuous experience and less on the creation of 'perfect' artifacts. Mistakes are allowed. It is also allowed to use suggested techniques in a sketchy way. Perhaps this facilitates a combination of child-like playfulness and adult-like rationality as recommended in [9].

The case study might be used to illustrate several points. For example, none of the students was trained in conducting interviews. Of course, we made mistakes. The first tutor showed some surprise when students started to record the interview. We never forgot again to ask and to emphasize that we don't want to 'test' the interviewees. Suggestive questions were asked. One interviewer asked a tutor: *Do you REALLY read the documents of student's project?* What can he answer? As mentioned, interviews were not thoroughly analyzed. However, it is possible to hand out and discuss a description like the following (it only takes five minutes). "The interviews were recorded and transcribed. Analysis included open coding for thematic analysis, selective coding and constant comparison between analysis products and raw data...". Students can recognise themselves in the description but also see that much more knowledge, experience, and work(!) is required. Perhaps, this helps to create a deeper understanding of other stakeholder's activities, an appreciation of diverse viewpoints, and mutual respect.

In the specific study described in Sec. 2, the authors were responsible for the RE course. Participants were graduate students in software engineering and business informatics. They analysed a basic course in software engineering with activities of second-year students, the authors, and other tutors. Most of them attended this basic course some semesters ago. Hence, students were teachers and teachers were learners in a way. Who were the users and who the developers, who the observers and who the observed? As it turned out, a 'frame' was set up which was convenient to support.

- Multiple, sometimes blurred roles and actions with multiple motives,
- Intertwined vertical and horizontal development,
- Deep reflection,
- Mutual respect and shared understanding,
- The idea of design as ongoing intervention.

Vertical and Horizontal Development
SE projects are basically guided by the waterfall system life cycle. In a way, the older students 'observed' their own activity of two or three years ago but now through the lenses of their increased knowledge and skills in software engineering. Some of the suggested early design techniques are not yet applied in the 'real world' of software development. They require an understanding and skills which are often not conveyed in 'traditional' software engineering. The case study might be a modest example of an intertwined vertical and horizontal development. The $^{—}$ in the above mentioned T-model is deeply related to the $|$ and yet different ways of thinking and acting are needed.

Deep Reflection
In [10], ongoing and off-loop reflection is required for a professional participatory design process. Off-loop reflection is seen as an opportunity to reify and discuss past experiences, and to establish a firm link to possible future practices. As already described, both forms of reflections were evoked. Two small examples from the 8th meeting about new registration practices for projects may serve for illustration. One group of participants applied use cases [11], the other used the concept of "rough QOC" [12]. Then, we looked at the notes of both groups to compose a proposal. The 'nature' of the approaches literally emerged. The use case with its focus on action sequences looked like a 'first-best solution' in comparison with the QOC diagram. Though the three questions in Fig. 1 seem to be trivial they don't have simple answers, let alone a best one. However, look at Fig. 1 again to understand the following situation in the QOC discussion (written from the tutor's perspective who 'served' as QOC scribe to record the discussion): *One student said that there are fewer conflicts and more continuous work if students can form their own groups. They know each other, their skills and so on. So, I drew a solid line between the appropriate option and the criterion. Then, another student said that he is not sure about that argument. It could also be a handicap to be friends and work in a team. I changed to a pencil and drew a dashed line between the same option and the same criterion. After two more arguments I drew a big question mark over this part of the paper. A student asked: Are we allowed to do it?! I said: Of course. This is a sheet of paper and we write and draw what we want to. This led us to a 10 minutes 'philosophical' talk about modeling, programming, the need for intertwining different activities in software design and so on. One student described, for example, some of his problems with modeling. There is a term for that: premature commitment to structure.* This situation may reveal much about how we teach and live with cognitive artifacts like methods. Is it allowed to draw a circle in a diagram which normally consists of rectangles and arrows? Or, is it allowed to perform step 4 of a method before step 2? And doing this without rejecting the whole method? It looks like a paradox. On the one hand, there is often rejection of methods or rules, on the other hand, a kind of faith in them.

Mutual Respect and Shared Understanding

We think one reason why the students became engaged in the analysis was that they were not detached observers. For example, the interviews were sometimes more like an exchange of experience and knowledge. One interviewer explained to a group who didn't use a version management system what it is good for. Of course, the participants were more experienced and had better understanding than the second-year students. However, they were still students and saw us as teaching staff though in a more relaxed way. We think there was much potential in this tension. The group started to see their own assumptions and was sometimes a kind of mediator. This might be illustrated by the following interview situation: *The students started to complain about a tutor (not theirs). The interviewer said he notices it but it has no consequences for anyone. The students said that they would like to let us know about it. The interviewer said: "Okay, this analysis is about improving the SE course. And teachers who are not committed will be chained to the wall and whipped. You are all invited to come." Laughter and the interview could continue.*

Design as Ongoing Intervention

Even in a "reflective design practice" with an intertwined goal shaping and problem solving the problem is still the main underlying concept - whether wicked or tame. In contrast, the idea of design as an ongoing process of a double intervention "in the Earth's cycles and processes, and simultaneously in the human culture of needs and techniques" [13] may be better supported by Bohm's idea of embedding problem solving into *awareness of paradoxes*. What is called for in the case of a paradox is not some procedure that solves the problem. Rather, it is to pause and to give attention to it in order "to bring the root of the paradox into awareness" [14]. Bohm suggests that the treatment of paradoxes as problems and the attempt to solve them does not contribute to their dissolving but results in "ever-increasing confusion". In the case study presented there are paradoxes between education and practice, between the desire of students to get good (individual) marks and yet to learn teamwork, between methods and actual situations... Take note that the brainstorming session was in the second half of the tutorial. We think that the relatively long first phase was an important experience for the participants. It helped to suspend activities of problem solving and to become aware of paradoxes. Perhaps this resulted in more 'modest' suggestions for changes at the workshop. Some of them are considered in the actual SE course, some of them were the basis for actual SE project topics.

4 Summary

"[T]hrough centuries of habit and conditioning, our prevailing tendency is now to suppose that 'basically we ourselves are all right' and that our difficulties generally have outward causes, which can be treated as problems" [14]. The paper is not about another method 'to bridge the gap' between SE and HCI. It looks instead for ways to facilitate a cooperative internalisation of non-familiar ideas and perspectives in order to question and change one's own practices. The case study presented describes a modest attempt to demonstrate this with future software engineers and managers. Though not a spectacular study it is a small example of a relatively tight network of activities and roles over time with feedback loops supporting deep reflection, mutual

awareness and respect (including self-awareness and self-respect). We are not able to validate our suggestions but we would like to encourage others to look for 'seeds' for adaptations in their own (design) attitudes and activities. Human-centred software engineering has to be treated as paradox, not as problem. There are no answers in terms of solutions (or methods). Design concepts and methods like those mentioned in this paper are artifacts that can guide this process. However, they cannot free humans from the need to be aware of the actual situation and the need to adapt it in a sensitive way. This includes the questioning and revision of the very same artifacts.

References

1. Diaper, D.: Understanding Task Analysis for Human-Computer Interaction. In: Diaper, D., Stanton, N.A. (eds.) The handbook of task analysis for human-computer interaction. Lawrence Erlbaum, Mahwah (2004)
2. Cockton, G.: A Development Framework for Value-Centred Design. In: Proc. CHI 2005. ACM Press, New York (2005)
3. Thimbleby, H.: Press On: Principles of interaction programming. MIT Press, Cambridge (2007)
4. Blevis, E.: Sustainable Interaction Design: Invention & Disposal, Renewal & Reuse. In: Proc. CHI 2007. ACM Press, New York (2007)
5. Ackoff, R.L.: Transforming the Systems Movement. In: ICSTM 2004 (2004), http://www.acasa.upenn.edu/RLAConfPaper.pdf
6. Engeström, Y.: Development as Breaking Away and Opening Up: A Challenge to Vygotsky and Piaget. Swiss Journal of Psychology 55, 126–132 (1996)
7. Dix, A.: Controversy and Provocation (Keynote). In: Proceedings of HCIE 2004, The 7th Educators Workshop: Effective Teaching and Training in HCI (2004)
8. Schön, D.A.: The reflective practitioner: how professionals think in action. Harper Collins (1983)
9. Dix, A.: Being playful: learning from children. In: Proc. IDC 2003: Interaction Design and Children. ACM Press, New York (2003)
10. Bødker, S., Iversen, O.: Staging a Professional Participatory Design Practice - Moving PD beyond the Initial Fascination of User Involvement. In: Proc. NordiCHI (2002)
11. Cockburn, A.: Writing Effective Use Cases. Addison-Wesley, Reading (2001)
12. Buckingham Shum, S., MacLean, A., Bellotti, V., Hammond, N.: Graphical Argumentation and Design Cognition. Human-Computer Interaction 12(3) (1997)
13. Knapp, R.: Sustainable Design, http://diac.cpsr.org/cgi-bin/diac02/pattern.cgi/public?pattern_id=798
14. Bohm, D.: On Dialogue. Routledge (1996)

Involving End Users in Distributed Requirements Engineering

Steffen Lohmann, Jürgen Ziegler, and Philipp Heim

University of Duisburg-Essen,
Lotharstrasse 65, 47057 Duisburg, Germany
{lohmann,ziegler,heim}@interactivesystems.info

Abstract. Active involvement of end users in the development of interactive systems is both highly recommended and highly challenging. This is particularly true in settings where the requirements of a large number of geographically distributed users have to be taken into account. In this paper, we address this problem by introducing an integrated, web-based approach that enables users to easily express their ideas on how the interaction with a system could be improved. In addition, the user input is contextualized, allowing for highly structured means to access, explore, and analyze the user requirements.

Keywords: Distributed Requirements Engineering, User Involvement, Global Software Development, Web-based Participation, Distributed Participatory Design.

1 Motivation

The active involvement of end users in the analysis and design of interactive systems has become to be known as *Participatory Design (PD)* [8][12]. Over the years, a couple of methods, techniques, and tools have been developed to support PD [2]. However, though most of these approaches work well for co-located stakeholders, they lack supporting the engineering of interactive systems where needs and desires of a large number of geographically dispersed users have to be met. As this becomes increasingly common in a globalized world, PD has to face new challenges. This is addressed by the emerging research area of *Distributed Participatory Design (DPD)* [3] which investigates PD with regard to physical, temporal, and organizational distribution.

Against the background of DPD, we are working on methods and tools that support end user participation in distributed requirements engineering within the *SoftWiki* project [13]. In the following, we present an approach for the elicitation of user requirements in the evolutionary development of interactive systems. It enables distributed users to express requirements on basis of their interaction experience. We first give a brief overview on related work. Then, we describe the overall approach for distributed elicitation of user requirements, its implementation, and the underlying model. Subsequently, we provide a short insight into different ways to access, explore, and analyze the gathered user requirements and into the tools and visualizations

P. Forbrig and F. Paternò (Eds.): HCSE/TAMODIA 2008, LNCS 5247, pp. 221–228, 2008.

we are currently working on to support these activities. The paper ends with a short discussion and an outlook on future work.

2   Related Work

Research regarding the participation of distributed end users in the development of interactive systems is – next to DPD – mainly conducted under the terms of *Distributed* or *Global Software Development (DSD, GSD)*. The majority of the existing approaches are of a very general nature in that they consider support for as many stakeholder groups as possible rather than focusing specifically on the end user's expectations and needs. Furthermore – though the quantity is reduced – most approaches still heavily rely on physical meetings and direct communication (cp. e.g. *ARENA* [5] or *DisIRE* [4]).

Other attempts try to equip the users with extensive possibilities to annotate or even design the interface. Moore [10], for instance, proposes the use of GUI elements without functionality to allow end users to express their requirements: The users are enabled to create "mock user interface constructions" and augment them with textual descriptions. However, it cannot be expected that users normally have the time and skills to develop GUI proposals without any guidance. Thus, this approach is not feasible in most situations with large, distributed user groups.

A more promising approach for distributed settings is to allow users to express requirements on the basis of an existing application or test prototype. One possibility is *Digital Annotation (DA)*: Tools such as *Annotate!Pro* [1] can be used to enable end users to express requirements intuitively by annotating applications using free-form drawing and send in a snapshot of their annotations to the developing team. Rashid et al. [11] present a solution that specifically aims to support end user participation in requirements elicitation by providing a DA toolset and some predefined templates that have been developed with the needs of requirements formulation in mind.

Though DPD approaches that are based on DA can be very intuitive, they still require some effort and skills of the users in expressing their requirements and demand time-consuming interpretation in the course of analyzing and understanding the annotated screens. The possibilities for structured access or machine readability are very limited. It is nearly impossible, for instance, to automatically detect similar or identical requirements. For these reasons, the mentioned approaches do not sufficiently support settings with large user groups and provide only limited means for developers to explore, filter, and evaluate the collection of user requirements.

3   Web-Based Elicitation of User Requirements

Our approach focuses on the elicitation of user requirements for web-based systems. The implementation is seamlessly integrated into the end user's web browser and provides some advantages compared to stand-alone applications:

1. A contributing user does not have to change the environment. He can express his requirement immediately when it occurs while interacting with the system.

2. Parts of the usage and system context can be captured along with the user requirement, allowing for more structured means to analyze and utilize the requirements as well as a better understanding of their intended meaning.
3. The user is enabled to explicitly point at parts of the interface the requirement refers to. Thus, requirements can be directly linked to the application structure.

3.1 Scenario and Application

The general idea of our approach is best illustrated by a brief scenario that uses the application we developed for the elicitation of user requirements (cp. Fig. 1).

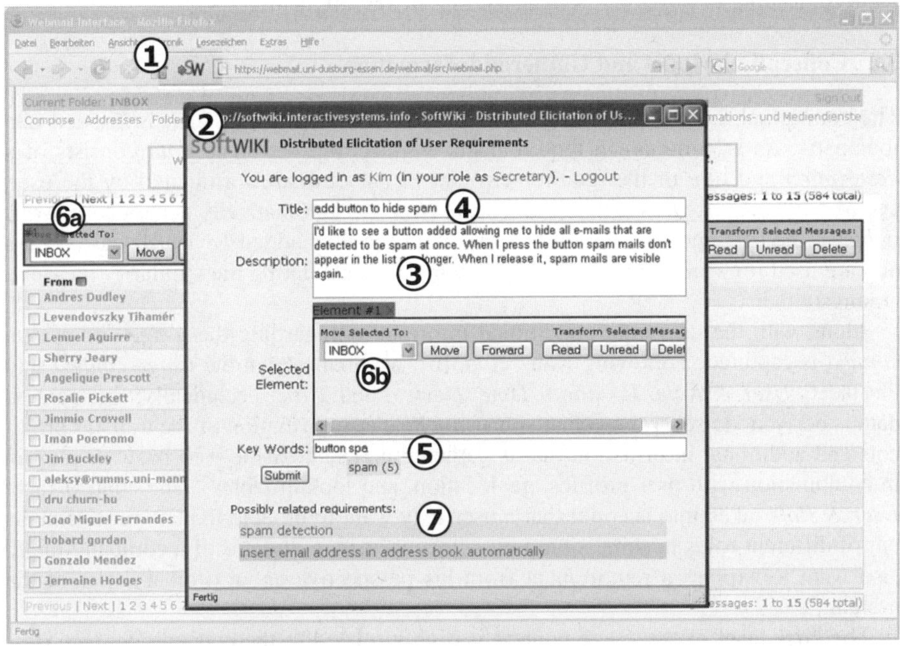

Fig. 1. Web-based interface for the submission of requirements

Imagine an employee who uses the company's web-based mail application in her daily business. While checking her e-mails, the employee misses a feature that she would like to see realized in one of the next releases, in this case, a possibility to hide all e-mails that have been detected to be spam at one click. Thus, she presses a button that is integrated in the user interface of her web browser (1). A pop-up window appears (2) containing a web form where she enters a description of her requirement (3) and optionally adds an adequate title (4) and some keywords (5). If her requirement refers to an element of the visible web page, she does not have to textually describe the element but can directly point to it as follows: While the pop-up window is opened, selected elements are highlighted (6a) and can be copied to the web form (6b) simply with a click[1]. Finally, the employee submits her requirement, receives a confirmation, the pop-up window closes and she returns to the web application where she continues to check her e-mails.

The user interface is reduced to its essential elements so that it is immediately understandable, minimizes user effort and hence encourages participation. In the example given, the user does not even have to classify her requirement into a pre-defined taxonomy or a collection of existing requirements but is simply asked to provide some meaningful, freely chosen keywords. In order to further ease participation, requirements that are identified as similar to the one the user is entering are displayed below the web form (7)[2]: That way, the user does not need to formulate a requirement a second time that already exists. Furthermore, the amount of redundant requirements is reduced, leading to lower effort in analyzing the requirements.

3.2 Conceptual Model and Gathered Information

The conceptual model underlying our approach is shown in Fig. 2. It is divided into four parts. As is common in requirements engineering, the *basic data* consists of a *description* and *title* of the requirement that in our case are formulated by the user, and an automatically assigned *identification (ID)*. An automatically generated full-*text index* of the title and description together with the user added *keywords* ease access and are used for searching in the requirements and calculating the similarity measure, amongst others.

Along with the user input, additional information regarding the *usage* and *system context* is captured. Following Kaltz et al. [6], we break down the *usage context* into the facets *User & Role*, *Location*, *Time*, *Device*, and *Task*. Technically, this context data is derived via several mechanisms using header information of the transfer protocols and additional information that is gathered and sent by the web browser plug-in in combination with user profiles, geolocation, and lookup tables[3]. The context facet *User & Role* takes into account that a user may want to be able to state requirements out of different roles in some situations – for instance, a director of a company might also want to express a requirement from his perspective as an ordinary user of the system.

The *Task* facet of the usage context is highly related to the concepts *System State* and *System Pointer* that together form the system context. The former expresses that each user requirement occurs within a specific state of the system that it can be linked with[4]. The latter represents elements that the user explicitly refers to when formulating his requirement (see Sec. 3.1). Depending on the implementation of the web application and its internal structure, these general model concepts can be further broken down and filled accordingly. For instance, if a model-driven web engineering

---

[1] Hyperlinks in the web page are temporarily deactivated for this purpose.

[2] The similarity measure is calculated in the background while the user types in her requirement using asynchronous server requests as well as statistical and linguistic algorithms.

[3] Depending on the particular use case, the derived context data cannot be expected to be perfectly correct.

[4] The state of the system and usage context when the requirement is entered by the user is, strictly speaking, not necessarily identical to that when the requirement occurs; but in most situations this is likely to be the case.

approach [9] has been used to develop the application, links between requirements and parts of the system models can be explicitly set. However, this requires that the models are accessible by the web browser plug-in at runtime and that the corresponding system state is represented in these models accordingly.

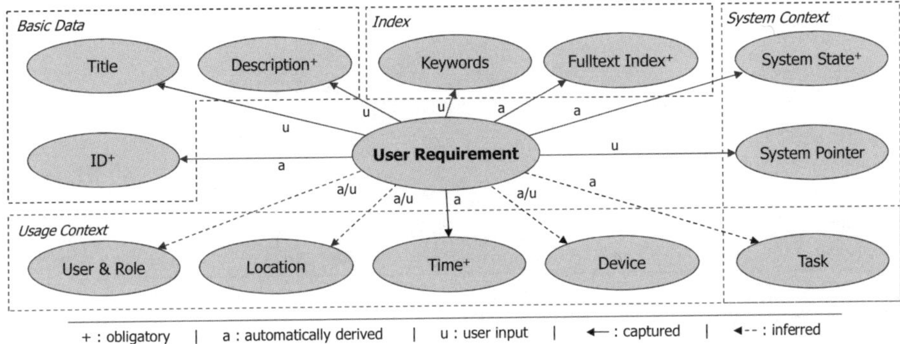

Fig. 2. The user requirement is linked to a number of model concepts

Our basic implementation follows a generic approach to determine the system context: The *System State* is derived from the URL of the corresponding web page and variables provided by the transfer protocol. The *System Pointer* consists of the paths of the selected elements according to the *Document Object Model (DOM)*. Of course, the expressiveness of relations to the system context is limited in this generic approach.

As already mentioned, information regarding the task that the user performs when the requirement occurs might be inferred from the system models to some degree. Such as in case of the other model concepts, the *Task* concept can be further broken down depending on the implementation of the specific use case.

4 Analyzing the User Requirements

The information that is captured along with each requirement provides multiple ways to access the requirements collection and thus eases its exploration and analysis. Again, this is best illustrated by an example:

Figure 3a shows a screenshot of a web-based prototype we developed for analyzing the requirements that are elicited on the basis of the tool and underlying model described in Sec. 3. The interface consists of a main view on the requirements collection and a sidebar containing visualizations that offer various options for filtering the requirements according to the model facets. Two visual filters are implemented in the current prototype: a map visualization that shows the requirements according to their geo-coordinates and can be used for location-based filtering, and a tag cloud visualization that alphabetically lists the user-assigned keywords, each with a size that corresponds to its usage frequency.

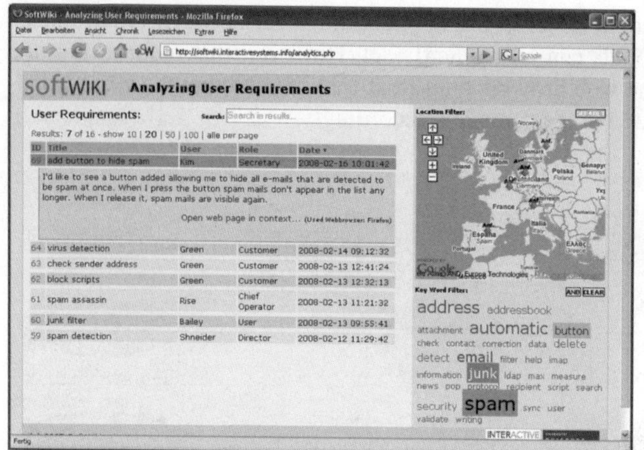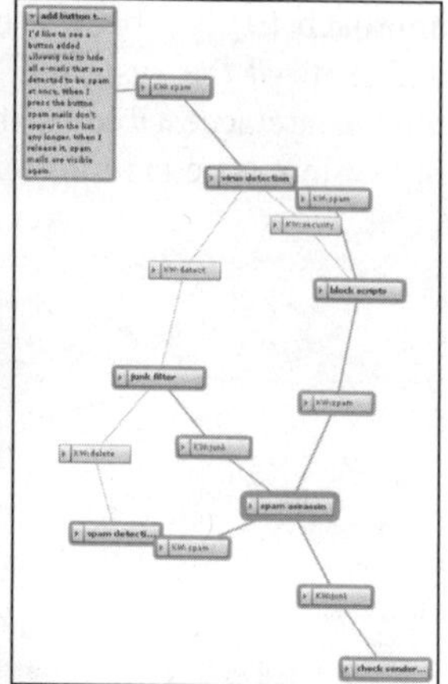

Fig. 3. a) Web interface for the analysis of user requirements, b) Alternative graph visualization

Continuing the scenario outlined in Sec. 3.1, one of the developers of the company's webmail application is going to define specifications for the next software release. Assume that the developer is particularly interested in all user requirements regarding the topic spam that have been stated by the employees working at company sites in Europe. He thus changes the visible area of the map so that only Europe is shown. Then, he selects all keywords that deal with the topic spam – in this case he chooses the synonyms spam and junk – and defines that these keywords should be interconnected by the logical OR operator. As a result, only requirements are listed that meet these criteria. Furthermore, the developer can take a look at the contextual situation as it was when a specific requirement has been entered by an employee. For this purpose, a pop-up window simulates the presentation of the application according to the context data that has been captured along with the requirement (e.g., the corresponding web page, the size of the content area, etc.). If references to parts of the web page were set by the employee (see Sec. 3.1), these elements are highlighted in the simulated view[5].

Besides the map and tag cloud visualization, further filter options are possible according to the model presented in Sec. 3.2. Furthermore, we investigate alternative ways of presenting the requirements collection in the main view. Figure 3b shows a prototype of a graph visualization that helps the analyst to reveal relationships, similarities, and conflicts between requirements that are otherwise hidden in the list view.

5 Discussion and Future Work

The presented approach differs from related work in that it is integrated into the user's web browser. That way, the user does not have to change the environment to express

---

[5] In our current prototype, the highlighting works properly only in cases where the DOM path to the selected web page elements remains the same.

an idea on how the interaction with a web-based system could be improved. The user input can furthermore be related to the system and usage context. This is possible mainly due to the fact that web applications are predominantly based on script languages that are interpreted by the web browser at runtime. However, with the advent of user interface markup languages for operating systems (e.g., XAML [14]), the application of a slightly adapted approach is also increasingly feasible outside the web browser.

We paid special attention to the balancing of our approach by minimizing the effort for users who express requirements and, at the same time, capturing sufficient metadata to enable structured analysis and further processing of the requirements. This is best demonstrated by the possibility to select interface elements a requirement refers to (see Sec. 3.1): On the one hand, the user does not have to describe GUI elements but can simply point at them, and, on the other hand, the developer does not have to guess what element is meant and can work with the reference, for instance, aggregate all requirements that have been related to one GUI element.

Generally, the presented approach can be used in all settings where users shall be enabled to give feedback regarding a web-based system, ranging from feature requests and bug tracking to remote usability testing. The overall aim is to establish a closer relationship between users and developers in settings with large and distributed user groups. First tests showed that the general approach and the developed tools are quickly understood by users. Currently, we are preparing a comprehensive case study that examines the developed applications within the larger context of the *SoftWiki* project.

In order to increase participation and create an awareness of what happens with the user input, we are investigating different requirements tracking, user feedback, and gratification mechanisms. In addition, we study how users might discuss, reformulate, or vote for a requirement that has already been stated by someone else and is identified as possibly related.

References

1. Annotate!Pro (June 11, 2008), http://www.annotatepro.com/
2. Bødker, K., Kensing, F., Simonsen, J.: Participatory IT Design – Designing for Business and Workplace Realities. MIT Press, Cambridge (2004)
3. Danielsson, K., Naghsh, A.M., Gumm, D., Warr, A.: Distributed Participatory Design. In: Extended Abstracts of the 2008 Conference on Human Factors in Computing Systems (CHI 2008), Florence, Italy, pp. 3953–3956. ACM, New York (2008)
4. Geisser, M., Heinzl, A., Hildenbrand, T., Rothlauf, F.: Verteiltes, internetbasiertes Requirements-Engineering. Wirtschaftsinformatik 49(3), 199–207 (2007)
5. Grünbacher, P., Braunsberger, P.: Tool Support for Distributed Requirements Negotiation. In: Cimititle, A., De Lucia, A., Gall, H. (eds.) Cooperative Methods and Tools for Distributed Software Processes, FrancoAngeli, Milano, pp. 56–66 (2003)
6. Kaltz, J.W., Ziegler, J., Lohmann, S.: Context-aware Web Engineering: Modeling and Applications. Revue d'Intelligence Artificielle 19(3), 439–458 (2005)
7. Kaser, O., Lemire, D.: Tag-Cloud Drawing: Algorithms for Cloud Visualization. In: Proceedings of the WWW 2007 Workshop on Tagging and Metadata for Social Information Organization (2007)

8. Kensing, F., Blomberg, J.: Participatory Design: Issues and Concerns. Computer Supported Cooperative Work 7, 167–185 (1998)
9. Moreno, N., Romero, J.R., Vallecillo, A.: An Overview of Model-Driven Web Engineering and the MDA. In: Rossi, G., Pastor, O., Schwabe, D., Olsina, L. (eds.) Web Engineering: Modelling and Implementing Web Applications, pp. 353–382. Springer, Heidelberg (2008)
10. Moore, J.M.: Communicating Requirements Using End-User GUI Constructions with Argumentation. In: Proceedings of the 18th IEEE International Conference on Automated Software Engineering (ASE 2003), Montreal, Canada, pp. 360–363. IEEE, Washington (2003)
11. Rashid, A., Meder, D., Wiesenberger, J., Behm, A.: Visual Requirement Specification in End-User Participation. In: Proceedings of the 1st International Workshop on Multimedia Requirements Engineering. IEEE, Washington (2006)
12. Schuler, D., Namioka, A.: Participatory Design: Principles and Practices. Erlbaum, Hillsdale (1993)
13. SoftWiki – Research project, funded by the German Federal Ministry of Education and Research (BMBF). For more information, `http://softwiki.de/`
14. Extensible Application Markup Language (XAML) (June 11, 2008), `http://msdn.microsoft.com/en-us/library/ms752059.aspx`

Concepts for Analysis and Design of Mobile Healthcare Applications

Joseph McKnight[1], Gavin Doherty[1], Bridget Kane[1,2], and Saturnino Luz[1]

[1] Department of Computer Science, Trinity College Dublin, Dublin 2, Ireland
[2] Trinity Centre for Health Sciences, St. James's Hospital, Dublin

Abstract. In complex domains such as healthcare, careful analysis of user requirements is an important aspect of the development process. In recent years, ethnographic study has become a popular tool for building up an understanding of the healthcare domain. However, linking observational data with the design and development process is a challenging problem. A range of conceptual frameworks have been proposed which can aid in transforming these data into concrete requirements. In this paper, we argue that the framework and associated design concepts used will have a strong influence on shaping the outcome of design, and that the development team should consider carefully which are most appropriate to the problem they face. We use a case study based around a patient review process as an illustrative example.

Keywords: Conceptual Analysis, Concepts, Healthcare, Ethnographic Study, Mobility.

1 Introduction

The healthcare environment raises many challenges for design, with many different roles and stakeholders involved, safety critical tasks being performed, large volumes of information, and highly mobile workers carrying out their activities in a variety of different settings. Standard user-centered design processes can be difficult to apply to such complex work environments, and while techniques such as participatory design are useful they are not going to fully address the problem [7].

In recent years, ethnographic studies have become a popular tool for getting to grips with the complexity of the healthcare environment, with a number of projects producing ethnographically-informed designs. Take-up has been such that commercially driven initiatives are now making use of these techniques. Typically, an observational investigation will yield a lot of information on the different users, working practices, activities as they currently happen, use of artefacts and information. However such studies do not necessarily produce actual design guidance, and in particular they are not a sufficient basis for reasoning about the effects of changes on the work, the workers, and the environment. These are dynamic environments, and are subject to many external factors, including evolving "best practice", changing regulations and organizational structures, and continuous upgrading of information systems.

P. Forbrig and F. Paternò (Eds.): HCSE/TAMODIA 2008, LNCS 5247, pp. 229–236, 2008.

A number of different analytic frameworks have been proposed, which can help to transform this ethnographically derived information into input to the design process. Hence teams looking at the development of such information systems are faced with the choice of which framework to use. In the following sections we argue that this choice will have a strong effect on shaping the designs which are produced, and will also impact on the ability to reason about evolution of the overall system in response to higher level changes within the organisation (for example, the push towards multi-disciplinary team meetings). The concepts considered in this paper have previously been applied to the healthcare environment and due to the nature of the environment many of these have an explicitly mobile aspect.

2 Case Study - Patient Case Review

The case study concerns a large tertiary referral and cancer treatment healthcare facility, where the cardio-thoracic surgery unit receives 5 to 10 new case referrals per week. Each new referral must be processed in order to determine the patient's suitability for surgery. This involves gathering the information needed to discuss the patient at a multi-disciplinary team meeting (MDTM), which *stages* (classifies) the patient's cancer, followed by an outpatient assessment before deciding if surgery is required, followed then by the surgery itself and aftercare. Given the large number of specialist staff that collaborate through the MDTM, it is vital that the necessary tests have been carried out and reviewed prior to the MDTM. The work of managing the patients through the surgical process is mainly carried out by the consultant cardio-thoracic surgeon and specialist oncology coordinator nurse (hereafter referred to as the coordinator), aided by administrative staff.

The processing of patients is tracked by various paper based artefacts that are maintained by the coordinator. The artefacts used include paper notebooks with the most relevant patient information, lists of patients in treatment with status, and a file with all documents related to the patient. This is necessary because typically patients in process are not physically located at the hospital ward and may not technically be a patient of the hospital until outpatient assessment or surgery. Even though patient treatment is managed from the tertiary referral hospital, scans and tests may be carried out by proxy at the referring hospital. As a result, the system is highly dependent on the coordinator and paper based artefacts to function. For example, a patient's processing may be on hold until a scan is completed at another hospital or a test result becomes available. Unless these actions are followed up by the coordinator, using paper files, notebook and various artefacts, a delay in processing could result, with potentially serious consequences. While the use of a paper-based system may seem atypical, the constant evolution of processes means that often workers have to fall back on ad-hoc methods while they wait for formal structures and technological support to emerge.

In order to investigate requirements prior to the introduction of electronic support for these activities, an ethnographic study was performed with the relevant clinicians and administrative staff at the hospital. This study is based on semi-structured interviews with clinicians, examination of paper-based artefacts, and observations of a number of key locations within the working environment. A previous and highly detailed ethnographic study of the MDTM was also of much benefit in understanding these activities (Kane and Luz, 2006).

The patient review process
When a patient is referred to the cardio-thoracic surgeon a letter of referral is received at the tertiary referral hospital and transferred to the coordinator for the cardio-thoracic unit. The coordinator will record the patients' details to a note book and store the letter of referral along with any other documents received to a file, which is then placed in a portable carry case. The patients' case will not be discussed again until the weekly meeting of the coordinator and surgeon. Current and new patients are discussed at this meeting in order to decide on tests that are needed before the patients case can be discussed at an MDTM. The coordinator records the tests required and follows up on the actions required with the patient and referring hospital to ensure they are carried out. Until these actions have been completed the patient is not yet 'active': these tests must be completed before deciding if the patient is ready to be discussed at the MDTM. Scans carried out at other hospitals will be forwarded to the tertiary referral hospital to be examined by the specialist radiologist.

When this initial processing is complete the patients are put on a list for discussion at a weekly MDTM, or referred back to the initial process if more information is needed. The coordinator is responsible for ensuring that the patient names are on the MDTM list and that the patient information needed at the MDTM is available. The surgeon discusses the patient cases with other clinicians at the MDTM, while the coordinator records follow up actions needed and decisions made. Once again the coordinator is responsible to implement follow up actions needed.

The patients that have been recommended for surgery at the MDTM come to the hospital for an outpatient assessment of general health before a final decision on surgery is made. While the assessment is carried out by a member of the surgical team the coordinator records the information on a self made artefact. The patients assessed will then have their cases discussed at the next meeting between the coordinator and surgeon. The coordinator will have to manage the patients requiring discussion after the outpatient assessment and weekly meeting, along with other follow up actions. In addition to the work described above in processing patients there are other tasks that need to be carried out. For instance the coordinator must answer queries on information related to patient processing from patients themselves, other hospitals, and colleagues. From the patient processing information the surgeon is mainly interested in the numbers in process, at each phase, awaiting MDTM, outpatient assessment and surgery.

3 Design Frameworks

We consider in this section concepts which have been used in ethnographically informed healthcare case studies on hospital wards, with a view to informing design. It is important to note that while these frameworks are not orthogonal, each contributes a unique conceptual lens through which the ethnographic data is analysed and interpreted. We briefly consider the relevance of each framework to the case study, and the degree to which they can shape design activities.

Table 1. Concepts and Abstractions used in Analysis and Design in Healthcare

Concept	Purpose
Rhythms	Conceptual framework to explore relationship between information seeking and temporal coordination.
Mobility Work	Conceptual framework to explore effects of moving people and things (artefacts, equipment) to accomplish work.
Common Information Space	Conceptual framework for analysis of a hospital CIS to reveal issues that affect information system design.
Cognitive Artefacts	An approach to uncover and understand the cognitive work in healthcare for the design of digital artefacts.
Coordinative Artefacts	To understand how coordination and cooperation of workers on a ward is enabled through a network of artefacts.
Activity-Based Computing	Abstraction that bases support systems around main activities that clinicians perform daily.

Temporal Rhythms

The concept of *temporal rhythms* (repeating daily patterns of work) is used [11] to analyse the information seeking activities of clinicians working on a ward. These typical working rhythms include shift change, morning rounds, medication, meetings and new arrivals etc, with each rhythm necessitating different information seeking activities. For example, a clinician might order a lab test knowing they will need the results for the following morning rounds; a nurse finishing a shift prepares all the information required for the handover. The rhythms concept leads us to concentrate on the information seeking and providing activities of clinicians that are a part of these working rhythms.

Although working rhythms in the case study are not occurring on a daily basis the concept still proves useful in analysing the information seeking and providing activities of the clinicians. The patient case discussion is the central provider and seeking rhythm in the system. The information sought in this patient case discussion process is provided to the MDTM. The MDTM often also acts as a source of information for future case discussions. This reciprocal relationship is also true between the case discussions and outpatient assessment.

Mobility Work

The concept of mobility work is used by [3] to describe the spatial aspect of co-operative work that is necessary for clinicians to accomplish tasks on a hospital ward. This entails that the correct configuration of **people**, **places**, **resources** and **knowledge** to be achieved to accomplish a task, while operating in an environment where these resources are also mobile. In general terms, mobility work is the work that must be performed so that clinicians can carry out tasks at specific locations.

Analysis of the case study reveals multiple resources required at the MDTM, outpatient and angiogram rooms to support task accomplishment. MDTM and PTF equipment are fixed to the room location where they are needed. However other resources are mobile such as patient files and notebooks, while the radiology scans and reports are available where network or PC access is present. As only the patients who must have their case discussed at the next MDTM or angiogram room meetings are required, the coordinator must organise this information ahead of the meetings. This involves creating a list of patients to be discussed while ensuring that other relevant information is also ready. Overall, the concept was found to be applicable to our case study, and suggests increased support for mobilisation of resources.

Common Information Space
The concept of a common information space (CIS) [2] is used by [13] to analyse co-operative work of heterogeneous workers on an ICU ward, which is based on the use of a common information repository, HealthStat. Their observations revealed a number of issues, firstly that physical proximity of co-workers does not equate to mutual understanding to enable smooth coordination and interpretation of each other's work; this was not the case in other studies of a hospital CIS [5]. Secondly, those heterogeneous workers have a different representation of the underlying information stored in HealthStat, so coordinating activities relies on each representation reflecting accurate shared data, with any change propagated to each representation.

An obvious issue identified from our CIS analysis is the reliance on the coordinator to relay information verbally to the consultant when discussing cases due to access restrictions to paper artefacts. The consultant must perform a similar CIS transfer at the MDTM, and is able to use the HIS to show scans and reports, but must refer to the coordinator for non medical processing information. This temporary immersion and information transfer in a "foreign" CIS for the duration of a task could be supported by mobile devices that facilitate shared views on data. While there are many potential issues surrounding the introduction of such technology [1], the framework is found to be relevant to the case study and design.

Cognitive Artefacts
The failure of automation in healthcare to improve clinical performance is examined by [14] who suggest that this is due to the design concepts on which these systems are based. Current healthcare displays do not represent the underlying domain semantics [12] and therefore are not suited to assisting clinicians in the cognitive work that they must perform, which forces them to perform extra work to overcome these deficiencies. To design displays that support clinicians in the work they actually perform requires a significant investigation of the *technical work* [10], i.e. non clinical work, that is performed in order to enable clinical work to happen. One way of uncovering this technical work is creation and usage of *cognitive artefacts* [9].

The cognitive artefacts concept focuses investigation on the artefacts that are created by clinicians so that we can uncover the work that the artefact is designed to support. This will reveal the goals and strategies employed by the artefact users during their work. Investigation of the work the artefact supports will ensure that any digital replacement is created with an understanding of how work is managed using the artefact, and provide appropriate support. It is important to perform such analysis as simply mimicking a paper based artefact may not equate to supporting the work it was designed to help.

The coordinator in our case study creates patient lists to act as external representations of the patients. These are not annotated or stored, but guide case discussions. A digital replacement could be created to support this task. This could involve the coordinator dynamically managing these lists using a mobile device in situ as required instead of en-masse prior to meetings. The coordinator also uses a notebook to record summary patient processing information such as scans, tests and patients status for quick reference. This is also used during case discussions and MDT meetings. Digitising this notebook requires an understanding of these multiple roles it plays and the work processes it is used within. As patient lists are created from and are a subset of the notebook information, its electronic counterpart should support this creation and migration of information. The recorded scans, tests and reports in the notebook could also be linked to the HIS, which could track and update patient processing status automatically, instead of requiring a search for patient details on the HIS and recording them to the notebook. Again, we can see that the framework is relevant to the case study, with a particular focus to the type of support suggested.

Activity Based Computing

The concept of Activity-Based Computing (ABC) is explored by [6] to investigate providing support for healthcare work. The *activity* abstraction is used due to concerns about the suitability of traditional paradigms, such as application and document centered systems, to an environment where work is "nomadic, collaborative, intensive and often interrupted". ABC is designed to allow activities to be suspended and resumed when interrupted and handed over to colleagues to support ad-hoc collaboration.

Activity Based Computing was proposed as an alternative to document and application centred system due to the nomadic, collaborative intensive and often interrupted nature of work in healthcare. While activity management is an important aspect of the work, and the issues targeted by the framework (collaborative, intensive, nomadic, interruptions) are relevant, the framework was found to apply more to the wider context of the application, rather than design for the review process itself.

Coordinative Artefacts

Bardram and Bossen [4] look at coordination and collaboration on a hospital ward by analysing usage of non digital *coordinative artefacts*. It was found that these artefacts (worksheets, whiteboards etc) facilitated locating patients and staff, cooperative planning, continuous coordination, status overview and passing messages. This has implications for development that digitises these artefacts as the functionality afforded to clinicians must be retained.

The study in [4] was focused on a heterogeneous group of workers on a hospital ward and is not directly applicable to our case study as the non digital artefacts created by our clinicians are primarily created for their own personal use, with some minor exceptions. While it is possible that the work system could well benefit from making greater use of such artefacts, it was not found to be immediately applicable to the case study.

4   Future Work

The question of how to choose an appropriate framework has not yet been fully addressed. We would argue that the closer the symmetry between the chosen concept and work system under study, the easier it will be to elucidate and communicate requirements for design. Specifically we need to address what constitutes a "fit" between a work system and concept and how we can extract requirements or design recommendations from analysis.

While each concept will prove more or less applicable to any given work system, the range of relevant design concepts goes beyond those considered in this paper. It could be that the process of attempting to apply a number of concepts to analysis of a particular setting may facilitate selection or development of a more suitable framework for conceptual description. Another interesting and related issue is the effect of such frameworks on interpretation of evaluation data from prototyping activities which might be conducted as part of a human-centered design process. A further question to be addressed is the role of such frameworks in the context of broader methodologies for analysis and design.

5 Discussion and Conclusions

Analysis of our case study has revealed that the existing design frameworks probe different aspects of the work performed and suggest different forms of technology intervention. A question which arises is whether development teams should seek to adopt a single framework for a particular project, or whether it would be better to consider multiple points of view, starting from the same ethnographic data. Another question is whether there a case for "unifying" frameworks which bring together multiple design concepts, or is it sufficient to have a checklist of things to consider in design, which is derived from a variety of frameworks.

In conclusion, the decision of which conceptual framework to adopt should not be made lightly; ideally the development team should have a palette of concepts, from which they can choose according to the context. Designers should be wary of influence of the analysis framework on the design space. Furthermore, the relationship of the design framework with further stages of design process remains to be investigated.

Acknowledgements

J. McKnight is supported by an IRCSET/Intel Enterprise Partnership award.

References

1. Ash, J.S., Berg, M., Coiera, E.: Some Unintended Consequences of Information Technology in Health Care: The Nature of Patient Care Information System-related Errors. Journal of the American Medical Informatics Association 11(2), 104–112 (2004)
2. Bannon, L., Bødker, S.: Constructing Common Information Spaces. In: Proceedings of ECSCW 1997, pp. 81–96. Kluwer Academic Publishers, Norwell (1997)
3. Bardram, J.E., Bossen, C.: Mobility Work: The Spatial Dimension of Collaboration at a Hospital. Computer Supported Cooperative Work 14(2), 131–160 (2005)
4. Bardram, J.E., Bossen, C.: A Web of Coordinative Artifacts: Collaborative Work at a Hospital Ward. In: ACM Conference on Supporting Group Work. ACM Press, New York (2005)
5. Bossen, C.: The parameters of common information spaces: the heterogeneity of cooperative work at a hospital ward. In: Computer supported cooperative work. ACM Press, New York (2002)

6. Christensen, H., Bardram, J.E.: Supporting Human Activities - Exploring Activity-Centered Computing. In: 4th International Conference on Ubiquitous Computing (2002)
7. Hartswood, M., Procter, R., Slack, R., Voß, A., Büscher, M., Rouncefield, M., Rouchy, P.: Co-realisation: towards a principled synthesis of ethnomethodology and participatory design. Scand. J. Inf. Syst. 14(2), 9–30 (2002)
8. Kane, B., Luz, S.: Multidisciplinary medical team meetings: An analysis of collaborative working with special attention to timing and teleconferencing. Computer Supported Cooperative Work 15(5), 501–535 (2006)
9. Nemeth, C., Cook, R.: Discovering and Supporting Temporal Cognition in Complex Environments. In: CogSci. 2004, Chicago, USA (2004)
10. Nemeth, C., Cook, R., et al.: The Messy Details: Insights from the Study of Technical Work in Healthcare. IEEE Trans. Syst. Man Cybern. 34(6), 689–692 (2004)
11. Reddy, M., Dourish, P., et al.: A Finger on the Pulse: Temporal Rhythms and Information Seeking in Medical Work. In: CSCW 2002, New Orleans, USA (2002)
12. Woods, D.D., Hollnagel, E.: Mapping Cognitive Demands in Complex Problem Solving Worlds. International Journal of Man Machine Studies 26, 257–275 (1987)
13. Reddy, M., Dourish, P., et al.: Coordinating Heterogeneous Work: information and Representation in Medical Care. In: European Conference on CSCW, Bonn, Germany (2001)
14. Nemeth, C., O'Connor, M., Klock, P., Cook, R.: Mapping Cognitive Work: The way out of IT System Failures. In: AMIA 2005 Annual Symposium, Washington, DC (2005)

ShaMAN: An Agent Meta-model for Computer Games

Steve Goschnick, Sandrine Balbo, and Liz Sonenberg

Interaction Design Group, DIS, University of Melbourne, 3010, Australia
`{stevenbg,sandrine,l.sonenberg}@unimelb.edu.au`

Abstract. In this paper, we detail recent research on agent meta-models. In particular, we introduce a new agent meta-model called ShaMAN, created with a specific focus on computer game development using agent systems. ShaMAN was derived by applying the concept of Normalisation from Information Analysis, against a superset of agent meta-model concepts from the meta-models investigated. A number of features are identified, including human-agent *locales* and *socialworlds*, that might be usefully added to a generic AO meta-model.

Keywords: Agent-oriented, Agent Architecture, Multi-Agent Systems, Meta-model, Agent Meta-models, Agents in Computer Games, HCI.

1 Introduction

Agent-oriented (AO) architectures and methodologies are the main interest area of the research outlined here, with a focus on the application domain of computer games. While we are specifically interested in extending current AO concepts to further facilitate game specification and development, a consequence of this study identifies possible generic features to add to an AO meta-model.

1.1 Motivation

Computer games invariably have a graphic user interface (GUI) whether they are on PCs, dedicated game consoles or mobile phones. Additionally, many games are multiuser over either a proprietary network or the Internet, and as such, some data is often shared between multiple users. Neither graphic interfaces nor their associated event models, nor distributed data are well considered in the current AO architectures and frameworks, but computer games make heavy use of all three.

There is a precedent early on in the Object-oriented (OO) paradigm for an underappreciation of these same facets of application programs, which ought to be instructive for the newer AO paradigm. At about the time that mainstream developers moved to OO languages, in particular C++ (early 1990's), GUI interfaces became the default in mainstream operating systems (OS). GUI and mouse/pointer interfaces made it necessary for application programmers to handle non-sequential *event-handling*, a significant change in programming practice from sequential processing in most character-based applications. Prior to more modern OO languages such as Java, both the GUI and event-handling was *not* a part of the language proper, e.g. C++. For

P. Forbrig and F. Paternò (Eds.): HCSE/TAMODIA 2008, LNCS 5247, pp. 237–245, 2008.

exam-ple, on the Unix OS events were handled via X-Windows and Motif *class libraries*. Thus, the application programmer in the early 1990s moved to an OO paradigm in language constructs, but their dealings with the GUI and event-driven programming, initially happened outside of the OO paradigm. So, an *event-driven paradigm* of pro-gramming happened concurrently by necessity, but it initially went unheralded in the shadow of the OO language paradigm.

1.2   A Gap in Agent Architectures

From the start AO has been socially-oriented such that *inter-agent communication* – a form of event - is typically allowed for with an Agent Communication Language (ACL). However, the AO paradigm has followed the initial OO programming languages, in not doing anything within the architecture or the constructs of the languages themselves, with regard to the GUI interface or non-agent event-handling.

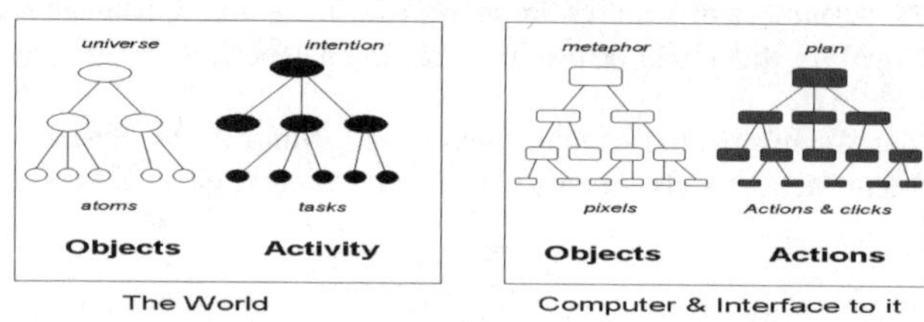

Fig. 1. Real world and the Object Action Interface Model

Interaction events and GUI interface objects are at the core of all mainstream computing platforms today, whether it be workstation, desktop, laptop, PDA or mobile phone. Figure 1 is an adaption of Shneiderman's Object Action Interface Model [20], showing a high-level representation of the physical world and what is done on a computer to supplement it, when a user interacts with an application program, via a computer screen and input mechanisms (e.g. mouse and keyboard).

The gap addressed by our research, is to achieve an AO architecture that engages with the user at the level of a GUI metaphor rendered down to the pixel level (left-hand side of right box in figure 1), with events down to the keyboard and mouse-click level, (right-hand side of figure 1). Our architecture is expressed as a meta-model.

1.3   Meta-models

Much of the research discussed here is centred around meta-models expressed in UML class diagram notation. Meta-models expressed in UML as such are now commonly used in both AO [1,12,13] and OO [17] research and development domains: to represent state-holding entities; to communicate base ideas; and as a useful means to compare different agent systems or architectures [6,12].

1.3.1   Agent Concepts

Given that there is currently no universally accepted single meta-model for AO systems, when we first looked to agent concepts and architectures with computer games in mind, we examined the meta-models of several agent architectures and methodologies - AAII [16], GAIA [22,23], Tropos [1,11], TAO/MAS-ML [5], ROADMAP [13,14], ShadowBoard [8,9] - to explore the commonalities and differences between them. In addition, given our identification of a gap in the AO paradigm at the input device event level, we studied several well-known meta-models from the *Task Modelling* field, with its roots in the interaction between human users and computational devices, covered elsewhere [10].

1.3.2 Normalisation

A technique from Information Analysis (IA) used to improve ER models [2] that did not crossover into the later OO paradigm is the concept of *Data Normalisation* [15]. In this process derived from relational mathematics by Codd [3], the ER model is put into *normal form*. The model resulting from normalising a preliminary model, is considered to be in a state ideal for future change, and one that causes the least anomalies to operations upon the state held in the current entities. It is usually applied in IA to a model as a quality control procedure, however, Normalisation can also be used as a *bottom-up design technique* enabling the analyst to methodically deduce a well-formed model from a set of relevant concepts. In this research we applied it to a superset of the agent concepts found in agent and task meta-models, and arrived at a normalised agent meta-model named ShaMAN. From the perspective of a multi-agent system at *runtime*, a normalised meta-model is best for *insertion*, *update* and *deletion* of state information as it is happening in real-time.

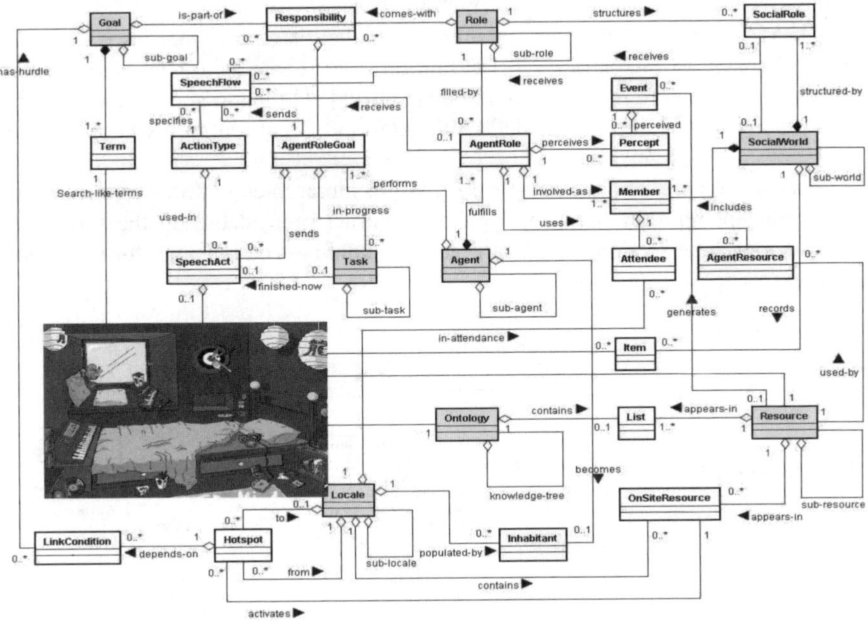

Fig. 2. The ShaMAN Agent Meta-model (with insert of a concrete game Locale)

1.3.3 Overview

In Section 2 we introduce the ShaMAN agent meta-model. To explain some of the entities in it, we present two groupings of the entities from the meta-model in detail, and then describe the flexibility it brings to building applications. In Section 3 we compare the concepts from the ShaMAN meta-model with those other agent meta-models investigated. In Section 4 we conclude and look to future work related to ShaMAN.

2 The ShaMAN Meta-model

We arrived at the ShaMAN meta-model depicted in figure 2 by taking concepts from a number of existing AO meta-models and a number of Task Analysis meta-models [10] – analysed them for similarities and differences, added some extra requirements from the games application genre, and then normalised the resultant set of entities. The following sections describe some aspects of the ShaMAN meta-model in more detail.

2.1 Locales for Computer Games

Computer games invariably interact with the player through the usage of a human-machine interface, for example a screen of one size or another. The Locale sub-section of ShaMAN lets us model the visual metaphors and the screen interaction between player/user and screen characters of a game, right in the AO model itself, rather than leaving it to some other paradigm such as OO. While some agent meta-models do have constructs for the agent *environment*, none of those investigated specifically model the computer screen as the primary representation of that environment.

In ShaMAN, this screen representation of an agent's environment is called a *Locale* - in homage to Fitzpatrick's [7] definition of a Locale as a generalised abstract representation of where members of a Social World [21] inhabit and interact. Figure 3 represents the sub-section of the ShaMAN meta-model that represents Locales within games.

A *Locale* entity may have sub-locales within hierarchies of Locales. Locale is a generic concept representing some spatial construct presentable on the screen, e.g. room, outdoor area, sections of a board-game - suitably broad enough for novel game interfaces.

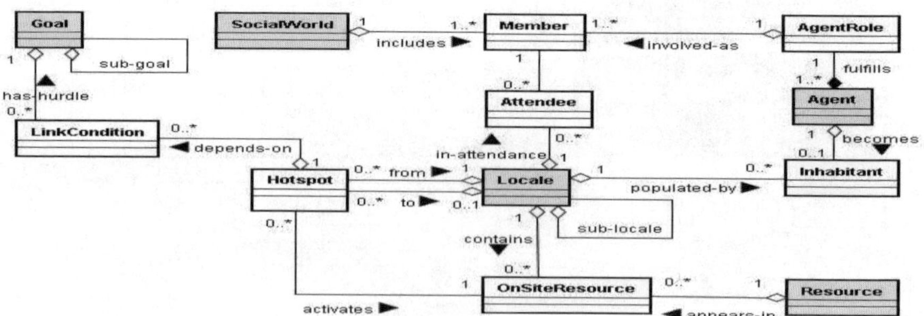

Fig. 3. The Locale sub-section of the meta-model

The insert in figure 2 is a concrete example of a Locale. It depicts the bedroom of a player's character within a game, which is represented as a Locale in ShaMAN. The *HotSpot* entity represents any area on the screen that is interactive, in the sense that whenever the user either clicks or passes over that area on the screen (or has *the focus*, from a keystroke point-of-view), certain interaction between the user and the game may take place. Whether the game presents a 2D or 3D scene, or an abstraction, the interaction with a standard display is 2D and involves *area*. The HotSpot entity has two relationships with Locale, one named *to* and the other named *from* – enabling navigation between Locales.

A HotSpot may also link to an *OnSiteResource* entity. These are *Resources* that live in the Resource entity (which may involve a hierarchy of Resources). Resources are typically programmed entities that are not Agent-oriented. E.g. clicking on the digital clock on the bedside table opens a window that displays a fully-functioning *clock* object, which is a Resource. OnSiteResource is an associate entity – a representation that allows the same Resource to be used in multiple Locales, e.g. a clock in many rooms drawing upon the same programmed code. Resource may also represent real objects in the real world, such as in a robot or a sensor application based upon the ShaMAN meta-model.

A HotSpot may also have a relationship with the entity *LinkCondition*, which in turn links to a *Goal* via a relationship called *has-hurdle*. This allows the game developer to enforce conditions to be met. Locale is also linked to the entities *Attendee* and *Inhabitant*. Attendee is an associative entity that records all occupants in a particular Locale over time, retaining a record of when agents (or human avatars) entered and left a Locale. It is linked to the agent's Role during that occupation via *AgentRole*, and also to the *SocialWorld* they were engaged in when they did so. This *history* aspect of the Attendee is usefull in providing and/or recording a back-story for any particular agent-oriented game character – a necessary aspect of realistic game creation.

2.2   The Goals, Roles, Responsibilities and Tasks of Agents

Computer games often have the need for intelligent, intentional, proactive and autonomous game characters that interact both with the human players and with other char-acters in a game. These properties are the harbingers of AO systems, and the sub-group of entities from ShaMAN meta-model in left and centre of figure 4,

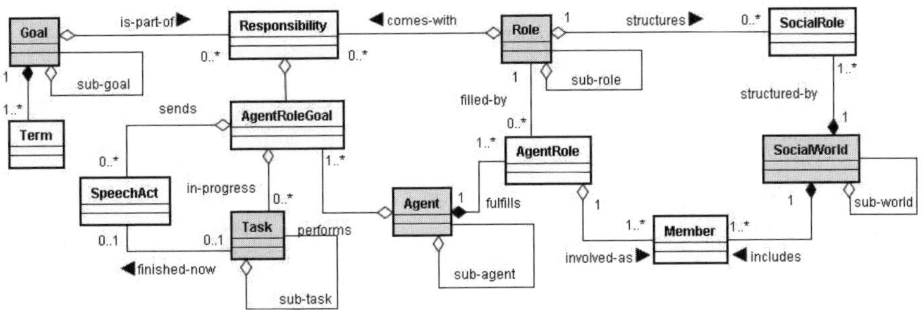

Fig. 4. Goals, Roles and Tasks in ShaMAN

represent the entities that appear most frequently (but not consistently) in one form or another, in many of the agent meta-models that we examined.

Figure 4 shows five entities in this sub-model of ShaMAN that have hierarchies of sub-elements of the same type, namely: *Goal, Role, Agent, Task* and *SocialWorld*. The associate entity between Goal and Role called *Responsibility* represents the responsibilities of a particular Role. A given Responsibility instance is fulfilled via an

Table 1. ShaMAN meta-model comparison with other agent architectures and meta-models

ShaMAN	KGR /BDI	GAIA V1	GAIA V2	RoadMap	Tropos	MAS-ML	DigitalFriend
AgentRole		Role	Role	(pointers)		Play	AgentRole
Percept							Percept
Event						Event	Event
SocialWorld (tree)	Acquaintance	System	Organisation, Pattern		Actor/ Social Agent	Organisation	
SocialRole		System			Actor/ Position	Ownership	
Member							
Item							
AgentRole-Goal	Capability, Service	Services, Activity	Service, Activity	Services	Dependency	Actions	AgentRoleGoal
Task (tree)		Activity	Activity		Plan		Task
SpeechAct	Interaction	Activity				Message	SpeechAct
ActionType	Action, performative						Action
SpeechFlow	Acquaintance, Permissions, Protocols	Protocol, Acquaintance model[5]	Protocol			Protocol	MessageFlow
Resource (tree)	Resource	Resource	Resource	Protocol (tree)	Resource	Object	Resource
Agent-Resource	Service	Permissions	Permissions		Dependency		AgentResource
Ontology (tree)				Knowledge-Component			Ontology (tree)
List	Knowledge						ResourcList
Locale (tree)			Environment	Environment-Zone		Environment	
Attendee							
Inhabitant						Inhabit	
OnSite Resource							
HotSpot							
Link-Condition							
R,A,D,I,T,Rt	A,D,I	A,D	A,D	R,A,D,Rt	R,A,D,I	R,A,D	R,A,D,I,Rt

Note 1. R,A,D,I,T,Rt lifecycle phases: Requirements, Analysis, Design, Implementation, Testing, Run-time.
Note 2. The DigitalFriend V1 tool [9] is an implementation of the ShadowBoard agent architecture [8].
Note 3. AO models for Prometheus [18] and GoalNet [19] were in the study but not here, for space rea-sons.

instance in the *AgentRoleGoal* entity, by being enacted or performed by an Agent that takes on that Role. An Agent may have many Roles via *AgentRole.*

Goals will often have sub-goals in a hierarchy of goals to be achieved. One such sub-goal will be associated with a matching sub-role, and an agent will be assigned via an instance of the AgentRole entity. During execution of a ShaMAN application, sub-agents can be called upon in a downward direction via the need to achieve the sub-goals of parent goals, which is termed *goal-driven execution.* Or, they can be called upon from below, where a SpeechAct has been sent from further down the sub-agent chain, and the upper level goal has to be solved or rerun, termed *data-driven execution.* Data-driven execution often eventuates when a sub-agent retrieves new information from an external service such as a Web service, or from another agent across agent hierarchies or across Social Worlds.

2.3 Social Worlds in ShaMAN

Individual *Agents* can be members of one or more *SocialWorlds.* Their membership begins with an instance in the *Member* entity. Agents are related to the Member entity via the *AgentRole* entity. SocialWorld's have a number of SocialRoles, such as 'Captain' or 'Treasurer', which is useful in the design phase before specific agents are instantiated.

3 A Comparison of Agent Meta-models

Our motivation for collecting and comparing agent meta-models was for their agent concepts, as the primary input into a normalisation process, to arrive at a well-formed agent meta-model. Hence our initial interest in the comparison was analytic only.

Table 1 is a comparative format representing a sub-set of agent concepts that we used as input into the meta-model normalisation process in deriving the ShaMAN entities (the first table column). All models have some entity similar to the ShaMAN's *Goal, Role, Responsibility* and *Agent,* so these have been excluded from the table in this paper. Even so, a particular comparison (e.g. ShaMAN's *Goal(tree)* and Tropos's *Soft Goal/Hard Goal*) only *approximately* equates the concepts. Sometimes a comparison is close in meaning, other times it is close in name but distant in meaning, and sometimes there is wide variance in both name and the semantics. In the full study we did examine each twin comparison of concept in detail, but it cannot be presented in this paper for space reasons.

What is more useful in this paper is to highlight where ShaMAN has entities that have little or no comparison across the other agent meta-models examined. The darker shaded cells in the table shows that entities around *Locale* are unique to ShaMAN. Similarly, the lighter shaded cells show several of the entities related to *SocialWorld* are unique to ShaMAN. These entities were discussed explicitly above in the discussion of figures 3 and 4.

4 Conclusions and the Future

Agent-oriented architectures and frameworks lend themselves well to Human-Centred Software Engineering, given that several of them are derived from branches of psychology and mentalistic notions (e.g. BDI – from Folk Psychology; ShadowBoard – from Analytical Psychology). We set out to extend current AO concepts to further facilitate game specification and development. While the entities unique to ShaMAN were introduced specifically for that purpose, most of them have a more generic usage, particularly for intelligent applications, with multiple users, many agents and rich user interfaces. It has not been our intent to develop a generic agent meta-model, however others are endeavouring to define an all-inclusive agent meta-model: Hahn et al [12] demonstrate the usefulness of the MDA (model driven architecture, see OMG [17]) approach to software development with AO tools. Fischer et al [6] propose that a *unified agent meta-model* is a worthy goal and could provide interoperability between many of the current disparate agent meta-models, methodologies and technology platforms. Theirs is a work-in-progress that we intend to align ShaMAN development with, as much as possible.

References

1. Bresciani, P., Perini, A., Giorgini, P., Guinchiglia, F., Mylopoulos, J.: Tropos: An Agent-Oriented Software Development Methodology. Autonomous Agents and Multi-Agent Systems, 203–236 (2004)
2. Chen, P.: The Entity-Relationship Model - Toward a Unified View of Data. ACM Transactions on Database Systems 1, 9–36 (1976)
3. Codd, E.F.: A relational model of data for large shared data banks. Communications of the ACM 13, 377–387 (1970)
4. Cossentino, M.: Different perspectives in designing multi-agent systems. In: AgeS 2002, workshop at NodE 2002, Erfurt, Germany (2002)
5. Da Silva, V.T., De Lucena, C.J.P.: From a Conceptual Framework for Agents and Ob-jects to a Multi-Agent System Modeling Language. Autonomous Agents and Multi-Agent Systems 9, 145–189 (2004)
6. Fischer, K.: Agent-oriented software engineering: a model-driven approach. International Journal of Agent-Oriented Software Engineering 1(3/4), 334–369 (2007)
7. Fitzpatrick, G.: The Locales Framework: Understanding and Designing for Wicked Problems. Kluwer Academic Publications, London (2003)
8. Goschnick, S.B.: ShadowBoard: an Agent Architecture for enabling a sophisticated Digital Self. Thesis, Dept. of Computer Science, University of Melbourne, Australia (2001)
9. Goschnick, S.B.: The DigitalFriend: the First End-User Oriented Multi-Agent System. In: OSDC 2006, the third Open Source Developers' Conference, Melbourne, Australia, December 5-8 (2006)
10. Goschnick, S., Balbo, S., Sonenberg, L.: From Task to Agent-Oriented Meta-models, and Back Again. In: Tamodia 2008, Pisa, Italy (2008)
11. Guinchiglia, F., Mylopoulos, J., Perini, A.: The Tropos Software Development Methodology: Processes, Models and Diagrams. In: AAMAS 2002. ACM, New York (2002)
12. Hahn, C., Madrigal-Mora, C., Fischer, K., Elvesaeter, B., Berre, A., Zinnikus, I.: Meta-models, Models, and Model Transformations: Towards Interoperable Agents. In: Fischer, K., Timm, I.J., André, E., Zhong, N. (eds.) MATES 2006. LNCS (LNAI), vol. 4196, pp. 123–134. Springer, Heidelberg (2006)
13. Juan, T., Sterling, L.: The ROADMAP Meta-model for Intelligent Adaptive Multi-Agent Systems in Open Environments. In: 4th International Workshop on Agent Oriented Software Engineering, Melbourne (2003)

14. Juan, T., Pearce, A., Sterling, L.: ROADMAP: Extending the Gaia Methodology for Complex Open Systems. In: Autonomous Agents and Multi-Agent Systems AAMAS 2002 (2002)
15. Kent, W.: A Simple Guide to Five Normal Forms in Relational Database Theory. Communications of the ACM 26(2), 120–125 (1983)
16. Kinny, D., Georgeff, M., Rao, A.: A Methodology and Modelling Technique for Systems of BDI Agents. In: Van de Velde, W., Perram, J.W. (eds.) The Seventh European Workshop on Modelling Autonomous Agents in a Multi-Agent World. Springer, Berlin (1996)
17. OMG: MDA Guide Version 1.0.1 (2003),
    `http//www.omg.org/docs/omg/03-06-01.pdf`
18. Padgham, L., Winikoff, M.: Prometheus: A Methodology for Developing Intelligent Agents. In: AOSE Workshop, AAMAS-20, Bologna, Italy (2002)
19. Shen, Z., Li, D., Miao, C., Gay, R.: Goal-oriented Methodology for Agent System Development. In: International Conference on Intelligent Agent Technology, IAT 2005 (2005)
20. Shneiderman, B.: Designing the User Interface, Strategies for Effective Human-Computer Interaction, 3rd edn. Addison-Wesley, USA (1997)
21. Strauss, A.: A Social World Perspective. Studies in Symbolic Interaction 1, 119–128 (1978)
22. Wooldridge, M., Jennings, N.R., Kinny, D.: The Gaia Methodology for Agent-Oriented Analysis and Design. Autonomous Agents and Multi-Agent Systems 3, 285–312 (2000)
23. Zambonelli, F., Jennings, N.R., Wooldridge, M.J.: Developing Multiagent Systems: The Gaia Methodology. ACM Transactions on Software Engineering and Methodology 12, 417–470 (2003)

A Study on Appropriate Plant Diagram Synthesis for User-Suited HMI in Operating Control

Mieczyslaw Metzger and Grzegorz Polaków

Faculty of Automatic Control, Electronics and Computer Science
Silesian University of Technology,
Akademicka 16, 44-100 Gliwice, Poland
`{mieczyslaw.metzger,grzegorz.polakow}@polsl.pl`

Abstract. In this paper a study on appropriate plant diagram synthesis for user-suited HMI in operating control is presented. Discussion is based on the long-term personal experience and illustrated with excerpts of existing HMIs developed for research and industrial use. The HMI notion is defined for operating control and for operator training. The paper present three aspects of plant diagrams design. The first aspect deals with task-oriented usage of screen space for plant diagram and other GUI elements. Second aspect covers all methods of image creation for process diagrams, including photography, schematic diagrams, use of predefined normalised 3D graphical elements, and creative possibilities of 3D scene. The third aspect stresses capability of dynamic visualisation with the use of animated graphics.

Keywords: Usability of HMI for operating control, software engineering for user-suited HMI, plant diagram for GUI, visualisation, SCADA.

1 Introduction

Proper design of a plant diagram, according to the needs of a specific plant operator (or group of operators), is an important task, since the comfort of the plant operators' is the key issue influencing efficiency of their work, and implicitly accuracy of their decisions. Design of graphical user interfaces in, for example, computer entertainment industry, backed up by large finances due to potential profits, is nearly insignificant and hardly related to the importance of work and responsibilities of industrial process' operators.

Modern automation systems are equipped with operating panels implementing human-machine interface (HMI) for communication between a human operator and an industrial process being automated. HMI is the main part of the SCADA (Supervisory Control and Data Acquisition) application. The quality of the HMI determines a comfort of the human operator, and indirectly influences a productivity of one's work, therefore it should be designed in a user-suited way. A specific operator of a plant has his own partialities and habits, as humans, in general, have individual preferences for tools used in their everyday work and life. Therefore, a task of synthesising HMI suited to the specific human operator is worth considering.

P. Forbrig and F. Paternò (Eds.): HCSE/TAMODIA 2008, LNCS 5247, pp. 246–254, 2008.

Publications and manuals for HMI synthesis deal mainly with the technical issues of GUI, like design of numerical control and indication fields, spatial layout of alert indicators, way of process trends presentation, etc. A very important part of the GUI, i.e. plant diagram, its design and synthesis, affecting human operator's perception and sense of aesthetics, is hard to normalise and should be suited to the specific user and tasks. In this paper a study on appropriate plant diagram synthesis for user-suited HMI in operating control is presented. Discussion is based on the long-term personal experience and illustrated with excerpts of existing HMIs developed for research and industrial use.

The paper is organised as follows. The next section presents much shortened overview of the related work in the bibliography. After that, the HMI notion is defined for the operating control and for the operator training. The following next three sections present three aspects of plant diagrams design. The first aspect deals with task-oriented usage of screen space for plant diagram and other GUI elements. Second aspect covers all methods of image creation for process diagrams, including photography, schematic diagrams, use of predefined normalised graphical elements, and creative possibilities of 3D graphics. Third aspect stresses capability of dynamic visualization with the use of animated graphics. Finally, a summary of major contributions is presented as concluding remarks.

2   Related Work

In this paper a discussion on synthesis of plant diagram for industrial HMI is presented. Hence, the shortened literature review here focuses on works dealing with cognitive and aesthetic aspects of industrial HMI. Recent developments in the area of usability in the human centred software engineering introduce some formal methods (see for example [1-5]), while fundamentals of human centred software engineering (HCSE) are well summarised in the books [6-7]. A special attention should be paid for the work of Seffah et.al. [5], in which 25 criterions for measuring usability are discussed. It should be also noticed, that there exist several attempts to standardisation, such as ISO/IS 9241, ISO/IS 13407, ISO/TR 18529, ISO 16071.

Different, slightly non-technical, approach for solving problems of the user interface design for effective human-computer interaction was presented in the books [8-9]. Ecological aspects of visual perception were discussed e.g. in [10], where it is stated that humans work more efficiently when interacting with three dimensional images as they are more analogous to the real world.

To mention particular ideas dedicated for synthesis of GUI being central part of HMI in industrial SCADA applications, earlier, more specialised publications must be referenced. It was 1986 when Norman in his note [11] introduced very important statement, that from the user's point of view it is the system's interface what is received as the actual system. A similar statement relating to simulators of industrial processes are found in [12].

In works [13-15] the investigation of colours and complexity of plant diagrams are presented. It is researched, how choice of colours and level of diagram's complexity influence the perception of the diagram. Wittenberg's work [15] additionally discusses three aspects of plant diagram design i.e. virtual process elements, task-oriented diagrams, and visualization of both goals and present condition. In our paper there are also three aspects of GUI synthesis discussed, from the other point of view.

3   HMI for Operating Control and for Operator's Training

After the revolution caused by common use of computers in nearly every sphere of everyday life, Human-Machine Interfaces (HMI) are used and required in many various applications, including very extensive and profitable area of computer entertainment. Before PCs spread and became popular, HMIs were used mainly in industrial systems requiring an operational control. Those systems (implemented as expensive specialised operating consoles) were designed by control instrumentation manufacturers and supplied by an investor as a part of whole industrial process. End-users had to accept the interfaces exactly as they were delivered.

Current wide availability of personal computers changed the situation. Operating consoles based on PC are cheap and readily obtainable. Diversity of the operating control software and the competition on the market makes it possible to easily and cheaply develop operating panels (nowadays called SCADA for Supervisory Control And Data Acquisition) according to the needs of a specific user. This paper focuses on proper choice and design of GUI being the main part of the HMI for the SCADA control operating system.

Fig. 1 symbolically presents the role of the GUI as perceived by the user of the system – in this case an operator of industrial process. As it was stated in the literature review, it is a GUI itself what is perceived by an operator as the system (see e.g. [11]). This statement is physically backed up by the fact, that in real plants, operating stations are located in the control room, which is spatially distant from the process. Until an emergency situation arises, there is no need for an operator to see and/or interact with the process, all the physical phenomena are represented for him with the GUI.

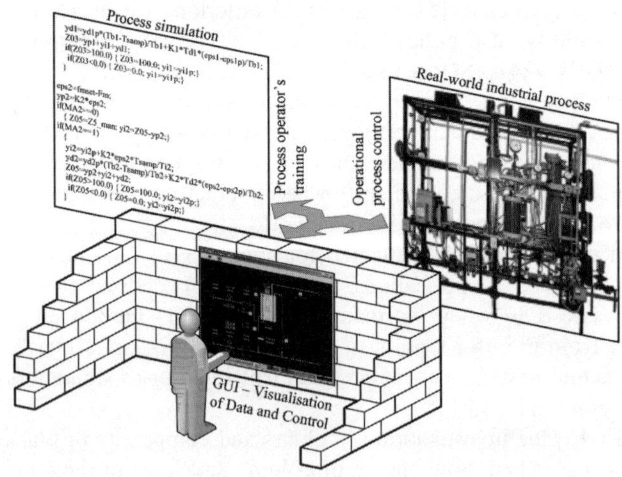

Fig. 1. General interpretation of GUI for process control

A common availability of computers with a relatively high processing power enabled the possibility of creating real-time simulators of industrial processes, used to train potential system operators. As it was cited above, simulator (numerical software application) of an industrial process has to substitute the real process in such a way, that user believes that he interacts with the real process – see Fig. 1.

This implies the need for proper GUI, with which the user might interact exactly in the same way as in the case of real-world process. Hence, it should be noticed, that for proper training the same GUI should be designed both for the SCADA and for the simulator. In such case the operator is even unable to distinct if he controls the real-world process or the simulator at the time. Such possibilities are known and exploited in aerial and military applications for a long time, however it is the availability of computer hardware and software which enables those possibilities in civil domains. The discussion in this paper deals with such a GUI, which can be used both for operating control of a real process and for control of a real-time simulated process for operators training.

4 Task-Oriented Usage of Screen Space for Plant Diagram

Basing on twenty-year experience in the design of the HMI/GUI for industrial and research purposes, a following statement can be presented. In the majority of cases the usage of screen space depends on the task for which a particular GUI is designed.

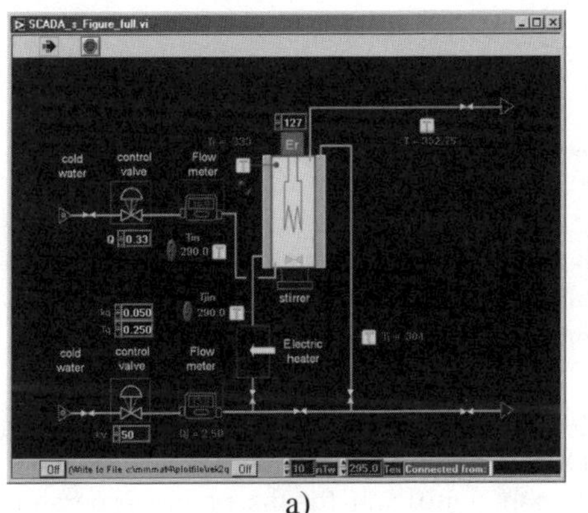
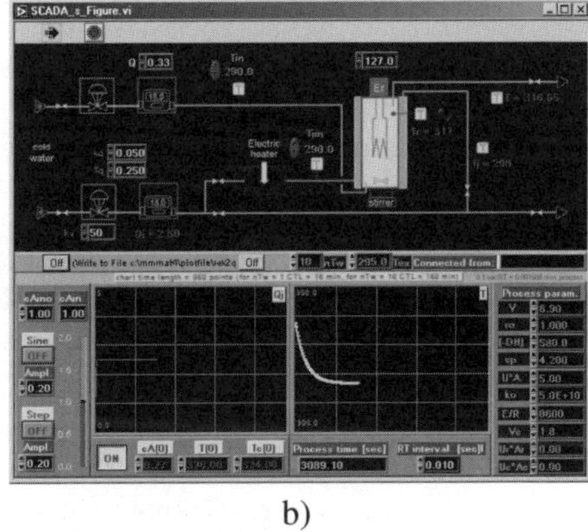

a)   b)

Fig. 2. a) GUI for hybrid exothermic reactor during the normal production, b) GUI for hybrid exothermic reactor in the case of operating control for research experimentation

In Fig. 2a the GUI for operating control system of the industrial process during normal operation is presented. The discussion below is illustrated with excerpts of GUIs developed for our semi-industrial pilot plants that are presented in [16]. Specifically, in Fig. 2a the GUI for pilot hybrid exothermic reactor is shown. As in the typical industrial systems, the background of the diagram is black. During normal operation conditions, process diagram fills whole display space, because additional data (e.g. variable trends) are needed during exceptional conditions only, and typically the operator doesn't need them, as he is not conducting any researches. When these additional information are needed to be displayed, there can be temporarily placed in movable window in any preferable place of the diagram.

If process is being investigated, for example during start-up of the process, periodic checkout, and redesign of installation, there is a need to constantly watch and keep track of changes of variables' values and their trends. Because of this, an alternate GUI has to be designed for such conditions, in which the display space is divided into several parts in which there is a place for the plant diagram, charts of variables' trends, and increased number of controls supporting the investigations to be conducted. The diagram itself, in this case, requires scaling-down or trimming, so it fits to the limited display space. In Fig. 2b the GUI is presented for the already introduced exothermic reactor, augmented with research capabilities.

5 Plant Diagram Selection

While there are both formal and informal attempts to standardisation of process diagrams, it seems that more user-centred approach could be possible, as colour-palette and aesthetics can modified on the fly for specific user needs. This could increase efficiency of process operator's work and improve accuracy of his decisions, according to the literature cited above.

Current state-of-art offers main four possibilities of process diagram creation technique (see Fig. 3):

a) Photograph of the real-world process;
b) Technical flowsheet;
c) 2D diagram composed of 3D and pseudo 3D elements;
d) Rendered full 3D scene.

For all the four stated techniques, research SCADA systems were developed (which are more complicated than typical exploitation SCADA). Basing on experiences gained during the synthesis of these applications and during their exploitation, following findings can be formulated.

The quickest and cheapest technique during creation and processing is photography. At the same time, its final effect is the least legible, because in the real installation there are many components, which are non-significant for the process operator. Controls and indicators are lost in the clutter, implying increased operator's reaction times. Nevertheless, photography, instead of simplification, shows the real looks of the process, which can be sometimes an advantage.

A technological chart based on a flow sheet uses the intentionally simplified diagram, displaying the most important process components only. Such design requires creativity and proper graphical tools. However, with no doubt, it is the most convenient and the most popular technique used in the practice. Software development environments for operating diagrams synthesis are usually supplied with a wide set of glyphs for the typical industrial instrumentation.

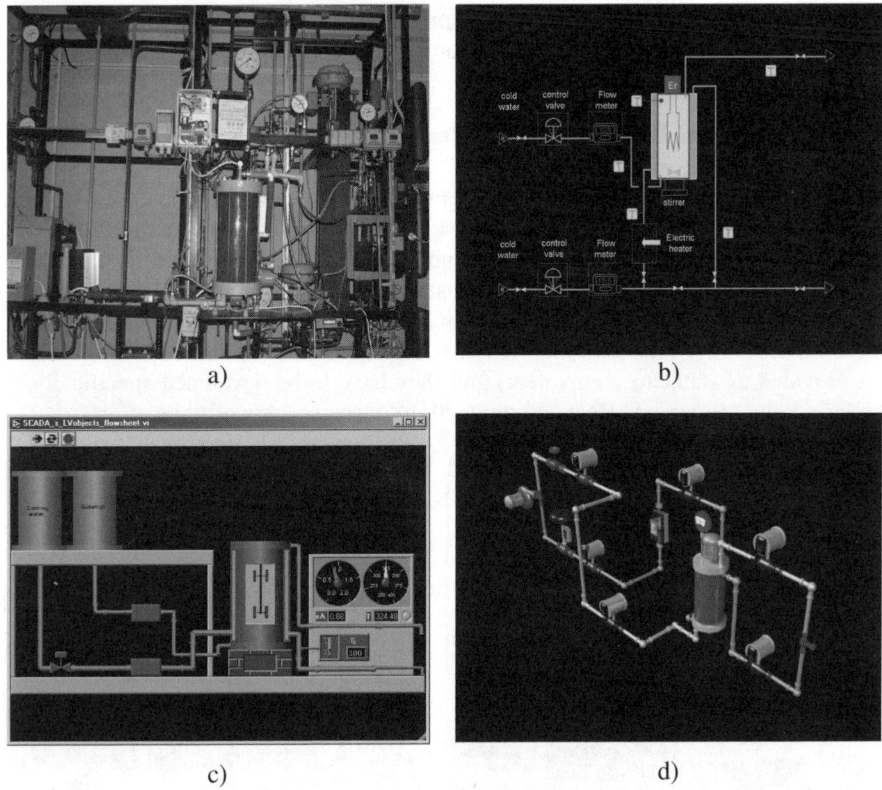

Fig. 3. Most important possibilities of plant diagram creation: a) photograph, b) technical flowsheet, c) 2D diagram with 3D elements, d) rendered full 3D scene

The third technique requires a proper software environment capable of SCADA systems development, equipped with the 3D components, which could be placed in the diagram space. A representative example of such environment is the National Instruments LabVIEW [17], which was used to develop examples presented in this paper. Using the supplied libraries of components including numerical controls and indicators, an improved (when compared to the previous technique) diagram can be synthesised. Because the components are designed to be perceived as three dimensional by a human, the diagram is more readable and easier accepted by the operator. A significant shortcoming of this approach is the limited set of ready components supplied.

Three dimensional rendered scene is very attractive from visual point of view and contains (as two previous cases) only selected components of the system, which are important from operating control's point of view. However, this technique of diagram synthesis is the most difficult and complicated, as it requires expensive software tools, non typical for an industrial control. Time required for the development (modelling of the scene) is also significantly larger than in other techniques. It should be taken into account, that the instrumentation of the presented example is exceptionally simple when compared to industry-grade installation.

6   Animation in Diagrams for Operating Control

Animated graphics is still reluctantly accepted in the industrial applications, which is surprising as it can significantly increase capabilities of on screen visualisation.

In Fig. 4a the GUI for operating control of sequencing reactor in wastewater treatment process is presented. The key tasks of control in this process is turning the stirring and aeration on and off adequately. Because of this, proper diagram elements are animated when corresponding action is in progress. Such animated elements are not provided as standard components and they have to be developed specifically for the task, however gained effect and productivity increase are worth the effort.

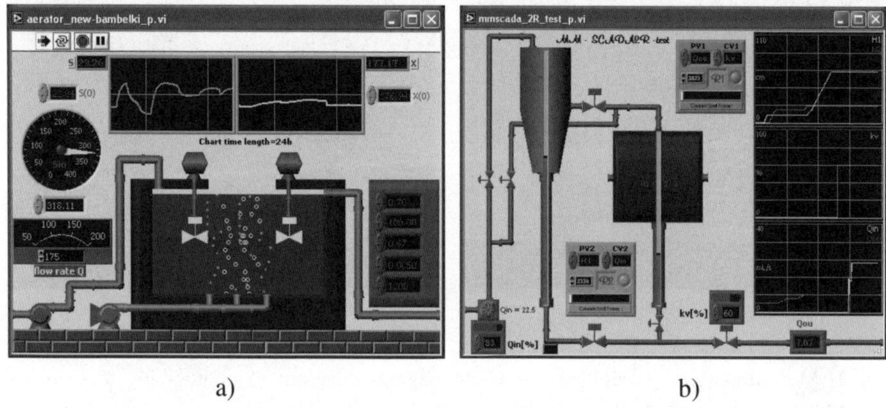

a)   b)

Fig. 4. a) GUI for sequenced biotechnological process with animated elements (switching-on and switching-off paddle mixers and floating bubbles of air), b) GUI for hydraulic process with changeable architecture (only pipes which are open at the moment are displayed in the diagram)

Some industrial processes are designed to have changeable structure of components connection, for example by cutting a flow of a liquid in a pipe. To enhance the visualisation, this modified structure may by presented in the GUI. For example, pipes closed with valves may disappear from the diagram completely. Fig. 4b presents such a GUI. For illustrative purposes, all the pipes are shown, but during the runtime only the current configuration of the piping is displayed.

7   Concluding Remarks

In this paper a study on appropriate plant diagram synthesis for user-suited HMI in operating control is presented. Discussion is based on the long-term personal experience and illustrated with excerpts of existing HMIs developed for research and industrial use.

After defining the HMI notion for the operating control and for the operator training, the paper describes three areas of the plant diagrams design process. The proper usage of a screen space for the plant diagram and other HMI elements is described. Then, four methods of image creation for process diagrams are depicted, i.e. photography, schematic 2D diagrams, pseudo-3D diagrams composed of predefined graphical elements, and ray-traced full 3D scene. At last, dynamic visualisation capabilities of the animated graphics are outlined.

The approach proposed here is not opposed to the one based on the formal methods, but it rather complements that methods with the point of view of industrial HMIs developers. The practice shows that users often prefer specific solutions, and their preferences are not based on any objective measurable principles, but are extremely subjective. Enabling the user to choose the variant of the graphical layout of the interface on his own is therefore highly desirable. The presented survey of methods can be used as a start point for the process of user-suited HMI design.

Acknowledgements. This work was supported by the Polish Ministry of Scientific Research and Education.

References

1. Vicente, K.J., Rasmussen, J.: Ecological Interface Design: Theoretical foundations. IEEE Transactions on Systems, Man and Cybernetics 22, 589–606 (1992)
2. Paterno, F.: Formal reasoning about dialogue properties with automatic support. Interacting with computers 9, 173–196 (1997)
3. Jamieson, G.A., Vicente, K.J.: Ecological interface design for petrochemical applications: supporting operator adaptation, continuous learning, and distributed, collaborative work. Computers and Chemical Engineering 25, 1055–1074 (2001)
4. Seffah, A., Forbrig, P., Javahery, H.: Multi-devices "Multiple" user interfaces: development models and research opportunities. The Journal of Systems and Software 73, 287–300 (2004)
5. Seffah, A., Donyaee, M., Kline, R.B., Padda, H.K.: Usability measurement and metrics: A consolidated model. Software Qual. J. 14, 159–178 (2006)
6. Burns, C.M., Hajdukiewicz, J.R.: Ecological Interface Design. CRC Press, Boca Raton (2004)
7. Seffah, A., Gulliksen, J., Desmarais, M.C.: Human-Centered Software Engineering – Integrating Usability in the Software Development Lifecycle. Springer, Heidelberg (2005)
8. Rasmussen, J.: Information processing and human-machine interaction: An approach to cognitive engineering. North-Holland, Amsterdam (1986)
9. Shneiderman, B.: Designing the user interface - strategies for effective Human-Computer Interaction. Addison-Wesley, Reading (1998)
10. Gibson, J.J.: The ecological approach to visual perception. Houghton Miffin (1979)
11. Norman, D.A.: Cognitive Engineering. In: User Centered System Design: New Perspectives On Human-Computer Interaction, p. 61. Erlbaum, Hillsdale (1986)
12. Metzger, M.: A new concept of industrial process simulation - cybernetic approach using distributed access control schemes. SAMS 15, 185–202 (1994)
13. Inverso, D., Sokoll, R.: Optimum Human-Interface. Control Engineering, 93–98 (September 1997)

14. Johnson, D.: Conveing understandable process information to an operator requires more than dazzling HMI graphics in real time. Control Engineering, 80–88 (September 1997)
15. Wittenberg, C.: A pictorial human-computer interface concept for supervisory control. Control Engineering Practice 7, 865–878 (2004)
16. Metzger, M., Polaków, G.: Holonic Multiagent-Based System for Distributed Control of Semi-industrial Pilot Plants. In: Mařík, V., Vyatkin, V., Colombo, A.W. (eds.) HoloMAS 2007. LNCS (LNAI), vol. 4659, pp. 338–347. Springer, Heidelberg (2007)
17. Official National Instruments LabVIEW website, http://www.ni.com/labview/

Preserving Rich User Interface State in Web Applications across Various Platforms

Fabio Paternò, Carmen Santoro, and Antonio Scorcia

ISTI-CNR, Via G. Moruzzi, 1
56124 Pisa, Italy
{Fabio.Paterno,Carmen.Santoro,Antonio.Scorcia}@isti.cnr.it

Abstract. This paper aims to provide thorough discussion of the aspects that compose the state of a Web application user interface, and show how it can be preserved across multiple devices with different interaction resources when the user interface dynamically migrates. The approach proposed exploits a migration server along with logical user interface descriptions.

1 Introduction

The Web is the most common user interface. There are currently hundreds of millions of Web sites and it is increasingly rare to find someone who has never used a Web application. In the meantime, Web technologies have evolved in many directions: the Web 2.0, Rich Interactive Applications, Multimodal Interfaces, ... Another important technological trend is the increasing availability in the mass market of many types of interactive devices, in particular mobile devices, which has enabled the possibility of ubiquitous applications.

In such environments migratory interfaces are particularly interesting. They allow users to move about freely, change device and still continue the interaction from the point where they left off. Thus, in order to obtain usable migration two aspects are important: preserving the user interface state across multiple devices and adaptation to the changing interaction resources. In this paper, we focus on the former aspect (state preservation) in the context of Web applications, identify a broad set of relevant aspects, and show how they can be addressed by our migration environment.

After discussing related work, we first identify seven relevant aspects that can be used to define the state of Web User Interfaces, including Web 2.0 applications with Ajax scripts. Then, we introduce our architecture for supporting Web application migration, and explain how it has been extended in order to be able to support the various aspects that have been deemed useful for defining the user interface state.

2 Related Work

ICrafter [1] is a solution to generate adaptive interfaces for accessing services in interactive spaces. It generates interfaces that adapt to different devices starting with XML-based descriptions of the service that must be supported. However, ICrafter is

P. Forbrig and F. Paternò (Eds.): HCSE/TAMODIA 2008, LNCS 5247, pp. 255–262, 2008.

limited to creating support for controlling interactive workspaces by generating user interfaces for services obtained by dynamic composition of elementary ones and does not provide support for migration and, consequently, continuity of task performance across different devices.

Aura [2] provides support for migration but the solution adopted has a different granularity. In Aura for each possible application service various applications are available and the choice of the application depends on the interaction resources available. Thus, for example for word processing, if a desktop is available then an application such as MS-Word can be activated, whereas in the case of a mobile platform a lighter editing application is used. Thus, Aura aims to provide a similar support but this is obtained mainly by changing the application depending on the resources available in the device in question, while we generate interfaces of the same application that adapt to the interaction resources available.

Bharat and Cardelli [3] addressed the migration of entire applications (which is problematic with limited-resource devices and different CPU architectures or operating systems) while we focus on the migration of the user interface part of a software application. Kozuch and Satyanarayanan [4] identified a solution for migration based on the encapsulation of all volatile execution state of a virtual machine. However, their solution mainly supports migration of applications among desktop or laptop systems by making copy of the application with the current state in a virtual machine and then copy the virtual machine in the target device. This solution does not address the support of different interaction platforms supporting different interaction resources and modalities, with the consequent ability to adapt to them. Chung and Dewan [5] proposed a specific solution for migration of applications shared among several users. When migration is triggered the environment starts a fresh copy of the application process in the target system, and replays the saved sequence of input events to the copy in order to ensure that the process will get the state where it left off. This solution does not consider migration across platform supporting different interaction resources and modalities and consequently does not support run-time generation of a new version of the user interface for a different platform. We follow a different approach: we assume that the desktop version of an application exists, without posing any restriction on the method or tool used for its development. Then, during the user session, we dynamically generate the version for the platform at hand exploiting model-based techniques.

We introduced some preliminary ideas on how to obtain automatic generation of migratory Web interfaces in [6]. In this paper we are able to present a solution supporting migration of rich information state, including application with Ajax scripts.

3   The Many Aspects of the Web Interface State

In our study we have identified at least eight aspects that can be relevant for defining the state of Web user interfaces and that can have an impact on the overall user experience. The first element is associated with the *user input*. People make selections, enter text and modify the state of various input controls during a session, and such modifications should not be lost when moving to a new device if we want to maintain continuity. An associated element is *client-side variables* associated with small functionalities (e.g. Javascript variables).

Another component that can be dynamically modified is the *content* of a Web application. While this can be easily managed with dynamic Web sites using PhP, JSP and similar languages because whenever a new request is performed then a different page is uploaded, with Ajax scripts this aspect becomes more problematic. Indeed, in this case the content of the page can vary without requiring the loading of a new page. Thus, it becomes more complex to detect what is actually composing the currently displayed page.

Cookies are more and more used and they allow an application to provide small pieces of information to the client in such a way that whenever the client accesses the application, then the client identifiers are inserted in the HTTP protocol. It is important that if and when a user changes device, then the current application preserves the same cookies in order to be recognised by the application server. A related technique is the *session*: it is a server-side mechanism, which stores information related to the user session, which is in turn associated with a specific identifier.

Another important aspect is the *history* of user accesses, which is maintained by the Web browser and drives the behaviour of the frequently used browser back button. Since the user is still the same, even if she has changed device, then she would appreciate still being able to easily return to recently accessed pages, even if through a different device. It is clear that the pages accessed through the new device may be adapted to the currently available interaction resources. In some cases (e.g. migration from desktop to mobile), it may even happen that the original desktop page is split into multiple mobile pages, thus accessing all its content may require further navigation.

Bookmarks are another interesting aspect that can be considered part of the user interface state. Users often use them to quickly find and access favourite pages. In migration, the devices change but not the user, who still has the same interests and may appreciate the possibility to find in the current bookmarks including the pages that were bookmarked in the previous device. Another element that has similar characteristics is the browser home page: in some cases users may be interested to migrate it to different platforms as well.

A last element that can be considered part of the state is the *query string* included in a URL after the "?" symbol. It is usually used to specify parameters for a dynamic site, which define some data that are presented in the associated page. By modifying the query string we will access the same Web site but since the parameters vary, then the corresponding page varies in terms of content.

4 An Architecture for Migratory Interfaces

Our architecture for migratory interfaces is based on a migration/proxy server. The advantage of this choice with respect to installing the necessary functionalities on the application servers is that we can concentrate them in a single server without the need for replication in the servers supporting the various possible applications. Indeed, we want to apply the migration support to a wide set of applications, and we do not want to force the application developers to use any specific authoring environment or to apply specific annotations to ease the migration process. In general, we consider that a wide set of Web applications for desktop systems already exist and they can be the target for a migration infrastructure.

Our migration infrastructure exploits logical descriptions of user interfaces. In such description there is an abstract level, which is platform independent and a concrete level, which refines the previous one by adding concrete elements and attributes. The environment has a service-oriented architecture based on four main functionality:

- *Reverse Engineering*, takes the existing Web pages for desktop systems and builds the corresponding logical descriptions;
- *Semantic Redesign*, this module is in charge to perform the adaptation to the target device. For this purpose it takes the abstract elements identified by the reverse engineering module and maps then into concrete elements more suitable for the target device. It also splits the source presentations into multiple presentation if they are too expensive for the interaction resources of such target device.
- *State Mapper*, once a concrete description for the target device has been obtained then the state resulting from the user interactions in the source use interface is associated with it. The abstract elements are used to identify which concrete element in the source interface correspond to the concrete elements in the target interface.
- *User Interface Generator*, this module generates the user interface in some implementation language. One concrete description for a given platform, for example a graphical form-based interface, can be associated with various implementations languages (such as Java, XHTML, C#). The generated user interface is then uploaded on the target device.

In addition, when the host acting as a migration/proxy server passes the Web pages to the client, it adds Ajax scripts, which are used to communicate to the server the interface state accessed through DOM when the migration is triggered.

All the devices that are involved in the migration should run a migration client, which is used for two purposes: in the device discovery phase, when the devices interested in migration are identified and provide information about themselves, and to trigger migration. Users can trigger migration through an interface separated from the application interface, which shows the list of available devices from which the user can select the target one.

5   Migration Preserving Rich Information State

In this section we discuss how our migration infrastructure has been modified in order to support rich state information, which includes various aspects additional to the changes due to the user input in some controls.

The use of Ajax scripts implies that the content of a Web page changes dynamically without loading an entire new page. This means that when the migration server starts the reverse engineering process to build the logical description of the current page it should work on the page version currently loaded in the client browser and not that in the application server, because they may be different.

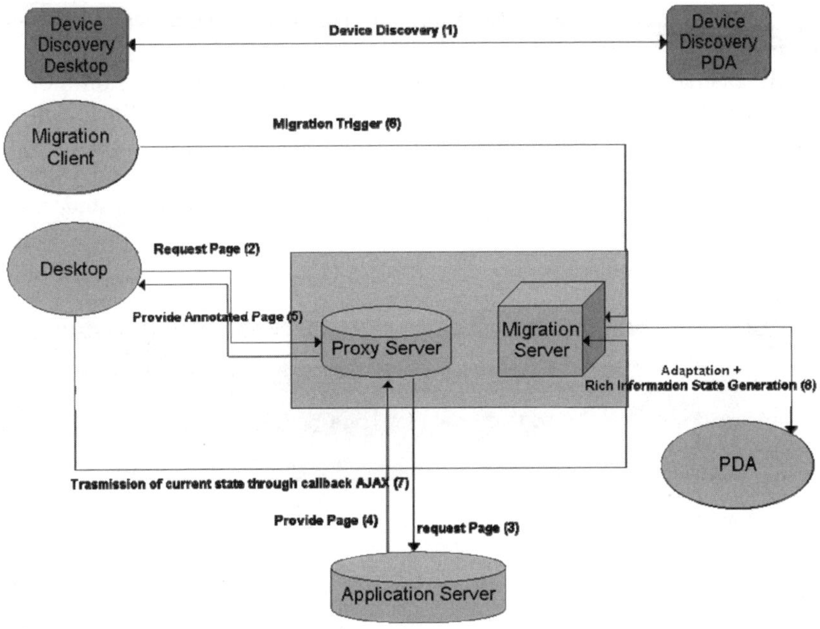

Fig. 1. The Migration Architecture Preserving Rich Information State

Figure 1 describes the current architecture of the environment. After the device discovery phase (1), there is an access to the Web page through the migration/proxy server (2), which downloads the page from the application server (3, 4) and annotates it by adding an Ajax script (5) whose goal is to collect the rich information state of the client device and send its description to the migration/proxy server. Among the functionalities that are included in such an AJAX script, we first mention a functionality performing a continuous monitoring (polling), whose objective is detecting whether or not a migration has been triggered by the migration client. In addition, a piece of invisible script code (since it uses a IFRAME element) is added to the page downloaded by the server with the aims of getting the cookies and the current history, storing their content, and continuously updating such information to maintain the state consistent in an automatic and transparent way. This is managed, again, by AJAX scripts: indeed, both the list of addresses (URLs) representing the history, and the set of cookies generated during the user session can be rewritten in the IFRAME and can be sent to the migration server without the user's awareness. While the user navigates through the source device browser without sending any migration request, the loaded Web page sends an invisible HTTP request to the Migration Server, which is suspended until a migration request is activated through the migration client.

When a migration trigger is generated (6), the AJAX callback function is automatically activated and thus sends (7) the DOM file (containing the state of the current page), together with the portion of the invisible content (IFRAME) previously mentioned. Then, the migration server will first associate the content state of the page on the source device accessed through the DOM to the concrete description of the version for the target device, and will add a new portion of invisible content (IFRAME) containing the AJAX functions to re-create the rich state on the target client device (8) in the corresponding generated implementation. Such rich state information will be obtained through the functions able to read the cookies and re-create them in the target device, as well as functions that will re-load within the IFRAME the addresses connected with the chronology and create the history accordingly on the target device.

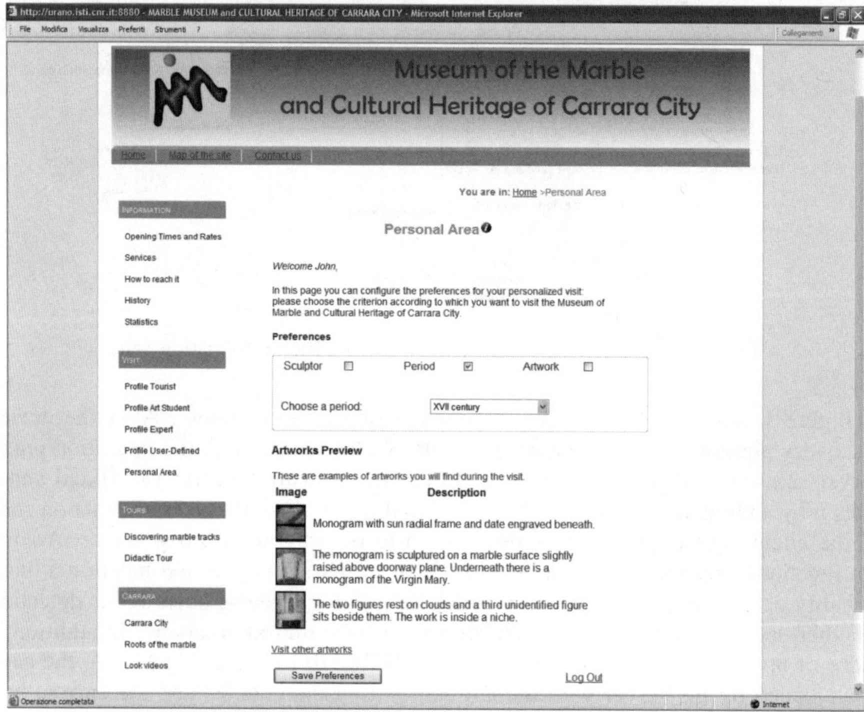

Fig. 2. The Example Ajax Application

6   An Example Application

In this section we describe an example to show how our approach concretely works. The scenario considered regards a user who starts interacting with a digital museum application providing information about artworks. At some point the user accesses a page, which allows him to specify preferences regarding artworks in the museum. While the various preference options are specified, the application using an Ajax script provides a preview of artworks that satisfy them (see Figure 2) without requiring access to a new page. Then, the user asks for migration to a mobile device in order to continue by means of indicating preferences on the move.

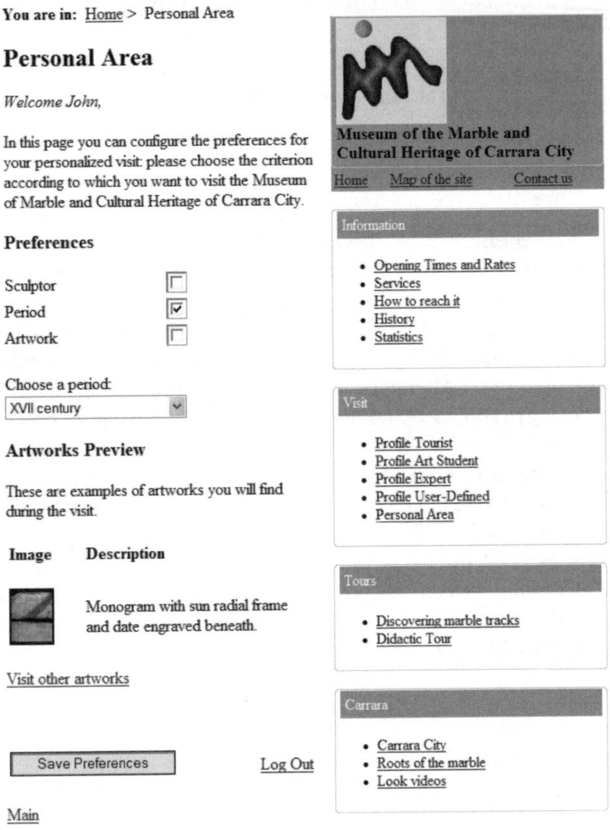

You are in: Home > Personal Area

Personal Area

Welcome John,

In this page you can configure the preferences for your personalized visit: please choose the criterion according to which you want to visit the Museum of Marble and Cultural Heritage of Carrara City.

Preferences

Sculptor

Period

Artwork

Choose a period:

XVII century

Artworks Preview

These are examples of artworks you will find during the visit.

Image   Description

Monogram with sun radial frame and date engraved beneath.

Visit other artworks

Save Preferences   Log Out

Main

Museum of the Marble and Cultural Heritage of Carrara City

Home   Map of the site   Contact us

Information
- Opening Times and Rates
- Services
- How to reach it
- History
- Statistics

Visit
- Profile Tourist
- Profile Art Student
- Profile Expert
- Profile User-Defined
- Personal Area

Tours
- Discovering marble tracks
- Didactic Tour

Carrara
- Carrara City
- Roots of the marble
- Look videos

Fig. 3. The Ajax Application after Migration to a Mobile Device

The left side in Figure 3 shows the user interface activated in the mobile device immediately after migration. Since the cookies are also migrated, the application still recognises the user (John). The desktop page is too large for the mobile device and, consequently, the adaptation component of the migration platform splits it into two pages for the mobile device after analysing its logical structure obtained by the reverse engineering functionality. One mobile page is dedicated to the interactive form enriched with the Ajax script for the preview, which is the page immediately uploaded because the user was interacting with it when migration was triggered. The other the page (Figure 3 right) is the main page including the navigational structure of the application. In the uploaded page some other adaptations take place: the check-box is lined up vertically because it would not fit horizontally and the preview of only one artwork is shown at a given time.

7 Conclusions and Future Work

In this paper we have discussed the many aspects that characterise the state of a Web application from the user point of view. Then, we have presented a solution for migration of Web applications, including those with Ajax scripts, able to preserve this rich state information and have shown an example application.

Future work will be dedicated to testing the usability of the proposed solution and its integration to a more general migration platform.

References

1. Ponnekanti, S.R., Lee, B., Fox, A., Hanrahan, P., Winograd, T.: ICrafter: A service framework for ubiquitous computing environments. In: Abowd, G.D., Brumitt, B., Shafer, S. (eds.) UbiComp 2001. LNCS, vol. 2201, pp. 56–75. Springer, Heidelberg (2001)
2. Garlan, D., Siewiorek, D., Smailagic, A., Steenkiste, P.: Project Aura: Toward Distraction-Free Pervasive Computing. IEEE Pervasive Computing 21(2), 22–31 (2002)
3. Bharat, K.A., Cardelli., L.: Migratory Applications. In: Proceedings of User Inteface Software and Technology (UIST 1995), Pittsburgh, PA, USA, November 15-17, 1995, pp. 133–142 (1995)
4. Kozuch, M., Satyanarayanan, M.: Internet Suspend/Resume. In: Proceedings of the Fourth IEEE Workshop on Mobile Computing Systems and Applications (WMCSA 2002). IEEE Press, Los Alamitos (2002)
5. Chung, G., Dewan, P.: A mechanism for Supporting Client Migration in a Shared Window System. In: Proceedings UIST 1996, pp. 11–20. ACM Press, New York (1996)
6. Bandelloni, R., Mori, G., Paternò, F.: Dynamic Generation of Migratory Interfaces. In: Proceedings Mobile HCI 2005, pp. 83–90. ACM Press, Salzburg (2005)

From Desktop to Tabletop: Migrating the User Interface of AgilePlanner

Xin Wang, Yaser Ghanam, and Frank Maurer

Department of Computer Science, University of Calgary, Canada
{xin,yghanam,maurer}@cpsc.ucalgary.ca

Abstract. Digital tabletops are emerging interactive systems that support group collaborations. To utilize digital tabletops for agile planning meetings, we migrated a desktop based planning tool – AgilePlanner to a digital tabletop. This paper reports on challenges of the migration and illustrates differences between user interactions on a digital tabletop and on a desktop. Moreover, lessons and experiences learnt from our design process are highlighted to facilitate future tabletop application design.

Keywords: desktop computer, digital tabletop, user interface design, agile planning tool.

1 Introduction

Desktop computers have dominated computer applications for several years. Many activities such as browsing websites and online shopping involve interactions between a desktop system and a computer user. Typical desktop computers are characterized by three basic facts: a vertical display, a single keyboard & mouse and a relatively small screen. Personal computers are called "personal" because they primarily only support interactions of a single individual with the computer.

However, today's business looks at supporting an increasing number of group interactions. A typical example is an agile planning meeting which requires the software developers, project managers and customers working together as a group to derive release and iteration plans for the next development step. To support agile planning meetings, we had developed a desktop-based application – AgilePlanner [1]. However, some usability problems were observed:

- It is difficult for collocated meeting attendees to share the AgilePlanner interface since it was limited by the small screen size of personal computers. Some agile teams use projectors to get a large display. However, the screen resolution is still limited. Also, the location of the projection screen focuses their attention to the screen and face-to-face interactions are reduced.
- The single input devices impacted group interactions. To use AgilePlanner, meeting participants have to share the mouse and keyboard. That was commented "unnatural", "inflexible" and "annoying". It also slowed down interactions when compared to index cards and pen.

P. Forbrig and F. Paternò (Eds.): HCSE/TAMODIA 2008, LNCS 5247, pp. 263–270, 2008.

To overcome usability problems of the desktop AgilePlanner, we started to use a digital tabletop with a large, horizontal and multi-touch screen (see Figure 1). In a tabletop-based meeting, participants could sit or stand around the table, communicate with each other and use their finger touches to interact with the tabletop. User interaction with the tabletop is more intuitive than that with the desktop [2].

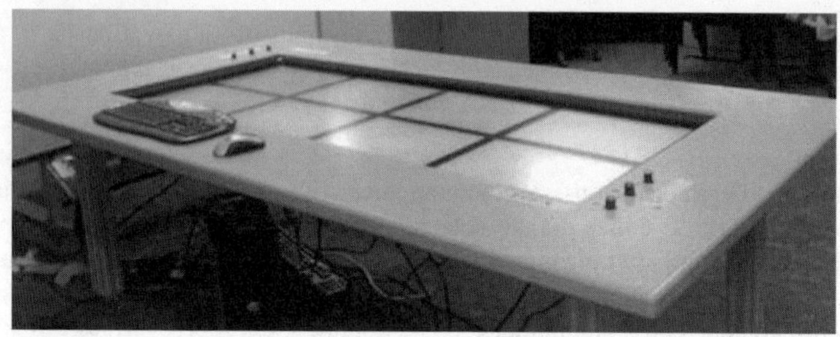

Fig. 1. The 183cm x 122 cm digital tabletop with 10 mega pixels output resolutions

Then we migrated our agile planning tool to a digital tabletop. The migration process kept the core functions of desktop AgilePlanner, initially utilized the existing user interface design, and then integrated tabletop usability features. Moreover, lessons and experiences learnt from the migration provide insights into the interaction design of tabletop applications.

This paper is organized as follows: Section 2 discusses related work on user interface migrations. Section 3 illustrates the 4-phase process for migrating AgilePlanner. Section 4 lists the key findings from the migration process. A conclusion is drawn in Section 5.

2   Related Works

There is some research on the migration of user interfaces but none specifically looking into migrating UIs to digital tabletops. Bandelloni et al presented a new environment to support the migration of Web based user interface through different modalities [3]. Mori et al migrated a user interface between Digital TV and mobile devices [4]. Other studies of user interface migrations involve the automatic translation and generation of different Web based user interface languages.

Web based applications are basically running on a similar hardware platform as personal computers, PDAs and cell phones. The main difference is screen resolution and the use of HTML instead of native widget libraries. The interactions for user interfaces are similar. However, a digital tabletop has different user interaction features:

- Tabletop supports touch and gesture recognition. Using a fingertip instead of a mouse reduces accuracy and makes precise selections difficult.
- The relatively large physical size screen combined with touch input makes reaching objects on the screen difficult as human arms have a limited length.

- The orientation independent display makes it difficult to read text for some meeting participants as it is upside down from their perspective.
- People are aware and often take ownership of parts of the table surface. "Territoriality" in the tabletop workspace was studied in [5].
- Studies of multiple input approaches (mouse, keyboard, finger and pen) for tabletop applications are required [6].

However, experiences about migrating desktop software applications to the digital tabletop are – to the best of our knowledge – not yet reported. Our project, in particular, explored a concrete migration of a desktop based application to tabletop devices.

3   The Migration Process

In this section, we will show a migration process that converts the desktop AgilePlanner to the tabletop environment. The migration was organized in four basic phases: analyzing the desktop AgilePlanner, evaluating AgilePlanner on the digital tabletop, redesigning the AgilePlanner UI and continued improvement of the redesign. Usability evaluations are conducted often to validate changes for AgilePlanner. The evaluations included task centered walkthroughs, questionnaire surveys, field studies and interviews with AgilePlanner users.

3.1   Phase 1: Analyzing Desktop Based AgilePlanner

Desktop AgilePlanner is a groupware tool for agile planning meetings. Compared to a traditional agile planning meeting that uses paper index cards and a table, the tool provides a flexible, computer-aided, distributed environment. It is easy to operate, e.g. create, modify and resize electronic index cards. Moreover, the meeting results, such as the card contents and the card order that represent task significance, are saved and can be recovered for the next planning meeting.

The user interface design of AgilePlanner (see Figure 2) provides basic functionalities. A large, scrollable workspace is provided to organize the index cards. A vertical legend bar shows card icons that can be dragged to create index cards on the workspace. The horizontal menu makes basic functions such as server connection and card print available to the user. The main user interactions include creating, deleting, resizing and moving index cards. A keyboard is used to conduct card editing and modifications.

Desktop AgilePlanner is designed for the typical personal computer featuring a small, vertical display with single keyboard & mouse control that supports individual interactions. But in a multi-user collocated team, some limitations are observable. For example, suppose there is an 11-person team which consisted of 2 collocated groups (one in Vancouver with 5 people and the other in Calgary with 6 people). To conduct an 11-person meeting which is distributed between Vancouver and Calgary but collocated inside the two groups, the attendees have to use their individual computers and thus, face to face communication of the collocated teams is changed. A possible alternative is using projectors to enlarge and project the AgilePlanner interface to a shared screen. However, the projected screen becomes the focus of attention of onsite team members, thus reducing the effectiveness of collocated communication. Moreover, some natural behaviors in traditional agile meetings, such as passing card among several participants, rotating cards and concurrently operating cards, are not supported by AgilePlanner or similar tools as a single user is controlling the mouse & keyboard.

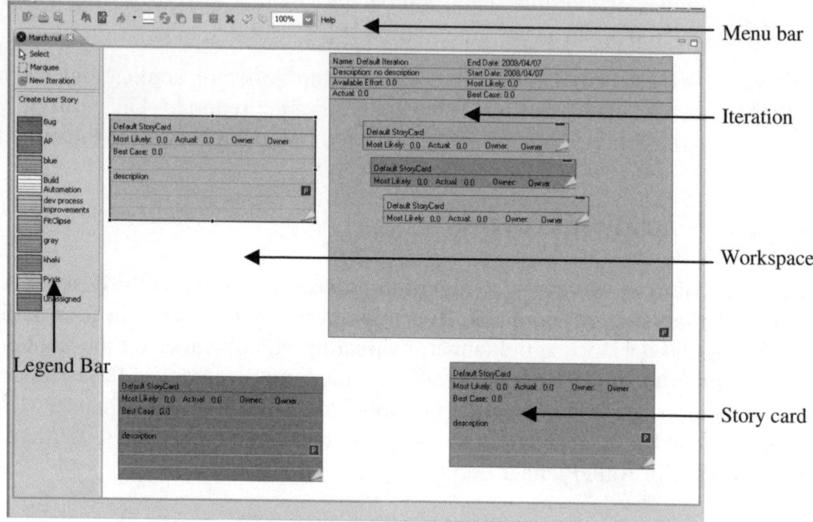

Fig. 2. User interface of desktop AgilePlanner

3.2   Phase 2: Evaluating AgilePlanner on the Tabletop

In this phase, we conducted a usability evaluation of the desktop AgilePlanner tool after deploying it on a digital tabletop. The goal of this evaluation is to highlight the differences of desktop and tabletop systems, in particular, the size of screens, the horizontal versus vertical display, as well as the single versus concurrent users. The evaluation was designed as a task-centered walkthrough that employed 6 testers. During the evaluation, the testers were required to complete some sample tasks using the desktop AgilePlanner which was running on the digital tabletop. We discovered several usability problems through this study. Design guidelines for a redesigned tabletop-based AgilePlanner were developed based on an analysis of the problems. The following subsections illustrate the basic differences of desktops and tabletops.

Vertical vs. horizontal display

A typical desktop computer often provides a vertical screen which only requires a top-down (vertical) orientation: there is a defined upper edge and a defined lower edge. Desktop applications are designed with this in mind. Using AgilePlanner as an example, story cards are all placed vertically. However, horizontal displays are orientation independent and require rotating cards to show them to people on the other side of the table.

Single vs. concurrent interaction

Desktop computers are based on single mouse-keyboard interactions. The desktop AgilePlanner can only respond to one mouse-keyboard action at the same time.

However, a real collocated planning meeting often involves several participants who operate story cards simultaneously. The lack of simultaneous interactions reduced the agile developers' motivation to use AgilePlanner. For example, if a meeting participant wants to edit a story card, she must negotiate with other participants to get the keyboard and mouse control. Moreover while she was editing story cards, other participants could not input information till the completion of her operation. Our testers noticed the inconvenience caused by the single mouse-keyboard interaction. They commented it *"unnatural"* and *"interrupt communications"*.

However, the digital tabletop support multi-touch input. Meeting attendees are able to use their fingers to operate the story cards simultaneously. For example, two or more meeting attendees could use their fingertips to write text, and their handwriting strokes would be kept and converted to text.

Small vs. large display

Several usability problems from the evaluation are related to the different screen sizes of desktops and tabletops. For instance, a popup dialog box is a common interaction component. AgilePlanner often shows these at the center of the computer screen. However, our physical tabletop surface is at least 8 times larger than a normal screen of a desktop computer. Thus, the pop up position of the dialog box might be out of reach of a user sitting at the end of the table. One of our study subjects mentioned that he was often stopped by the pop-up dialog box. He commented that *"finding and clicking the pop-up dialog box are both annoying"*.

Recommendations

The following guidelines for redesigning the AgilePlanner user interface were derived from our study:

1. UI components of AgilePlanner should be moveable and rotatable.
2. Use gesture recognition for user interactions and avoid traditional menus.
3. Use handwriting instead of the keyboard to input text.
4. Consider concurrent interaction while designing the UI.
5. The size of widgets of the tabletop AgilePlanner should be large enough to facilitate touch input.
6. Avoid using pop up dialog boxes and other similar components.
7. Since the size of tabletops varies a lot, it is necessary to make the application interface scalable.

3.3   Phase 3: Redesigning the AgilePlanner User Interface

Based on the guidelines from the phase 2, AgilePlanner was redesigned. We found that Microsoft WPF (Windows Presentation Foundation) better supported tabletops than Java SWT (the framework underlying the desktop version of AgilePlanner). WPF provides a sound basis for tabletop applications. UI components of WPF can easily be transformed in size, position and angularity. Handwriting, gesture and voice recognition engines are provided by the WPF environment.

We abandoned the traditional WIMP (window, icon, menu, pointer device) approach in the desktop applications. The menus and legend bars are integrated into a *control palette* which can be moved and rotated on the table surface to allow access from any seat around the table. A rotation and translation (RNT) algorithm was implemented to facilitate the movement of the story cards, iterations and the control palette. Moreover, we implemented handwriting recognition to translate strokes into text. The original handwritings are kept and displayed on the story card surface. The control flow of AgilePlanner is also simplified. Instead of clicking buttons with a mouse, users can make simple gestures to complete the card operations. Figure 3 lists some gestures defined for card operations. A story card is created by a "Chevron-Down" gesture. The "Square" gesture creates iteration. To delete an index card, a "ScratchOut" gesture is required to exceed the whole card boarder. Our evaluation indicates that gestures are flexible, learnable and easy to use. Moreover, pop up dialog boxes are replaced by customized windows which have a large size and can be moved on the table surface. System warnings are displayed on the control palette. The new user interface of tabletop AgilePlanner is shown on the Figure 4:

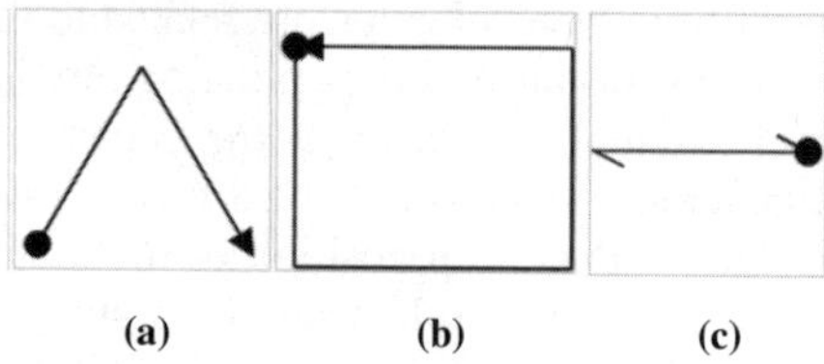

(a)   (b)   (c)

Fig. 3. Gestures commands for Tabletop based AgilePlanner (a) create story card, (b) create iteration, (c) delete card

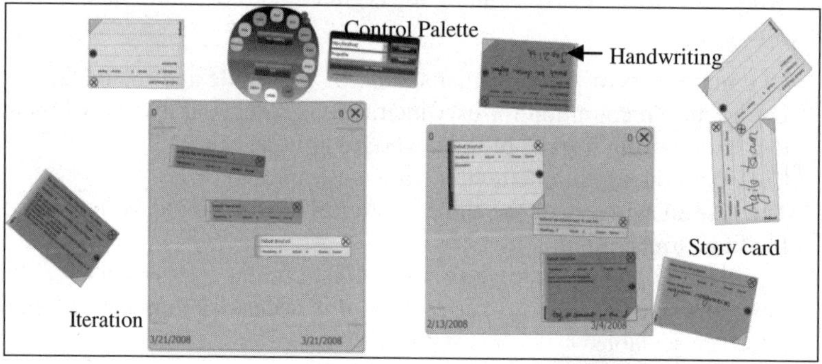

Fig. 4. User interface of tabletop based Agile Planner

To validate the new UI, we conducted a pilot evaluation which included 14 subjects. They were asked to complete sample tasks and filled out a questionnaire afterwards. Unstructured interviews were used to collect the testers' comments. The results of the pilot evaluation showed the users' satisfactions with the new UI and interaction design. Most of the testers felt comfortable when using the tabletop based AgilePlanner. Some negative comments and usability issues were arisen. For example, some testers suggested the "deleting card" gesture (see Figure 4(d)) was confusing while others commented the handwriting *"cool but sometimes unreadable"*.

3.4 Phase 4: Continued Improvement

We continue development to solve the usability problems found in Phase 3. We analyzed the card deletion gestures and found out that most of testers were not aware the deletion gesture should go through the whole card. Moreover, when the card is very large, drawing the deletion gesture will be difficult. As an alternative approach, a card deletion button is placed at the right corner of an index card. We also studied the problems of handwriting readability and found out that the fingertips of testers were very thick so that it was difficult to draw tiny ink strokes accurately. Moreover, some testers mentioned that using their fingers to write on the table surface was *unnatural* because, while writing with fingers, their fists were not allowed to touch the table.

We reevaluated the system after making corresponding changes. 9 testers showed their satisfactions (see Figure 5) to the functionalities provided by AgilePlanner. But the usability of handwriting on tabletop still requires the improvements.

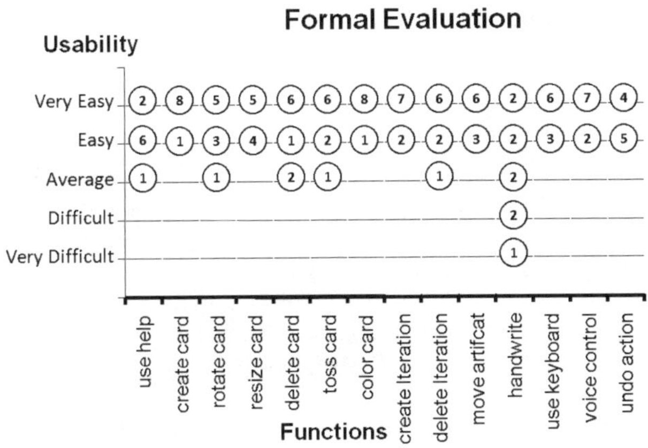

Fig. 5. Formal evaluation result

4 Discussion

From the migration process, we gathered experiences that can help other developers of tabletop applications.

The horizontal display brings the orientation independence to the user interface. Thus, rotating the UI elements of AgilePlanner became necessary. The physical screen sizes of tabletops vary a lot. On a large tabletop (like ours), menu bars or popup windows with fixed positions and small sizes are hard to find and click. Thus, the UI components need to be scalable to fit different tabletop surfaces.

Tabletop devices are touch sensitive. Tabletop developers can make use of the touch recognition to support a gesture and handwriting. However, "unnatural" gesture definitions might cause severe confusions. Thus, although a gesture and finger interaction is often more flexible than the mouse actions, its implementation must be based on careful design and evaluation.

5 Conclusion

The digital tabletop is gaining its popularity as an emerging technology to support group activities. However, not many tabletop based applications for real end users exist. We migrated the desktop AgilePlanner to the tabletop environments to gain a better understanding of issues involved in application engineering for tabletop-based software systems.

The migration had 4 phases. The first phase helped to understand the UI and interaction design of the source application. In the second phase, we evaluated the existing application in the new environment. A new tabletop AgilePlanner was designed in Phase3. The focus of the redesign was on utilizing the capabilities of tabletops and improving the application usability. In Phase 4, continued improvements were made to fulfill new user requirements or solve usability problems.

We discussed the differences of the desktop and tabletop interactive systems. Some UI design experiences provide rough guidelines to help tabletop application developers in migrating other applications.

References

1. Liu, L., Erdogmus, H., Maurer, F.: An environment for collaborative phase planning. In: Proceedings of Agile Conference, pp. 80–89. ACM, New York (2005)
2. Morgan, R., Walny, J., Kolenda, H., Ginez, E., Maurer, F.: Using Horizontal Displays for Distributed & Collocated Agile Planning. In: Concas, G., Damiani, E., Scotto, M., Succi, G. (eds.) XP 2007. LNCS, vol. 4536, pp. 38–45. Springer, Heidelberg (2007)
3. Bandelloni, R., Paternò, F., Santoro, C., Scorcia, A.: Web User Interface Migration through Different Modalities with Dynamic Device Discovery. In: Proceedings AEWSE 2007, Como, pp. 58–72 (2007)
4. Mori, G., Paternò, F., Santoro, C., Sansone, S.: Migrating the User Interface between the Digital TV and Mobile Devices. In: Proceedings Interacive TV: A shared experience, Amsterdam, Holland, pp. 73–77 (2007)
5. Scott, S.D.: Sheelagh M., C.T.I. Kori: Territoriality in collaborative tabletop workspaces Tabletop design. In: Proceedings of ACM Conference on Computer-Supported Cooperative Work, pp. 294–303. ACM Press, New York (2006)
6. Tse, E., Shen, C., Greenberg, S., Forlines, C.: Enabling interaction with single user applications through speech and gestures on a multi-user tabletop. In: Proceedings of the conference on Advanced visual interfaces, pp. 336–343. ACM Press, New York (2006)

Learning Key Contexts of Use in the Wild for Driving Plastic User Interfaces Engineering

Vincent Ganneau[1,2], Gaëlle Calvary[2], and Rachel Demumieux[1]

[1] Orange Labs, 2 avenue Pierre Marzin, 22307 Lannion Cedex, France
{Vincent.Ganneau,Rachel.Demumieux}@orange-ftgroup.com
[2] Laboratoire LIG, 385 rue de la Bibliothèque, BP 53, 38041 Grenoble Cedex, France
{Vincent.Ganneau,Gaelle.Calvary}@imag.fr

Abstract. This paper addresses software plasticity, i.e. the ability of interactive systems to adapt to context of use while preserving user-centered properties. In plasticity, a classical approach consists in concentrating design efforts on a set of pre-defined contexts of use that deserve high quality User Interfaces (UIs), and switching from one to another according to variations of context of use at runtime. However, key contexts of use cannot be finely envisioned at design time, especially when dealing with the specific field of mobility. Thus, we propose a designer's partner tool running on the end-user's mobile device to probe key contexts of use in the wild. The underlying principles are data gathering, bayesian learning, and clustering techniques. Probing key contexts of use can save design efforts.

Keywords: Mobility, plasticity, context of use, probing, bayesian network, learning, clustering.

1 Introduction

In ubiquitous computing [11], context-aware adaptation has been widely investigated to cope with the increasing number of platforms, users, and environments, i.e. the diversity of contexts of use. This paper addresses the notion of *plasticity*, i.e. the ability of interactive systems to withstand variations of context of use while preserving user-centered properties [10]. In plasticity, most of the works so far make the implicit hypothesis that the contexts of use to be considered are identified at design time. In practice, this is far from being easy. As known in human-computer interaction, laboratory tests make it possible to observe usability issues with the system [9] but are limited to understand usage and system's impacts in a very few envisioned contexts of use such as home, street, work, etc. [5]. In the specific field of mobility, the number of contexts of use is unpredictable. Limiting them to predefined rough ones may result in not fully meeting the user's expectations. As a result, there is a need for partner tools that help the designers in identifying the *key* contexts of use in the wild on mobile devices such as cell phones.

Recent works in the field of end-user development underline the need for monitoring the end-user's environment (task, place, time, etc.) in order to provide

P. Forbrig and F. Paternò (Eds.): HCSE/TAMODIA 2008, LNCS 5247, pp. 271–278, 2008.

context-aware adaptivity [6]. In addition, experience shows that users tend to have distinct contexts of use when in mobility. In this paper, we propose a Windows Mobile embedded tool that collects objective data from user's actions in the wild and provides algorithms for learning key contexts of use from these observations. The process is based on bayesian user modeling and clustering techniques. The tool aims at separating relevant contexts of use from marginal situations by asking the end-user through a dedicated User Interface (UI). Such a probing task has to be taken in the early phases of the development process to save design efforts. Some frequent or critic contexts may require specific prototyping for ensuring high quality UIs.

2 EMMA: Embedded Manager for Mobile Adaptation

EMMA (Embedded Manager for Mobile Adaptation) is our running system for probing key contexts of use on Windows Mobile devices. EMMA relies on a user model that learns from user's actions gathered in mobility. The overall process is based on the functional decomposition given in Fig. 1. Three steps are identified. The system starts by collecting objective data from the observation of context of use and person-system interaction. Then these data are processed by the user model through learning algorithms. Finally, clustering techniques are performed to discover the best set of key contexts of use given knowledge inferred from the user model.

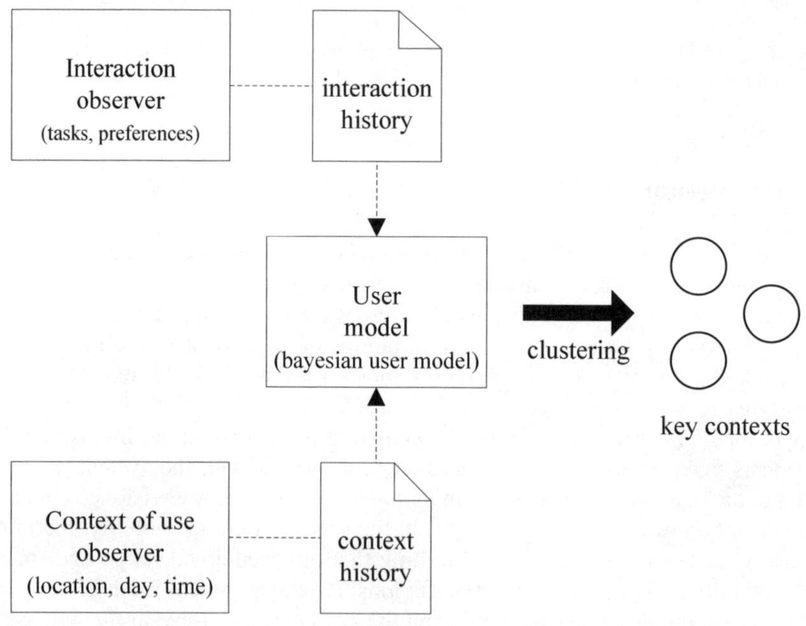

Fig. 1. Overall process for the identification of key contexts of use

Key context identification may be placed under the end-user's control through a dedicated UI (Fig. 2) that helps in reinforcing system's perception as well as validating the correctness of data. When a new key context of use is detected, the end-user is put in the loop: he/she can customize system's propositions and set the name of the new context (Fig. 3).

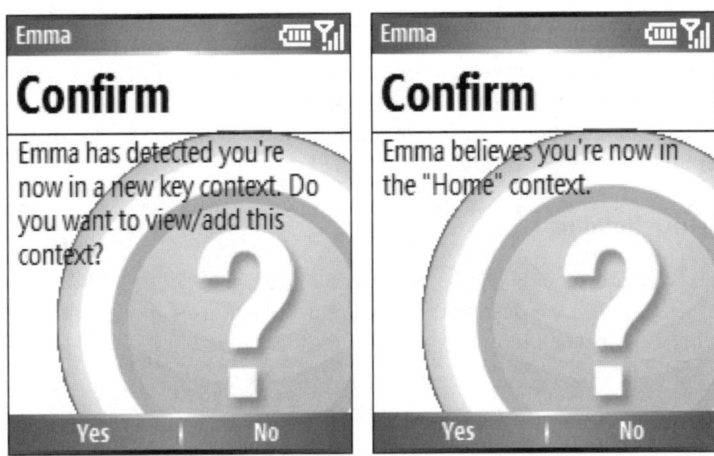

Fig. 2. Key context identification and change may be negotiated with the end-user

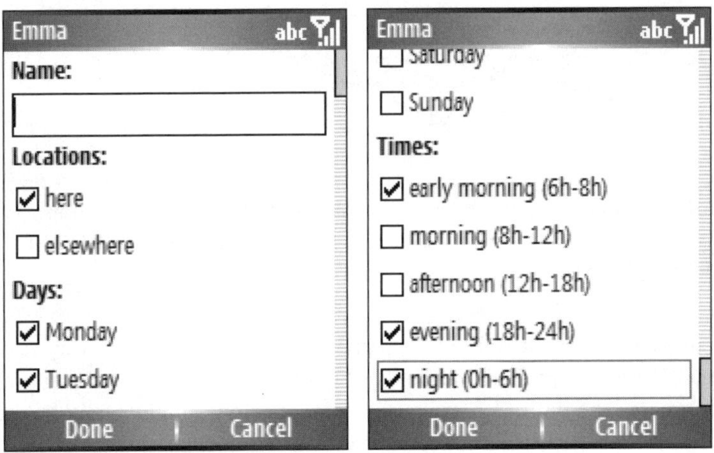

Fig. 3. When adding a new key context, system's propositions may be customized by the end-user. A key context is identified by its name.

3 Bayesian User Modeling

EMMA's user model is based on a bayesian network. Bayesian networks are graphical models that consist in both a qualitative and a quantitative part. The qualitative part is the structure of the network: a directed acyclic graph where vertices are variables and edges denote influences between variables. The quantitative part provides the Conditional Probabilities Tables (CPTs), i.e. the parameters of the network.

Bayesian networks are powerful tools provided with inference and learning algorithms. Inference relies on Bayes' theorem for propagating knowledge along the network. Learning applies for both the structure and the parameters of the network. It can be done from either complete or incomplete raw data. Bayesian networks are usually used for diagnosis, prediction, modeling, and monitoring. A key point is their ability to deal with incompleteness, which argues for their use when dealing with imperfect context information [3]. Bayesian user modeling has been investigated in previous works [4]. On mobile phones, bayesian learning has been used to discover when and how a user changes his/her profile over time [1].

3.1 Structure Building

In practice, bayesian models can be built from expert knowledge and/or automatically from data. As experts, we designed the structure of the user model for daily probing the user's behaviour when interacting with a mobile device in the wild (Fig. 4).

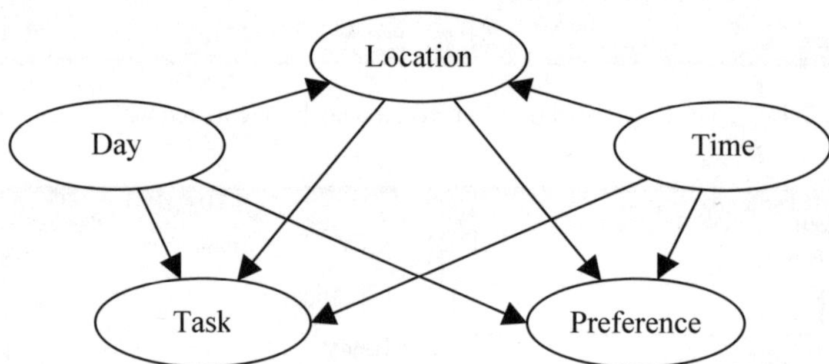

Fig. 4. EMMA's bayesian user model: the impact of context of use (day, time, location) on user's activity (tasks, preferences) is represented by causal links among nodes. User's location is time-context dependent.

In our model, we assumed that user's tasks and preferences may vary according to the context of use. We probed two kinds of context changes: changes in time (day of the week, time of the day) and space (location). Probing might easily be enlarged to additional information. In addition, we assumed that context changes might give rise to repetitive tasks (e.g. switching to silent mode when joining a meeting). Thus, each node of the model was dedicated to a particular function. We distinguished two kinds of functions depending on whether the node was in charge of sensing and identifying the context of use (i.e. *Day*, *Time*, and *Location* nodes), or tracking user's tasks and preferences (i.e. *Task* and *Preference* nodes). Extending the prototype to other context changes and tasks would be simply done by adding new nodes and causal links in the network. The structure defines the format of the gathered data.

3.2 Data Gathering

Data gathering in mobility has been investigated in previous works [2]. As motivated above, we need to collect two kinds of data to be processed by the user model: context and interaction data. As discussed, time and space contribute to the context identification when processed by the user model. Day and time changes are probed through the corresponding system states. We parse time into five intervals as following: night (0h-6h), early morning (6h-8h), morning (8h-12h), afternoon (12h-18h), and evening (18h-24h). Alike in [7], we use the nearest GSM cell-tower to track changes in the user's location. At any time, the mobile phone is connected to a particular cell-tower unless the user is not in a mobile phone receiving area. Each cell-tower is identified by its Cell IDentifier (CID) and its Location Area Code (LAC). Both CID and LAC are integers. We use the Radio Interface Layer (RIL) provided with Windows Mobile powered devices to catch cell changes. We match each cell change with the day and time within which it occurs.

We probe two kinds of interactions on mobile phones (Fig. 4): applicative tasks – *Task* node – (e.g., messaging, calls, games, etc.) and customization tasks – *Preference* node – (e.g., phone's profile, look and feel, etc.). Every time the active application changes, the interaction observer reports the application the user is interacting with in the interaction history. Observations are matched with day, time, and location (see Table 1). User's preferences are gathered in the same way.

Table 1. Interaction history gathered in mobility

Location	Day	Time	Application
CID40506LAC4354	Thursday	morning	Settings
CID40511LAC4354	Thursday	morning	Calendar
CID40511LAC4354	Thursday	morning	Contacts
CID58063LAC4354	Thursday	morning	Call History
CID40511LAC4354	Thursday	afternoon	Calendar
CID40506LAC4354	Thursday	afternoon	Messaging
CID40511LAC4354	Thursday	afternoon	Settings
CID58063LAC4354	Thursday	afternoon	Games
CID58063LAC4354	Thursday	evening	Settings
CID64457LAC4354	Thursday	evening	Call History
CID22057LAC4354	Thursday	evening	Messaging

3.3 User Model Implementation

From an implementational point of view, the bayesian user model is developed with Netica™ [8], a software provided by Norsys Software Corp. Netica is a complete software package which includes a graphical editor and an Application Programming Interface (API). The API is available under several operating systems and is accessible within different programming languages. We use a C version specially crafted for Windows Mobile devices. The Netica-C API is a compact Dynamic Link Library (DLL) of ultra-fast C-callable functions.

3.4 Parameters Learning

In order to process bayesian inference, we need to specify the joint probability distribution of each node of the network. As discussed earlier, the structure of the network drives data gathering. In turn, the collected data are processed by a parameter learning algorithm to adapt the CPTs. Netica supports parameter learning from raw case files. Once parameters are learnt, the user model can be used to infer knowledge.

User's tasks and needs evolve over time as user's experience increases. This is an important issue to take into account. Before running the parameter learning algorithm, we therefore fade the CPTs of nodes to indicate greater uncertainty, which accounts for the idea that user's tasks and needs may evolve over time. Thus, what has been recently learned is more strongly weighted than what was learned long ago. The amount of fading to be done is $1 - r^{\Delta t}$, where Δt is the amount of time since the last fading was done, and r is a number less than but close to 1.

4 Clustering

We have experimented clustering techniques for merging atomic contexts of use (days, times, locations) into key contexts of use. Merging is based on past user's actions similarities. For instance, we merge two locations in which the user has set the same phone's profile and used almost the same set of applications. Many clustering methods exist. We use two of them: K-Means and Hierarchical clustering. K-Means clustering is a partitioning method while Hierarchical clustering is an agglomerative one. We use Hierarchical clustering at the beginning when no key context of use has been identified yet. Then we use K-Means to reinforce existing key contexts. Before performing clustering, we first eliminate non-significant variables, i.e. variables of the context (day, time, or location) for which the standard deviations computed for tasks and preferences are close to zero. Standard deviations are computed as follow:

$$\sigma(X) = \sqrt{\frac{1}{N} \sum_{i=1}^{N} \left(x_i - \overline{x}\right)^2}$$

where X is either *Task* or *Preference*, N is the number of states for node X, and x_i are the conditional probabilities p_i of P($X \mid variable$).

Hierarchical clustering starts by putting each data in a separate cluster. Then, at each step, the algorithm chooses the pair of closest clusters and merges them into a new one (Fig. 5). Hierarchical clustering produces clusters for all possible number of clusters. Distances between clusters can be computed from one of single-link, complete-link, average-link, and centroid methods.

We use K-Means clustering to reinforce existing key contexts. K-Means assumes a fixed number of clusters, k. The goal is to create compact clusters. The classic K-Means algorithm starts by randomly initializing clusters. Here, we start by initializing the first n clusters with existing key contexts, and then we randomly initialize the $k - n$ remaining ones. Then each data is assigned to the nearest cluster based on a similarity measure. Clusters are then recomputed (Fig. 6). The algorithm repeats the last two operations until convergence.

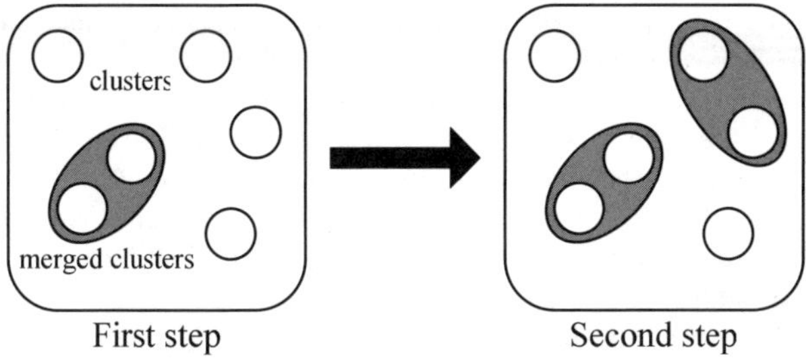

Fig. 5. Two steps of hierarchical clustering

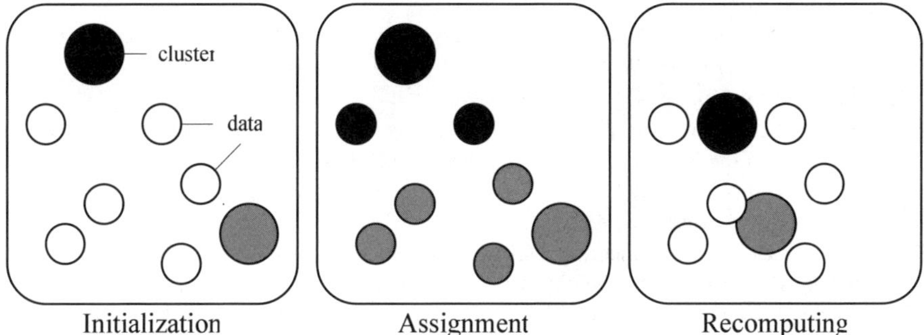

Fig. 6. First step of K-Means clustering

5 Results and Perspectives

EMMA is still under evaluation. However, the early results based on six people show that users tend to have two key contexts of use at least. This calls for further evaluation to (1) understand whether contexts of use can be matched with user's profiles, (2) measure minimum and maximum numbers of contexts of use, and (3) elaborate a methodology that takes into account this first probing in the wild. In the near future, EMMA will act as an end-user's tool for managing context-aware adaptation. Envisioned adaptations are phone's profile managing and phone's menu reordering.

References

1. Bridle, R., McCreath, E.: Improving the Mobile Phone Habitat – Learning Changes in User's Profiles. In: Zhang, S., Jarvis, R. (eds.) AI 2005. LNCS (LNAI), vol. 3809, pp. 970–974. Springer, Heidelberg (2005)
2. Demumieux, R., Losquin, P.: Gather Customer's Real Usage on Mobile Phones. In: Proceedings of the 7th International Conference on Human Computer Interaction with Mobile Devices & Services, Salzburg, Austria, September 19 – 22. MobileHCI 2005, vol. 111, pp. 267–270. ACM, New York (2005)

3. Henricksen, K., Indulska, J.: Modelling and Using Imperfect Context Information. In: Workshop on Context Modeling and Reasoning (CoMoRea), Proceedings of the 2nd IEEE Annual Conference on Pervasive Computing and Communications Workshops, Orlando, FL, March 14–17. PerCom 2004, pp. 33–37. IEEE Computer Society, Washington (2004)
4. Horvitz, E., Breese, J., Heckerman, D., Hovel, D., Rommelse, K.: The Lumière Project: Bayesian User Modeling for Inferring the Goals and Needs of Software Users. In: Proceedings of the 14th Annual Conference on Uncertainty in Artificial Intelligence, Madison, WI, July 1998. UAI 1998, pp. 256–265. Morgan Kaufmann, San Francisco (1998)
5. Kellar, M., Reilly, D., Hawkey, K., Rodgers, M., MacKay, B., Dearman, D., Ha, V., MacInnes, W.J., Nunes, M., Parker, K., Whalen, T., Inkpen, K.M.: It's a Jungle Out There: Practical Considerations for Evaluation in the City. In: CHI 2005 Extended Abstracts on Human Factors in Computing Systems, Portland, OR, April 2 – 7. CHI 2005, pp. 1533–1536. ACM, New York (2005)
6. Klann, M., Paternò, F., Wulf, V.: Future Perspectives in End-User Development. In: Lieberman, H., Paternò, F., Wulf, V. (eds.) End User Development. Human-Computer Interaction Series, vol. 9, pp. 475–486 (2006)
7. Laasonen, K.: Where Are You Going? Predicting user movement from cellular data. In: Proceedings of the Proactive Computing Workshop, Helsinki, Finland, November 25 – 26. PROW 2004, pp. 121–124 (2004)
8. Netica, http://www.norsys.com
9. Nielsen, J.: Usability Engineering. Morgan, San Francisco (1994)
10. Thevenin, D., Coutaz, J.: Plasticity of User Interfaces: Framework and Research Agenda. In: Sasse, A., Johnson, C. (eds.) Proceedings of the 7th IFIP International Conference on Human-Computer Interaction, Edinburgh, Scotland, August 30 – September 3, 1999. INTERACT 1999, pp. 110–117. IOS Press Publ., Amsterdam (1999)
11. Weiser, M.: The Computer for the 21st Century. Scientific American 256(3), 94–104 (1991)

The Ecology of Participants in Co-evolving Socio-technical Environments

Gerhard Fischer[1], Antonio Piccinno[2], and Yunwen Ye[1,3]

[1] Center for LifeLong Learning & Design (L3D), Department of Computer Science, University of Colorado, Boulder, USA
gerhard@colorado.edu
[2] Dipartimento di Informatica, Università di Bari, Bari, Italy
piccinno@di.uniba.it
[3] SRA Key Technology Lab, Tokyo, Japan
yunwen@colorado.edu

Abstract. The traditional notions of developer and user are unable to reflect the fact that many software systems nowadays are developed with the participation of many people of different interests and capabilities. The sharp distinction between users and developers gets blurred. Many researchers have used different concepts such as end-user developer, prosumer, pro-am to describe those new in-between roles. This paper provides a conceptual framework for characterizing varied activities that all people involved in using and developing software systems from a socio-technical perspective. The conceptual framework clarifies the spectrum of different use and development activities by a continuum of participants with different roles. Based on the framework, we analyze how participants change their roles to migrate from users to developers through interactions, and how such interactions co-evolve both the community and software artifacts.

Keywords: Open-source software, ecology of participants, Software Shaping Workshop, end-user development, meta-design.

1 Introduction

Users and developers are considered two distinct groups of people: users are those people who own a problem, and developers are those who implement software systems for supporting users to solve problems. Nowadays, with the widespread use of web-based software systems, the sharp distinction between users and developers is quickly disappearing: they are no more considered as two mutually exclusive groups of people. A lot of users are not only using software but also getting involved in designing software. In this way users increasingly take an active role in the development of software tools suited to their needs. This results in a continuum ranging from passive consumer, to meta-designer [1], to developer. It is also the case that the same person is and wants to be a consumer in some situations and in others a designer; therefore "consumer/designer" is not an attribute of a person, but a role assumed in a

P. Forbrig and F. Paternò (Eds.): HCSE/TAMODIA 2008, LNCS 5247, pp. 279–286, 2008.

specific context. Our aim is to study and characterize virtual organization in which richer ecologies of participants, i.e., *professional amateurs* [2], *prosumers* [3], *power users, local developers, and gardeners* [4], and *communities of practice* [5], can develop according to their own needs. A deeper understanding of this ecology, needs to be exploited to create multi-faceted computational environments [6] tailored to the interests, needs and expertise of different stakeholders to support the *migration path* [7] between the different roles.

To face with end-user needs, the challenge is to develop software environments that support end users in performing their activities of interest, but also allow to tailor their software environments to better adapt them to their needs, and even to create or modify software artifacts. The latter are defined as activities of End-User Development (EUD), to which a lot of attentions are currently devoted by various researchers in Europe and all over the world. EUD requires the active participation of end users in the software development process and tasks that are traditionally performed by professional software developers need to be transferred to the users, who need to be specifically supported in performing these tasks.

To allow EUD activities, we have to consider a two-phase process, the first devoted to design the design environment, the second one to design applications using the design environment. These two phases are not clearly distinct, and are executed several times in an interleaved way; because the design environments evolve both as a consequence of the progressive insights the different stakeholders gain into the design process and as a consequence of the comments of end users at work. This two-phase process requires a shift in the design paradigm, which must move from user-centered and participatory design to *meta-design* [8]. Through meta-design, design environments can be created that permit applications to be designed and evolved at the hands of end users in accordance with their own culture, skills and languages.

This paper is organized as follows. Section 2 presents a spectrum of participants in socio-technical environments. Section 3 presents Open Source Systems as an example of socio-technical environments, the ecology of involved participants. Section 4 discusses the role migration in the considered ecology of participants, and Section 5 provides conclusions.

2   A Spectrum of Participants in Socio-technical Environments

To support EUD with meta-design, it is imperative to break down the sharp boundaries between users and developers. Being a user or a developer is a continuum ranging from passive consumer, to well-informed consumer [9], to end user, to power users [4], to domain designer [10] all the way to meta-designer (a similar role distribution for domain-oriented design environments is defined in [1]). Moreover, the same user is often a consumer in some situations and in others a designer.

A critical challenge is to support a *migration path* [7] between the different mentioned roles: consumers, power-users, and designers are nurtured and educated, not born, and people must be supported to assume these roles. Supporting migration requires to view software systems not only as a technical system but also a *socio-technical environment* [11] in which the functionality of the software system is shaped by the interaction of all stakeholders that constitute an ecology of participants for the software system. Figure 1 depicts the ecology of participants in a software system from the socio-technical perspective. The x axis represents the user expertise in software design and y axis represents the technical complexity of participating activities. A zone delineates a participation space. The top-right space is called "Software design space" in which development activities are mainly carried out by professional software developers and meta-designers. The bottom-left space is the "Software consuming space" whose participants are mainly passive consumers or users of software systems and they are not actively involved in the development process of the software. In between, an EUD space exists, in which users, thanks to available techniques made available in their software system are able to modify their software. Rather than being distinct, these three areas usually overlap and their boundaries are blurred.

3   OSSs as Co-evolving Socio-technical Environments

EUD and meta-design shares many common features with Open-Source Software (OSS) development practices that actively seeking the participation and contributions of users at different levels. There are abundant lessons in OSS to be discovered and learned for the success of EUD systems, especially in the aspects of understanding what motivates so many people to dedicate their time, skills, and knowledge to OSS systems, and how users of OSS system become developers.

OSS grants not only developers but also all users, who are potential developers, the right to read and change its source code. Developers, users, and user-turned-developers form a *community of practice* [5]. A community of practice is a group of people who are informally bounded by their common interest and practice in a specific domain. Community members interact with each other for knowledge sharing and collaboration in pursuit of solutions to a common class of problems. An OSS project is unlikely to be successful unless there is an accompanied community that provides the platform for developers and users to collaborate with each other. Members of such communities are volunteers whose motivation to participate and

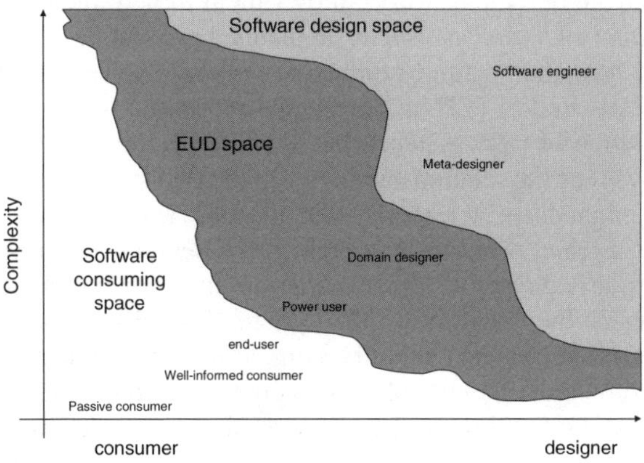

Fig. 1. The ecology of participants in a socio-technical environment

contribute is of essential importance to the success of OSS projects. In OSS users are usually developers, professionals or beginners. OSS refers to software systems that are free to use and whose source code is fully accessible to anyone who is interested. Most OSS systems start out with developers who want to solve their own particular problem and make the system available to others for free. It often attracts many users who have a similar problem, and because of the free access of source code, some interested users become co-developers by extending or improving the initial system. Together with the original developer, users and co-developers create a collaborative and evolving OSS community around the system [12]. OSS exploits meta-design techniques to empower their users to be able to develop the system, even if they are not professionals.

3.1 Mapping the Ecology of Participants in OSS

We will use OSS as an example to illustrate the ecology of participants in socio-technical environments. In OSS, the right to access and modify source code itself does not make OSS projects different from most "Closed Source Software" ones. All developers in a project in any software company would have the same access privilege. The fundamental difference is the *role migration* of the people involved in a project. In Closed Source Software projects, developers and users are clearly defined and strictly separated. In OSS projects, there is no clear distinction between developers and users: all users are potential developers. Borrowing terms from programming languages, *developers* and *users* are types, and *persons* involved in a project are data objects, Closed Source Software projects are static, binding languages in which a *person* is bound to the type of *developers* or *users* statically, and OSS projects are dynamic-binding languages in which a *person* is bound to the type of *developer* or *user* dynamically, depending on his or her involvement with the project at a given time.

Most OSS systems are not completely designed in advance. They evolve in response to the needs of users in the OSS community, and the evolution is carried out by contributing (co-)developers of the same community. Although the evolution of an OSS system is not well planned, "giving users of a product access to its source code and the right to create derivative works allows them to help themselves, and encourages *natural product evolution* as well as preplanned product design [13]."

To understand how the "natural product evolution" happens in OSS systems, we have conducted case studies [12] and presented a broader perspective by examining not only the evolution of OSS systems, but also the evolution of the associated OSS communities, as well as the relationship between the two types of evolution. Although an OSS project might have a leader (often the one who initiates the project), the leader neither has a grand plan for the system at the beginning, nor dictates the evolution of the system. It is the whole OSS community that collaboratively drives, as both users and developers, the evolution of the system. Therefore, a full understanding of the evolution of an OSS system cannot be complete without understanding the evolution of the OSS community and its role in driving the evolution of the system.

Participants of an OSS community assume a role by themselves according to their personal interest in the project, rather than being assigned by someone else; the different roles are the following [12]:

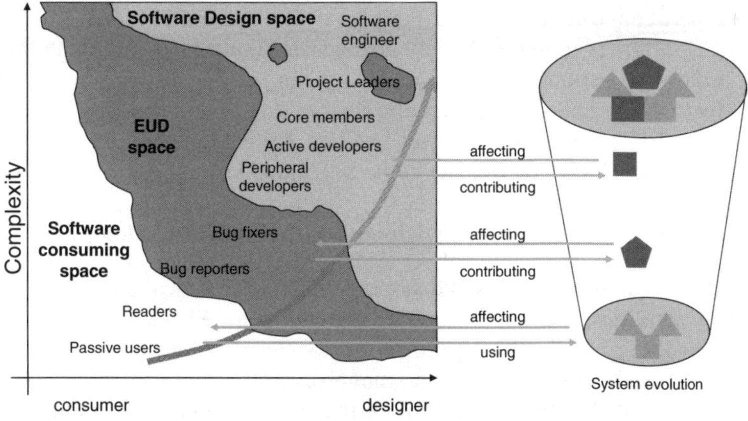

Fig. 2. Role migration in the co-evolution of participants and systems

- *Passive User* just uses the system in the same way as most of us use commercially available Closed Source Software. They are attracted to OSS mainly due to its high quality and the potential to be changed when needed.
- *Reader* refers to those active users of the system; they not only use the system, but also try to understand how the system works by reading the source code. Given the high quality of OSS systems, some Readers read the systems to learn programming. Another group of Readers exists who read an OSS system not for the purpose of improving the system per se but for understanding its underlying model and then using the model as a reference model to implement similar systems [14].
- *Bug Reporter* discovers and reports bugs. They assume the same role as testers of the traditional software development model. The existence of many Bug Reporters assures the high quality of OSS, because "given enough eyeballs, all bugs are shallow" [15].
- *Bug Fixer*, that are called to fix bugs that either they discover by themselves or are reported by other members.
- *Peripheral Developer*, that occasionally contributes new functionality or features to the existing system. Their contribution is irregular, and the period of involvement is short and sporadic.
- *Active Developer*, that is the person that regularly contributes new features and fixes bugs; they are one of the major development forces of OSS systems. *Core Member*, that is responsible for guiding and coordinating the development of an OSS project. Core Members are those people who have been involved with the project for a relative long time and have made significant contributions to the development and evolution of the system.
- *Project Leader*, that is the person who has initiated the project and is responsible for the vision and overall direction of the project.

Not all of the eight types of roles exist in all OSS communities, and the percentage of each type varies. Different OSS communities may use different names for the above roles. For example, some communities refer to Core Members as Maintainers. The difference between Bug Fixers and Peripheral Developers is rather small because Peripheral Developers might be mainly engaged in fixing bugs. Mapping those roles into the ecology of participants of Figure 2, we can see that Readers and Passive Users participate in the Software Consuming Space; Bug Fixers and Bug Reporters participate in the EUD Space; and Project Leaders, Core Members, Active Developers and Peripheral Developers participate in the Software Design Space.

3.2 Supporting the Ecology of Participants with SSW Methodology

To support co-evolution of users and systems in socio-technical environments and to allow EUD activities, we have proposed the Software Shaping Workshop (SSW) design methodology [16]. This approach views the development of an interactive system as the results of the interaction among several virtual software environments, each of them is called virtual workshop. Furthermore, when a complex activity has to be performed by a team of people of different cultures, each member of the team performing different tasks, the SSW methodology prescribes the development of a network of environments, each being devoted to the performance of specific tasks by well identified members of the team, while the overall environment has to be customized to the culture and skills of the people who will use it.

Overall, according to the SSW methodology an interactive system to support the work practice in a given application domain is developed as a set of interconnected virtual workshop. There are two types of virtual workshop: *application workshop* is a software environment used by a community of end users to perform their daily tasks in a certain domain, it is properly designed for the specific needs of that community of end users; *system workshop* is a software environment used by a community of experts in the design team to generate and update other workshops. An interactive system is always organized as a network of system and application workshops, always presenting three main levels. *Meta-design level*, in which software engineers use a system workshop to provide the software tools necessary to the development of the overall interactive system, and to participate in the design, maintenance, and validation of application and system workshops. Software engineers produce the initial programs, which generate the virtual workshop to be used and refined at the same or at lower levels, and participate in the maintenance of virtual workshops by modifying them to satisfy specific requests coming from lower levels. *Design level*, in which HCI experts, and domain experts cooperate in design, maintenance, and validation of application workshops through their own system workshops. *Use level*, in which end users (not participating to the development process) belonging to a certain community participate in task achievement using the application workshop devoted to their community. The network is thus organized, as in OSSs, so that it reflects the working organization of users and developers. Both meta-design and design levels include all the system workshops that support the design team in performing the activity of participatory design.

According to the ecology of participants (Figure 2) and to the SSW methodology, we identified a mapping between the network levels involved in the virtual workshops network devoted to participants in OSS with the three main areas in the framework characterizing the ecology of participants in the development process in OSS. At meta-design level there are software environments supporting user in the Software

Design Space (see Figure 2); Project Leaders, Core Members, Active Developers and Peripheral Developers will find here the virtual workshop devoted to them. At design level two system workshops are identified to support Bug Fixers and Bug Reporters activities. At use level Readers and Passive Users participating in the Software Consuming Space will have application workshops to accomplish to their tasks. In each of the three levels, communication paths among virtual workshop belonging to are provided to support the co-operation in the development process.

4   Role Migration in the Ecology of Participants

The ecology of participants (Figure 1) depicts the varied roles that participants assume in using and developing software systems. The software systems are developed and evolved through the intensive interactions among all the participants, and the interaction between users and software systems. At the same time, participants also evolve through the same process and assume bigger roles in shaping the functionality of the software systems. At this aim, they are supported by the Software Shaping Workshop methodology that foresees a virtual workshop for each role in the ecology of participants in the OSS development process. The network of virtual workshops allows them to communicate and collaborate to the system design, implementation, use and evolution by working with a workshop customized to them and using their own languages and notations, so that they are not disoriented and may overcome the gaps existing among them. Figure 2 describes the co-evolution that we have observed in OSS systems. Many participants started as users, and during their interactive use of the software system, some of the participants become interested in reading and making bug reports of the system, migrating into the roles of readers and bug reporters. Some got more involved and continued their migration path into bug fixers and peripheral developers as they gain more knowledge of the system. Some even became active developers and core members by contributing more development the system. As the members migrated into bigger roles, their contributions made the system evolve, and the evolution of the system in turn relied on the active participation and contributions of different levels of participants.

5   Conclusions

In this paper we discussed a conceptual framework to characterize the rich and varied ecology of participants, at various levels, in open, evolvable and living socio-technical environments. Nowadays, the sweeping kinds of end users are increasingly involved in the design and development of the tools they use, thus they need to be supported through techniques that are suitable for them. In particular we explored the ecology of participants in Open-Source Software, by analyzing the various roles of involved end users in the development process belonging to three different spaces (software consuming, EUD and Software design space) and matching them with the three different levels (use, design and meta-design level) required by the Software Shaping Workshop design methodology. Finally we provided some insights about the evolution and the consequent migration of user roles along the migration path.

References

1. Fischer, G., Giaccardi, E.: Meta-Design: A Framework for the Future of End User Development. In: Lieberman, H., Paternò, F., Wulf, V. (eds.) End User Development, vol. 9, pp. 427–457. Springer, Dordrecht (2006)
2. Leadbeater, C., Miller, P.: Pro-Am Revolution. How enthusiasts are changing our economy and society. Demos, London (2004)
3. Tapscott, D., Williams, A.D.: Wikinomics: How Mass Collaboration Changes Everything. Portofolio. Penguin Group, New York (2006)
4. Nardi, B.A.: A Small Matter of Programming. The MIT Press, Cambridge (1993)
5. Wenger, E.: Communities of Practice — Learning, Meaning, and Identity. Cambridge University Press, Cambridge (1998)
6. Myers, B.A., Ko, A.J., Burnett, M.M.: Invited Research Overview: End User Programming. Human Factors in Computing Systems, CHI 2006 (Montreal), pp. 75–80 (2006)
7. Burton, R.R., Brown, J.S., Fischer, G.: Analysis of Skiing as a Success Model of Instruction: Manipulating the Learning Environment to Enhance Skill Acquisition. In: Rogoff, B., Lave, J. (eds.) Everyday Cognition: Its Development in Social Context, pp. 139–150. Harvard University Press, Cambridge (1984)
8. Sutcliffe, A., Mehandjiev, N.: Introduction. Communications of the ACM 47, 31–32 (2004)
9. Beyond 'Couch Potatoes': From Consumers to Designers and Active Contributors. FirstMonday (Peer-Reviewed Journal on the Internet), http://firstmonday.org/issues/issue7_12/fischer/
10. Fischer, G.: Domain-Oriented Design Environments. Automated Software Engineering 1, 177–203 (1994)
11. Sutcliffe, A.G.: Requirements Engineering for socio-technical systems. In: Proceedings Fifth IEEE International Symposium on Requirements Engineering, pp. 27–31. IEEE Computer Society Press, Los Alamitos (2001)
12. Nakakoji, K., Yamamoto, Y., Nishinaka, Y., Kishida, K., Ye, Y.: Evolution Patterns of Open-Source Software Systems and Communities. In: International Workshop on Principles of Software Evolution (IWPSE 2002), Orlando, FL, pp. 76–85 (2002)
13. O'Reilly, T.: Lessons from Open-Source Software Development. Communications of the ACM 42, 33–37 (1999)
14. Aoki, A., Hayashi, K., Kishida, K., Nakakoji, K., Nishinaka, Y., Reeves, B., Takashima, A., Yamamoto, Y.: A Case Study of the Evolution of Jun: An Object-Oriented Open-Source 3D Multimedia Library. In: 23rd International Conference on Software Engineering (ICSE 2001), pp. 524–533. IEEE Press, Toronto (2001)
15. Raymond, E.S., Young, B.: The Cathedral and the Bazaar: Musings on Linux and Open Source by an Accidental Revolutionary. O'Reilly, Sebastopol (2001)
16. Costabile, M.F., Fogli, D., Mussio, P., Piccinno, A.: End-User Development: the Software Shaping Workshop Approach. In: Lieberman, H., Paternò, F., Wulf, V. (eds.) End User Development, vol. 9, pp. 183–205. Springer, Dordrecht (2006)

User Interface Migration between Mobile Devices and Digital TV

Fabio Paternò, Carmen Santoro, and Antonio Scorcia

ISTI-CNR, Via G. Moruzzi, 1
56124 Pisa, Italy
{Fabio.Paterno,Carmen.Santoro,Antonio.Scorcia}@isti.cnr.it

Abstract. In this paper we present a demonstration of the Migrantes environment for supporting user interface migration through different devices, including mobile ones and digital TV. The goal of the system is to furnish user interfaces that are able to migrate across different devices, in such a way as to support task continuity for the mobile user. This is obtained through a number of transformations that exploit logical descriptions of the user interfaces to be handled. The migration environment supports the automatic discovery of client devices and its architecture is based on the composition of a number of software services required to perform a migration request.

Keywords: User Interface Migration, Adaptation to the Interaction Platform, Ubiquitous Environments.

1 Introduction

One important aspect of pervasive environments is the possibility for users to freely move about and continue interacting with the services available through a variety of interactive devices (i.e. cell phones, PDAs, desktop computers, digital television sets, intelligent watches, and so on). In this area, one important goal is to support continuous task performance, which implies that applications be able to follow users and adapt to the changing context of users and the environment itself. In practice, it is sufficient that only the part of an application that is interacting with the user migrates to different devices.

In recent years, research on issues related to user interfaces in ubiquitous environments has started (see for example [1] [2] [3]). For instance, a discussion of some high-level requirements for software architectures in multi-device environments is proposed in [1], although it is done without presenting a software architecture and implementation solution for these issues. In our work, we propose a specific architectural solution, based on a migration/proxy server, able to support migration of user interfaces associated with applications hosted by different content servers.

More in detail, in this demo, we show a solution for supporting migration of application interfaces among different types of devices. Such solution is able to detect any user interaction performed at the client level. Then, we can get the state resulting from the different user interactions and associate it to a new user interface version that is

P. Forbrig and F. Paternò (Eds.): HCSE/TAMODIA 2008, LNCS 5247, pp. 287–292, 2008.

activated in the migration target device. In particular, the solution proposed has been encapsulated in a service-oriented architecture and supports user interfaces with different platforms (fixed and mobile) and modalities (graphical, vocal, and their combination). The new solution also includes a discovery module, which is able to detect the devices that are present in the environment and collect information on their features. Users can therefore conduct their regular access to the Web application and then ask for a migration to any device that has already been discovered by the migration server. The discovery module also monitors the state of the discovered devices, automatically collecting their state-change information in order to understand if there is any need for a server-initiated migration. Moreover, we show how the approach is able to support migration across devices that support various implementation languages. This has been made possible thanks to the use of a logical language for user interface descriptions at different abstraction levels [4], which is independent of the implementation languages involved, and a number of transformations that incorporate design rules and take into account the specific aspects of the target platforms.

In the paper we first describe a scenario supported by our demo, next we briefly describe the underlying architecture, and lastly we discuss an example session showing the corresponding user interfaces provided to the users.

2   A Scenario Supported by the Demo

The demo regards a user returning home from work, who starts to prepare the shopping list through a mobile device (while s/he is on the bus or train) and then when s/he gets at home, s/he may look at what is actually available and realise that some items are still missing. Then, s/he completes the list by interacting with the digital TV with large screen while sitting comfortably on the couch.

Thus, using the PDA, the users can access the page dedicated to the products and specify the category they are interested in (for example "meat"). Depending on the selected category, the application allows a further refinement of the selection. In our scenario, the users are allowed to select which kind of meat they want to buy by means of choosing among beef, poultry and pork. Then, a number of options are visualised together with the associated amounts, and the user can start to select what s/he wants to buy. When the user enters home, the smart environment suggests the user the possibility to migrate the user interface to other devices which have been recognised as available in the new environment, since the agent-based architecture has recognised a situation where more comfortable interactions might take place (e.g.: the user could interact with the desktop PC which has a larger screen, or s/he can interact with the TV while comfortably sitting on the couch). Then, if the user decides to migrate the user interface to the digital TV, s/he can continue editing the shopping list through a larger screen without having to save their selections from the PDA and login again the application from the new device. After the interface migration, the user can find the items that were specified before, through the PDA (e.g. the request for three beef steaks, which was specified using the handheld device) and edit them or add new ones until lastly they send the request. The text can be entered by selecting a specific button on the TV controller, which activates a virtual keyboard on the screen.

3   The Migration between Mobile Device and Digital TV

The main characteristics of migration are: device change, adaptation, and continuity. The basic idea is that people would like to freely move and still be able to continue to perform their tasks and thus the interactive part of an applications should be able to follow them and adapting to the changing context of use.

Our migration environment is based on a service-oriented architecture involving multiple clients and servers: the architecture is aimed at providing interoperability between the different services, which can be also combined for delivering composite services, as it happens in the migration support. We assume that the desktop version of the considered applications already exists in the application servers. In addition, we have a migration platform, which is composed of a proxy service and a number of specific services and can be hosted by either the same or different systems.

The main services that have been identified to compose the migration platform:

- The *Discovery Manager*, which includes the functionalities for discovering the available devices and update the device list accordingly;
- The *Migration Manager/Proxy* is the core of the system: it handles the communication with the other modules, also including proxy functionalities.
- The *Reverse Engineering*, is in charge of reversing the desktop implementation into a logical user interface description;
- The *Semantic Redesign* module, which transforms the logical description of the user interface designed for the source platform into a logical description of the user interface for the target migration platform;
- The *State Mapper*, which updates the final user interface with the values of the current state, which have been saved at the time the request of migration occurred;
- The *UIGenerator*, which reifies the logical concrete description into an implementation language for the target platform.

The process starts with the source and target devices notifying their presence to the Discovery Manager, which is in charge of discovering the available devices and updating the list of devices accordingly, also showing their characteristics. Indeed, in order to allow for a good choice of the target device, information about the devices that are automatically discovered in the environment is displayed and saved. Such information mainly concerns device identification and interaction capabilities and, on the one hand, it enables users to choose a target migration device with more accurate and coherent information on the available targets and, on the other hand, it enables the system to suggest or automatically trigger migrations when the conditions for one arise. Thus, both the system and the user have the possibility to trigger the migration process, depending on the surrounding context conditions.

Users have two different ways of issuing migration requests. The first one is to graphically select the desired target device in their migration client. Users only have the possibility of choosing those devices that they are allowed to use and are currently available for migration. The second possibility for issuing migration requests occurs when the user is interacting with the system through a mobile device equipped with an RFID reader. In this case, users could move their device near a tagged migration target and keep it close from it for a number of seconds in order to trigger a migration to that device. In this case, in addition to a spatial threshold used to indicate when the user is sufficiently close to trigger a migration, a time threshold has been defined in order to avoid accidental migration, for example when the user is just passing by a tagged device. This second choice offers users a chance to naturally interact with the system, requesting a migration just by moving their personal device close to the desired migration target, in an easy manner. Migration can also be initiated by the system, skipping explicit user intervention in critical situations when the user session could accidentally be interrupted by external factors. Alternatively, the server can provide users with migration suggestions to improve the overall user experience.

The migration clients are supposed to access the various applications through the proxy available within the Migration Manager. Indeed this module works as a proxy since it is in charge of intercepting the clients' request of accessing a page, retrieving such a page from Internet and saving it locally together with the referred entities (images, CSS files, etc.). Afterwards, the Migration Manager receives from the source device the request for migration (which specifies the source device, the target device, and the page that has to be migrated), and it triggers the sequence of actions needed for fulfilling such a request. It is worth noting that the application that triggers the migration – the so-called 'Migration Client'- can be contained in an application which is separated from the web browser. For instance, in the current implementation, the migration request is activated through a separate C# program which allows the user to select the devices available for migration (see Figure 1, Left).

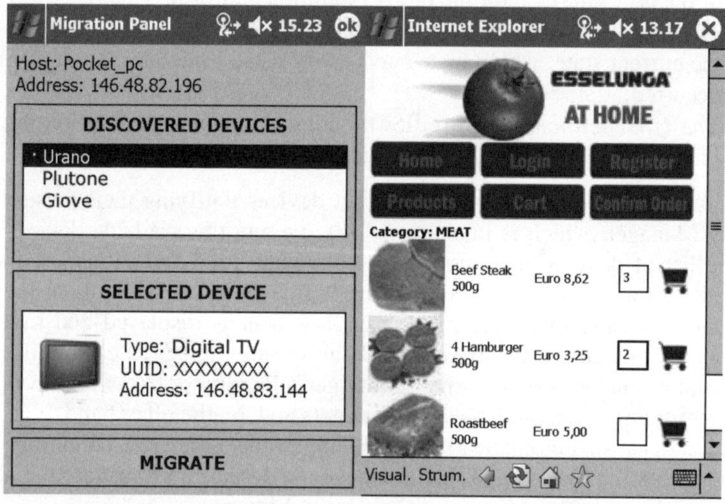

Fig. 1. Left, The Migration Client Interface, Right, the Application User Interface

Once the Proxy receives the Web page from the concerned Application Server, the Proxy modifies it by including JavaScript functions that are aimed at collecting information about the state of the migrating page, and afterwards it sends to the Web browser of the source device (PDA). The JavaScript functions that are automatically inserted by the proxy server are in charge of collecting the information that describes the state of the migrating page by accessing its DOM. The information is collected into a string formatted following a XML-based syntax and submitted to the server together with the IP of the target device. This information is sent to the server through an AJAX script. The reason for this is that only the application running on the client device can access the DOM and the AJAX callback can transmit the data without requiring any additional explicit action from the user.

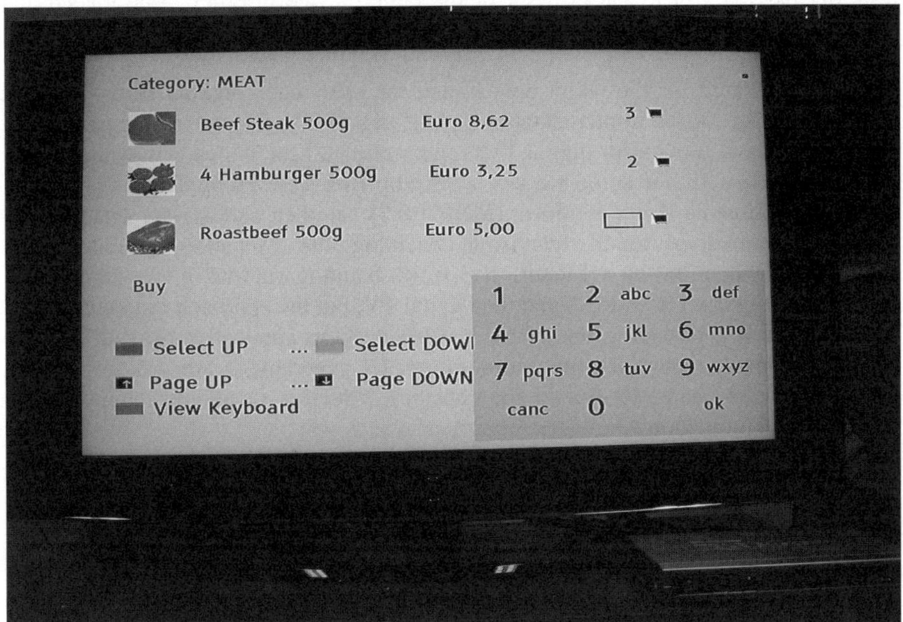

Fig. 2. The Application User Interface Migrated into the Digital TV

The Migration Server, after receiving the request of migration by the source device, interrogates the Migration Client of the target device asking about its availability/willingness for accepting a migrating UI: if the migration is accepted, the environment detects the state of the application modified by the user input (elements selected, data entered, ..) and identifies the last element accessed in the source device. Then, the Migration Manager gets information about the source device and, depending on such information it builds the corresponding logical descriptions, at a different abstraction level, by invoking the Reverse Engineering service of our system. At this point, the Migration Manager asks the Discovery Manager information about the target device in order to understand for which platform the redesign process has to be carried out. Indeed, the result of the reverse engineering process, together with information about source and target platforms is used as input for the Semantic Redesign service, in order to perform a redesign of the user interface for the target platform. This part of the migration environment transforms the logical description of the desktop version into the logical description for the new platform. This solution allows the environment to exploit semantic information contained in the logical description and obtain more meaningful results than transformations based only on the analysis of the specific implementation language used for the final UI. Once the application presentation to activate on the target device is identified, the Migration Manager asks the State Mapper to adapt the state of the concrete user interface with the values that have been saved previously. Then, once the concrete user interface adapted with the new values has been obtained, the reification of such a logical description into the final user interface for the target platform is performed by the UIGenerator module and lastly, the resulting page is sent to the browser of the target device in order to be loaded and rendered. Figure 2 shows the UI migrated into the Digital TV. It is possible to see that the values entered in the source device (see Figure 1) have been preserved in the user interface generated for the target device, and the users can continue from the point they left off. As for the implementation for the digital TV, it involves the generation of a file in a Java version for digital TVs representing a Xlet, which is downloaded on the Set-Top-Box. In our demo we use a Set Top Box Telesystem TS7.2 DT, which supports Multimedia Home Platform (MHP 1.0.2), an open middleware system standard for interactive digital television, enabling the execution of interactive, Java-based applications on a TV-set. It is worth pointing out that in this example we considered migration from PDA and the Digital TV, but the approach can be extended for any platform, providing that exists a Web desktop application version and the opportune software modules (migration client, UI generator,..) are provided taking into account the characteristics of the considered devices (available interaction resources, implementation languages supported, …).

4 Conclusions

In this paper we describe a system for enabling user interface migration through different devices: UI logical descriptions (with associated transformations) have been exploited for supporting the migration mechanisms, together with various technologies (e.g. AJAX scripts) for saving the current state of the user interface. Ongoing work is dedicated to further enrich the data associated with the current state of the user interface in order to support continuity in a wider set of user's interactions.

References

1. Balme, L., Demeure, A., Barralon, N., Coutaz, J., Calvary, G.: CAMELEON-RT: a Software Architecture Reference Model for Distributed, Migratable and Plastic User Interfaces. In: Markopoulos, P., Eggen, B., Aarts, E., Crowley, J.L. (eds.) EUSAI 2004. LNCS, vol. 3295, pp. 291–302. Springer, Heidelberg (2004)
2. Bandelloni, R., Mori, G., Paternò, F.: Dynamic Generation of Migratory Interfaces. In: Proceedings Mobile HCI 2005, Salzburg, September 2005, pp. 83–90. ACM Press, New York (2005)
3. Luyten, K., Coninx, K.: Distributed User Interface Elements to support Smart Interaction Spaces. In: IEEE Symposium on multimedia, Irvine, USA, December 12-14 (2005)
4. Mori, G., Paternò, F., Santoro, C.: Design and Development of Multi-device User Interfaces through Multiple Logical Descriptions. In: IEEE Transactions on Software Engineering, August, vol. 30(8), pp. 507–520. IEEE Press, Los Alamitos (2004)

Demonstration of Software Components for End-User Development

Mario Gleichmann[1], Thomas Hasart[2], Ilvio Bruder[3], Andreas Heuer[4],
and Peter Forbrig[5]

[1] IT Science Center Rügen gGmbH, Germany
gleichmann@it-science-center.de
[2] IT Science Center Rügen gGmbH, Germany
hasart@it-science-center.de
[3] IT Science Center Rügen gGmbH, Germany
bruder@it-science-center.de
[4] IT Science Center Rügen gGmbH, Germany
heuer@it-science-center.de
[5] University of Rostock, Germany
peter.forbrig@uni-rostock.de

Abstract. This paper demonstrates how "End-User-Development" can be implemented with the Qt4 designer of Trolltech. It provides an example showing how users modify user interfaces by adding functionality that originally was not available.

Keywords: end user development, design, user interface.

1 Introduction

This paper demonstrates the design process of user defined user interfaces for accessing OLAP data (Pendse, 1998) at runtime. As an example, a simple dashboard for a controller is designed.

2 Project Monicca

Our Monicca project on "Model-Driven Account Management in Data Warehouse Environments" aims at adapting OLAP applications of the user interface to the functional layer. Thereby, a tool is developed for Key Accounts [6]. With this tool one can offer clients different data from the Data Warehouse or other external resources. It gives key account managers a special interface to the data of key customers. Additionally, this allows applications to offer broad, suitable and adjusted analysis functionalities. The general problem of adaptation of OLAP applications will be solved by using techniques based on metadata. To generate the user views, a model language will be developed which can describe necessary OLAP operations for the views, relations, the definition of the outputs and the following interactions. This model-based

P. Forbrig and F. Paternò (Eds.): HCSE/TAMODIA 2008, LNCS 5247, pp. 293–298, 2008.

approach is the basis for the "end-user development" that aims at adapting and extending applications.

3 Demonstration

Figure 1 shows the embedded Qt-Designer [15] with an empty new window (Ui-Container). On the right hand side the current available UI components are listed. These components can be dragged and dropped on the empty window. From the dock window "Widget Box/BI-Suite Widgets", which holds the custom designer plug-ins, "ESumGrid" was selected and dragged on the new widget (Figure 2).

Now, a data cube must be specified representing the data of this table. Therefore, a cube from the list in the "Cube Selection" tab window is dropped on the table (Figure 3).

Following the same procedure, the node for the horizontal and the vertical axis (Figure 4) can be assigned.

Measures and plan scenarios can be designed in the same way like the axis definition by drag and drop of the needed items.

To demonstrate the layout mechanism, some more items must be created - in this example two speedometers and one button (Figure 6). As first step the two speedometers are laid out horizontally (Figure 7). The button is being placed at the lower left corner. Therefore, a vertical spacer is created and a layout with the button is horizontally performed. Afterwards all created elements are laid out vertically. Figure 8 shows the final layout of the sample dashboard.

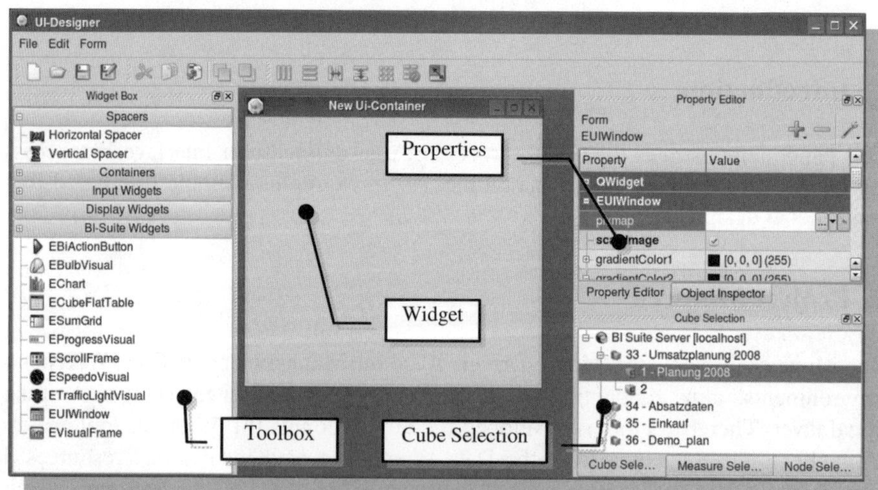

Fig. 1. Designer

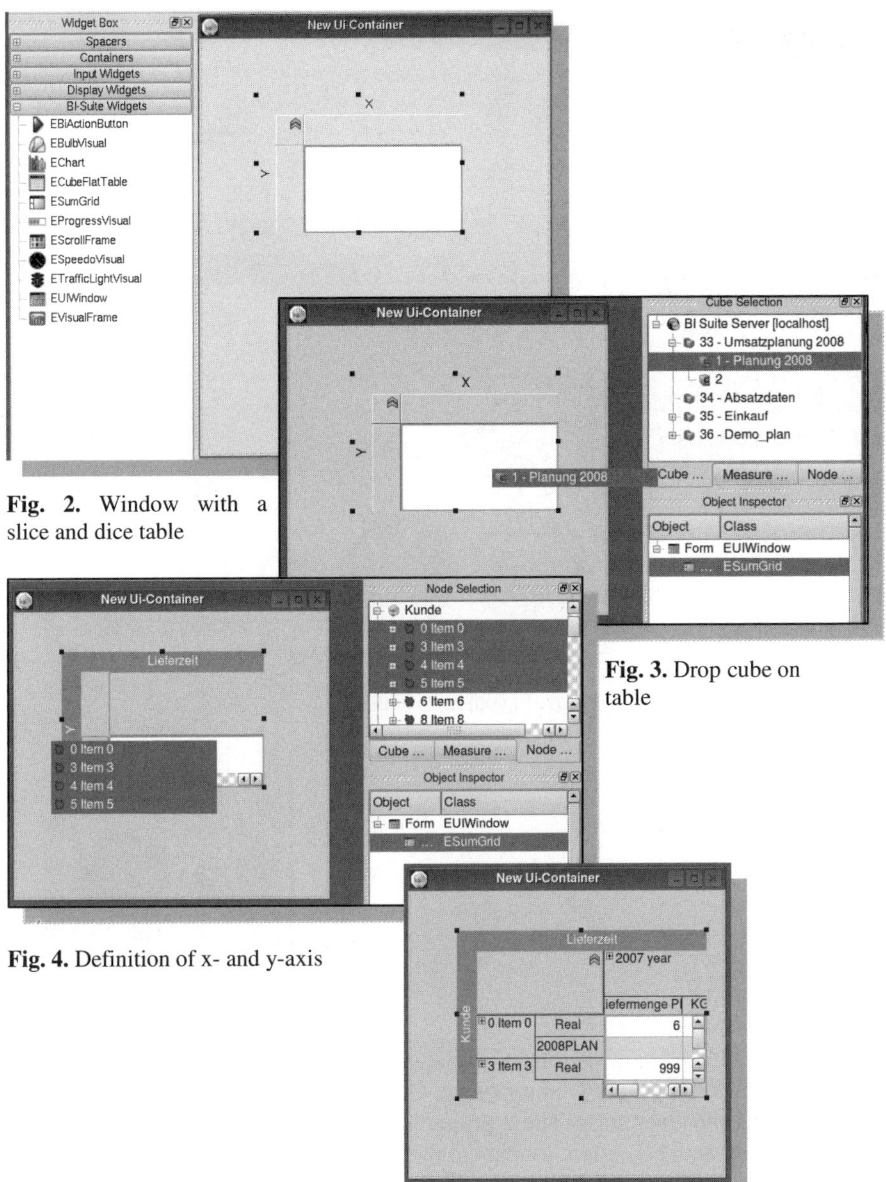

Fig. 2. Window with a slice and dice table

Fig. 3. Drop cube on table

Fig. 4. Definition of x- and y-axis

Fig. 5. Finished axis definition

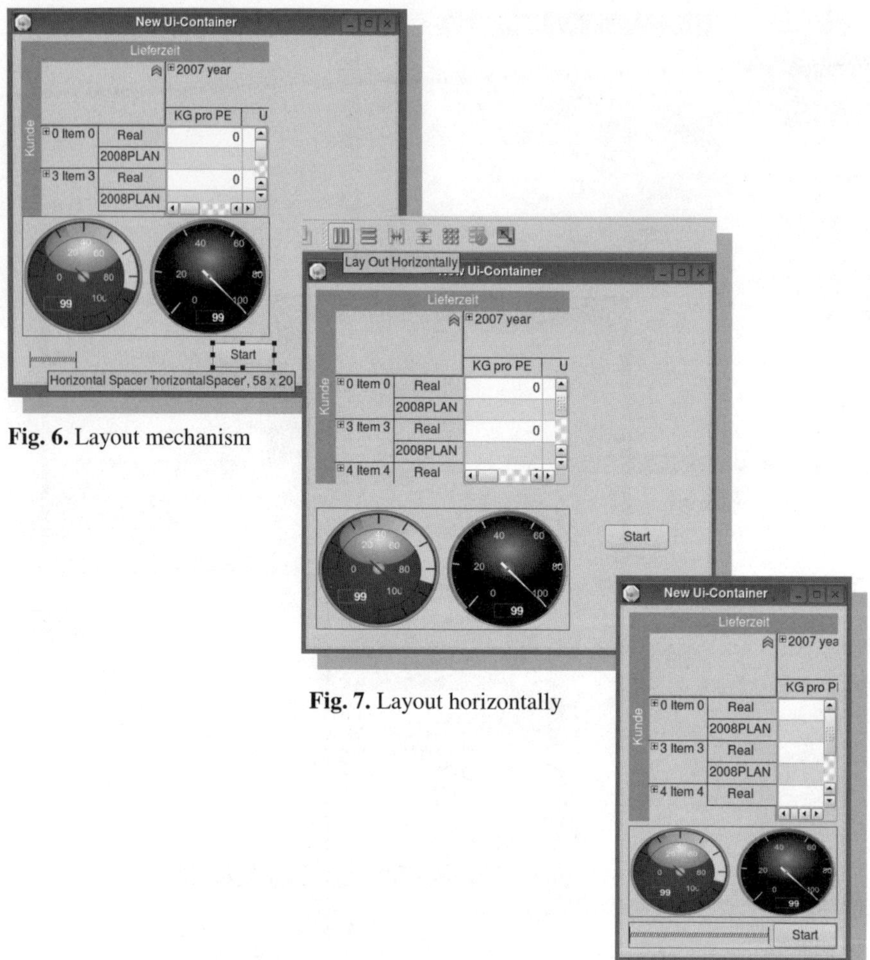

Fig. 6. Layout mechanism

Fig. 7. Layout horizontally

Fig. 8. Final layout

Figure 9 shows the property editor of the Qt-Designer. Most of the properties are provided by the QWidget class. These properties are needed to define the look of the selected component. They allow to change the font or the background image. In the example, a new property "onClick" for the BIActionButton is implemented. Within this property, a script can be defined which is executed if the button is clicked by the user. Currently, functions for switching to another container and for executing external commands are implemented.

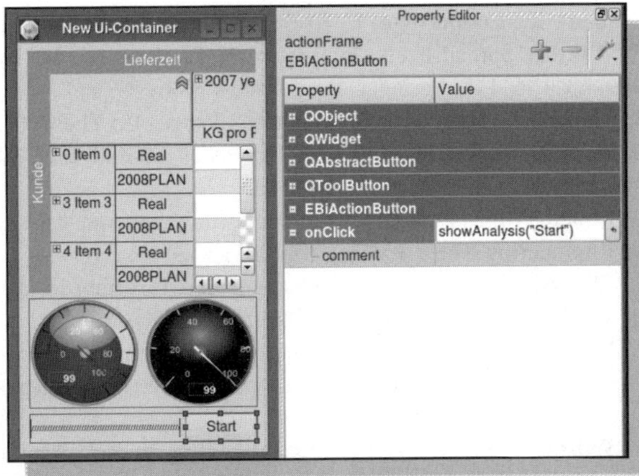

Fig. 9. Component properties

4 Summary and Future Work

With the developed plug-ins, we allow users to design interactive applications according to their own needs. A first big step in the direction of "End-User-Development" has been realized. Our approach provides opportunities to represent OLAP cubes as spreadsheet metaphors for end users. Limitation and problems in forms creation are no longer only solvable by software developers. Initial experiments with key account managers (without any programming knowledge) showed very positive results.

As a challenge still remains defining dependencies between visualization components. This would allow users to specify the consequences of interacting with one object by state changes in other objects. A selection box could restrict the data area of all elements or a chart could show the currently selected row in a table.

Indeed, experiments demonstrated that user would like to have these possibilities in existing applications.

It is also planned to consider visualization proposals for spreadsheets discussed in [1]. Constrains analogous to [2] would be more meaningful expansions to a wider security of the programs.

In the current stage of development, very limited opportunities for process control are available. At the moment there are no conditional jumps to other analysis elements. It is also not possible to unlock actions depending on properties of the elements.

For enterprise applications it is not enough to have good individual (local) user interface elements. Complex enterprise models are needed to get the software usable. It must e.g. be possible to specify various user roles in these models.

References

1. Ballinger, D., Bidle, R., Noble, K.: Spreadsheet Visualisation to Improve End-user Understanding. In: Australiean Symposium on Information Visualisation, Adelaide, Australia (2003)
2. Burnett, M., Cook, C., Pendes, O., Rothermel, G., Summet, J., Wallace, C.: End-User Software Engineering with Assertions in the Spreadsheet Paradigm. In: Proc. International Conference on Software Engineering, pp. 93–103. Portland, Oregon, USA (2003)

3. Erwig, M., Abraham, R., Cooperstein, I., Kollmansberger, S.: Automatic Generation and Maintenance of Correct Spreadsheets. In: Inverardi, P., Jazayeri, M. (eds.) ICSE 2005. LNCS, vol. 4309, pp. 136–145. Springer, Heidelberg (2006)
4. Hodgins, J., Bruckman, A., Hemp, P., Ondrejka, C., Vinge, V.: The Potential of End-User Programmable Worlds: Present and Future. In: Panel SIGGRAPH 2007: ACM SIG-GRAPH 2007 panels (2007)
5. Ruthruff, J.R., Burnett, M.: Six challenges in supporting end-user debugging. ACM SIG-SOFT Software Engineering Notes 30(4), 1–5 (2005)
6. McDonald, M., Rogers, B.: Key Account Management – Learning from supplier and customer perspectives. Butterworth Heinemann, Oxford (1998)
7. Meyer, R.M., Masterson, T.: Towards a better visual programming language: critiquing prograph's control structures. The Journal of Computing in Small Colleges 15(5), 181–193 (2000)
8. Millman, A.F., Wilson, K.J.: From Key Account Selling to Key Account Management. Journal of Marketing Practice: Applied Marketing Science 1(1), 9–21 (1995)
9. Mørch, A.I., Stevens, G., Won, M., Klann, M., Dittrich, Y., Wulf, V.: Component-Based Technologoies for End-User Development. Communications of the ACM 47(9), 59–62 (2004)
10. Myers, B., Burnett, M.M., Wiedenbeck, S., Ko, A.J.: End User Software Engineering. In: CHI 2007 Special Interest Group Meeting, San Jose, California, USA. CHI (2007)
11. Pendse, N.: What is OLAP?, The OLAP Report (1998) (visited: March 13 (2008), `http://www.olapreport.com/fasmi.htm`
12. Scaffidi, C., Shaw, M., Myers, B.: An Approach for Categorizing End User Programmers to Guide Software Engineering Research. In: First Workshop on EndUser Software Engineering (WEUSE I), Saint Louis, Missouri, May 21 (2005)
13. Scaffidi, C.: A Data Model to Support End User Software Engineering. In: 29th International Conference on Software Engineering, ICSE 2007 Companion (2007)
14. Sidow, H.D.: Key Account Management. Landsberg am Lech: mi-Fachverlag (2007)
15. Trolltech (2008) (visited: March 11, 2008), `http://trolltech.com/`

Transactions in Task Models

Daniel Reichart and Peter Forbrig

University of Rostock, Department of Computer Science
`{daniel.reichart,peter.forbrig}@uni-rostock.de`

Abstract. In this paper we propose a method to model the behaviour of task models in error situations. For these purposes we follow the idea of transactions in database systems. By encapsulating tasks in transactions the atomicity of complex tasks can be asserted. Corresponding tool support is presented which includes modelling and simulating task models. The tools themselves were developed in a model-based way.

Keywords: Transaction, Task Model, Tool Support.

1 Motivation

The diversity of mobile devices and platforms requires new methods to master the complexity of user-interface development. Abstract models can help to solve many issues so that model-based user interface development becomes more and more popular. Task models are widely used to specify interactive software. Many methods and tools using task models to develop user interfaces. But still there are many problems that can occur, when generating user interfaces from these models. Task models just describe interactions between user and system in an idealistic way. Exceptions to this default behaviour is hard to express or even can not be expressed. But in real world applications errors occur and developers have to specify fallback behaviour. What happens, if a system task fails, because a required resource is not available? Which tasks have to be undone to get back to a consistent state? The cascading selective undo mechanism presented in [1] can help to address the second question but has another motivation. Instead of undoing selective, already successfully completed tasks and their impact on application state we propose an approach to handle error recovery strategies for task models using the concept of transactions.

2 Transactions

Transactions were originally developed to be used in database management systems to avoid inconsistencies of data. Such problems can arise when two processes write the same data concurrently or in case of hardware or network failures. The idea of this paper is to encapsulate more than one task into one transaction. The three new operations *begin*, *commit* and *rollback* define the boundaries of the transaction. Transactions in databases are required to ensure the following constraints:

P. Forbrig and F. Paternò (Eds.): HCSE/TAMODIA 2008, LNCS 5247, pp. 299–304, 2008.
© IFIP International Federation for Information Processing 2008

- Atomicity: Atomity guarantees, that either all of the operations are performed or none of them.
- Consistency: The database remains in a consistent state before the start and after the end of the transaction.
- Isolation: Isolation ensures, that each transaction appears to be isolated from all other transactions. This means, an operation outside a transaction can not see intermediate data of the transaction causing unwanted side effects.
- Durability: Durability guarantees, that once a transaction was performed successful it will persist.

These so called ACID criteria are too strict to be used in workflow systems or task models. To loosen some of the restrictions there are advanced transaction models to specify nested transactions [1], long-living transactions [3] or multi-level transactions [4]. We make use of some of these ideas and concepts in modeling transactions in task models.

3 Task Models

The task models we are dealing with are derived from the CTT notation [5].

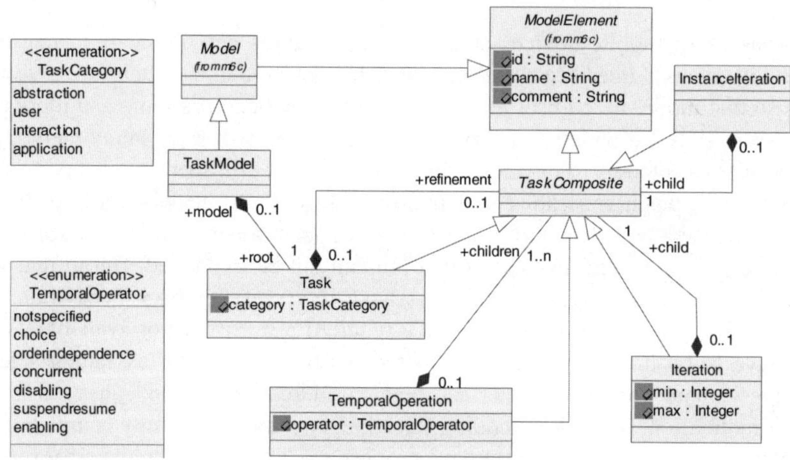

Fig. 1. Task-meta-model

A task model is basically a tree of tasks and subtasks. Iterations and optional tasks can be specified as well as different temporal relations between subtasks.

Figure 1 shows the important parts of our task-meta-model. This meta model is an integral part of our tool development process [7, 8]. Using Eclipse [9] and some frameworks like EMF [10], GEF [11] and GMF [12] we developed a set of model-based user interface design tools.

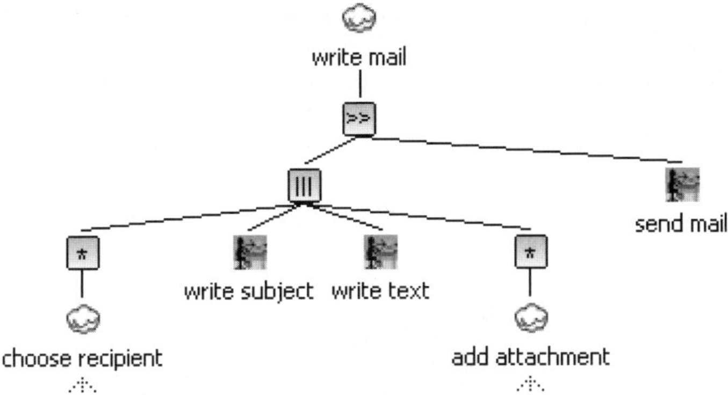

Fig. 2. Task model "write mail"

Figure 2 shows an example task model created with one of our tools. It differs a little bit from the CTT notation. Temporal relations and iterations are nodes in our models instead of attributes respectively associations. One advantage of this notation, that one can immediately see the order of applied temporal operations without knowing operator priorities like in CTTE.

3.1 Lifecycle of Tasks

Each task passes different states during its lifetime. A state chart can be used to specify the states and possible transitions between them, like in [13]. We developed our own state chart that fits our needs.

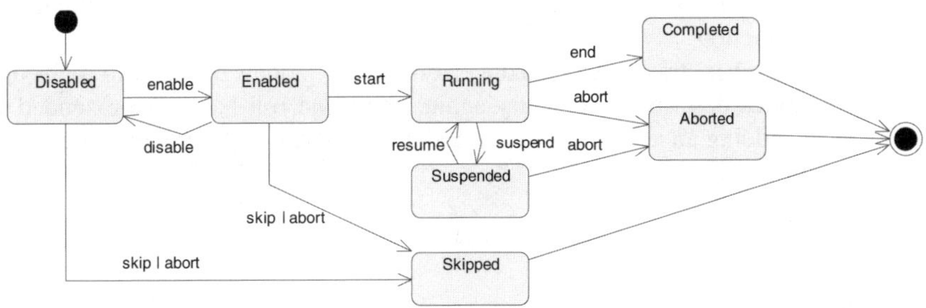

Fig. 3. Lifecycle of a task

This state chart of Fig. 3 is applicable for basic (leaf) tasks as well as complex tasks. At the beginning, a task is in the state *Disabled*. In the default case, the event *enable* causes a state change to *Enabled*, *start* changes the state to *Running* and *end* results in the final state *Completed*. Variations of this behaviour arise by using different temporal operators. For example, using a *Choice* operator between two tasks A and B, *skip* is send to task A when the user chooses to start task B, effecting in state *Skipped*. The operator *OrderIndependence* takes care that while one task is running the other task will be temporarely disabled by sending *disable*. The events *suspend* and *resume* occur using the temporal operator *Suspend/Resume* and *abort* is sent by the operator *Disabling* to cancel task A when task B starts.

To simulate a complete task model, for each task an instance is created first. This instance contains amongst other things the current state of execution, following the above state chart. The temporal operators act like agents between these instances and take care to reproduce the specified behaviour. For example, the temporal operator *Enabling* between two tasks A and B achieves this by observing the state of A and send the event *enable* to B when A changes his state to *Completed*.

3.2 Transactions in Task Models

The reason to introduce the concept of transactions into task models was to model the behaviour in case of an error. First, we had to reflect error situations in our runtime models. We inserted a new state *Failed* into the state chart and a transition from *Running* to *Failed*, reflecting an error situation. When a task enters the state *Failed*, interesting questions arise: What happens with the state of following tasks and the parent task? How can the task model get back to a consistent state?

We take a look at some examples first: Let's assume, in figure 2 the task *send mail* cannot be performed due to connection problems. The reasonable behaviour here is to give the user the opportunity to retry the task *send mail* when the network connection is working again.

In another task model we describe a complex calculation. If on of it steps cannot be performed, e.g. if some data is missing, the whole calculation fails due to missing intermediate data.

A third task model contains the task of booking a journey. This includes amongst other things the booking of a flight, a hotel and a rental car and the payment process. If one of these steps goes wrong (no hotel available, not enough money, ...) any already performed task has to be undone. This behaviour is similar to the rollback operation of a transaction.

There may be other strategies to handle errors in task models but we will focus upon the three strategies described above: try again, abort and roll back. We extended our task models by adding an attribute for each task to specify, which strategy to apply.

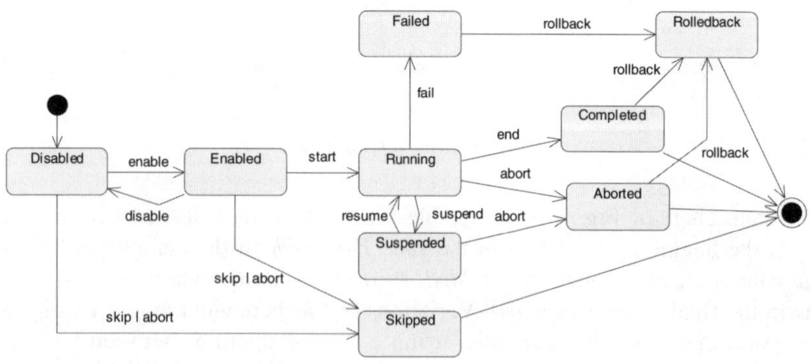

Fig. 4. Extended lifecycle with transaction concepts

Figure 4 shows the extended lifecycle of a task, including the two new states, *Failed* and *Rolledback*. We also defined for each combination of temporal operator and strategy, how to behave, when a tasks state switches into the state Failed.

The strategy "Abort" generally causes a failure of the task when a subtask fails. Using this strategy all over the task model, each failure in one of the subtasks causes the whole model to fail.

"Try again" resets the task and all of its subtasks when a subtask fails. Using this strategy we can stop the error propagation from a leaf task to the root task resulting from the application of the strategy "Abort".

The strategy "Roll back" revokes already performed tasks by executing the opposite tasks in reversed order, for example the cancelation of orders or accounting transactions. Using this strategy we create an effect similar to transactions in database systems: Either the whole tasks is performed or nothing. Of course, not all criteria of database transactions are fulfilled, but this is not required.

3.3   Tool Support for Transactions in Task Models

To test the above ideas we implemented them in a few of our tools. First of all, we enhanced the meta model in figure 1 and added an attribute to specify for each task, which strategy to apply and how many times the user can retry a task. For example, the task model designer can specify, that the user has 3 attempts to perform "enter PIN", until this task fails finally. These meta-model-changes are reflected directly in our editors.

Further modifications are related to our task model simulation engine: The introduction of the new task states *Failed* and *Rolledback* and the implementation of error strategies. The user interface to control the task model simulation has changed too: Users are able to send the message *Crash* to a task to simulate an error as seen in figure 5.

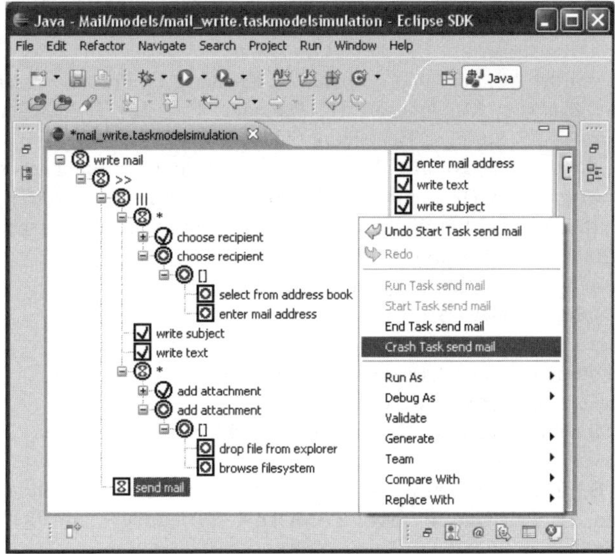

Fig. 5. Simulation of a task model

Additionally, the order of already performed tasks can be seen now on the right side to keep an eye on how the rollback mechanism works. In this example, the tasks *enter mail address, write text, write subject* and *drop file from explorer* (hidden by the popup menu) are already completed.

4 Summary and Future Work

The paper discussed an approach to address error situation in task models, using ideas from the concept of transactions. In the process of developing user interfaces we need to use this method to specify non-standard cases in task execution. This approach works on a very basal level. It does not consider consistency on the object level. For example, if a task modifies the state of an object and is rolled back later, the object's state will not be restored.

In the future we want to readjust our other tools, like the dialog graph editor [8] to the task model transaction approach. We have to develop new concepts for dialog graphs in order to react reasonable to error situations in task models.

References

1. Cass, A., Fernandes, C.: Using Task Models for Cascading Selective Undo. In: Coninx, K., Luyten, K., Schneider, K.A. (eds.) TAMODIA 2006. LNCS, vol. 4385, pp. 186–201. Springer, Heidelberg (2007)
2. Moss, J.: Nested Transactions and Reliable Distributed Computing. In: Proc. Of the 2nd Symposium on Reliability in Distributed Software and Database Systems (1982)
3. Garcia-Molina, H., Salem, K.: Sagas. In: Proc of ACM SIGMOD Conference on Management of Data (1987)
4. Weikum, G., Schek, H.: Concepts and Applications of Multilevel Transactions and Open-nested Transactions. In: Database Transaction Models for Advanced Applications (1992)
5. CTTE: The ConcurTaskTree Environment,
   `http://giove.cnuce.cnr.it/ctte.html`
6. Sinnig, D., Wurdel, M., Forbrig, P., Chalin, P., Khendek, F.: Practical Extensions for Task Models. In: Winckler, M., Johnson, H., Palanque, P. (eds.) TAMODIA 2007. LNCS, vol. 4849, pp. 42–55. Springer, Heidelberg (2007)
7. Brüning, J., Dittmar, A., Forbrig, P., Reichart, D.: Getting SW Engineers on Board: Task Modelling with Activity Diagrams. In: EIS 2007, Salamanca, Spain (2007)
8. Forbrig, P., Reichart, D.: Ein Werkzeug zur Spezifikation von Dialoggraphen. Mensch and Computer 2007, Weimar, Germany (2007)
9. Eclipse (visited: June 8, 2008), `http://www.eclipse.org`
10. Eclipse Modeling Framework (visited: June 08, 2008),
    `http://www.eclipse.org/emf`
11. Graphical Editing Framework (visited: June 08, 2008),
    `http://www.eclipse.org/gef`
12. Graphical Modeling Framework (visited: June 08, 2008),
    `http://www.eclipse.org/gmf`
13. Bomsdorf, B.: The WebTaskModel Approach to Web Process Modelling. In: Winckler, M., Johnson, H., Palanque, P. (eds.) TAMODIA 2007. LNCS, vol. 4849, pp. 240–253. Springer, Heidelberg (2007)

Author Index

Printing: Mercedes-Druck, Berlin
Binding: Stein+Lehmann, Berlin

Lecture Notes in Computer Science

Sublibrary 2: Programming and Software Engineering

For information about Vols. 1– 4591
please contact your bookseller or Springer

Vol. 4954: C. Pautasso, É. Tanter (Eds.), Software Composition. X, 263 pages. 2008.

Vol. 4951: M. Luck, L. Padgham (Eds.), Agent-Oriented Software Engineering VIII. XIV, 225 pages. 2008.

Vol. 4949: R.M. Hierons, J.P. Bowen, M. Harman (Eds.), Formal Methods and Testing. XIII, 367 pages. 2008.

Vol. 4937: M. Dumas, R. Heckel (Eds.), Web Services and Formal Methods. IX, 169 pages. 2008.

Vol. 4922: M. Broy, I.H. Krüger, M. Meisinger (Eds.), Model-Driven Development of Reliable Automotive Services. XVIII, 183 pages. 2008.

Vol. 4916: S. Leue, P. Merino (Eds.), Formal Methods for Industrial Critical Systems. X, 251 pages. 2008.

Vol. 4909: I. Eusgeld, F.C. Freiling, R. Reussner (Eds.), Dependability Metrics. XI, 305 pages. 2008.

Vol. 4906: M. Cebulla (Ed.), Object-Oriented Technology. VIII, 204 pages. 2008.

Vol. 4902: P. Hudak, D.S. Warren (Eds.), Practical Aspects of Declarative Languages. X, 333 pages. 2007.

Vol. 4899: K. Yorav (Ed.), Hardware and Software: Verification and Testing. XII, 267 pages. 2008.

Vol. 4895: J.J. Cuadrado-Gallego, R. Braungarten, R.R. Dumke, A. Abran (Eds.), Software Process and Product Measurement. X, 203 pages. 2008.

Vol. 4888: F. Kordon, O. Sokolsky (Eds.), Composition of Embedded Systems. XII, 221 pages. 2007.

Vol. 4880: S. Overhage, C.A. Szyperski, R. Reussner, J.A. Stafford (Eds.), Software Architectures, Components, and Applications. X, 249 pages. 2008.

Vol. 4849: M. Winckler, H. Johnson, P. Palanque (Eds.), Task Models and Diagrams for User Interface Design. XIII, 299 pages. 2007.

Vol. 4839: O. Sokolsky, S. Taşıran (Eds.), Runtime Verification. VI, 215 pages. 2007.

Vol. 4834: R. Cerqueira, R.H. Campbell (Eds.), Middleware 2007. XIII, 451 pages. 2007.

Vol. 4829: M. Lumpe, W. Vanderperren (Eds.), Software Composition. VIII, 281 pages. 2007.

Vol. 4824: A. Paschke, Y. Biletskiy (Eds.), Advances in Rule Interchange and Applications. XIII, 243 pages. 2007.

Vol. 4821: J. Bennedsen, M.E. Caspersen, M. Kölling (Eds.), Reflections on the Teaching of Programming. X, 261 pages. 2008.

Vol. 4807: Z. Shao (Ed.), Programming Languages and Systems. XI, 431 pages. 2007.

Vol. 4799: A. Holzinger (Ed.), HCI and Usability for Medicine and Health Care. XVI, 458 pages. 2007.

Vol. 4789: M. Butler, M.G. Hinchey, M.M. Larrondo-Petrie (Eds.), Formal Methods and Software Engineering. VIII, 387 pages. 2007.

Vol. 4767: F. Arbab, M. Sirjani (Eds.), International Symposium on Fundamentals of Software Engineering. XIII, 450 pages. 2007.

Vol. 4765: A. Moreira, J. Grundy (Eds.), Early Aspects: Current Challenges and Future Directions. X, 199 pages. 2007.

Vol. 4764: P. Abrahamsson, N. Baddoo, T. Margaria, R. Messnarz (Eds.), Software Process Improvement. XI, 225 pages. 2007.

Vol. 4762: K.S. Namjoshi, T. Yoneda, T. Higashino, Y. Okamura (Eds.), Automated Technology for Verification and Analysis. XIV, 566 pages. 2007.

Vol. 4758: F. Oquendo (Ed.), Software Architecture. XVI, 340 pages. 2007.

Vol. 4757: F. Cappello, T. Herault, J. Dongarra (Eds.), Recent Advances in Parallel Virtual Machine and Message Passing Interface. XVI, 396 pages. 2007.

Vol. 4753: E. Duval, R. Klamma, M. Wolpers (Eds.), Creating New Learning Experiences on a Global Scale. XII, 518 pages. 2007.

Vol. 4749: B.J. Krämer, K.-J. Lin, P. Narasimhan (Eds.), Service-Oriented Computing – ICSOC 2007. XIX, 629 pages. 2007.

Vol. 4748: K. Wolter (Ed.), Formal Methods and Stochastic Models for Performance Evaluation. X, 301 pages. 2007.

Vol. 4741: C. Bessière (Ed.), Principles and Practice of Constraint Programming – CP 2007. XV, 890 pages. 2007.

Vol. 4735: G. Engels, B. Opdyke, D.C. Schmidt, F. Weil (Eds.), Model Driven Engineering Languages and Systems. XV, 698 pages. 2007.

Vol. 4716: B. Meyer, M. Joseph (Eds.), Software Engineering Approaches for Offshore and Outsourced Development. X, 201 pages. 2007.

Vol. 4709: F.S. de Boer, M.M. Bonsangue, S. Graf, W.-P. de Roever (Eds.), Formal Methods for Components and Objects. VIII, 297 pages. 2007.

Vol. 4680: F. Saglietti, N. Oster (Eds.), Computer Safety, Reliability, and Security. XV, 548 pages. 2007.

Vol. 4670: V. Dahl, I. Niemelä (Eds.), Logic Programming. XII, 470 pages. 2007.

Vol. 4652: D. Georgakopoulos, N. Ritter, B. Benatallah, C. Zirpins, G. Feuerlicht, M. Schoenherr, H.R. Motahari-Nezhad (Eds.), Service-Oriented Computing ICSOC 2006. XVI, 201 pages. 2007.

Vol. 4640: A. Rashid, M. Aksit (Eds.), Transactions on Aspect-Oriented Software Development IV. IX, 191 pages. 2007.

Vol. 4634: H. Riis Nielson, G. Filé (Eds.), Static Analysis. XI, 469 pages. 2007.

Vol. 4620: A. Rashid, M. Aksit (Eds.), Transactions on Aspect-Oriented Software Development III. IX, 201 pages. 2007.

Vol. 4615: R. de Lemos, C. Gacek, A. Romanovsky (Eds.), Architecting Dependable Systems IV. XIV, 435 pages. 2007.

Vol. 4610: B. Xiao, L.T. Yang, J. Ma, C. Muller-Schloer, Y. Hua (Eds.), Autonomic and Trusted Computing. XVIII, 571 pages. 2007.

Vol. 4609: E. Ernst (Ed.), ECOOP 2007 – Object-Oriented Programming. XIII, 625 pages. 2007.

Vol. 4608: H.W. Schmidt, I. Crnković, G.T. Heineman, J.A. Stafford (Eds.), Component-Based Software Engineering. XII, 283 pages. 2007.